★ 1319 ★
Helicopter Services (SIC 4522)

Helicopter Service Industry in the Gulf of Mexico

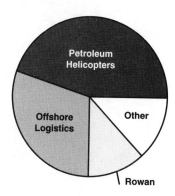

The industry refers to the ferrying of people from land to deep sea oil rigs. With the increase of off-shore drilling and the rise of oil prices, the industry has been booming.

Petroleum Helicopters	45.0%
Offshore Logistics	30.0
Rowan	12.0
Other	13.0

Source: *Investor's Business Daily*, April 26, 2001, p. A8, from R.W. Baird & Co.

★ 1320 ★
Airlines (SIC 4581)

Top Airlines at Boston, MA

Market shares are shown based on planned mergers.

US Airways	23.0%
Delta	22.1
American	14.9
United	11.2
Other	28.8

Source: *Air Transport World*, March 2001, p. 38.

★ 1321 ★
Airlines (SIC 4581)

Top Airlines at Denver International

Market shares are shown in percent.

United Airlines	65.0%
Air Wisconsin	6.0
Great Lakes Aviation	2.0
Other	27.0

Source: *Denver Post*, January 31, 2001, p. C2.

★ 1322 ★
Airlines (SIC 4581)

Top Airlines at La Guardia Airport, NY

Market shares are shown based on planned mergers.

US Airways	30.06%
Delta	22.38
American	16.43
United	7.90
Other	23.23

Source: *Air Transport World*, March 2001, p. 38.

★ 1323 ★
Airports (SIC 4581)

Largest Air Cargo Airports in the East

Airports are ranked by cargo traffic, in thousands of tons.

NY Kennedy	1,825.9
Miami	1,642.4
Newark, NJ	1,082.6
Atlanta	871.6
Philadelphia	562.7
Boston	465.7
Washington Dulles	384.2
Orlando	271.0
Ft. Lauderdale	236.6

Source: *Air Cargo World*, June 2001, p. 32, from Airports Council International.

★ 1324 ★

Airports (SIC 4581)

Largest Cargo Airports

Airports are ranked by tonnage transported.

Memphis, TN	2,412,905
Chicago O'Hare	1,531,809
Louisville, KY	1,486,205
Indianapolis, MD	1,107,985
Dayton, OH	894,389
Dallas/Ft. Worth, TX	844,075
Wilmington, OH	492,165
Toledo, OH	490,352
Cincinnati, OH	384,486
Minneapolis/St. Paul, MD	366,356

Source: *Air Cargo World*, August 2000, p. 30, from Airports Council International, Airborne Express, Hillwood Properties, and Willow Run Airport.

SIC 46 - Pipelines, Except Natural Gas

★ 1325 ★

Pipelines (SIC 4610)

Largest Pipeline Firms

Firms are ranked by revenues in millions of dollars.

Enron	$ 100,789
Dynegy	29,445
El Paso	21,950
Williams	11,481
Transmontaigne	5,071
Kinder Morgan	3,731

Source: *Fortune*, April 16, 2001, p. F61.

SIC 47 - Transportation Services

★ 1326 ★
Tourism (SIC 4720)

Top States for Domestic Tourism

Spending by domestic travelers is shown in billions of dollars.

California	$ 54
Florida	37
Texas	28
New York	26
Illinois	20

Source: *USA TODAY*, May 21, 2001, p. B1, from Travel Industry Association of America.

★ 1327 ★
Tourism (SIC 4720)

Top States for International Tourism

Spending by international travelers is shown in billions of dollars.

Florida	$ 17
California	13
New York	9
Hawaii	7
Texas	3

Source: *USA TODAY*, May 22, 2001, p. B1, from Travel Industry Association of America.

★ 1328 ★
Travel (SIC 4720)

Domestic Travel Market Shares

Data show the states that received the greatest share of domestic travelers.

Florida	11.37%
California	10.27
Texas	5.75
Nevada	4.88
Other	67.73

Source: *Arizona Republic*, June 10, 2000, p. D1, from D.K. Shifflet & Associates.

★ 1329 ★
Ticket Reservations (SIC 4724)

Electronic Ticket Reservations

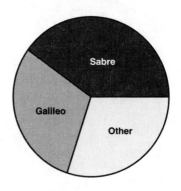

Market shares are shown in percent.

Sabre	40.0%
Galileo	30.0
Other	30.0

Source: *Mergers & Acquisitions Report*, October 30, 2000, p. 1.

★ 1330 ★
Travel (SIC 4724)

Time Share Industry

Florida	18.0%
California	10.0
South Carolina	9.0
Colorado	5.0
North Carolina	5.0
Tennessee	5.0
Texas	4.0
Hawaii	3.0
Virginia	3.0
Alabama	2.0
Other	64.0

Source: *Hotel & Motel Management*, February 5, 2001, p. 18, from D.K. Shifflet & Associates.

★ 1331 ★
Travel (SIC 4724)

Top U.S. Destinations

Data show where the top destinations Americans plan to visit Summer 2000.

Florida	34.0%
California	26.0
New York	13.0
Texas	10.0
Hawaii	9.0
Colorado	8.0
Washington D.C.	7.0
Nevada	7.0
Arizona	7.0

Source: *Washington Post*, May 27, 2000, p. E1.

★ 1332 ★
Travel Agencies (SIC 4724)

Largest Travel Agencies, 2000

Firms are ranked by airline ticket sales in millions of dollars.

American Express	$ 11.40
Navigant/Sato	3.99
Carlson Wagonlit Teavel	3.90
Worldtravel BTI	3.80
Rosenbluth International	2.72
TQ3 Maritz Travel Solutions	1.67
Travel and Transport	0.75
Omega World Travel	0.71

Total Travel Management	$ 0.71
VTS Travel Enterprises	0.63

Source: *New York Times*, June 7, 2001, p. C8, from *Business Travel News*.

★ 1333 ★
Cruise Lines (SIC 4725)

Caribbean Cruise Industry

Data show market shares of North American operators.

Carnival	31.7%
RCI	22.0
Norwegian Cruise Lines	8.0
Disney	7.2
Princess	5.5
Celebrity	4.5
HAL	4.5
Other	16.6

Source: "Caribbean Market Focus." Retrieved June 28, 2000 from the World Wide Web: http://www.cruiseindustrynews.com, from *Cruise Industry News*.

★ 1334 ★
Cruise Lines (SIC 4725)

Leading Cruise Lines

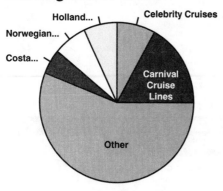

Shares are shown based on total capacity and double occupancy.

Carnival Cruise Lines	17.45%
Celebrity Cruises	7.66
Holland America Line	7.27
Norwegian Cruise Line	6.82
Costa Crusies	5.05
Other	55.75

Source: "Berth Capacity Marketshare." Retrieved January 11, 2001 from the World Wide Web: http://www.traveltrade.com.

SIC 48 - Communications

★ 1335 ★

Broadcasting (SIC 4800)

Interactive Broadcast Video Market, 2005

The market is forecast to reach $4.2 billion in 2005. Roughly 71% of cable and broadcast channels support on-screen or PC program enhancements. PVR stands for personal video recorder. VOD stands for video on demand.

	($ mil.)	Share
Internet on TV	$ 1,135.7	27.14%
Net PVR advertising	1,105.2	26.41
VOD	526.2	12.57
Streaming video	454.4	10.86
Broadband video content	430.8	10.29
On-screen overlays	364.0	8.70
Datacasting	168.4	4.02

Source: "Interactive Broadcast Video Market." Retrieved February 1, 2000 from the World Wide Web: http://www.businesswire.com, from DFC Intelligence.

★ 1336 ★

Telecommunications (SIC 4810)

U.S. Telecom Market

The market is expected to grow from $609 billion to $954 billion.

	2000	2004
Transport services	46.0%	40.0%
Support services	27.0	35.0
Equipment and software	26.0	23.0
Specialized services	1.0	2.0

Source: *Investor's Business Daily*, May 4, 2001, p. A5, from Telecommunications Industry Association.

★ 1337 ★

Cellular Services (SIC 4812)

Largest Cellular/PCS Firms

Shares are shown based on revenue.

AT&T Wireless	18.0%
SBC Wireless	12.0
Vodafone Airtouch	11.0
Bell Atlantic Mobile	9.0
Bell/South Wireless	8.0
Other	42.0

Source: *Computer Reseller News*, July 31, 2000, p. 81, from International Data Corp.

★ 1338 ★

Cellular Services (SIC 4812)

Leading Cellular Service Providers in Mexico

Operators are ranked by millions of subscribers.

Telcel	11.90
Lusacell	1.80
Telefonica	1.40
Pegaso	0.71
Unefon	0.39

Source: *Financial Times*, May 16, 2001, p. 20.

★ 1339 ★

Cellular Services (SIC 4812)

Top Cellular Service Providers, 2000

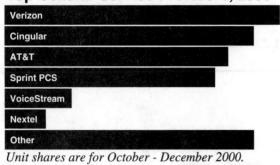

Verizon

Cingular

AT&T

Sprint PCS

VoiceStream

Nextel

Other

Unit shares are for October - December 2000.

Verizon	21.4%
Cingular	19.2
AT&T	16.7
Sprint PCS	15.9
VoiceStream	4.7
Nextel	3.0
Other	19.1

Source: "NPD Intelect Reports." Retrieved March 21, 2001 from the World Wide Web: http://www.businesswire.com, from NPD Intelect.

★ 1340 ★

Cellular Services (SIC 4812)

Top Cities for Cell Phones

Data show the cities with the highest percentage of cell phone owners.

Anchorage, AL	56.0%
Chicago, IL	55.0
Honolulu, HA	54.0
Atlanta, GA	52.0
Detroit, MI	52.0
Lake Charles, LA	51.0

Source: *USA TODAY*, June 5, 2000, p. B1, from Polk.

★ 1341 ★

Wireless Communications (SIC 4812)

CTI Vertical Market Shares

CTI stands for computer-telephony integration.

Financial services	21.0%
Telecommunications	12.8
Manufacturing	12.5
Transportation	9.2
Other	44.5

Source: *Business Communications Review*, May 2000, p. 16, from Telecommunications Industry Association and Multimedia Telecommunications Association.

★ 1342 ★

Wireless Communications (SIC 4812)

Largest PCS Firms

Firms are ranked by millions of customers. PCS stands for personal communication services.

Sprint PCS	7.40
Nextel Communications	5.60
VoiceStream Wireless Corp.	3.10
AT&T Wireless Services Inc.	1.90
Powertel Inc.	0.72
Qwest Communications	0.65
Telecorp Holdings	0.31
Triton PCS Inc.	0.30

Source: *RCR Wireless News*, October 9, 2000, p. 22.

★ 1343 ★

Wireless Communications (SIC 4812)

Largest Wireless Firms in Canada, 2001

Market shares are shown in percent based on March 31, 2001.

Bell Wireless Alliance	36.0%
Rogers AT&T	28.4
Telus Mobility	24.8
Microcell	10.8

Source: *Marketing Magazine*, June 4, 2001, p. NA, from Yankee Group.

★ 1344 ★

Wireless Communications (SIC 4812)

Leading DSL Providers

Data show number of subscriber lines. DSL stands for digital subscriber line.

	Lines	Share
SBC	767,000	33.0%
Verizon	540,000	23.0
Covad	274,000	12.0
Qwest	255,000	11.0
BellSouth	215,000	9.0
NorthPoint	100,000	4.0
Rhythms	67,000	3.0
Other	129,084	5.0

Source: *VAR Business*, May 28, 2001, p. 26, from Yankee Group.

★ 1345 ★

Wireless Communications (SIC 4812)

Leading Wireless Carriers, 2000

Shares are shown for the fourth quarter.

Verizon Wireless Inc.	29.0%
Cingular Wireless	20.0
AT&T Wireless	17.0
Sprint PCS Group	10.0
Nextel	7.0
Alltel Corp.	6.0
Voicestream Wireless Corp.	5.0
Other	6.0

Source: *Detroit Free Press*, May 14, 2001, p. 4F, from Cellular Telecommunications & Internet Association.

★ 1346 ★

Wireless Communications (SIC 4812)

Mobile Data Revenue, 2005

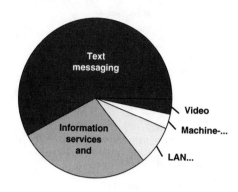

Machine to machine includes such things as a vending machine sending a message to a supplier that it needs to be refilled.

Text messaging and email	58.0%
Information services and m-commerce	28.0
LAN access	8.0
Machine-to-machine (telemetry)	3.0
Video	3.0

Source: *M Business*, April 2001, p. 79, from Yankee Group.

★ 1347 ★

Wireless Communications (SIC 4812)

U.S. PON Market Segments

The market for passive optical networks is forecast by locations served. This market has been estimated at $158 million this year and $394 million in 2002 by The Yankee Group. Communications Industry Researchers says $84 million today and $762.9 million by 2004.

	2000	2004	Share
Curb	12.4	468.5	61.41%
Building	24.0	225.1	29.51
Home	0.5	69.3	9.08

Source: *Telephony*, February 12, 2001, p. 80, from Communications Industry Researchers Inc.

★ 1348 ★

Wireless Communications (SIC 4812)

Wireless Service in Mexico

Market shares are shown in percent.

Telcel 70.0%
Other 30.0

Source: *Latin Trade*, March 2001, p. 56.

★ 1349 ★

Telephone Services (SIC 4813)

Long-Distance Market

Market shares are shown in percent.

AT&T 40.0%
MCI WorldCom 25.0
Sprint 10.0
Other 25.0

Source: *Newsbytes*, January 24, 2001, p. NA.

★ 1350 ★

Telephone Services (SIC 4813)

Long-Distance Market in Canada, 2001

Market shares are shown in percent based on total revenue of $3.1 billion.

Bell Canada 49.0%
Telus 19.0
AT&T Canada 14.0
Sprint Canada 6.0
Aliant 3.0
Other 9.0

Source: *Marketing Magazine*, June 4, 2001, p. NA, from Yankee Group.

★ 1351 ★

Telephone Services (SIC 4813)

Long-Distance Market Leaders

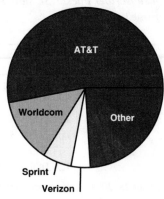

Market shares are shown in percent.

AT&T 53.0%
Worldcom 13.0
Sprint 6.0
Verizon 4.0
Other 24.0

Source: *New York Times*, October 26, 2000, p. C13, from Yankee Group and Paul Kagan Associates.

★ 1352 ★

Telephone Services (SIC 4813)

New York Phone Market

Market shares are shown in percent.

AT&T 50.0%
WorldCom 20.0
Bell Atlantic 11.5
Sprint 8.5
Other 10.0

Source: *Investor's Business Daily*, August 15, 2000, p. A6, from company reports and *Crain's New York Business*.

★ 1353 ★

Telephone Services (SIC 4813)

Telephone Service In New Jersey

Market shares are shown in percent.

Verizon 95.0%
Other 5.0

Source: *Knight-Ridder/Tribune Business News*, February 28, 2001, p. NA.

★ 1354 ★
Telephone Services (SIC 4813)

U.S. Telephone Revenue, 1999

Local service 41.0%
Toll/long-distance 40.0
Wireless service 19.0

Source: *Investor's Business Daily*, March 28, 2001, p. A4.

★ 1355 ★
Electronic Commerce (SIC 4822)

Comparison Shopping Engine Market

CSEs are expected to play a significant role in B-to-B commerce. By 2005, they may influence roughly 10% of sales. They can compare pricing or other desired qualities. Data show millions of dollars in influenced sales.

	($ mil.)	Share
Pure play	$ 591	41.0%
Portal associated	528	36.7
Leisure travel	289	20.0
Niche	30	2.1
Softward download	3	0.2

Source: *Direct*, April 2001, p. NA.

★ 1356 ★
Electronic Commerce (SIC 4822)

E-Commerce in North America

Sales are shown in billions of dollars.

	2000	2001	Share
United States	$ 488.7	$ 864.1	95.09%
Canada	17.4	38.0	4.18
Mexico	3.2	6.6	0.73

Source: *Supply House Times*, January 2001, p. 41, from Forrester Research.

★ 1357 ★
Electronic Commerce (SIC 4822)

E-Commerce Revenues, 2000

Revenues are forecast in billions of dollars.

	($ bil.)	Share
Travel	$ 11.0	42.15%
Computer hardware and software . .	7.3	27.97
Books, music, video	2.8	10.73
Apparel	1.6	6.13
Groceries	0.8	3.07
Consumer electronics	0.6	2.30
Health	0.6	2.30
Flowers and specialty gifts	0.5	1.92
Movie and event tickets	0.5	1.92
Other	0.4	1.53

Source: *Industry Standard - Supplement*, December 2000, p. 115, from Jupiter Communications.

★ 1358 ★
Electronic Commerce (SIC 4822)

Government Web Sites, 2000

The federal government generated $3.6 billion in sales from its 164 web sites. It sold train tickets, T-bills, repossessed Winnebagos, satellite images and much, much more. Figures are in thousands of dollars. As a comparison Amazon.com, the top e-tailer, took in $2.8 billion in sales last year.

Treasury Department	$ 3,300,000
U.S. Postal Service	27,000
Administrative Office of the U.S. Courts .	12,000
U.S. Geological Survey	7,500
National Park Service	5,400
American Battle Monuments Comm. . .	85
Bureau of Land Management	48

Source: *U.S. News & World Report*, June 11, 2001, p. 12.

★ 1359 ★

Electronic Commerce (SIC 4822)

Holiday 2000 Sales

Data show thousands of average daily visitors.

Amazon.com	1,600
Mypoints.com	1,400
AmericanGreetings.com	538
Half.com	511
BizRate.com	510
WebStakes.com	446
Walmart.com	370
CDNow.com	320
Buy.com	316
eToys.com	310

Source: *Wall Street Journal*, January 22, 2001, p. B7, from Jupiter Research, Media Metrix, and AdRevelance.

★ 1360 ★

Electronic Commerce (SIC 4822)

Holiday Shopping Online

Home Internet users spent $1.04 billion during the week ended December 24, 2000. It was a substantial drop from $1.6 billion spent the previous week. However, 94% of customers reported the same or better service over 1999.

	Sales	Share
Electronics	$ 118,639	13.13%
Computer hardware	116,844	12.93
Travel	109,485	12.12
Apparel	98,738	10.93
Personal accessories	60,462	6.69
Pet supplies	50,901	5.63
Books	43,105	4.77
Video/DVD	42,856	4.74
Computer software	34,655	3.84
Music	33,694	3.73
Other	194,122	21.49

Source: "Press Release." Retrieved January 8, 2001 from the World Wide Web: http://www.prnewswire.com.

★ 1361 ★

Electronic Commerce (SIC 4822)

How Electronic Bills Are Delivered

Market shares are shown in percent.

	1998	2005
Web	61.0%	38.0%
Proprietary	19.0	20.0
E-mail	18.0	40.0
Other	2.0	2.0

Source: *Infoworld*, September 11, 2000, p. 10, from Killen & Associates.

★ 1362 ★

Electronic Commerce (SIC 4822)

Internet Frauds

Online auction frauds cost victims an average of $326 in 2000.

Online auctions	78.0%
General merchandise sales	10.0
Work-at-home	3.0
Internet access services	3.0
Advance fee loans	2.0
Information adult services	1.0
Nigerian money offers	1.0
Computer equipment/software	1.0
Travel/vacations	0.5
Credit card offers	0.5

Source: *Globe and Mail*, February 15, 2001, p. B1, from National Fraud Information Center.

★ 1363 ★

Electronic Commerce (SIC 4822)

Largest Internet Retailers

Firms are ranked by estimated online sales in millions of dollars.

Ebay	$ 3,700
Amazon.com	1,900
Dell	1,300
Buy.com	800
Egghead.com	600
Gateway	600

Continued on next page.

★ 1363 ★ *Continued*
Electronic Commerce (SIC 4822)

Largest Internet Retailers

Firms are ranked by estimated online sales in millions of dollars.

Quixtar	$ 450
Barnes & Noble	325
uBid	325
Cyberian Outpost	250

Source: *Stores*, September 2000, p. R5.

★ 1364 ★
Electronic Commerce (SIC 4822)

Leading IT Providers to the Web Marketplace

Leading technology providers to industry-sponsored marketplaces.

Ariba	24.0%
I2 Technologies	19.0
CommerceOne	17.0
IBM	15.0
SAP	13.0
Oracle	12.0

Source: *Forbes*, May 21, 2001, p. 24, from Jupiter Communications.

★ 1365 ★
Electronic Commerce (SIC 4822)

North America Electronic Business Market

The North American business-to-business e-marketplace market grew 171% in 1999, propelled by "brick-to-click" distributors and established dot-com marketplaces, according to the source. Market shares are shown based on revenues.

Ingram Micro	26.4%
Tec Data	12.2
Arrow Electronics	11.9
Grainger	7.6
Avnet	7.6

VerticalNet	4.0%
FreeMarkets	3.2
Altra Energy Techniques	3.0
Others	24.1

Source: *EC World*, November 2000, p. 40, from Gartner Group.

★ 1366 ★
Electronic Commerce (SIC 4822)

Online Booking Sales, 1999

Market shares are shown in percent.

Air	68.5%
Lodging	14.8
Car	12.7
Cruise	2.1
Package	1.9

Source: *Investor's Business Daily*, December 26, 2000, p. A6, from Forrester Research.

★ 1367 ★
Electronic Commerce (SIC 4822)

Online Consumer Sales in Canada by Year

Sales are shown in billions of dollars.

2002	$ 10.2
2001	6.2
2000	3.6
1999	2.0
1998	0.8

Source: *Toronto Star*, October 3, 2000, p. C5, from Retail Council of Canada and Boston Consulting Group.

★ 1368 ★

Electronic Commerce (SIC 4822)

Online Consumer Spending

Spending is shown in billions of dollars and pro-jected for 1999 and 2003.

	1999	2003
Air travel	$ 5.0	$ 13.6
PCs	3.8	10.2
Groceries	0.2	7.5
Apparel	0.8	6.7
Hotels	1.0	5.2
Books	1.3	4.9
Software	0.9	3.5
Event tickets	0.3	2.6
Music	0.3	2.6
Toys	0.3	1.6

Source: *Wall Street Journal*, October 23, 2000, p. R4, from Jupiter Research.

★ 1369 ★

Electronic Commerce (SIC 4822)

Online Music Sales

Sales are shown in millions of dollars.

	2002	2003	2004
Song	$ 88	$ 189	$ 339
Subscription	63	278	581

Source: *U.S. News & World Report*, February 26, 2001, p. 46, from Jupiter Communications.

★ 1370 ★

Electronic Commerce (SIC 4822)

Online Plane Ticket Sales

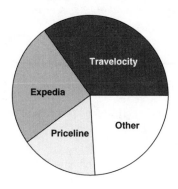

Market shares are shown in percent.

Travelocity	35.0%
Expedia	25.0
Priceline	16.0
Other	24.0

Source: *Infoworld*, June 4, 2001, p. 35, from Phocuswright.

★ 1371 ★

Electronic Commerce (SIC 4822)

What We Buy Online

Figures show the results of a survey of 1,632 women and 1,761 men who had had made online purchase in the last 90 days.

	Men	Women
CDs	21.0%	18.0%
Computer software	17.0	10.0
Clothing	13.0	20.0
Videos	10.0	7.0
Pet supplies	6.0	9.0

Source: *Business Week*, December 25, 2000, p. 14, from Greenfield Online.

★ 1372 ★
Electronic Publishing (SIC 4822)

Corporate Market for E-Learning

Revenue from e-learning will surge from $550 million in 1998 to $11.4 billion in 2003, an 84% growth rate. The market includes public and private sectors, but not academic. Figures are in billions of dollars.

	2000	2001	2002
Content	$ 1.33	$ 2.27	$ 3.91
Learning services	0.55	1.22	2.42
Delivery solutions	0.35	0.56	0.78

Source: *Washington Technology*, June 5, 2000, p. 25, from International Data Corp.

★ 1373 ★
Internet (SIC 4822)

Favorite Online Games

Data show the percent of online games who play. More than 75 million cybersurfers visit online game sites.

Cards	30.0%
Strategy	14.0
Fantasy	8.0
Word puzzles	6.0
Trivia	5.0
Sports	5.0
Board	5.0

Source: *Business Week*, February 19, 2001, p. 12, from Cyber Dialogue and PC Data.

★ 1374 ★
Internet (SIC 4822)

Households Using the Internet

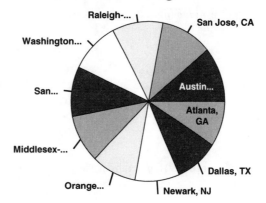

Austin-San Marcos, TX	69.7%
San Jose, CA	67.6
Raleigh-Durham-Chapel Hill, NC	67.0
Washington D.C.	64.9
San Francisco, CA	62.5
Middlesex-Somerset-Hunterdon, NJ	60.7
Orange County, CA	59.1
Newark, NJ	58.5
Dallas, TX	58.4
Atlanta, GA	58.2

Source: *Yahoo! Internet Life*, April 2001, p. 103.

★ 1375 ★
Internet (SIC 4822)

How We Access the Internet

	1999	2002
Direct dial-up	92.0%	65.0%
Cable modem	4.0	14.0
DSL	3.0	12.0
Satellite/wireless	1.0	9.0

Source: *Critical Mass*, Fall 2000, p. 60, from eMarketer.

★ 1376 ★
Internet (SIC 4822)
Internet Access by Region

Data show the cities with the highest penetration of Internet access.

Portland, OR	70.0%
Seattle, WA	70.0
San Francisco, CA	69.0
Boston, MA	68.0
San Diego, CA	66.0
Washington D.C.	65.0
Denver, CO	63.0

Source: *USA TODAY*, April 3, 2001, p. D1, from Nielsen/NetRatings.

★ 1377 ★
Internet (SIC 4822)
Internet Backbone Leaders, 1999

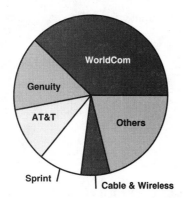

Firms are ranked by revenue in millions of dollars.

	Rev. ($ mil.)	Share
WorldCom	$ 3,000	38.0%
Genuity	1,200	15.0
AT&T	924	11.0
Sprint	728	9.0
Cable & Wireless	459	6.0
Others	1,700	21.0

Source: *Forbes*, June 12, 2000, p. 238, from TeleGeography Inc. and Sanford C. Bernstein & Co.

★ 1378 ★
Internet (SIC 4822)
Internet Backbone Services, 2000

Data show thousands of ISP connections, as of May 2000.

UUNet (MCI/WorldCom)	2,682
Sprint	1,483
Cable and Wireless	818
AT&T	810
GTE Internetworking	589

Source: *New York Times*, January 15, 2001, p. C6, from Sprint, Federal Communications Commission, *Boardwatch*, and Lehman Brothers.

★ 1379 ★
Internet (SIC 4822)
Largest Web Hosting Companies

Market shares are shown in percent. Data for 2000 are based on the first six months.

	1999	2000
IBM Global Services	14.6%	12.7%
Exodus	10.0	12.5
Qwest	6.4	4.1
Verio	6.4	4.1
UUNet/WorldCom	3.7	3.7
Digex	2.8	2.9
GlobalCenter	2.2	2.4
Other	53.9	57.6

Source: *Infoworld*, January 29, 2001, p. 16, from International Data Corp.

★ 1380 ★
Internet (SIC 4822)
Most-Visited Web Sites

Millions of visitors are shown for September 2000.

AOL Network	61.0
Yahoo	52.7
Lycos	51.4
Lycos	30.8
Excite Network	27.0
Go Network	23.0

Continued on next page.

★ 1380 ★ *Continued*
Internet (SIC 4822)

Most-Visited Web Sites

Millions of visitors are shown for September 2000.

About.com	20.6
Altavista Network	19.2
Time Warner Online	15.9
Amazon.com	15.3

Source: *Wall Street Journal*, October 31, 2000, p. B6, from Media Metrix.

★ 1381 ★
Internet (SIC 4822)

Online Pharmaceutical Sales

Online pharmaceutical sales are expected to hit $2.5 billion to $3.5 billion by 2004. Drugstore.com and Planetrx.com offer convenience, competitive pricing and current info.

Anti-aging products (cleansers, moisturizers)	30.0%
Sunscreen	20.0
Acne remedies	10.0
Other	40.0

Source: "Leading Online Drugstores." Retrieved October 9, 2000 from the World Wide Web: http://www.prnewswire.com, from Kalorama Information.

★ 1382 ★
Internet (SIC 4822)

Top Dot.Com Startups

The table shows the top earners during the second quarter. Figures are in millions.

EqualFooting.com	$ 54
Adauction.com	53
Supplyforce.com	52
OneMediaPlace (formerly Peoplesupport.com	50
DataPlay.com	50
NetFlix.com	50
Homepage.com	48
Everypath.com	48
Gator.com	44
BuyandHold.com	42

Source: *Computer Reseller News*, October 9, 2000, p. 45, from Prudential Securities.

★ 1383 ★
Internet (SIC 4822)

Top Entertainment Sites For Kids

Sites are ranked by number of unique visitors in April 2001.

Disney online	7,300
CartoonNetwork.com	2,400
Nick.com	2,100
NickJr.com	971
Yahooligans.com	944
FoxKids.com	743
PBSKids.org	645
gURL.com	599
Kbkids.com	574
KidsDomain.com	516

Source: *USA TODAY*, June 5, 2001, p. B1, from Jupiter Media Metrix.

★ 1384 ★
Internet (SIC 4822)

Top Finance Sites

Data show unique users for October 2000.

X.com	3.39
Nextcard.com	2.31
aria.com	2.01
americanexpress.com	1.64
Wellsfargo.com	1.27
MarketWatch.com	1.19
1st-netcard.com	1.14
Etrade.com	1.13
Fidelity.com	1.11
Bankofamerica.com	1.08

Source: *PC Magazine*, February 2, 2001, p. 78, from PC Data.

★ 1385 ★
Internet (SIC 4822)

Top Health Care Sites

Data show millions of unique visitors.

webmd.com	9,393
nih.gov	1,710
drkoop.com	1,262
healthandage.com	1,258
allhealth.com	1,193
healthscout.com	1,148
mayohealth.org	963

Continued on next page.

★ 1385 ★ *Continued*
Internet (SIC 4822)

Top Health Care Sites

Data show millions of unique visitors.

intelihealth.com	832
medscape.com	795
merckmedco.com	715

Source: "Consumer Market Share." Retrieved January 30, 2001 from the World Wide Web: http://www.aishealth.com.

★ 1386 ★

Internet (SIC 4822)

Top Internet Domains

Data show share of registrations.

.com	48.94%
.net	6.34
.edu	5.08
.de (Germany)	4.78
.org	4.76
.jp (Japan)	4.31
.uk (United Kingdom)	4.01
.tw (Taiwan)	1.20
.nl (Netherlands)	1.10
.fr (France)	1.00

Source: *Wired*, December 2000, p. 118.

★ 1387 ★

Internet (SIC 4822)

Top Newspaper Sites

Data show unique visitors, in thousands, for November 2000.

NYTimes	3,957
Usatoday.com	3,948
WashingtonPost.com	3,251
LATimes.com	2,232
WSJ.com	1,605
Boston.com	1,123
SFGate.com	899
Herald.com	897
DallasNews.com	841

Source: *Inside*, February 6, 2001, p. 35, from Media Metrix.

★ 1388 ★

Internet (SIC 4822)

Types of Email Delivered

Almost 400 billion emails were delivered in the United States in 1999. The number is expected to hit 509 billion by 2000 and 675 billion by 2001. The Post Office delivers about 209 billion pieces of mail in 1999.

	(bil.)	Share
Noncommercial	314.6	80.01%
Permission	40.1	10.20
SPAM	38.5	9.79

Source: *Business 2.0*, June 27, 2000, p. 311, from eMarketer.

★ 1389 ★

Online Services (SIC 4822)

Internet Service Provider Industry, 2000

Firms are ranked by millions of cutomers as of October 31, 2000.

America Online	20.3
EarthLink	4.3
Juno Online Services	3.7
NetZero	3.6
MSN Internet	3.5
Spinway	2.8
Excite@Home	2.3
Prodigy Comm.	2.2
AT&T WorldNet	1.5

Source: *Wall Street Journal*, November 16, 2000, p. A16, from ISP-Planet.

★ 1390 ★

Online Services (SIC 4822)

Leading E-Recruiting Providers

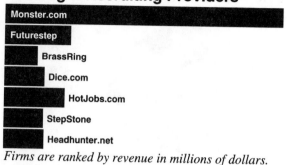

Firms are ranked by revenue in millions of dollars.

	1999	2000
Monster.com	$ 108.0	$ 349.2
Futurestep	21.9	82.0
BrassRing	20.0	40.0
Dice.com	15.9	48.5
HotJobs.com	15.6	74.7
StepStone	12.9	48.1
Headhunter.net	9.3	49.2

Source: *Infoworld*, March 26, 2001, p. 18, from International Data Corp.

★ 1391 ★

Online Services (SIC 4822)

Top Cable Modem Service Providers

Data show number of customers.

	No.	Share
ExciteAtHome	1,500,000	65.89%
Road Runner	730,000	32.07
HAS	17,000	0.75
ISP Channel	16,000	0.70
Online System Services	6,000	0.26
Power Link	5,000	0.22
CyberCable	1,350	0.06
PerKINet	1,200	0.05

Source: *Industry Standard*, May 22, 2000, p. 195, from Telecommunications Reports International.

★ 1392 ★

Online Services (SIC 4822)

Top Internet Service Providers in Canada, 2001

Market shares are shown in percent based on subscribers for the year ended March 24, 2001.

Sympatico	24.1%
Telus	11.9
Rogers@Home	7.2
Shaw@Home	6.6
Sprint Canada	4.7
LookTV	3.8
PSINet	3.7
AOL Canada	3.6
Videotron	3.2
Netcom Canada	2.3
Other	28.9

Source: *Marketing Magazine*, June 4, 2001, p. NA.

★ 1393 ★

Radio Broadcasting (SIC 4832)

Largest Radio Groups

Firms are ranked by revenue in millions of dollars. Clear Channel has roughly 20% of the $16 billion in radio revenue for the year.

Clear Channel	$ 3,100.0
Infinity	2,100.0
ABC Radio	406.9
Cox Radio	385.2
Entercom	358.6
Citadel	319.5
Emmis	244.4
Cumulus	239.1
Radio One	233.0
Susquehanna	221.6

Source: *Broadcasting & Cable*, September 18, 2000, p. 50, from BIA Research.

★ 1394 ★

Radio Broadcasting (SIC 4832)

Leading Radio Groups

Groups are ranked by ad revenue in billions of dollars.

Clear Channel	$ 3.52
Viacom	2.35
Cox Radio	0.45
ABC Radio	0.44
Entercom	0.42

Source: *Wall Street Journal*, March 19, 2001, p. B10, from BIA Financial Network.

★ 1395 ★

Radio Broadcasting (SIC 4832)

Popular Radio Webcasters

Shares are shown based on total hours online listeners tuned in during August 2000. Figures based on analysis of 75 channels.

NetRadio Corp.	50.5%
ABC Radio	16.2
Enigma Digital	4.7
Scottish Media Group	3.6
New Wave Broadcasting	3.1
Fisher Broadcasting	3.0
Other	18.9

Source: *Inside*, December 12, 2000, p. 41, from Arbitron.

★ 1396 ★

Radio Broadcasting (SIC 4832)

Radio Market in Atlanta, GA

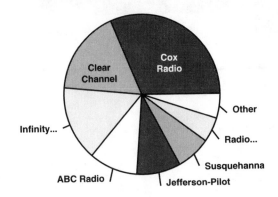

Shares are shown based on revenues.

Cox Radio	31.3%
Clear Channel	17.2
Infinity Broadcasting	14.9
ABC Radio	10.4
Jefferson-Pilot	9.4
Susquehanna	6.9
Radio One	5.1
Other	4.8

Source: *Mediaweek*, October 9, 2000, p. 26.

★ 1397 ★

Radio Broadcasting (SIC 4832)

Radio Market in Canada, 1998-2000

Adult contemporary	26.8%
News/talk	21.7
Contemporary hit radio	18.9
Album-oriented rock	7.2
Classical	7.0
Country	5.8
Classic rock	3.3
Gold	3.1
Full service	2.1
Others	4.1

Source: *Marketing Magazine*, October 16, 2000, p. 15, from Bohn & Associates Media.

★ 1398 ★
Radio Broadcasting (SIC 4832)

Radio Market in Detroit, MI

Shares are shown based on revenues.

Clear Channel Communications	34.0%
Infinity	26.5
ABC Radio	16.3
Greater Media	11.9
Radio One	3.4
Crawford Broadcasting	0.6
Other	7.3

Source: *Mediaweek*, October 16, 2000, p. 26.

★ 1399 ★
Radio Broadcasting (SIC 4832)

Radio Market in Houston, TX

Clear Channel Communications
Infinity
Radio One
Cox Radio
El Dorado Communications
Other

Shares are shown based on revenues.

Clear Channel Communications	39.6%
Infinity	13.2
Radio One	12.6
Cox Radio	11.0
El Dorado Communications	3.0
Other	20.6

Source: *Mediaweek*, October 23, 2000, p. 26.

★ 1400 ★
Radio Broadcasting (SIC 4832)

Radio Market in Los Angeles, CA

Shares are shown based on revenues.

Infinity Broadcasting	33.2%
Clear Channel Communications	30.5
Hispanic Broadcasting	8.4
ABC Radio	6.4
Emmis Communications	6.4
Radio One	4.8
Other	10.3

Source: *Mediaweek*, October 9, 2000, p. 26.

★ 1401 ★
Radio Broadcasting (SIC 4832)

Streaming Radio Market Shares

Figures are baased on an aggregate of 16.8 million listening hours during October 2000.

Netradio	27.6%
Global Media	12.7
ABC Radio	10.5
Live365	9.8
Broadcast America	8.0
Enigma Digital	3.0
Other	28.4

Source: *Inside*, March 6, 2001, p. 27.

★ 1402 ★
Radio Broadcasting (SIC 4832)

Top Radio Stations, 2000

Stations are ranked by estimated revenue in millions of dollars.

KIIS-FM	$ 65.5
WFAN-AM	65.2
WXRK-FM	61.0
WLTW-FM	60.7
WINS-AM	57.4
WHTZ-FM	49.0
KROQ-FM	48.7
KGO-AM	48.1
WKTY-FM	48.0
WCBS-AM	47.6

Source: *Inside*, April 3, 2001, p. 41, from BIA Financial Network.

★ 1403 ★
Radio Broadcasting (SIC 4832)

Top Webcasting Stations

Data show time spent listening, in hours.

WABC-AM	107,409
The Beat LA	59,590
WBAP-AM	53,188
KSFO-AM	49,237
WLS-AM	40,116

Source: *Wall Street Journal*, December 11, 2000, p. B12, from Measurecast.

★ 1404 ★

Television Broadcasting (SIC 4833)

Digital TV Stations by State

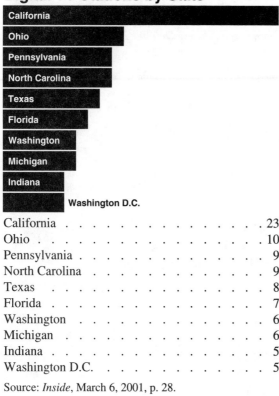

California	
Ohio	
Pennsylvania	
North Carolina	
Texas	
Florida	
Washington	
Michigan	
Indiana	
Washington D.C.	

California	23
Ohio	10
Pennsylvania	9
North Carolina	9
Texas	8
Florida	7
Washington	6
Michigan	6
Indiana	5
Washington D.C.	5

Source: *Inside*, March 6, 2001, p. 28.

★ 1405 ★

Television Broadcasting (SIC 4833)

Largest TV Networks

Companies are ranked by revenue in billions of dollars.

NBC	$ 4.7
ABC	4.3
CBS	3.5
QVC	3.3
ESPN	2.1
Fox	1.7
HBO	1.7
HSN	1.5
TNT	1.1
Nickelodeon	1.0

Source: *Broadcasting & Cable*, November 27, 2000, p. 54.

★ 1406 ★

Television Broadcasting (SIC 4833)

Spanish TV Market

Market shares are shown in percent.

Univision	74.0%
Telemundo	26.0

Source: *Hollywood Reporter*, September 12, 2000, p. 84.

★ 1407 ★

Broadcasting (SIC 4841)

Broadcasting Market Shares

Low-power satellites include large backyard dishes, also known as c-band dishes.

	2000	2004
Cable	66.9%	70.5%
Satellite	15.1	22.6
Low-power satellite	1.3	0.3
Telephone	0.5	1.4

Source: *USA TODAY*, August 14, 2000, p. 2B, from Merrill Lynch.

★ 1408 ★

Cable Broadcasting (SIC 4841)

Cable Market in Southeast Michigan

Market shares are shown in percent. Comcast is the fifth largest cable company in the United States, with estimated subscribers of 5.7 million.

Comcast	81.0%
Other	19.0

Source: *Detroit Free Press*, January 4, 2001, p. C1.

★ 1409 ★

Cable Broadcasting (SIC 4841)

Cable Market in Washington/ Baltimore Area

Market shares are shown in percent.

Comcast	80.0%
Other	20.0

Source: *Warren's Cable Regulation Monitor*, January 29, 2001, p. 1.

★ 1410 ★
Cable Broadcasting (SIC 4841)

Children's Favorite Networks

Data show thousands of viewers.

Nickelodeon	1,600
TBS	1,200
Lifetime	1,000
Cartoon Network	1,000
TNT	878
USA	830
ESPN	827
A&E	801
Disney Channel	734
CNN	654

Source: *USA TODAY*, January 12, 2001, p. 2E.

★ 1411 ★
Cable Broadcasting (SIC 4841)

Interactive Television Subscriber Market

DBS stands for direct broadcast satellite.

	2001	2006
Digital cable	26.0%	52.0%
DBS	43.0	43.0
Stand-alone	31.0	5.0

Source: *Broadcasting & Cable*, December 18, 2000, p. 60, from The Carmel Group.

★ 1412 ★
Cable Broadcasting (SIC 4841)

Largest Cable Markets

Data show thousands of subscribers.

New York City, NY	1,180
Tampa Bay, FL	903
Central Florida	669
Houston, TX	665
Raleigh/Fayetteville, N.C.	441
Milwaukee, MN	426

Source: *Wall Street Journal*, December 15, 2000, p. B1.

★ 1413 ★
Cable Broadcasting (SIC 4841)

Largest Cable/Satellite Broadcasters

Data show millions of subscribers.

Time Warner	12.7
AT&T	11.1
DirecTV	7.4
Comcast	7.1
Charter	6.2
Cox	6.1
Adelphia	5.0
MediaOne	4.9
EchoStar	3.9
Cablevision	2.8

Source: *Investor's Business Daily*, June 6, 2000, p. A6, from The Yankee Group.

★ 1414 ★
Cable Broadcasting (SIC 4841)

Leading Cable Channels, 2000

Data show average millions of prime time viewers from December 27, 1999 - October 29, 2000.

USA Network	1.7
HBO	1.6
Turner Broadcasting	1.5

Continued on next page.

★ 1414 ★ *Continued*

Cable Broadcasting (SIC 4841)

Leading Cable Channels, 2000

Data show average millions of prime time viewers from December 27, 1999 - October 29, 2000.

Lifetime	1.3
Nickelodeon	1.3
TNT	1.3
A&E	1.1
Cartoon Network	1.1
ESPN	1.0
Disney Channel	0.9

Source: *New York Times*, November 13, 2000, p. C18, from Nielsen Media Research.

★ 1415 ★

Cable Broadcasting (SIC 4841)

Top Cable Companies in Canada

Firms are ranked by millions of subscribers.

Rogers Communications	2.2
Cogeco	1.5
Shaw Communications	1.5
Groupe Videotron	0.8
Moffat Communications	0.3

Source: *Globe and Mail*, August 10, 2000, p. B4, from company reports.

★ 1416 ★

Cable Broadcasting (SIC 4841)

Top Cable Firms

Market shares are shown in percent.

AT&T	24.0%
Time Warner	19.0
SBC/Comcast	11.0
Charter Comm.	9.0
Cox Comm.	9.0
Other	28.0

Source: *New York Times*, October 26, 2000, p. C13, from Yankee Group and Paul Kagan Associates.

★ 1417 ★

Satellite Broadcasting (SIC 4841)

Mexico's Satellite TV Industry

Market shares are shown in percent.

DTH	76.0%
Other	24.0

Source: "First and Final Add." Retrieved October 30, 2000 from the World Wide Web: http://www.prnewswire.com.

★ 1418 ★

Satellite Broadcasting (SIC 4841)

Satellite TV Market Shares

Market shares are shown in percent.

DirecTV	65.3%
Echostar	34.7

Source: *Satellite News*, November 20, 2000, p. 1.

★ 1419 ★

Satellite Broadcasting (SIC 4841)

Satellite TV Market Shares in Canada, 2000

Shares are shown for the second quarter of the year.

Bell ExpressVuy	55.8%
Star Choice	44.2

Source: *TV International*, August 21, 2000, p. 8.

★ 1420 ★

Satellite Broadcasting (SIC 4841)

Subscription TV Market

DirecTV	10.0%
EchoStar	5.0
Others	85.0

Source: *Financial Times*, October 7, 2000, p. 9, from Primark Database, Carmel Group, and FCC.

SIC 49 - Electric, Gas, and Sanitary Services

★ 1421 ★

Energy (SIC 4900)

Energy Consumption in California

Data are in thousands of gigawatt hours.

	(000)	Share
Commercial	93,999	35.93%
Residential	79,067	30.22
Industrial	55,060	21.05
Agriculture	18,035	6.89
Other	15,434	5.90

Source: *Financial Times*, January 19, 2001, p. 4.

★ 1422 ★

Energy (SIC 4900)

U.S. Energy Consumption

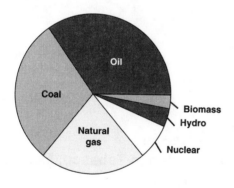

Oil	38.0%
Coal	32.0
Natural gas	24.0
Nuclear	8.0
Hydro	4.0
Biomass	3.0

Source: *Christian Science Monitor*, December 14, 2000, p. 16, from Carbon Sequestrian Research and Development.

★ 1423 ★

Home Heating (SIC 4900)

Home Heating Market in the Northeast

Natural gas	46.4%
Fuel oil	35.9
Electricity	11.9
Propane	1.9
Other	3.6

Source: *USA TODAY*, September 28, 2000, p. 3B, from U.S. Energy Information Administration and Housing Characteristics.

★ 1424 ★

Home Heating (SIC 4900)

Home Heating Market in the South

Electricity	48.7%
Natural gas	38.3
Propane	5.7
Fuel oil	3.1
Other	3.9

Source: *USA TODAY*, September 28, 2000, p. 3B, from U.S. Energy Information Administration and Housing Characteristics.

★ 1425 ★

Home Heating (SIC 4900)

Home Heating Market in the West

Natural gas	58.1%
Electrcity	32.6
Propane	2.5
Fuel oil	1.1
Other	5.2

Source: *USA TODAY*, September 28, 2000, p. 3B, from U.S. Energy Information Administration and Housing Characteristics.

★ 1426 ★

Nuclear Power (SIC 4911)

Largest Nuclear Generating Plants

Plants are ranked by net generation in megawatt hours.

Palo Verde (Arizona Public Services)	30.41
Oconee (Duke Energy)	19.83
South Texas (Reliant Energy)	19.41
Sequoyah (Tennessee Valley)	18.96
Braidwood (Commonwealth Edison)	18.95
Alvin W. Vogtle (Southern Nuclear Operating)	18.48
Browns Ferry (Tennessee Valley)	18.29
Limerick (PECO)	18.29

Source: *Wall Street Journal*, May 2, 2001, p. A25.

★ 1427 ★

Utilities (SIC 4911)

How Electricity Is Sold

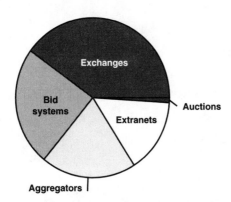

The majority of wholesale transactions among traders in the energy markets are still conducted by telephone trading networks. But by 2004, nearly 20% will occur online. The total online energy business trade: $57 billion in 2000, $111 billion in 2001, $204 billion by 2004. Data show projected location of market transactions in 2004.

Exchanges	40.0%
Bid systems	24.0
Aggregators	20.0
Extranets	15.0
Auctions	1.0

Source: *Industry Standard*, April 17, 2000, p. 189, from Forrester Research.

★ 1428 ★

Utilities (SIC 4911)

Leading Power Marketers

Firms are ranked by sales in megawatt hours.

Enron Power Marketing	392
AEP	306
Aquila Power Corporation	236
PG&E Energy Trading	222
Southern Company Energy	219
Avista Energy	135
Reliant Energy Services	112

Source: *Electric Perspectives*, July/August 2000, p. 7.

★ 1429 ★

Utilities (SIC 4911)

Nuclear Ownership, 2000

In 1995, 46 companies owned 108 plants. There are now 24 owners of 103 plants.

Exelon/Amergen	17.0%
Entergy/FP&L	13.0
NUMCO	7.0
Duke	7.0
Southern	6.0
Dominion	6.0
Progress Energy	5.0
TVA	5.0
Other	34.0

Source: *Utility Business*, April 2001, p. 26, from Constellation.

★ 1430 ★

Gas Distribution (SIC 4923)

Gas Distribution in Tabasco, Mexico

Market shares are shown in percent.

Pemex	75.0%
Other	25.0

Source: *South American Business Information*, March 19, 2001, p. NA.

★ 1431 ★

Gas Distribution (SIC 4923)

Leading Gas Distribution Utilities

Companies are ranked by millions of customers.

Southern California Gas Co.	4.93
Pacific Gas & Electric Co.	3.79
Nicor Gas	1.94
Dominion	1.90
Consumers Energy Co.	1.58
Public Service Electric & Gas Co.	1.57
AGL Resources Inc.	1.52
Reliant Energy Entex	1.46
ONEOK Inc.	1.43
TXU Gas Company	1.38

Source: *Pipeline & Gas Journal*, November 2000, p. 53.

★ 1432 ★

Trash Disposal (SIC 4950)

Largest Trash Haulers

Shares are shown for the top 100 firms.

Waste Management	56.8%
Allied Waste Industries Inc.	16.6
Republic Services Inc.	9.8
Norcal Waste Systems Inc.	1.4
Waste Connections Inc.	1.4
Other	14.0

Source: *Waste News*, June 12, 2000, p. 23.

SIC 50 - Wholesale Trade - Durable Goods

★ 1433 ★
Wholesale Trade - Home Improvement (SIC 5030)

Leading Home Improvement Distributors

Firms are ranked by sales in millions of dollars.

Georgia-Pacific	$ 4,850.0
TruServ	4,505.0
Weyerhaeuser	3,800.0
Ace Hardware	3,181.8
Do it Best	2,377.0
Lumbermen's Merchandising	2,063.0
Universal Forest Products	1,440.0
Boise Cascade	1,273.0
North Pacific Group	1,200.0

Source: *National Home Center News*, July 17, 2000, p. 9.

★ 1434 ★
Wholesale Trade - Business Forms (SIC 5044)

Top Business Form Distributors

Firms are ranked by business form sales in thousands of dollars.

Precept Business Products	$ 104,400
American Business Forms	70,400
ProForma	61,250
SFI	54,768
Data Supplies	51,399

GBS	.$ 40,668
Global DocuGrphix	37,365
Data Source	14,748
The Graphics and Technology Group	14,677

Source: *Business Forms, Labels & Systems*, October 20, 2000, p. 34.

★ 1435 ★
Wholesale Trade - Office Supplies (SIC 5044)

Top Office Supply Stores, 1999

Companies are ranked by revenues in billions of dollars. The office supply business is a $22 billion a year industry.

Office Depot	$ 10.3
Staples	8.8
OfficeMax	4.8

Source: *Dallas Morning News*, July 5, 2000, p. 1D.

★ 1436 ★
Wholesale Trade - Electronics (SIC 5060)

Largest Electronics Distributors, 1999

Market shares are shown among publicly traded companies.

Arrow Electronics	29.0%
Avnet	24.0
Wesco Intl.	10.6
Anixter Intl.	8.4
Pioneer Std.	7.6
Premier Farnell	3.7
Bell Micro	3.5
Kent Electronics	3.0
Reptron	1.2
Other	9.0

Source: *Investor's Business Daily*, June 19, 2000, p. A10.

★ 1437 ★

Wholesale Trade - Batteries (SIC 5065)

Battery Market for OEM Companies

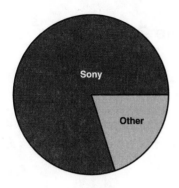

The leading suppliers of batteries to original equipment manufacturers are shown.

Sony	80.0%
Other	20.0

Source: *MMR*, January 8, 2001, p. 42.

★ 1438 ★

Wholesale Trade - Gardening Supplies (SIC 5080)

Where Landscapers Buy Goods

Figures are based on a survey.

Buy from dealer	68.0%
Buy from distributor	67.0
Buy from service vendor	35.0
Buy from manufacturer	34.0
Bid process	25.0
Buying cooperative	12.0
Buy via the Internet	10.0

Source: *Landscape Management*, November 2000, p. 18.

SIC 51 - Wholesale Trade - Nondurable Goods

★ 1439 ★
Contracted Sales Organizations (SIC 5122)
Contract Sales Organization Market

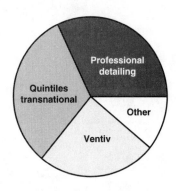

Contract sales organizations, or CSOs, contract with big drug makers and then employ teams of sales reps to peddle their drugs to tens of thousands of doctors every year.

Professional detailing	32.0%
Quintiles transnational	32.0
Ventiv	25.0
Other	11.0

Source: *Investor's Business Daily*, February 14, 2001, p. A10, from company data and W.R. Hambrecht & Co.

★ 1440 ★
Wholesale Trade - Drugs (SIC 5122)
Largest Drug Delivery Firms

Companies are ranked by revenue in millions of dollars.

Elan Corp.	$ 1,007.8
Alza Corp.	795.9
Andrx Corp.	476.0
Dura Pharmaceuticals Inc.	301.4
MiniMed Inc.	212.3
Biovail Corp.	176.5
Alkermes Inc.	43.7

Inhale Therapeutic Systems Inc.	$ 41.4
Meridian Medical Technologies Inc. . . .	40.7

Source: *Med Ad News*, June 2000, p. 1.

★ 1441 ★
Wholesale Trade - Drugs (SIC 5122)
Largest Drug Wholesalers

Market shares are shown in percent.

McKesson HBOC	17.0%
Cardinal	14.0
Bergen Brunswig	12.0
AmeriSource	9.0
Bindley Western	5.0
Other	43.0

Source: *Wall Street Journal*, December 5, 2000, p. A8, from EGS Securities.

★ 1442 ★
Wholesale Trade - Beverages (SIC 5140)
Office Coffee Industry

The market continues with roughly 5% a year growth in revenue. Operators have expanded their products into specialty coffee and advanced brewing systems: airpot, thermal and countertop and single-cup brewers. Coffee makes up 75% of the office productservice industry, with the remainder held by creamer, paper products and other beverages. Table shows the 100,500 single-cup brewers.

	No.	Share
Filterfresh	30,000	29.85%
Crane	25,000	24.88
Keurig	13,000	12.94
Unibrew	9,000	8.96
Flavia	8,000	7.96
Avalon	7,500	7.46

Continued on next page.

332

★ 1442 ★ *Continued*
Wholesale Trade - Beverages (SIC 5140)
Office Coffee Industry

The market continues with roughly 5% a year growth in revenue. Operators have expanded their products into specialty coffee and advanced brewing systems: airpot, thermal and countertop and single-cup brewers. Coffee makes up 75% of the office productservice industry, with the remainder held by creamer, paper products and other beverages. Table shows the 100,500 single-cup brewers.

	No.	Share
Brio	5,000	4.98%
APPART	3,000	2.99

Source: *Automatic Merchandiser*, November 2000, p. 32.

★ 1443 ★
Wholesale Trade - Groceries (SIC 5141)
Top Grocery Distributors

Market shares are shown in percent.

Sysco	12.5%
Ahold/US Foodservice	7.5
Other	80.0

Source: *Forbes*, October 2, 2000, p. 78, from *Supermarket News*.

★ 1444 ★
Wholesale Trade - Groceries (SIC 5141)
Top Grocery Wholesalers, 1999

Firms are ranked by sales in billions of dollars.

Supervalu Inc.	$ 12.2
Fleming Cos.	10.9
C&S Wholesale Grocers Inc.	7.1
NashFinch Co.	4.1
Wakefern Food Corp.	3.9
Associated Wholesale Grocers	3.3
Unified Western Grocers	3.0
Giant Eagle Co.	2.7
Roundy's Inc.	2.6
Penn Traffic Co.	2.4

Source: *Food Institute Report*, November 6, 2000, p. 5.

★ 1445 ★
Wholesale Trade - Chemicals (SIC 5160)
Appearance Chemicals Industry in Ohio

Applied Chemical Technologies has a dominant share of detergents, waxes, tire cleaners and other rinsing agents used at independent car washes.

ACT	75.0%
Other	25.0

Source: *Knight-Ridder/Tribune Business News*, April 17, 2001, p. NA.

★ 1446 ★
Wholesale Trade - Periodicals (SIC 5192)
Magazine Distribution Market

There are roughly 4,700 titles in the marketplace now, a jump from roughly 1,300 25 years ago. The groups are all losing money and often receive cushioning from other profitable businesses.

Anderson Corporation	40.0%
Jim Pattison Group	25.0
Chas. Levy Circulating	17.0
Hudson News	10.0
Other	8.0

Source: *New York Times*, October 23, 2000, p. C20.

★ 1447 ★
Wholesale Trade - Periodicals (SIC 5192)
Magazine Wholesaling in North America

Market shares are shown in percent.

Anderson News	32.0%
News Group	27.0
Chas. Levy Circulating	13.0
Hudson News	11.0
Other	17.0

Source: *Wall Street Journal*, March 5, 2001, p. A6, from Harrington Associates.

★ 1448 ★

Wholesale Trade - Tobacco & Candy (SIC 5194)

Largest Convenience Wholesalers, 1999

Firms are ranked by sales in millions of dollars.

McLane Co. Inc.	$ 14,900
Eby-Brown Co. L.P.	3,010
Core-Mark International	2,800
H.T. Hackney Co.	1,800
GSC Enterprises	1,112
Spartan Stores/Convenience Store	934
Miller & Hartman Co. Inc.	868
S. Abraham & Sons Inc.	819
Harold Levinson Associates	526
Fleming Convenience Marketing & Distribution	508
Minter-Weisman Co.	500

Source: *Convenience Store News*, October 22, 2000, p. 205.

SIC 52 - Building Materials and Garden Supplies

★ 1449 ★
Retailing - Building Materials (SIC 5211)

Top Building Material Markets, 1999

Metro areas are ranked by building material and hardline sales in millions of dollars.

Chicago, IL	$ 5.05
Los Angeles-Long Beach, CA	4.61
Boston, Worcester, Lawrence, Lowell, Brockton, MA	3.74
Detroit, MI	3.08
Washington D.C.-MD-VA-WV	2.95
Philadelphia, PA-NJ	2.72
Minneapolis, St. Paul, MN	2.65
Nassau-Suffolk, NY	2.64
Atlanta, GA	2.60
New York City, NY	2.58

Source: *National Home Center News*, May 22, 2000, p. 114.

★ 1450 ★
Retailing - Home Improvement (SIC 5211)

Home Improvement Industry

Home centers/lumberyards	68.6%
Discount & dept. stores	9.4
Hardware stores	8.9
Lawn & garden stores	5.7
Paint stores	5.1
Variety & general merch. Stores	2.0

Source: *Forest Products Journal*, no. 9, 2000, p. 33.

★ 1451 ★
Retailing - Home Improvement (SIC 5211)

Home Improvement Market, 2005

Sales are shown in billions of dollars.

	($ bil.)	Share
Lumber materials	$ 64.7	28.6%
Lawn & garden	30.2	13.3
Paint	15.1	6.7
Electricals	12.5	5.5
Plumbing	12.5	5.5
Tools	11.9	5.3
Hardware	9.7	4.3
Flooring	6.3	2.8

Source: *National Home Center News*, January 22, 2001, p. 30, from Home Improvement Research Institute.

★ 1452 ★
Retailing - Home Improvement (SIC 5211)

Home Security Sales

The market includes locks, alarms, fire extinguishers and carbon monoxide detectors.

Home centers	42.0%
Lumberyards	33.0
Hardware stores	25.0

Source: *Do-It-Yourself Retailing*, August 2000, p. 278, from National Retail Hardware Association.

★ 1453 ★
Retailing - Home Improvement (SIC 5211)

Largest Home Improvement Retailers, 1999

Firms are ranked by sales in billions of dollars.

Home Depot	$ 38.43
Lowe's	15.90
Menard	4.50

Continued on next page.

★ 1453 ★ *Continued*
Retailing - Home Improvement (SIC 5211)

Largest Home Improvement Retailers, 1999

Firms are ranked by sales in billions of dollars.

Sherwin-Williams	$ 3.00
Payless Cashways	1.82
Carolina Holdings	1.81
84 Lumber	1.78
ICI Paints	1.67
HomeBase	1.53
Builders FirstSource	1.50

Source: *National Home Center News*, August 7, 2000, p. 159.

★ 1454 ★

Retailing - Home Improvement (SIC 5211)

Largest Home Improvement Retailers in Canada

Firms are ranked by sales in millions of dollars.

Canadian Tire	$ 3,705
Home Depot Canada	2,300
Revy Home Centre	800
Beaver Lumber	755
Reno Depot	570
Alpa Lumber	330
Cashway Building Centres	322
ICI Canada	300
Kent Building Supplies	150
Totem Building Supplies	150

Source: *National Home Center News*, May 22, 2000, p. 111.

★ 1455 ★

Retailing - Home Improvement (SIC 5211)

Leading Home Improvement Stores in Milwaukee, WI

Data show the top stores, based on a survey of shoppers.

Home Depot	37.0%
Menards	35.0
Ace	31.0
True Value	17.0

Source: *Milwaukee Journal Sentinel*, March 24, 2001, p. 1.

★ 1456 ★

Retailing - Paint (SIC 5231)

Retail Architectural Paint Sales

Market shares are shown in percent.

Stores	56.0%
Dealers	26.0
Mass merchant	18.0

Source: *Paint & Coatings Industry*, July 2000, p. 114.

★ 1457 ★

Retailing - Paint (SIC 5231)

What People Shop For At Paint Stores, 1999

Figures are based on a survey of respondents who said they had made at least one purchase in each category.

Paint, interior	26.3%
Paint brush/roller/pan/pad	22.7
Caulk	16.1
Tape	15.1
Spray paint	12.7
Paint, exterior	12.1
Sandpaper/steel wool	11.9
Varnish/polyurethane	9.6
Stain	9.4
Adhesive/glue	7.5

Source: *National Home Center News*, October 23, 2000, p. 16, from *HIRI Product Purchase and Product Activity Study, 2000*.

★ 1458 ★

Retailing - Hardware (SIC 5251)

Leading Hardware Chains in Canada, 2000

Market shares are shown based on sales of $24.5 billion.

Canadian Tire	20.3%
Home Hardware	12.1
Home Depot	11.3
Rona	8.2
Revy Home Centres	3.3
Reno Depot	2.7
Other	42.1

Source: *Marketing Magazine*, June 4, 2001, p. NA, from *Hardware Merchandising*.

★ 1459 ★

Retailing - Hardware (SIC 5251)

Retail Hardware Sales

Sales are shown in millions of dollars. Figures are at mass merchandisers.

	($ mil.)	Share
Garden supplies	$ 5,438.1	31.99%
RTA	2,828.3	16.64
Paint & wallpaper	2,230.3	13.12
Batteries, flashlights	1,057.6	6.22
Electrical supplies	760.3	4.47
Hand tools	632.4	3.72
Power tools	614.3	3.61
Security hardware	583.7	3.43
Fasteners	544.1	3.20
Plumbing supplies	529.7	3.12
Heating supplies	257.6	1.52
Lighting fixtures	245.0	1.44
Other	1,277.5	7.52

Source: *Retail Merchandiser*, July 2000, p. 37.

★ 1460 ★

Retailing - Lawn & Garden (SIC 5261)

Leading Lawn & Garden Retailers

Firms are ranked by sales in millions of dollars.

Home Depot	$ 5,490.0
Lowe's Inc.	2,780.0
Wal-Mart	1,317.1
Kmart	1,262.0
Orchard Supply Hardware/Sears	577.5
Frank's Nursery & Crafts	500.0
Target Stores Inc.	376.0
Menard's Inc.	310.0
Price Costco Company	274.7
Albertson's Inc.	230.0

Source: *Nursery Retailer*, April/May 2000, p. 70.

SIC 53 - General Merchandise Stores

★ 1461 ★
General Merchandise (SIC 5300)

Top General Merchandise Markets

Chicago, IL	
Los Angeles/Long Beach, CA	
Detroit, MI	
Washington D.C.	
Atlanta, GA	
Houston, TX	
Philadelphia, PA	
New York City, NY	
Dallas, TX	
Minneapolis/St. Paul, MN	

Markets are ranked by general merchandise sales in millions of dollars.

Chicago, IL	$ 8.64
Los Angeles/Long Beach, CA	7.84
Detroit, MI	6.68
Washington D.C.	5.64
Atlanta, GA	5.44
Houston, TX	5.30
Philadelphia, PA	4.60
New York City, NY	4.59
Dallas, TX	4.42
Minneapolis/St. Paul, MN	4.19

Source: *MMR*, June 26, 2000, p. 12, from *Sales & Marketing Management*.

★ 1462 ★
Retailing (SIC 5300)

Largest Retailers in the Eastern North Central U.S.

Chains are ranked by estimated sales in billions of dollars.

Wal-Mart/Sam's Club	$ 20.9
Meijer	10.0
Kmart	7.9
Walgreens	5.8
Target Stores	5.0
CVS	4.3
Rite Aid	2.3
ShopKo/Pamida	1.3

Source: *Retail Merchandiser*, December 2000, p. 30.

★ 1463 ★
Retailing (SIC 5300)

Largest Retailers in the Pacific U.S.

Chains are ranked by estimated sales in billions of dollars.

Costco	$ 12.4
Wal-Mart/Sam's Club	9.0
Target Stores	5.0
Rite Aid	4.8
Kroger/Fred Meyer	4.7
Long's Drug	4.1
Kmart	4.0
Osco Drug/Sav-On Drug	2.3

Source: *Retail Merchandiser*, December 2000, p. 30, from Trade Dimensions.

★ 1464 ★
Retailing (SIC 5300)

Largest Retailers in the South Atlantic U.S.

Chains are ranked by estimated sales in billions of dollars.

Wal-Mart/Sam's Club	$ 29.8
Kmart	7.6
Eckerd Drug	6.1
CVS	5.3
Target Stores	4.9
Walgreens	3.7
Costco	3.3
Rite Aid	1.8

Source: *Retail Merchandiser*, December 2000, p. 30, from Trade Dimensions.

★ 1465 ★
Retailing (SIC 5300)

Largest U.S. Retailers, 1999

Firms are ranked by revenues in millions of dollars.

Wal-Mart	$ 166.80
Kroger Co.	45.35
Sears, Roebuck and Co.	41.07
Home Depot	38.43
Albertson's	37.47
Kmart Corp.	35.92
Target Corp.	33.70
J.C. Penney	32.51
Safeway	28.85
Costco	27.45

Source: *Chain Store Age*, August 2000, p. 4A.

★ 1466 ★
Retailing (SIC 5300)

Retail Market Shares

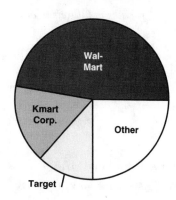

Market shares are shown in percent.

Wal-Mart	47.8%
Kmart Corp.	15.6
Target	11.5
Other	25.1

Source: *Detroit Free Press*, August 17, 2000, p. C1.

★ 1467 ★
Retailing (SIC 5300)

Retail Stores by Classification, 1999

Sales are shown in millions of dollars.

Discount department stores	$ 149,608
Supercenters	70,975
Warehouse clubs	58,256
Specialty mass retailers	46,262
Consumer electronics retailers	30,937
Off-price apparel chains	24,111
Office supplies superstores	16,080
Automotive aftermarket chains	10,995
PX retailers	10,008
Toy superstores	9,042
Home furnishings chains	7,732
Electronic retailers	7,395

Source: *Discount Store News*, July 10, 2000, p. 10.

★ 1468 ★
Retailing (SIC 5300)

Top Retail Sales Areas

Metro areas are ranked by sales in billions of dollars.

Chicago, IL	$ 101.5
Los Angeles-Long Beach, CA	99.8
New York City, NY	80.1
Detroit, MI	62.2
Atlanta, GA	59.6
Washington D.C.	58.2
Philadelphia, PA	58.2
Boston-Lawrence-Lowell-Brockton, MA	56.2

Source: *Sales & Marketing Magazine Survey of Buying Power, 2000*, Annual, p. 6.

★ 1469 ★
Department Stores (SIC 5311)

Leading Department Stores in Canada, 2000

Market shares are shown in percent.

Wal-Mart	36.4%
Zellers	25.9
Sears Canada	22.2
The Bay	15.6

Source: *Marketing Magazine*, June 4, 2001, p. NA, from Kubas Consultants.

★ 1470 ★
Convenience Stores (SIC 5331)

Convenience Store Sales

Tobacco	36.0%
Foodservice	14.0
Beer/wine/liquor	12.0
Packaged beverages	11.0%
Candy/gum	5.0
Publications	3.0
Breads cake	3.0
Salty snacks	3.0
Milk products	3.0
Groceries	1.0
Other	9.0

Source: *Research Alert*, May 4, 2001, p. 1.

★ 1471 ★
Discount Merchandising (SIC 5331)

Discount Merchandising by State

Sales are shown in billions of dollars. Data include clubs and supercenters.

California	$ 9.3
Texas	8.4
Ohio	6.3
Michigan	5.9
Florida	5.1
Washington	3.4
Indiana	3.3
Illinois	3.2
Virginia	3.1
New York	3.1

Source: *DSN Supercenter & Club Business*, August 14, 2000, p. 1, from *Supermerchants Market Guide, 1999*.

★ 1472 ★
Discount Merchandising (SIC 5331)

Discount Merchandising in Dallas/Ft. Worth, TX, 1999

Market shares are shown in percent.

Wal-Mart Supercenter	56.3%
Sam's Clubs	43.7

Source: *DSN Supercenter & Club Business*, August 28, 2000, p. 1, from *Supermerchants Market Guide, 1999*.

★ 1473 ★
Discount Merchandising (SIC 5331)

Largest Dollar Stores

Companies are ranked by number of stores.

Dollar General Corp.	4,889
Family Dollar Stores	3,817
Dollar Tree Stores	1,729
Bill's Dollar Stores	500
Dollar Discount Stores of America	135
99 Cents Only Stores	100

Source: *Chain Store Age*, February 2001, p. 36.

★ 1474 ★
Discount Merchandising (SIC 5331)

Leading Discount Retailers

Firms are ranked by sales in billions of dollars.

Wal-Mart	$ 165.0
Kmart	35.9
Costco	27.0
Target	26.1
Meijer	9.0
Zellers	4.6
B.J.'s	4.1
Shopko	3.9
Ames	3.8
Bradlee's	1.5

Source: *MMR*, 5/08/00, p. 31.

★ 1475 ★
Discount Merchandising (SIC 5331)

Membership Club Market in Baltimore/ Washington D.C.

Market shares are shown in percent.

Costco	54.7%
Sam's	24.6
BJ's	20.7

Source: *DSN Supercenter & Club Business*, November 27, 2000, p. 1, from *Supermerchants Market Guide*.

★ 1476 ★
Discount Merchandising (SIC 5331)

Membership Club Market in Chicago, IL

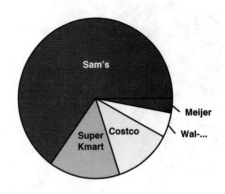

Market shares are shown in percent.

Sam's	64.9%
Super Kmart	15.2
Costco	12.0
Wal-Mart Supercenters	4.7
Meijer	3.2

Source: *DSN Supercenter & Club Business*, October 23, 2000, p. 1, from *Supermerchants Market Guide*.

★ 1477 ★
Discount Merchandising (SIC 5331)

Membership Club Market in San Francisco, CA

Market shares are shown in percent.

Costco.	97.0%
Other	3.0

Source: *DSN Supercenter & Club Business*, November 6, 2000, p. 1, from *Supermerchants Market Guide*.

★ 1478 ★

Discount Merchandising (SIC 5331)

Membership Club Market in Virginia

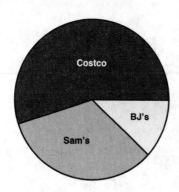

Market shares are shown in percent.

Costco 54.9%
Sam's 33.2
BJ's 11.9

Source: *DSN Supercenter & Club Business*, July 10, 2000, p. 1, from *Supermerchants Market Guide* and J.M. Degen & Company Inc.

★ 1479 ★

Discount Merchandising (SIC 5331)

Membership Club Market in Washington

Market shares are shown in percent.

Costco 50.3%
Fred Meyer 45.4
Sam's Club 4.3

Source: *DSN Supercenter & Club Business*, June 16, 2000, p. 1, from *Supermerchants Market Guide, 1999* and J.M. Degen & Co.

★ 1480 ★

Discount Merchandising (SIC 5331)

Top Supercenters in Colorado, 1999

The supercenter and club market was valued at $2.1 - $2.3 billion.

Wal-Mart 76.8%
Super Kmart 16.8
Biggs 6.4

Source: *DSN Supercenter & Club Business*, April 24, 2000, p. 1.

★ 1481 ★

Discount Merchandising (SIC 5331)

Top Supercenters in Georgia

Market shares are shown in percent.

Wal-Mart 92.3%
Other 7.7

Source: *DSN Supercenter & Club Business*, June 26, 2000, p. 1.

★ 1482 ★

Discount Merchandising (SIC 5331)

Top Supercenters in Ohio

Market shares are shown in percent.

Wal-Mart 42.5%
Meijer 37.0
Sam's Clubs 17.0
Super Kmart 3.5

Source: *DSN Supercenter & Club Business*, July 10, 2000, p. 1, from *Supermerchants Market Guide* and J.M. Degen & Company Inc.

SIC 54 - Food Stores

★ 1483 ★
Grocery Stores (SIC 5411)

Largest Food Retailers in Hampton Roads, VA

Market shares are shown in percent. Among super-markets only, Food Lion took 46.9% of the market.

Food Lion	24.7%
Farm Fresh	17.2
Other	58.9

Source: *Knight-Ridder/Tribune Business News*, June 23, 2001, p. NA.

★ 1484 ★
Grocery Stores (SIC 5411)

Largest Grocery Stores

Total sales reached $515.1 billion.

Wal-Mart Supercenters	11.1%
Kroger Co.	9.6
Albertson's	7.1
Safeway	6.4
Ahold USA	5.3
Supervalu	4.5
Fleming	2.9
Publix Super Markets	2.7
Winn-Dixie Stores	2.7
Loblaw Cos.	2.7
Delhaize America	2.5
A&P	2.1
Other	40.4

Source: *Supermarket News*, January 22, 2001, p. 1, from U.S. Department of Commerce.

★ 1485 ★
Grocery Stores (SIC 5411)

Leading Online Grocers in Canada, 2000

Grocery sales are shown in millions of Canadian dollars.

	($ mil.)	Share
Grocery Gateway	$ 8	32.0%
Vancouver Organic Cos.	8	32.0
Peachtree Affiliates	3	12.0
Loblaw E-grocer	2	8.0
EZGrocer	1	4.0
IGA Cybergrocer	1	4.0
Other	2	8.0

Source: *Canadian Grocer*, March 2001, p. 1, from National Bank Financial, *The Green Report*.

★ 1486 ★
Grocery Stores (SIC 5411)

Top Grocery Stores in Richmond, VA

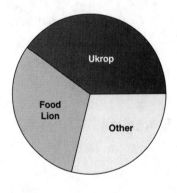

Market shares are shown in percent.

Ukrop	39.71%
Food Lion	31.13
Other	29.16

Source: *Knight-Ridder Tribune Business News*, June 14, 2000, p. NA.

★ 1487 ★

Grocery Stores (SIC 5411)

Top Grocery Markets

Markets are ranked by supermarket sales in millions of dollars.

Los Angeles/Long Beach, CA	$ 12.54
Chicago, IL	10.32
New York City, NY	8.64
Washington D.C.	8.34
Philadelphia, PA	8.19
Boston/Lawrence/Lowell/Brockton, MA	7.54
Houston, TX	7.43
Atlanta, GA	7.12
Phoenix/Mesa, AZ	6.17
Detroit, MI	5.59

Source: *MMR*, June 26, 2000, p. 12, from *Sales & Marketing Management*.

★ 1488 ★

Grocery Stores (SIC 5411)

Top Grocery Markets in Canada, 2000

Grocery sales are shown in billions of Canadian dollars.

	($ bil.)	Share
Ontario	$ 17.84	31.52%
Quebec	14.40	25.44
British Columbia	8.18	14.45
Alberta	6.76	11.94
Atlantic Provinces	5.26	9.29
Manitoba/Sakatchewan	4.16	7.35

Source: *Canadian Grocer*, January/February 2001, p. 1, from A.C. Nielsen MarketTrack.

★ 1489 ★

Grocery Stores (SIC 5411)

Top Grocery Stores, 1999

Market shares are shown in percent.

Kroger	12.4%
Albertson's	10.1
Safeway Inc.	7.9
Ahold USA	5.8
Costco Companies	4.8
Winn-Dixie Stores	3.7
Wal-Mart Supercenters	3.5
Publix Super Markets Inc.	3.3
Delhaize America	3.0

Great Atlantic & Pacific Tea Co.	2.8%
Sam's Club	2.5
H.E. Butt Grocery Co.	2.1
Other	42.7

Source: *Feedstuffs*, July 24, 2000, p. 6, from Food Marketing Institute.

★ 1490 ★

Grocery Stores (SIC 5411)

Top Grocery Stores in Arkansas

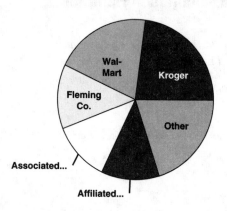

Market shares are shown in percent.

Kroger	23.3%
Wal-Mart	19.5
Fleming Co.	13.0
Associated Wholesale Grocers	12.0
Affiliated Foods Southeast	12.0
Other	20.2

Source: *Arkansas Business*, April 24, 2000, p. 1.

★ 1491 ★

Grocery Stores (SIC 5411)

Top Grocery Stores in Atlanta, GA

Data are for 1998.

Kroger's	26.2%
Publix	22.1
Winn-Dixie's	12.0
Other	39.7

Source: *Supermarket News*, August 21, 2000, p. 1.

★ 1492 ★
Grocery Stores (SIC 5411)

Top Grocery Stores in Austin, TX

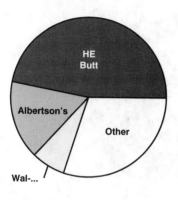

Data are for 1998.

HE Butt 46.8%
Albertson's 16.3
Wal-mart Supercenters 7.1
Other 29.8

Source: *Supermarket News*, August 21, 2000, p. 1.

★ 1493 ★
Grocery Stores (SIC 5411)

Top Grocery Stores in Canada

Market shares are shown in percent.

Loblaw Cos. Ltd. 35.0%
Sobey's Inc. 20.0
Canada Safeway Ltd. 9.0
Metro Inc. 7.0
A&P Canada 6.0
Overwaitea Food Group 4.0
Other 19.0

Source: *Progressive Grocer*, March 2001, p. 14, from Standard & Poor's and Toronto/AC Nielsen.

★ 1494 ★
Grocery Stores (SIC 5411)

Top Grocery Stores in Charlotte, N.C.

Selected shares are shown in percent.

Food Lion 32.21%
Hannaford 4.29
Other 64.50

Source: *Business Journal - Serving Charlotte and the Metropolitan Area*, June 9, 2000, p. 3, from Shelby Report.

★ 1495 ★
Grocery Stores (SIC 5411)

Top Grocery Stores in Dallas, TX

Market shares are shown in percent. The market is worth $10 billion a year.

Albertson's 23.1%
Tom Thumb 21.4
Other 55.5

Source: *Knight-Ridder/Tribune Business News*, March 1, 2001, p. NA.

★ 1496 ★
Grocery Stores (SIC 5411)

Top Grocery Stores in Detroit, MI

Shares are for 2000.

Farmer Jack 27.1%
Kroger 22.3
Meijer 10.5
Other 40.1

Source: *Crain's Detroit Business*, December 11, 2000, p. 25, from Food Marketing Institute.

★ 1497 ★

Grocery Stores (SIC 5411)

Top Grocery Stores in Fort Worth/Arlington, TX

Market shares are shown in percent.

Albertson's	28.0%
Winn-Dixie	16.7
Kroger	15.3
Minyard	13.0
Wal-Mart	3.0
Other	24.0

Source: *Florida Times Union*, June 6, 2000, p. F1, from FTC.

★ 1498 ★

Grocery Stores (SIC 5411)

Top Grocery Stores in Little Rock, Arkansas

Market shares are shown in percent.

Kroger	47.82%
Wal-Mart	18.11
Supermarket Inv.	15.88
Military	4.10
Knight's Inc.	3.84
Harp's Food	2.56
Sexton Food	1.02
Wild Oats	0.90
Save-A-Lot	0.64
Other	5.13

Source: *Arkansas Business*, November 6, 2000, p. 1, from Shelby Report/Trade Dimensions.

★ 1499 ★

Grocery Stores (SIC 5411)

Top Grocery Stores in New England

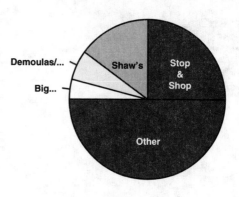

The grocery market in the region is valued at $27.1 billion.

Stop & Shop	24.75%
Shaw's	14.97
Demoulas/Market Basket of Tewksbury	6.38
Big Y Foods Inc. of Springfield	4.00
Other	49.90

Source: *Boston Business Journal*, December 22, 2000, p. 1.

★ 1500 ★

Grocery Stores (SIC 5411)

Top Grocery Stores in New York City, NY

Market shares are shown in percent.

ShopRite	18.1%
A&P	15.2
Pathmark	13.1
Grand Union	7.3
Edwards	6.1
Other	40.3

Source: *Supermarket Business*, July 15, 2000, p. 22, from Trade Dimensions Market Scope.

★ 1501 ★
Grocery Stores (SIC 5411)

Top Grocery Stores in Northern Virginia

Market shares are shown in percent.

SunTrust Banks Inc.	14.0%
First Union Corp.	11.0
Bank of America	11.0
Wachovia	9.0
Other	55.0

Source: *Knight-Ridder/Tribune Business News*, January 24, 2001, p. NA, from SNL Securities.

★ 1502 ★
Grocery Stores (SIC 5411)

Top Grocery Stores in Omaha, Nebraska

Market shares are shown based on number of outlets.

Bakers	24.5%
Hy-Vee	19.7
No Frills	10.6
Albertson's	9.9
Bag N Save	6.8
Wal-Mart Supercenter	3.0
Military	2.6
B&R Stores	2.5
Other	20.4

Source: *Supermarket Business*, October 15, 2000, p. 28.

★ 1503 ★
Grocery Stores (SIC 5411)

Top Grocery Stores in Ontario, Canada

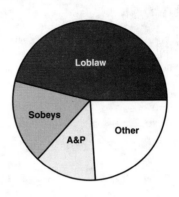

Market shares are shown in percent.

Loblaw	46.0%
Sobeys	17.0
A&P	13.0
Other	24.0

Source: *Progressive Grocer*, March 2001, p. 14, from Dlouhy Merchant Bank Inc.

★ 1504 ★
Grocery Stores (SIC 5411)

Top Grocery Stores in Philadelphia, PA

The industry is valued at $7.2 billion.

Acme Markets	26.7%
ShopRite	12.1
Genuardi's Markets Inc.	11.7
Pathmark	9.3
Other	40.2

Source: *Philadelphia Inquirer*, July 7, 2000, p. 1, from *Food Trade Network*.

★ 1505 ★

Grocery Stores (SIC 5411)

Top Grocery Stores in Phoenix, AZ

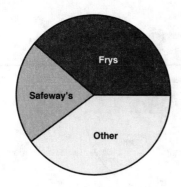

Market shares are shown in percent.

Frys	39.0%
Safeway's	21.0
Other	40.0

Source: *Knight-Ridder/Tribune Business News*, June 19, 2000, p. NA.

★ 1506 ★

Grocery Stores (SIC 5411)

Top Grocery Stores in Pittsburgh, PA

Market shares are shown in percent.

Giant Eagle	52.3%
Supervalu	36.5
Wal-Mart	2.7
Other	8.5

Source: *Knight-Ridder/Tribune Business News*, March 24, 2001, p. NA, from TradeDimensions.

★ 1507 ★

Grocery Stores (SIC 5411)

Top Grocery Stores in Salt Lake City, Utah

Market shares are shown in percent.

Smith's Food & Drug	24.9%
Albertson's	22.9
Harmons City	7.4
Macey's	6.1
Reams Food Stores	4.3
My Stores	3.4
Fred Meyer	3.2

Dans Foods	2.7%
Other	25.1

Source: *Supermarket Business*, July 15, 2000, p. 44.

★ 1508 ★

Grocery Stores (SIC 5411)

Top Grocery Stores in South Carolina

Market shares are shown in percent.

Food Lion	18.0%
Bi-Lo	14.8
Piggly Wiggly	14.1
Other	53.1

Source: *Knight-Ridder/Tribune Business News*, August 1, 2000, p. NA, from Market Scope.

★ 1509 ★

Grocery Stores (SIC 5411)

Top Grocery Stores in the Buffalo, N.Y. Area

Shares refer to the Buffalo/Niagara Falls/Rochester/ Erie P.A. area.

Tops	35.6%
Wegmans	35.1
Quality	10.0
Jubilee	8.0
Other	11.3

Source: *Knight-Ridder/Tribune Business News*, August 7, 2000, p. NA, from *Progressive Grocer*.

★ 1510 ★

Grocery Stores (SIC 5411)

Top Grocery Stores in the Triangle Area, North Carolina

Market shares are shown in percent.

Food Lion	40.0%
Harris Teeter	18.0
Kroger	14.0
Winn-Dixie	8.0
Other	20.0

Source: *News & Observer*, September 30, 2000, p. D1, from Shelby Report.

★ 1511 ★

Grocery Stores (SIC 5411)

Top Grocery Stores in Washington D.C.

Market shares are shown in percent.

Giant Food	41.2%
Safeway	25.6
Shoppers Food Warehouse	12.6
Food Lion	6.2
Other	14.4

Source: *Washington Business Journal*, April 27, 2001, p. 3.

★ 1512 ★

Retailing - Beverages (SIC 5411)

Retail Beverage Sales

Market shares are shown in percent.

Supermarkets	72.0%
Convenience stores & gas stations	19.0
Discount stores	9.0
Drug stores	4.0

Source: *MMR*, February 19, 2001, p. 16, from Coca Cola Co. and A.C. Nielsen.

★ 1513 ★

Retailing - Beverages (SIC 5411)

Retail Milk Sales

Sales are shown in millions of dollars.

	($ mil.)	Share
Supermarkets	$ 4,880	77.91%
Foodservice	526	8.40
Mass	282	4.50
Wholesale clubs	212	3.38
C-stores	197	3.14
Drug stores	76	1.21
Home delivery	52	0.83
Military	39	0.62

Source: *Dairy Foods*, February 2001, p. 17, from Beverage Marketing Corp., International Dairy Foods Association, and A.C. Nielsen.

★ 1514 ★

Retailing - Food (SIC 5411)

Retail Sports Beverage Sales, 1999

Sales reached $1.7 billion and 635.9 million gallons.

Convenience store/down the street	48.0%
Supermarkets	28.0
Mass merchandisers	8.0
Club stores	7.0
Vending	5.0
Drug stores	2.0
Foodservice	2.0

Source: *Beverage Aisle*, October 15, 2000, p. 22, from Beverage Marketing Corp.

★ 1515 ★

Retailing - Food (SIC 5411)

Where Ice Cream Is Sold

Market shares are shown in percent.

Supermarkets	54.1%
Scoop shops	24.5
Convenience stores	7.1
Vending	4.4
Other	9.9

Source: *Dairy Foods*, March 2001, p. 24, from Market Facts.

★ 1516 ★

Retailing - Confectionery Products (SIC 5441)

Candy and Gum Sales

Food stores	45.4%
Mass merchandisers	34.0
Drug stores	20.6

Source: *Brand Packaging*, July 2000, p. 4.

★ 1517 ★

Retailing - Confectionery Products (SIC 5441)

Where Candy is Sold

Candy and snacks have turned into a high profit category in mass merchants and drug stores.

	($ mil.)	Share
Food	$ 4,994	41.94%
Mass	2,342	19.67
Drug	2,329	19.56
Convenience	2,242	18.83

Source: *DSN Retailing Today*, May 21, 2001, p. 2, from A.C. Nielsen Convenience Track Major Markets.

SIC 55 - Automotive Dealers and Service Stations

★ 1518 ★

Auto Dealerships (SIC 5511)

Largest New/Used Car Dealerships

Dealerships are ranked by sales in millions of dollars. Sales include used and new cars, body shop business and auto parts.

Ricart Automotive	$ 469.2
Galpin Ford	394.9
Brown & Brown Chevrolet	310.1
Landmark Chevrolet	277.8
Fletcher Jones Motorcars	276.4
Prestige Ford	264.3
Earnhardt Ford Sales Co.	260.6
JM Lexus	256.7
Mullinax Ford South	256.2
Smythe European	251.1

Source: *Ward's Dealer Business*, June 2000, p. 30.

★ 1519 ★

Retailing - Auto Supplies (SIC 5531)

Auto Accessory Sales

Sales are shown in millions of dollars. Figures are at mass merchandisers.

	($ mil.)	Share
Motor oil	$ 1,947,725	24.01%
Accessories	1,118,664	13.79
Car stereos	856,664	10.56
Parts	807,158	9.95
Filters	602,732	7.43
Batteries	556,493	6.86
Antifreeze	492,407	6.07
Waxes & polishes	473,748	5.84
Ignition/electrical	412,096	5.08
Chemicals/additives	327,730	4.04
D-I-Y books	47,861	0.59
Other	468,865	5.78

Source: *Retail Merchandiser*, July 2000, p. 37.

★ 1520 ★

Retailing - Auto Supplies (SIC 5531)

Auto Air Freshener Sales, 2000

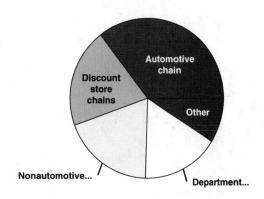

Total aftermarket sales reached $301 million.

Automotive chain	39.0%
Discount store chains	22.0
Nonautomotive chain	21.0
Department store chain	18.0
Other	10.0

Source: *Aftermarket Business*, April 2001, p. 24.

★ 1521 ★

Retailing - Auto Supplies (SIC 5531)

Largest Auto Store Chains

Companies are ranked by number of outlets.

AutoZone Inc.	2,854
Advance Auto Parts	1,617
CSK Auto Inc.	1,120
General Parts Inc.	1,055
Genuine Parts (NAPA Auto Parts)	908
Pep Boys	662
Discount Auto Parts	645
O'Reilly Automotive Inc.	628
Restoration Auto LLC	270
Fisher Auto Parts	260

Source: *Automotive Marketing*, July 2000, p. 1.

★ 1522 ★
Retailing - Auto Supplies (SIC 5531)

Largest Auto Supply Stores

Companies are ranked by sales in millions of dollars.

AutoZone . . . . $ 397
Advance 356
Pep Boys 250
CSK 249

Source: *Aftermarket Business*, May 2001, p. 1.

★ 1523 ★
Retailing - Auto Supplies (SIC 5531)

Retail Antifreeze Sales, 2000

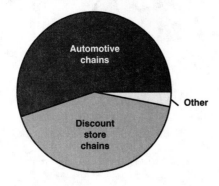

Total aftermarket sales reached $3 billion.

Automotive chains 55.0%
Discount store chains 42.0
Other 3.0

Source: *Aftermarket Business*, April 2001, p. 24.

★ 1524 ★
Retailing - Auto Supplies (SIC 5531)

Retail Auto Battery Sales, 2000

Total aftermarket sales reached $9.6 billion.

Automotive chains 52.0%
Discount store chains 38.0
Department stores 8.0
Nonautomotive chains 2.0

Source: *Aftermarket Business*, April 2001, p. 24.

★ 1525 ★
Retailing - Auto Supplies (SIC 5531)

Retail Auxiliary Lighting Sales, 2000

Total aftermarket sales reached $36 million.

Automotive chains 52.0%
Discount store chains 44.0
Other 4.0

Source: *Aftermarket Business*, April 2001, p. 24.

★ 1526 ★
Retailing - Auto Supplies (SIC 5531)

Retail Cargo Liner Sales, 2000

Total aftermarket sales reached $87 million.

Automotive chains 71.0%
Discount store chains 18.0
Department store chains 10.0
Nonautomotive chains 1.0

Source: *Aftermarket Business*, April 2001, p. 24.

★ 1527 ★
Retailing - Auto Supplies (SIC 5531)

Retail Dashboard Cover Sales, 2000

Market shares are shown in percent.

Automotive chains 78.0%
Discount store chains 19.0
Department store chains 2.0
Nonautomotive chains 1.0

Source: *Aftermarket Business*, April 2001, p. 24.

★ 1528 ★
Retailing - Auto Supplies (SIC 5531)

Retail Electronic Security Sales, 2000

Total aftermarket sales reached $355 million.

Non-automotive chains 38.0%
Automotive chains 32.0
Discount store chains 20.0
Department store chains 10.0

Source: *Aftermarket Business*, April 2001, p. 24.

★ 1529 ★

Retailing - Auto Supplies (SIC 5531)

Retail Floor Mat Sales, 2000

Total aftermarket sales reached $245 million.

Discount store chains	56.0%
Automotive chains	41.0
Other	3.0

Source: *Aftermarket Business*, April 2001, p. 24.

★ 1530 ★

Retailing - Auto Supplies (SIC 5531)

Retail Motor Oil Sales, 1999

Sales are shown in millions of dollars.

	($ mil.)	Share
Mass	$ 690.7	91.07%
Supermarkets	55.2	7.28
Drug chains	12.5	1.65

Source: *Lubricants World*, October 2000, p. 16, from *Private Label Merchandiser Association 2000 Private Label Yearbook*.

★ 1531 ★

Retailing - Auto Supplies (SIC 5531)

Retail Touchup Paint Sales, 2000

Total aftermarket sales reached $461 million.

Automotive chains	62.0%
Discount store chains	35.0
Nonautomotive chains	2.0
Department store chains	1.0

Source: *Aftermarket Business*, April 2001, p. 24.

★ 1532 ★

Retailing - Auto Supplies (SIC 5531)

Retail Wiper Blade Sales, 2000

Total aftermarket sales reached $723 million.

Automotive chains	53.0%
Discount store chains	42.0
Department store chains	4.0
Nonautomotive chains	1.0

Source: *Aftermarket Business*, April 2001, p. 24.

★ 1533 ★

Retailing - Tires (SIC 5531)

Largest Tire Dealerships

Companies are ranked by commercial sales in millions of dollars.

Treadco Inc.	$ 186.6
Les Schwab Tire Centers	169.8
Kal Tire	157.0
Purcell Tire & Rubber Co.	116.0
Parkhouse Tire Inc.	89.0
Pomp's Tire Service Inc.	89.0
Bauer Built Inc.	85.0
Cross-Midwest Tire	80.0
Snider Tire Inc.	66.0

Source: *Tire Business*, January 29, 2001, p. 4.

★ 1534 ★

Aftermarket Services (SIC 5541)

Automotive Aftermarket Services in North America

Sales are shown in millions of dollars.

	1999	2004
Mechanical	$ 18,755	$ 22,625
Exterior & structural	12,325	14,500
Electrical	7,210	8,935
Electronic	6,890	9,755

Source: *Autoparts Report*, October 19, 2000, p. NA, from Freedonia Group.

★ 1535 ★

Gas Stations (SIC 5541)

Largest Gas Retailers, 1999

Firms are ranked by trillions of gallons sold.

ExxonMobil	24.7
BP Amoco	14.2
Texaco	10.9
Marathon/Ashland Petroleum	10.9
Citgo	10.6
Chevron	10.2

Source: *USA TODAY*, October 17, 2000, p. 3B, from *National Petroleum News Market Facts*.

SIC 56 - Apparel and Accessory Stores

★ 1536 ★

Retailing - Apparel (SIC 5600)

U.S. Apparel Sales, 2000

Sales are shown in millions of dollars.

	($ mil.)	Share
Specialty stores	$ 50,580	27.74%
Department stores	36,515	20.03
Mass merchants	35,478	19.46
National chains	23,478	12.88
Off-price retailers	15,188	8.33
Direct mail/e-tailers	7,489	4.11
Factory outlets	4,866	2.67
Other	8,711	4.78

Source: "NPD Reports Soft Sales." Retrieved March 26, 2001 from the World Wide Web: http://www.businesswire.com, from NPD Group.

★ 1537 ★

Retailing - Apparel (SIC 5611)

Boy's Apparel Sales

Shares are as of February 2000.

Discount stores	33.8%
Chain stores	18.6
Specialty stores	17.9
Department stores	9.8
Off price	6.1
Other	13.8

Source: *DSN Retailing Today*, May 8, 2000, p. A6, from NPD Group.

★ 1538 ★

Retailing - Apparel (SIC 5611)

Men's Apparel Sales

Shares are as of February 2000.

Department stores	18.7%
Discount stores	18.6
Specialty stores	17.7
Chain stores	17.5
Off price	7.0
Direct mail	5.9
Other	14.6

Source: *DSN Retailing Today*, May 8, 2000, p. A6, from NPD Group.

★ 1539 ★
Retailing - Apparel (SIC 5621)

Women's Apparel Sales

Shares are as of February 2000.

Specialty stores	25.7%
Department stores	21.2
Discount stores	16.5
Chain stores	13.9
Direct mail	8.9
Off price	5.8
Other	8.0

Source: *DSN Retailing Today*, May 8, 2000, p. A6, from NPD Group.

★ 1540 ★
Retailing - Apparel (SIC 5631)

Largest Specialty Apparel Retailers

Firms are ranked by sales in millions of dollars.

The Gap	$ 11,635.0
The Limited Inc.	9,723.0
Ann Taylor Stores	1,084.5
Abercrombie & Fitch	1,042.0
The Talbots Inc.	903.6
Intimate Brands Inc.	896.0
American Eagle Outfitters	832.1

Source: *Apparel Industry*, August 2000, p. 40.

★ 1541 ★
Retailing - Apparel (SIC 5632)

Retail Lingerie Market, 1999

Intimate apparel sales reached $11.6 billion in 1999.

Discount/variety stores	28.7%
Specialty stores	19.3
Chain stores	17.5
Department stores	16.3
Direct mail	7.5
Factory outlets	4.8
Off price stores	3.2
Other	2.6

Source: *Body Fashions Intimate Apparel*, June 2000, p. 6, from NPD Group American Shoppers Panel.

★ 1542 ★
Retailing - Apparel (SIC 5641)

Children's Licensed Apparel Sales

Market shares are shown in percent.

Discount stores	29.0%
Specialty stores	19.0
Major chains	17.0
Off-price outlets	12.0
Department stores	11.0
Other	12.0

Source: *Sporting Goods Business*, October 11, 2000, p. 26, from NPD American Shoppers Panel.

★ 1543 ★
Retailing - Apparel (SIC 5641)

Leading Youth Apparel Retailers

Selected firms are ranked by 1999 sales in millions of dollars.

Abercrombie & Fitch	$ 1,042.0
American Eagle Outfitters	832.1
Wet Seal	539.3
Pacific Sunwear of California	436.8
Buckle	375.5
Urban Outfitters	253.7
Gadzooks	241.6

Source: *Chain Store Age*, August 2000, p. 11A.

★ 1544 ★
Retailing - Apparel (SIC 5641)

Top Children's Apparel Retailers, 1999

Stores are ranked by kidswear sales in millions of dollars.

Wal-Mart	$ 5,300
Kmart	2,400
J.C. Penney	1,800
Target	1,640
Federated	1,450
Sears	1,400
May Co.	1,100
GapKids	1,000

Continued on next page.

★ 1544 ★ *Continued*
Retailing - Apparel (SIC 5641)

Top Children's Apparel Retailers, 1999

Stores are ranked by kidswear sales in millions of dollars.

TJX Corp.	$ 870
J.C. Penney (catalog only)	830
Dillard	820
Kids R Us	760

Source: *Children's Business*, May 2000, p. 1.

★ 1545 ★
Retailing - Apparel (SIC 5651)

Largest Apparel Retailers

Firms are ranked by apparel sales in billions of dollars.

Wal-Mart Stores Inc.	$ 33.00
J.C. Penney Company Inc.	22.75
Federated Department Stores Inc.	12.40
The Gap Inc.	11.63
Target Corp.	10.11
The Limited Inc.	9.72
The May Department Stores Company	9.70
Sears, Roebuck and Co.	8.21
Kmart Corp.	7.18
The TJX Companies Inc.	6.15

Source: *Apparel Industry*, August 2000, p. 32.

★ 1546 ★
Retailing - Shoes (SIC 5661)

Boy's Footwear Market, 1999

Consumers purchased 78.1 million pairs in 1999. Athletic was the top segment, followed by sandals. Sales are shown in percent.

Discount	37.8%
Self service stores	21.0
Athletic shoe stores	7.7
Sears/J.C. Penney/Ward	7.2
High shoe stores	7.2
Department stores	3.9
Sporting goods	3.7%
Specialty stores	3.5
Moderate shoe	3.2
Factory outlets	3.0

Source: *Children's Business*, July 2000, p. 14, from Footwear Market Insights.

★ 1547 ★
Retailing - Shoes (SIC 5661)

Girl's Footwear Market, 1999

Sales are shown in percent. Girls' demand increased .8% to 35.6% share of the market.

Discount	45.8%
Self service stores	24.7
High shoe stores	5.3
Sears/J.C. Penney/Ward	5.0
Department stores	4.8
Moderate shoe	2.8
Specialty stores	2.6
Factory outlets	2.6
Athletic shoe stores	2.4
Other	4.0

Source: *Children's Business*, July 2000, p. 14, from Footwear Market Insights.

★ 1548 ★
Retailing - Shoes (SIC 5661)

Men's Footwear Sales

Sales were sluggish in the year overall, with retailers cutting prices and offering numerous discounts. Shares were essentially flat in the men's segment, with the athletic segment being the big market.

High-end retailers	58.0%
Discounters	17.9
Other	24.1

Source: *Footwear News*, January 8, 2001, p. 2, from Footwear Market Insights and NPD Group.

★ 1549 ★

Retailing - Shoes (SIC 5661)

Women's Shoe Sales

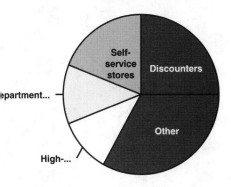

Market shares are shown in percent. Women's dress and sport shoes had 23% of the market.

Discounters	25.0%
Self-service stores	19.0
Department stores	12.0
High-end shoe stores	11.0
Other	33.0

Source: *Footwear News*, August 21, 2000, p. 10.

SIC 57 - Furniture and Homefurnishings Stores

★ 1550 ★

Furniture Stores (SIC 5712)

Largest Furniture/Home Décor Retailers, 1999

Firms are ranked by furniture revenues in millions of dollars.

Heilig-Meyers	$ 1,493.5
Ethan Allen	1,150.9
Office Depot	1,027.5
Federated Stores	883.9
Rooms To Go	860.0
Berkshire Hathaway	739.0
Pier 1	715.2
Staples	698.4
J.C. Penney	675.2
HomeLife	669.5

Source: *HFN*, August 21, 2000, p. 42.

★ 1551 ★

Furniture Stores (SIC 5712)

Top Furniture Retailers, 1999

Firms are ranked by estimated furniture and bedding shipments in millions of dollars.

Heilig-Myers	$ 1,639.9
Office Depot	944.2
Ethan Allen	$ 932.0
Wal-Mart	870.0
Federated Dept. Stores	824.6
Rooms To Go	791.2
JC Penney	723.0
Kmart	710.0
Berkshire Hathaway furniture division	671.0
La-Z-Boy	656.2

Source: *Furniture Today*, Winter 2000, p. 40.

★ 1552 ★

Furniture Stores (SIC 5712)

Top Furniture Retailers in Canada, 1999

Firms are ranked by furniture, bedding and accessory sales in millions of dollars.

Sears Canada	$ 650.0
Ikea	412.8
Leon's Furniture Ltd.	362.5
The Brick Warehouse Corp.	298.0
Groupe BMTC	211.5

Source: *Furniture Today*, Winter 2000, p. 46.

★ 1553 ★

Retailing - Floorcoverings (SIC 5713)

Largest Floor Retailers, 2000

Firms are ranked by sales in millions of dollars.

Home Depot	$ 2,660
Lowe's	602
Sears	487
Wal Mart	481
Flooring America	350
Sherwin Williams	216
Target Corp.	194
Federated Stores	178

Continued on next page.

★ 1553 ★ *Continued*
Retailing - Floorcoverings (SIC 5713)

Largest Floor Retailers, 2000

Firms are ranked by sales in millions of dollars.

Floors Inc.	$ 145
Menard	125

Source: *Floor Focus*, November 2000, p. 1.

★ 1554 ★
Retailing - Floorcoverings (SIC 5713)

Leading Carpeting Stores in Milwaukee, WI

Data show the top stores, based on a survey of shoppers.

Menard	13.0%
Home Depot	13.0

Source: *Milwaukee Journal Sentinel*, March 24, 2001, p. 1.

★ 1555 ★
Retailing - Floorcoverings (SIC 5713)

Leading Rug Retailers

Market shares are shown in percent.

	($ mil.)	Share
Discount stores	$ 2,142	42.0%
Home centers	1,071	21.0
Specialty chains	561	11.0
Department stores	459	9.0
Carpet/flooring stores	204	4.0
Warehouse clubs	153	3.0
Furniture stores	102	2.0
Ind. specialty stores	102	2.0
Sears and Wards	102	2.0
Catalogs	102	2.0
Military exchanges	51	1.0
Other	51	1.0

Source: *Home Textiles Today*, January 15, 2001, p. 6.

★ 1556 ★
Retailing - Floorcoverings (SIC 5719)

Retail Rug Sales

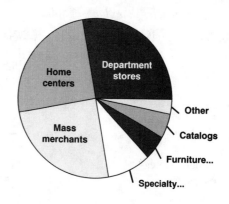

Market shares are shown in percent.

Department stores	28.0%
Home centers	25.0
Mass merchants	25.0
Specialty carpet stores	9.0
Furniture stores	5.0
Catalogs	5.0
Other	3.0

Source: *HFN*, March 12, 2001, p. 49.

★ 1557 ★
Retailing - Homefurnishings (SIC 5719)

Home Accessories Sales

	($ bil.)	Share
Mass merchants/discounters/ warehouse clubs	$ 14.5	21.94%
Gift specialty stores/chains	10.3	15.58
Home accent specialty stores/ chains	9.1	13.77
Furniture stores/chains	8.9	13.46
Department stores	7.9	11.95
Internet and other	6.1	9.23
Home textile specialty stores/ chains	3.9	5.90
Lamp/lighting stores/chains	2.9	4.39
Interior designers	2.5	3.78

Source: *Home Accents Today*, December 2000, p. S5.

★ 1558 ★

Retailing - Homefurnishings (SIC 5719)

Kids Homefurnishings Sales

Firms are ranked by sales in millions of dollars.

Target Stores	$ 2,300
Wal-Mart	2,200
Kmart	1,525
Babies R Us	775
Sears	515
J.C. Penney	375
Burlington Coat Factory	250
Toys R Us	235
Ames Department Stores	68
Rooms To Go For Kids	65
USA Baby	65

Source: *Home Textiles Today*, November 13, 2000, p. S20.

★ 1559 ★

Retailing - Homefurnishings (SIC 5719)

Largest Home Textile Retailers

Firms are ranked by sales in millions of dollars.

	($ mil.)	% of Group
J.C. Penney	$ 2,325	19.83%
Wal-Mart	2,275	19.40
Kmart	1,774	15.13
Target Stores	1,565	13.35
Bed Bath & Beyond	1,033	8.81
Sears	819	6.98
Linens'n Things	774	6.60
T.J. Maxx/Marshalls	430	3.67
Mervyn's	399	3.40
Fingerhut	333	2.84

Source: *Home Textiles Today*, Annual 2001, p. 40.

★ 1560 ★

Retailing - Homefurnishings (SIC 5719)

Largest Houseware Retailers, 1999

Firms are ranked by homefurnishing revenues in millions of dollars.

Wal-Mart	$ 7,510.7
Kmart	3,405.8
Target	2,180.3
Sears	1,391.3
Federated	1,159.2

May Co.	$ 908.8
Bed, Bath & Beyond	845.1
TruServ	773.9
Walgreens	685.8
QVC	564.2

Source: *HFN*, August 21, 2000, p. 42.

★ 1561 ★

Retailing - Homefurnishings (SIC 5719)

Retail Space/Closet Organizer Sales

	($ mill.)	Share
Discount stores/supercenters	$ 1,753	28.0%
Hardware stores/home centers	1,155	18.0
Specialty stores	543	9.0
Warehouse clubs	275	4.0
Department stores	122	2.0
Other	2,442	39.0

Source: *Do-It-Yourself Retailing*, January 2001, p. 52, from U.S. Consumer Price Index and U.S. Department of Commerce.

★ 1562 ★

Retailing - Homefurnishings (SIC 5719)

Top Bedding Retailers

Firms are ranked by sales in millions of dollars.

Select Comfort	$ 260.0
Mattress Discounters	238.3
Federated Department Stores	232.9
Heilig-Meyers	218.4
Sleepy's	154.8
Mattress Giant	142.0
May Department Stores	120.0
Homelife Furniture	105.0

Source: *Furniture Today*, Annual 2000, p. 38.

★ 1563 ★
Retailing - Appliances (SIC 5722)

Largest Appliance Stores

Circuit City recently stopped selling appliances.

Sears	38.0%
Circuit City	9.0
Lowe's	7.0
Best Buy	5.0
Other	41.0

Source: *The Record*, November 24, 2000, p. A56.

★ 1564 ★
Retailing - Appliances (SIC 5722)

Retail Air Cleaner Sales

Market shares are shown in percent.

	1998	1999
Mass merchants/clubs	35.0%	34.0%
Dept. stores/chains	34.0	28.0
Specialty stores	4.0	4.0
Hardware/home improvement stores	4.0	8.0
Drug stores/supermarkets	2.0	2.0
Catalogs	1.0	3.0
Other	20.0	21.0

Source: *HFN*, August 7, 2000, p. S6.

★ 1565 ★
Retailing - Electronics (SIC 5731)

DTH Satellite Sales, 1999

Market shares are shown in percent.

Satellite TV dealer	29.6%
Radio Shack	11.7
Circuit City	10.9
Appliance/TV	8.6
Best Buy	7.3
Other	31.9

Source: *Dealerscope*, August 2000, p. 20, from Consumer Electronics Association.

★ 1566 ★
Retailing - Electronics (SIC 5731)

Retail DVD Player Sales, 1999

Market shares are shown in percent.

Best Buy	21.5%
Circuit City	16.9
Appliance/TV stores	9.8
Sears	9.1
Hifi/stereo stores	7.7
Other	35.0

Source: *Dealerscope*, August 2000, p. 20, from Consumer Electronics Association.

★ 1567 ★
Retailing - Electronics (SIC 5731)

Retail TV Sales, 1999

Market shares are shown in percent.

Wal-Mart	20.5%
Appliance/TV stores	12.1
Best Buy	11.5
Sears	10.9
Kmart	7.1
Other	37.9

Source: *Dealerscope*, August 2000, p. 20, from Consumer Electronics Association.

★ 1568 ★
Retailing - Electronics (SIC 5731)

Retail VCR Sales, 1999

Market shares are shown in percent.

Wal-Mart	22.8%
Circuit City	10.3
Best Buy	9.3
Sears	8.8
Appliance/TV store	8.5
Other	40.3

Source: *Dealerscope*, August 2000, p. 20, from Consumer Electronics Association.

★ 1569 ★

Retailing - Computers (SIC 5734)

Where PCs Were Purchased, 2000

Manufacturer direct 23.0%
Consumer electronics store 19.0
Clone shop 9.0
Used PC 8.0
Office superstore 8.0
PC superstore 7.0
Other 26.0

Source: *Wall Street Journal*, January 4, 2001, p. B6, from Ziff Davis.

★ 1570 ★

Retailing - Video Games (SIC 5734)

Retail Nintendo Game Sales

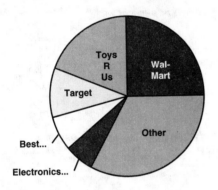

Total market reached $469 million for the first eight months of the year.

Wal-Mart 25.0%
Toys R Us 19.0
Target 10.0
Best Buy 7.0
Electronics Boutique 6.0
Other 33.0

Source: *New York Times*, September 2, 2000, p. C4, from International Development Group.

★ 1571 ★

Retailing - Video Games (SIC 5734)

Retail PC-Based Game Sales

Total market reached $604.6 million for the first eight months of the year.

Best Buy 16.0%
Electronics Boutique 13.0
Wal-Mart 12.0
Babbage's/Funco 11.0
Comp USA 11.0
Other 37.0

Source: *New York Times*, September 2, 2000, p. C4, from International Development Group.

★ 1572 ★

Retailing - Video Games (SIC 5734)

Retail Playstation Game Sales

Total market reached $766.2 million for the first eight months of the year.

Wal-Mart 19.0%
Best Buy 15.0
Toys R Us 15.0
Babbage's/Funco 13.0
Electronics Boutique 12.0
Other 26.0

Source: *New York Times*, September 2, 2000, p. C4, from International Development Group.

★ 1573 ★

Retailing - DVDs (SIC 5735)

Top DVD Retailers

Companies are ranked by DVD sales in millions of dollars. DVD sales have increased 175% over the previous year.

	($ mil.)	Share
Best Buy	$ 162	12.3%
Circuit City	127	9.6
Musicland Stores	110	8.3
Blockbuster	96	7.3
Wal-Mart	74	5.6
Express.com	60	4.5
Costco	58	4.4
Amazon.com	58	4.4
Tower Video	34	2.6

Source: *DVD Report*, May 8, 2000, p. 1, from *Video Store*.

★ 1574 ★
Retailing - Music (SIC 5735)

Leading Music Retailers in Canada, 2000

Market shares are shown in percent.

HMV Canada	19.0%
General retailers (Wal-Mart, Zellers)	14.0
Music World	8.0
A&B Sound	7.0
Archambault Musique	7.0
Sam the Record Man	7.0
Future Shop	6.0
Other	32.0

Source: *Marketing Magazine*, June 4, 2001, p. NA, from Statistics Canada.

★ 1575 ★
Retailing - Music (SIC 5735)

Retail Music Sales, 1999

Market shares are shown in percent.

Record store	44.5%
Tape/record club	7.9
Mail order	2.5
Internet	2.4
Other	42.7

Source: *Industry Standard*, August 28, 2000, p. 166, from Recording Industry Association of America.

★ 1576 ★
Retailing - Music (SIC 5735)

Retail Music Sales, 2000

Market shares are shown in percent.

Chains	54.8%
Mass	28.4
Nontraditional outlets	22.0
Independent stores	14.6

Source: *Billboard*, January 13, 2001, p. 1, from Soundscan.

★ 1577 ★
Retailing - Video (SIC 5735)

Leading Video Specialty Retailers, 2000

Firms are ranked by estimated sales in millions of dollars.

Blockbuster	$ 5,191
Hollywood Entertainment	1,818
Movie Gallery	1,027
Suncoast Motion Picture Co.	403
Video Update	257
West Coast Ent.	217
Video City	74
Video Warehouse	43

Source: *Video Store*, April 15, 2001, p. 24.

★ 1578 ★
Retailing - Video (SIC 5735)

Retail Video Sales, 2000

Market shares are shown in percent.

	($ mil.)	Share
Mass	$ 382.5	63.96%
Drug	151.3	25.30
Food	64.2	10.74

Source: *Drug Store News*, May 21, 2001, p. 44, from Information Resources Inc.

★ 1579 ★
Retailing - Musical Products (SIC 5736)

Leading Music Product Retailers

Firms are ranked by sales in millions of dollars.

Guitar Center Inc.	$ 620.0
Sam Ash Music Corp.	280.0
Mars Inc.	210.0
Brook Mays/H&H	83.0

Continued on next page.

★ **1579** ★ *Continued*

Retailing - Musical Products (SIC 5736)

Leading Music Product Retailers

Firms are ranked by sales in millions of dollars.

Hermes Music . . . .$ 72.0
Schmitt Music Company 66.5
Washington Music Center 50.4
Full Compass 50.0
J.W. Pepper 49.7
Music Go Round 47.5

Source: *Music Trades*, August 1, 2000, p. 84.

SIC 58 - Eating and Drinking Places

★ 1580 ★

Foodservice (SIC 5812)

Contract Chain Market Shares

Market shares are shown based on aggregate sales of the top contract chains in the source's top 100 list.

Aramark Global Food/Leisure Services	25.42%
LSG/Sky Chefs	8.94
Sodexho Marriott Corporate Services	7.92
Sodexho Marriott Healthcare Services	7.61
Sodexho Marriott Education Services	7.00
Canteen Services	6.91
Dobbs International Services	6.60
Eurest Dining Services	6.34
Other	23.26

Source: *Nation's Restaurant News*, September 26, 2000, p. 144.

★ 1581 ★

Foodservice (SIC 5812)

Hotel Market Shares

Market shares are shown based on aggregate sales of the top hotel chains in the source's top 100 list.

Marriott hotels, resorts & suites	25.42%
Hilton Hotels	16.99
Sheraton Hotels	16.43
Holiday Inns	11.41
Radisson	10.86
Ramada Inn	9.99
Hyatt Hotels	8.90

Source: *Nation's Restaurant News*, September 26, 2000, p. 148.

★ 1582 ★

Foodservice (SIC 5812)

Leading Contract Management Firms

Firms are ranked by food & beverage sales in millions of dollars. Data are for North America.

Aramark	$ 3,990.0
Sodexho Marriott Services	3,827.0
Compass Group USA	1,725.0
Delaware North Companies	1,375.0
Wood Dining Services	500.0
Volume Services America	431.5
Bon Appetit Management Co.	265.0

Source: *Restaurants & Institutions*, September 15, 2000, p. 51.

★ 1583 ★

Foodservice (SIC 5812)

Leading Food Purchasers

Firms are ranked by sales in thousands of dollars.

Premier	$ 1,150,000
HPSI	627,000
Healthshare Assoc. Inc.	410,000
Novation	360,000
UHF Purchasing Svcs.	210,000
Hospital Purchasing Svcs.	202,126
AmeriNet	190,000
Health Svcs. Corp. of America	153,000
Tidewater Group Purchasing	150,000

Source: *Food Service Director*, November 15, 2000, p. 45.

★ 1584 ★
Foodservice (SIC 5812)

Leading Self-Operated Corrections Operations

Firms are ranked by food & beverage sales in millions of dollars. Data are for North America.

California Department of Corrections . . .	$ 143.8
Federal Bureau of Prisons	94.8
Texas Department of Criminal Justice . . .	64.3
New Jersey Department of Corrections . . .	60.0
Illinois Department of Corrections	56.4
New York State Department of Corrections .	50.3
Virginia Department of Corrections	50.0
Ohio Department of Rehabilitation & Correction	48.0
Pennsylvania Department of Corrections . .	48.0

Source: *Restaurants & Institutions*, September 15, 2000, p. 51.

★ 1585 ★
Foodservice (SIC 5812)

Popular "Main Meal" Foods

Chciken accounts for 35% of all meat, poulty and fish consumption. It is also sold and processed in more ways than most other meat. Data show the most popular center-of-the-plate items in the non-commercial foodservice sector.

Fried chicken/nuggets	18.0%
Pasta	17.0
Pizza	15.0
Roast beef	7.0
Other	43.0

Source: *Food Service Director*, August 15, 2000, p. 91.

★ 1586 ★
Foodservice (SIC 5812)

Takeout Food Sales

CMS stands for convenience meal solutions, which are packaged meals that are not ready to eat, which distinguishes them from takeout meals.

	1999	2004	Share
Restaurants	$ 136	$ 174	48.33%
Takeout	111	150	41.67
CMS	31	36	10.00

Source: *Automatic Merchandiser*, October 2000, p. 64.

★ 1587 ★
Restaurants (SIC 5812)

Casual Italian Dining Market

Market shares are shown in percent.

Olive Garden	16.9%
Romano's Macaroni Grill	4.1
Pizzeria Uno	3.4
Other	75.6

Source: *Investor's Business Daily*, November 29, 2000, p. A12, from company reports, Technomic, and Salomon Smith Barney Holdings Inc.

★ 1588 ★
Restaurants (SIC 5812)

Casual Seafood Dining Market

Market shares are shown in percent.

Red Lobster	28.4%
Joe's Crab Shack	3.5
Landry's	1.7
Other	66.4

Source: *Investor's Business Daily*, November 29, 2000, p. A12, from company reports, Technomic, and Salomon Smith Barney Holdings Inc.

★ 1589 ★
Restaurants (SIC 5812)

Chicken Chain Market Shares

Market shares are shown based on aggregate sales of the top chicken chains in the source's top 100 list.

KFC	55.18%
Popeyes	12.66
Chick-fil-A	12.14
Boston Market	10.97
Church's Chicken	9.04

Source: *Nation's Restaurant News*, September 26, 2000, p. 110.

★ 1590 ★
Restaurants (SIC 5812)

Chicken Restaurant Sales

Between 1996 and 2000, sales at major fast-food chicken chains rose 11%. Market shares are shown in percent.

Kentucky Fried Chicken	48.0%
Popeyes	11.5
Church's	8.5
Other	32.0

Source: *Investor's Business Daily*, May 1, 2001, p. A8, from company reports and Deutsche Banc Alex. Brown.

★ 1591 ★
Restaurants (SIC 5812)

Dinner House Chain Market Shares

Market shares are shown based on aggregate sales of the top dinner house chains in the source's top 100 list.

Applebee's	14.99%
Red Lobster	12.95
Outback Steakhouse	11.17
Olive Garden	10.42
Chili's Grill & Bar	10.05
T.G.I. Friday's	8.61
Ruby Tuesday	5.94
Lone Star Steakhouse & Saloon	3.02
Romano's Macaroni Grill	3.01
Other	19.84

Source: *Nation's Restaurant News*, September 26, 2000, p. 134.

★ 1592 ★
Restaurants (SIC 5812)

Family Chain Market Shares

Market shares are shown based on aggregate sales of the top family chains in the source's top 100 list.

Denny's	22.75%
Cracker Barrel Old Country Store	12.72
International House of Pancakes	11.78
Shoney's	9.51
Perkins Restaurant and Bakery	8.65
Friendly's Ice Cream	7.34
Waffle House	6.78
Steak n Shake	4.64
Other	15.83

Source: *Nation's Restaurant News*, September 26, 2000, p. 134.

★ 1593 ★
Restaurants (SIC 5812)

Fast-Food Industry by Segment

	($ bil.)	Share
Hamburger	$ 44.1	38.79%
Pizza	23.5	20.67
Other sandwich	12.1	10.64
Chicken	10.8	9.50
Mexican	7.1	6.24
Ice cream/yogurt	5.5	4.84
Other	10.6	9.32

Source: *Akron Beacon Journal*, October 25, 2000, p. C7.

★ 1594 ★
Restaurants (SIC 5812)

Fast-Food Industry Leaders

Market shares are shown in percent.

	1997	1998	1999
McDonald's	16.3%	16.4%	16.3%
Burger King	7.5	7.8	7.4
Taco Bell	4.6	4.5	4.5
Wendy's	4.4	4.4	4.6
Other	67.2	66.9	67.2

Source: *USA TODAY*, February 21, 2001, p. 3B, from Technomic and Burger King.

★ 1595 ★
Restaurants (SIC 5812)

Grill Buffet Chain Market Shares

Market shares are shown based on aggregate sales of the top grill buffet chains in the source's top 100 list.

Golden Corral	32.13%
Ryan's Family Steak House	25.10
Ponderosa Steakhouse	19.71
Western Sizzlin'	11.71
Sizzler	11.34

Source: *Nation's Restaurant News*, September 26, 2000, p. 134.

★ 1596 ★
Restaurants (SIC 5812)

Hamburger/Sandwich Market Leaders, 1999

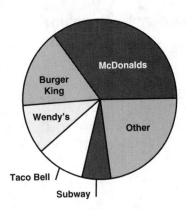

Market shares are shown in percent.

McDonalds	35.0%
Burger King	16.0
Wendy's	10.0
Taco Bell	10.0
Subway	6.0
Other	23.0

Source: *Dayton Daily News*, January 29, 2001, p. 2C.

★ 1597 ★
Restaurants (SIC 5812)

Largest Barbeque Chains

Tony Roma's	$ 289
Damon's	258
Sonny's	176
Bill Miller's Bar-B-Q	70
Red Hot & Blue	50

Source: *Restaurant Business*, August 1, 2000, p. 27, from Technomic.

★ 1598 ★
Restaurants (SIC 5812)

Largest Doughnut Chains in Canada

Firms are ranked by number of outlets.

Tim Horton's	1,863
Country Style	546
Coffee Time	359
Robin's Donuts	266
Dunkin Donuts	205

Source: *Chain Leader*, September 2000, p. 68.

★ 1599 ★
Restaurants (SIC 5812)

Largest Independent Restaurants

Restaurants are ranked by food & beverage sales in millions of dollars.

Windows on the World	$ 37,500
Tavern on the Green	37,015
Bob Chinn's Crab House	23,065
Joe's Stone Crab	22,841
Sparks Steak House	21,400
21 Club	18,759
Redeye Grill	17,451
The Russian Tea Room	16,838
Fulton's Crab House	16,344

Source: *Restaurants & Institutions*, April 1, 2001, p. NA.

★ 1600 ★
Restaurants (SIC 5812)

Leading Fast-Food Chains Chains in Canada, 1999

Market shares are shown for fiscal year.

McDonald's Restaurants	28.4%
Cara Operations	21.7
Tricon Global Restaurants	17.3
Subway Franchise Systems	6.5
Burger King Restaurants	5.8
Wendy's Restaurants	5.5
Other	13.8

Source: *Marketing Magazine*, June 4, 2001, p. NA.

★ 1601 ★
Restaurants (SIC 5812)

Pizza Restaurant Market

Market shares are shown in percent.

Pizza Hut	21.4%
Domino's Pizza	11.3
Little Caeser's	7.4
Papa Johns	5.2
Others	54.7

Source: *Detroit Free Press*, March 30, 2000, p. C1, from Technomic Inc.

★ 1602 ★
Restaurants (SIC 5812)

Texas Restaurant Industry

Market shares are shown in percent.

Bar/lounge	14.24%
American	11.32
Mexican	11.23

Hamburgers	8.21%
Secondary operation	7.47
Retail	6.50
Pizza	5.13
Other	6.60

Source: *Dallas Morning News*, November 5, 2000, p. H1, from Texas Restaurant Association.

★ 1603 ★
Restaurants (SIC 5812)

Top Chain Restaurant Companies, 1999

Firms are ranked by systemwide sales in billions of dollars.

McDonald's Corp.	$ 19.1
Tricon Global Restaurants Inc.	14.5
Diageo PLC	8.7
Wendy's International Inc.	5.4
Darden Restaurants Inc.	3.4
Doctor's Associates	3.2
CKE Restaurants Inc.	3.1
International Dairy Queen Inc.	2.9
Allied Domecq	2.8
Domino's Inc.	2.6

Source: *Quick Frozen Foods International*, July 2000, p. 98, from Technomic Inc.

★ 1604 ★
Restaurants (SIC 5812)

Top Multi-Concept Franchisees

Firms are ranked by revenue in millions of dollars.

RTM Restaurant Group	$ 610.0
Harman Management Corp.	315.0
Sydran Services	270.0
DavCo Restaurants Inc.	252.4
Cimms Inc.	167.0
ICH Corporation	145.0
Nath Corporation	144.0
Main Street and Main Inc.	140.2
Quality Dining Inc.	140.0
RMS Family Restaurants	130.0

Source: *Restaurant Business*, December 1, 2000, p. 22, from *Restaurant Finance Monitor's Monitor 2000*.

★ 1605 ★

Restaurants (SIC 5812)

U.S. Restaurant Sales, 2001

Sales are forecast in billions of dollars.

	($ bil.)	Share
Limited-service	$ 125.97	52.31%
Full-service	112.87	46.87
Bars & taverns	1.97	0.82

Source: *Restaurant Business*, October 15, 2000, p. 24, from Technomic and International Foodservice Manufacturers Association.

★ 1606 ★

Coffee Shops (SIC 5813)

Leading Coffee Chains in Canada, 1999

Market shares are shown for fiscal year.

TDL Group	62.2%
The Second Group	13.2
Coffee Time Donuts	5.5
Starbucks Coffee	4.9
Allied Domecq Retailing	4.9
Country Style Foodservice	4.7
mmmuffins Canada	1.7
Timothy's World Coffee	1.7
Baker's Dozen Donuts	1.3

Source: *Marketing Magazine*, June 4, 2001, p. NA, from *Foodservice & Hospitality*.

★ 1607 ★

Retailing - Beverages (SIC 5813)

Cold Beverage Sales

Market shares are shown in percent.

Supermarkets	31.0%
Fountain	23.0
Vending	12.0
C-stores	7.0
Small grocers	5.0
Mass merchants	4.0
Drug stores	2.0
Gas mini-marts	1.0
Other	15.0

Source: *Automatic Merchandiser*, October 2000, p. 58, from Beverage Marketing Corp.

SIC 59 - Miscellaneous Retail

★ 1608 ★

Drug Stores (SIC 5912)

Leading Drug Stores, 1999

Firms are ranked by sales in millions of dollars.

CVS	$ 18,098.3
Walgreens	17,838.8
Rite Aid	13,325.0
Eckerd	12,427.0
Longs	3,672.4
Phar-Mor	1,206.5
Drug Emporium	904.8
Duane Reade	839.7
Brooks	750.0
Kerr	535.0

Source: *Stores*, July 2000, p. S14.

★ 1609 ★

Drug Stores (SIC 5912)

Top Drug Stores in Las Vegas, NV

Firms are ranked by number of outlets.

	Outlets	Share
Sav-On	38	19.90%
Walgreens	36	18.85
Rite-Aid	31	16.23
Von's	14	7.33
Smith's	13	6.81
Raley's	10	5.24
Wal-Mart	10	5.24
Long's	8	4.19
Kmart	8	4.19
Other	23	12.04

Source: *Las Vegas Review - Journal*, March 18, 2001, p. 1F.

★ 1610 ★

Drug Stores (SIC 5912)

Top Drug Stores in Michigan

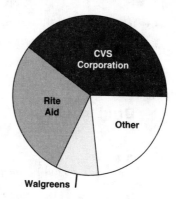

Market shares are shown in percent.

CVS Corporation	40.0%
Rite Aid	28.0
Walgreens	9.2
Other	22.8

Source: *Crain's Detroit Business*, October 9, 2000, p. 21.

★ 1611 ★

Drug Stores (SIC 5912)

Top Drug Stores in New York

Market shares are shown in percent.

Duane Reade	25.8%
CVS	22.7
Rite Aid	16.9
Eckerd/Genovese	11.2
Walgreens	3.6
Other	19.8

Source: *Investor's Business Daily*, March 8, 2001, p. A10, from company reports, Metro Market Studies, and J.P. Morgan.

★ 1612 ★

Retailing - Drugs (SIC 5912)

Mail Order Pharmacy Use

Mail order is up 23% over 1999. The most popular pharmacies in the survey were chain drug stores with 58%, independents with 15% and supermarkets with 12%.

Merck-Medco Rx Services	29.5%
Express Scripts/DPS/Value Rx	11.0
Caremark	8.8
Walgreen	7.5
PCS	6.4
Other	36.8

Source: *Drug Store News*, October 16, 2000, p. 1.

★ 1613 ★

Retailing - Drugs (SIC 5912)

Over-The-Counter Drug Industry, 2000

Market shares are shown in percent.

	($ mil.)	Share
Discount stores	$ 511.31	35.0%
Chain drug stores	9.69	30.0
Food/drug combos	8.40	26.0
Supermarkets	2.26	7.0
Independent drug stores	0.65	2.0

Source: *Chain Drug Review*, January 1, 2001, p. 39, from Racher Press.

★ 1614 ★

Retailing - Drugs (SIC 5912)

Pharmacy Sales in Canada, 1999

Market shares are shown in percent.

Supermarkets	50.7%
Drug stores	18.6
Discount stores	13.5
Warehouse clubs	6.7
Other	10.5

Source: *Chain Drug Review*, November 20, 2000, p. 1.

★ 1615 ★

Retailing - Drugs (SIC 5912)

Prescription Drug Leaders

Market shares are shown in percent.

Chain drug stores	44.0%
Independents	27.0
Supermarkets	13.0
Mass	11.0
Mail order	5.0

Source: *Supermarket Business*, December 15, 2000, p. 46, from IMS Health.

★ 1616 ★

Retailing - Drugs (SIC 5912)

Prescription Drug Sales

U.S. prescription drug sales grew 14.9% to $145 billion in the year 2000. New, more effective drugs and an aging population all fueled the growth.

	($ mil.)	Share
Chain stores	$ 54.9	37.8%
Independents	25.2	17.4
Mail order	16.1	11.1

Continued on next page.

★ 1616 ★ *Continued*
Retailing - Drugs (SIC 5912)

Prescription Drug Sales

U.S. prescription drug sales grew 14.9% to $145 billion in the year 2000. New, more effective drugs and an aging population all fuled the growth.

	($ mil.)	Share
Nonfederal hospitals	$ 15.6	10.7%
Food stores	13.1	9.0
Clinics	10.4	7.2
Long-term care	4.5	3.1
Federal facilities	2.4	1.7
Home health care	1.6	1.1
HMO	1.4	0.9

Source: *Marketletter*, June 11, 2001, p. NA.

★ 1617 ★
Retailing - Sporting Goods (SIC 5941)

Top Sports Stores, 1999

Market shares are shown based on industry sales.

The Sports Authority	3.4%
Champs	1.5
Sportmart	1.4
Dick's	1.2
Academy	1.0
Big 5	1.0
Jumbo Sport	0.7
Modell's	0.7
Oshman's	0.6
Other	88.5

Source: "Market Share Survey." Retrieved November 20, 2000 from the World Wide Web: http://www.activemedia-guide.com, from USBR.

★ 1618 ★
Retailing - Sporting Goods (SIC 5941)

Where People Purchase Irons

Golf specialty stores	41.0%
Pro shops	26.0
Sporting goods stores	11.0
Internet	9.0
Golf catalogs	6.0
Mass merchants	2.0
Other	5.0

Source: *Golf World Business*, January 2001, p. 43.

★ 1619 ★
Retailing - Books (SIC 5942)

Retail Book Sales, 1999

Market shares are shown in percent.

Large bookstore chains	24.6%
Book clubs	17.7
Independents	15.2
Warehouse clubs	6.5
Mass merchandisers	6.2
Internet	5.4
Mail order	4.4
Food/drug stores	3.5
Used bookstores	3.0
Discount stores	3.0
Multimedia	0.9
Other	9.6

Source: *Publishers Weekly*, June 2000, p. 9, from Consumer Research Study on Book Publishing.

★ 1620 ★
Retailing - Books (SIC 5942)

Retail Book Sales, 2000

Market shares are shown in percent.

Bookstores	34.0%
Book clubs/mail order/book fairs	24.0
Mass merchandisers	9.0
Discount/variety stores	8.0
Internet	6.0
Warehouse/price clubs	5.0
Other	14.0

Source: "Ipsos-NPD Reports Book Sales Flat in 2000." Retrieved March 12, 2001 from the World Wide Web: http://www.businesswire.com, from Ipsos and NPD.

★ 1621 ★

Retailing - Greeting Cards (SIC 5943)

Retail Greeting Card Sales

Card & gift stores	26.2%
Mass	18.0
Drug stores	15.6
Food	15.1
Discount card & gift stores	9.5
Dollar stores	5.3
Other	10.3

Source: *Supermarket Business*, September 15, 2000, p. 112, from Home Testing Institute and NPD Group.

★ 1622 ★

Retailing - Writing Instruments (SIC 5943)

Writing Instrument Sales, 2000

Shares are based on sales of $876.8 million for the second quarter of the year.

Discount stores	52.7%
Drug stores	29.5
Food stores	17.8

Source: *MMR*, November 13, 2000, p. 32, from A.C. Nielsen.

★ 1623 ★

Craft Chains (SIC 5945)

Largest Craft Chains, 1999

Chains are ranked by sales in millions of dollars.

Michaels Stores	$ 1,883
Jo-Ann	1,382
Hobby Lobby	798
Frank's Nursery & Crafts	487
Hancock Fabrics	382
A.C. Moore	223
Rag Shops	100

Source: *Discount Store News*, August 7, 2000, p. 49.

★ 1624 ★

Retailing - Toys (SIC 5945)

Top Online Toy Retailers, 1999

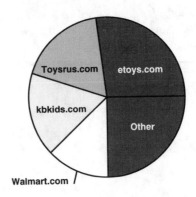

Market shares are shown in percent.

etoys.com	27.0%
Toysrus.com	18.0
kbkids.com	17.0
Walmart.com	13.0
Other	25.0

Source: *Smart Business*, November 2000, p. 160, from NPD Group.

★ 1625 ★

Retailing - Toys (SIC 5945)

Top Toy Retailers, 1999

Market shares are shown in percent.

Wal-Mart	17.4%
Toys R Us	15.6
Kmart	7.2
Target	6.8
KB Toys/Toy Works	5.1
Ames	1.6
J.C. Penney	1.2
Hallmark	1.1
Meijer	1.0
Shopko	0.8
Other	42.2

Source: "Press Release." Retrieved December 1, 2000 from the World Wide Web: http://www.npd.com, from NPD Group.

★ 1626 ★

Retailing - Toys (SIC 5945)

Top Toy Retailers, 2000

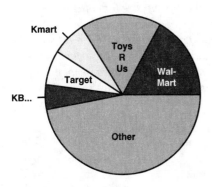

Market shares are shown in percent. The industry had sales of $23 billion; 53% of sales come in the final quarter of the year. The estimated amount spent per child per year on toys was $530.

Wal-Mart	17.4%
Toys R Us	16.5
Kmart	7.2
Target	6.8
KB Toys	5.1
Other	47.0

Source: *Akron Beacon Journal*, February 11, 2001, p. F4.

★ 1627 ★

Retailing - Cameras (SIC 5946)

Retail Digital Camera Sales

Distribution is shown in percent.

Computer/office superstore	42.0%
Electronic/specialty	31.0
Mass merchant	14.0
E-commerce	7.0
Other	6.0

Source: *New York Times*, April 23, 2001, p. C12, from NPD Intelect.

★ 1628 ★

Retailing - Cameras (SIC 5946)

Retail Disposable Camera Sales, 2000

Shares are shown based on sales of 95.2 million for the year ended May 21, 2000.

	Units	Share
Mass	.$ 44.9	47.11%
Drug	29.7	31.16
Food	20.7	21.72

Source: *Supermarket Business*, July 15, 2000, p. 88, from Information Resources Inc.

★ 1629 ★

Retailing - Candles (SIC 5947)

Retail Candle Sales

Sales are shown in millions of dollars for the year ended January 28, 2001.

	($ mil.)	Share
Mass	$ 473.6	51.97%
Food	324.6	35.62
Drug	113.1	12.41

Source: *Supermarket Business*, May 15, 2001, p. 50, from Information Resources Inc.

★ 1630 ★

Retailing - Luggage (SIC 5948)

Where Canadians Buy Luggage

Market shares are shown in percent.

Department stores	43.0%
Discount stores	22.2
Luggage stores	18.5
Leather goods stores	2.7
Other	13.6

Source: "2000 Canadian Consumer Research Result." Retrieved May 5, 2001 from the World Wide Web: http://www.llanda.com, from Luggage, Leathergoods Handbags & Accessories.

★ 1631 ★

Mail Order (SIC 5961)

Top Catalog Companies, 1999

Firms are ranked by sales in millions of dollars.

Dell Computer Corp.	$ 25.2
IBM Corp.	7.5
J.C. Penney Co.	3.9
Office Depot	3.2
CDW Computer Centers	2.5
Micro Warehouse	2.4
Henry Schein	2.2
Staples	2.0
Federated	1.8
Systemax	1.7

Source: "2000 Catalog Age 100." Retrieved November 2, 2000 from the World Wide Web: http://www.catalogagemag.com.

★ 1632 ★

Vending Machines (SIC 5962)

Best-Selling Candies in Vending Machines

Sales are for the year ended September 3, 2000. Figures are from roughly 25,000 vending machines nationwide.

Snicker's original 20-oz	4.40%
M&Ms peanut 1.74 oz.	4.07
Twix Bar 2-oz.	2.64
Reese's Peanut Butter Cup 1.6 oz.	1.97
M&M's/Mars Milk Chocolate 1.69 oz	1.64
Three Musketeers Original 2.3 oz	1.55
Skittles 1.42 oz	1.34
Starburst Original 2.07 oz	1.27
Butterfinger 2.1 oz	1.16
Other	79.96

Source: *Automatic Merchandiser*, January 2001, p. 10, from Vendiscape.

★ 1633 ★

Vending Machines (SIC 5962)

Coffee Cup Sales

While 8oz remains the top cup size for coffee sales, younger consumers are beginning to influence the sales of larger sizes. Larger cup sizes mean retailers can charge more and the cup has more surface area for advertising. Retailers have not alwayskept up with the new trends, however. Sales are shown in millions of units.

	(mil.)	Share
Quick-serve restaurants	63.00	62.0%
C-stores	6.60	6.0
Full-service restaurants	5.95	6.0
Recreation	5.80	6.0
Vending	5.15	5.0
Business & industry	4.52	4.0
Education	3.55	3.0
Health care	1.75	2.0

Source: *Automatic Merchandiser*, February 2001, p. 28, from Technomic and National Coffee Association.

★ 1634 ★

Vending Machines (SIC 5962)

Milk Sales in Schools

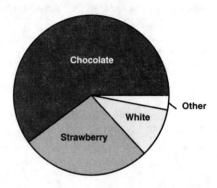

The dairy industry has partnered with a few vending equipment manufacturers to test dedicated milk machines. Various trends have aided in the industry's growth. Plastic containers have eliminated leaking problems. People drink more milk in order to embrace healthier lifestyles. Sales are at middle and high schools.

Chocolate	60.0%
Strawberry	27.0
White	10.0
Other	3.0

Source: *Automatic Merchandiser*, May 2001, p. 16.

★ 1635 ★

Vending Machines (SIC 5962)

Non-Commercial Foodservice Sales

Total vending sales in non-commercial foodservice units 9% to $109,1000, making the category one of the industry's highest growers. Vending now accounts for 14% of total food sales on college campuses, B&I, school and hospitals.

	1998	1999
Colleges	163,800	281,300
B&I	151,800	149,600
Hospitals	69,700	85,400
Schools	39,000	68,600

Source: *Food Service Director*, October 15, 2000, p. 63.

★ 1636 ★

Retailing - Propane (SIC 5984)

Largest Propane Retailers, 2000

Firms are ranked by sales in millions of gallons for fiscal year.

Ferrellgas Partners L.P.	947.0
AmeriGas Partners L.P.	771.2
Cenex Propane Partners	651.9
Suburban Propane Partners L.P.	523.9
Heritage Propane Partners L.P.	314.0
Cornerstone Propane	276.4
Columbia Propane Corp.	244.4
Level Propane Gases Inc.	111.0
Star Gas Propane L.P.	107.5
Agway Energy Products	92.2

Source: "Top 50 Retailers Rankings." Retrieved May 16, 2001 from the World Wide Web: http://www.lpgasmagazine.com.

★ 1637 ★

Retailing - Optical Goods (SIC 5995)

Largest Optical Goods Retailers

Firms are ranked by domestic sales in millions of dollars.

LensCrafters	$ 1,253.3
Cole Vision	1,022.0
Wal-Mart Sotes	368.5
Eye Care Centers of America	345.5
Vista Eyecare	300.0
Consolidated Vision Group	190.0
Costco Wholesale	189.0
U.S. Vision	147.5
Sterling Vision	119.5

Source: *20/20 Magazine*, April 2001, p. NA.

★ 1638 ★

Retailing - Optical Goods (SIC 5995)

Where Sunglasses Were Sold

Summer is the top time for sales, and the industry is optimistic for this year. Sales are for the year ended September 2000.

	($ mil.)	Share
Specialty	$ 637	29.03%
Optical	396	18.05
Mass	365	16.64
Convenience	158	7.20

Continued on next page.

★ 1638 ★ *Continued*
Retailing - Optical Goods (SIC 5995)

Where Sunglasses Were Sold

Summer is the top time for sales, and the industry is optimistic for this year. Sales are for the year ended September 2000.

	($ mil.)	Share
Department stores	$ 149	6.79%
Sport	110	5.01
Drug store	104	4.74
Grocery store	102	4.65
Chain apparel	83	3.78
Other	90	4.10

Source: *Drug Store News*, March 26, 2001, p. 93, from Sunglass Association of America and Jobson Optical Group.

★ 1639 ★

Retailing - Detergent (SIC 5999)

Liquid Laundry Sales

Sales are shown for the year ended December 3, 2000.

Supermarkets	60.7%
Mass merchandisers	34.0
Drug stores	5.3

Source: *Chemical Week*, January 24, 2020, p. 23, from Information Resources Inc.

★ 1640 ★

Retailing - Diapers (SIC 5999)

Retail Diaper Sales

Sales are shown in millions of dollars.

Discounters	46.0%
Supermarkets	43.8
Drug stores	10.2

Source: *MMR*, May 28, 2001, p. 35, from A.C. Nielsen.

★ 1641 ★

Retailing - Film (SIC 5999)

Retail Film Sales, 2000

Shares are shown based on sales of 245.1 million for the year ended May 21, 2000.

	Units	Share
Mass	$ 106.4	43.41%
Drug	82.5	33.66
Food	56.2	22.93

Source: *Supermarket Business*, July 15, 2000, p. 88, from Information Resources Inc.

★ 1642 ★

Retailing - First Aid Products (SIC 5999)

Retail First Aid Sales, 2000

Sales are for the year ended September 18, 2000.

	($ mil.)	Share
Drug stores	$ 340.3	45.90%
Food stores	200.7	27.07
Mass	200.4	27.03

Source: *Supermarket Business*, November 15, 2000, p. 68, from Information Resources Inc.

★ 1643 ★

Retailing - Party Supplies (SIC 5999)

Retail Party Supplies

Mass merchandisers have the leading segment in individual categories, with 24% of the market for greeting cards, 38% for wrapping paper, with 36% for party goods.

Supermarkets	67.9%
Mass merchandisers	11.5
Club stores	11.2
Bakeries	1.2
Delis/butchers	1.0
Party goods stores	0.5
Convenience stores	0.3
Drug stores	0.1
Other	6.3

Source: *Supermarket Business*, June 15, 2000, p. 105, from National Market Measures.

★ 1644 ★
Retailing - Personal Care Products (SIC 5999)
Retail Acne Product Sales

Unit sales are shown in millions of dollars for the year ended July 16, 2000.

	(mil.)	Share
Mass	30.7	43.55%
Food	20.1	28.51
Drug	19.7	27.94

Source: *Supermarket Business*, September 15, 2000, p. 112, from Information Resources Inc.

★ 1645 ★
Retailing - Personal Care Products (SIC 5999)
Retail Adult Incontinence Product Sales, 2000

Market shares are shown in percent.

	1998	2000
Chain drug stores	47.0%	42.0%
Discount stores	29.0	32.0
Food/drug	15.0	18.0
Supermarkets	5.0	5.0
Ind. Drug stores	4.0	3.0

Source: *Chain Drug Review*, January 1, 2001, p. 45, from Information Resources Inc.

★ 1646 ★
Retailing - Personal Care Products (SIC 5999)
Retail Bath Fragrance Sales

Sales are for the year ended June 2000.

Discounters	52.5%
Supermarkets	24.0
Drug stores	23.5

Source: *MMR*, October 2, 2000, p. 93, from Information Resources Inc.

★ 1647 ★
Retailing - Personal Care Products (SIC 5999)
Retail Contraceptive Sales, 2000

Market shares are shown in percent.

Chain drug stores	47.0%
Discount stores	24.0
Food/drug combo stores	20.0
Ind. drug stores	7.0
Supermarkets	2.0

Source: *Chain Drug Review*, January 1, 2001, p. 70, from Information Resources Inc.

★ 1648 ★
Retailing - Personal Care Products (SIC 5999)
Retail Eye/Lens Care Solution Sales

Unit sales reached 203.6 million for the year ended May 21, 2000.

	Units	Share
Mass	90.5	44.45%
Drug	60.0	29.47
Food	53.1	26.08

Source: *Supermarket Business*, July 15, 2000, p. 99, from Information Resources Inc.

★ 1649 ★
Retailing - Personal Care Products (SIC 5999)
Retail Face Moisturizer Sales, 2000

Sales are for the year ended June 2000.

Discounters	40.5%
Drug stores	39.7
Supermarkets	19.8

Source: *MMR*, October 2, 2000, p. 71, from Information Resources Inc.

★ 1650 ★
Retailing - Personal Care Products (SIC 5999)
Retail Family Planning Sales

Total sales reached $601.6 million for the year ended July 15, 2000.

Drug stores	58.1%
Discount stores	23.5
Supermarkets	18.4

Source: *MMR*, September 18, 2000, p. 1.

★ 1651 ★
Retailing - Personal Care Products (SIC 5999)

Retail Feminine Protection Sales in Mexico

Market shares are shown in percent.

Supermarkets	52.5%
Grocery stores	23.8
Stores and clinics, govt run	12.6
Pharmacies	11.1

Source: *InfoLatina S.A. de C.V.*, February 2, 2001, p. NA, from A.C. Nielsen.

★ 1652 ★
Retailing - Personal Care Products (SIC 5999)

Retail Foot Care Product Sales

Sales are for the year ended May 21, 2000.

Drug stores	40.4%
Discounters	38.8
Supermarkets	20.8

Source: "Foot Care Device Market Overview." Retrieved October 19, 2000 from the World Wide Web: http://www.exposemagazine.com, from Implus Corporation.

★ 1653 ★
Retailing - Personal Care Products (SIC 5999)

Retail Hair Coloring Sales

Market shares are shown in percent.

Drug store	40.8%
Mass	38.3
Food	20.9

Source: *Drug Store News*, October 16, 2000, p. 36.

★ 1654 ★
Retailing - Personal Care Products (SIC 5999)

Retail Hair Spray Sales

Sales are shown by outlet.

	1999	2000
Discount stores	36.0%	41.0%
Chain drug stores	26.0	26.0
Food/drug combo stores	21.0	20.0
Supermarkets	14.0	11.0
Ind. drug stores	3.0	2.0

Source: *Chain Drug Review*, January 29, 2001, p. 41, from Information Resources Inc.

★ 1655 ★
Retailing - Personal Care Products (SIC 5999)

Retail Hand/Body Care Cleaner Sales

Unit sales are shown in millions of dollars for the year ended July 16, 2000.

	(mil.)	Share
Mass	132.1	47.95%
Drug	74.8	27.15
Food	68.6	24.90

Source: *Supermarket Business*, September 15, 2000, p. 112, from Information Resources Inc.

★ 1656 ★
Retailing - Personal Care Products (SIC 5999)

Retail Hand/Body Lotion Sales

Market shares are shown in percent.

Mass	43.3%
Drug stores	31.8
Food	24.9

Source: *Drug Store News*, October 16, 2000, p. 36.

★ 1657 ★
Retailing - Personal Care Products (SIC 5999)

Retail Health & Beauty Sales

Market shares are shown in percent.

Discounters	38.1%
Drug chains	32.2
Supermarkets	29.7

Source: *MMR*, July 24, 2000, p. 22, from Information Resources Inc.

★ 1658 ★

Retailing - Personal Care Products (SIC 5999)

Retail Lip Balm Sales, 2000

Distribution is based on 180.7 million units sold for the year ended October 8, 2000.

Discounters	40.3%
Drug stores	33.2
Supermarkets	28.5

Source: *MMR*, December 19, 2000, p. 43, from Information Resources Inc.

★ 1659 ★

Retailing - Personal Care Products (SIC 5999)

Retail Liquid Soap Sales

Total sales reached $905.8 million.

Discount stores	40.0%
Food/drug combo stores	34.0
Chain drug stores	14.0
Supermarkets	11.0
Ind drug stores	1.0

Source: *Chain Drug Review*, January 29, 2001, p. 48, from Information Resources Inc.

★ 1660 ★

Retailing - Personal Care Products (SIC 5999)

Retail Men's Fragrance Sales

Sales are shown by outlet.

	1998	2000
Discount stores	44.0%	40.0%
Chain drug stores	34.0	33.0
Food/drug combo stores	15.0	17.0
Supermarkets	6.0	4.0
Indep drug stores	1.0	6.0

Source: *Chain Drug Review*, January 29, 2001, p. 41, from Information Resources Inc.

★ 1661 ★

Retailing - Personal Care Products (SIC 5999)

Retail Nail Care Sales

The category has been dominate for the last few years. Eye and lip color have been dominate. Sales are for the year ended July 16, 2000.

Drug stores	44.4%
Mass merchandisers	42.1
Food stores	13.5

Source: *DSN Retailing Today*, October 2, 2000, p. 37, from Information Resources Inc.

★ 1662 ★

Retailing - Personal Care Products (SIC 5999)

Retail Razor Sales, 2000

Market shares are shown in percent.

	1998	1999	2000
Discount stores	34.0%	36.0%	37.0%
Food/drug combo stores . . .	25.0	26.0	27.0
Chain drug stores	22.0	21.0	20.0
Supermarkets	17.0	16.0	15.0
Indep drug stores	2.0	1.0	1.0

Source: *Chain Drug Review*, January 29, 2001, p. 34, from Information Resources Inc.

★ 1663 ★
Retailing - Personal Care Products (SIC 5999)

Retail Sun Care Sales, 2000

Market shares are shown in percent.

Mass	41.0%
Drug	36.4
Food	22.6

Source: "Suncare Year to Year." Retrieved October 19, 2000 from the World Wide Web: http://www.exposemagazine.com.

★ 1664 ★
Retailing - Supplements (SIC 5999)

Retail Nonherbal Supplement Sales

Drug stores	42.0%
Mass	41.6
Food stores	16.4

Source: *Drug Topics*, March 5, 2001, p. 52.

★ 1665 ★
Retailing - Supplements (SIC 5999)

Retail Vitamin/Mineral Sales

Unit shares are shown in percent.

Discounters	36.6%
Drug stores	34.9
Supermarkets	25.5

Source: *MMR*, January 22, 2001, p. 18, from Information Resources Inc.

★ 1666 ★
Retailing - Supplements (SIC 5999)

Retail Vitamin Sales

Market shares are shown in percent.

Grocery/supermarket	22.0%
Pharmacy/drug stores	22.0
Mass market	18.0
Club stores	9.0
Direct mail/catalog	8.0
Vitamin/supplement stores	5.0
Natural/health food stores	4.0
Direct from sales rep	3.0
Other	8.5

Source: "Vitamins, Minerals, Herbs & Supplements." Retrieved October 19, 2000 from the World Wide Web: http://www.exposemagazine.com.

★ 1667 ★
Retailing - Weight Control Products (SIC 5999)

Retail Weight Control Sales

Sales are shown by channel.

	($ mil.)	Share
Mass	$ 143	43.33%
Drug stores	137	41.52
Supermarkets	50	15.15

Source: *Supermarket News*, January 8, 2001, p. 37.

SIC 60 - Depository Institutions

★ 1668 ★
Banking (SIC 6020)

Banking Market in Kansas City, MO

Market shares are shown in percent.

UMB Financial Corp.	13.80%
Bank of America	13.28
Firstar Corp.	13.12
Commerce Bancshares Inc.	11.98
Valley View Bancshares Inc.	6.45
Other	41.37

Source: *Kansas City Business Journal*, October 6, 2000, p. 1, from Federal Reserve Bank of Kansas City.

★ 1669 ★
Banking (SIC 6020)

Largest Independent Banks in Florida

Banks are ranked by total deposits in millions of dollars.

Century Bank	$ 229
First National Bank and Trust of Manatee	158
Peninsula Bank	93
Sarasota Bank	92
Englewood Bank	87
Charlotte State Bank	65
First State Bank	57
Community National Bank of Sarasota County	51
Community Bank of Manatee	50

Source: *Sarasota Herald-Tribune*, October 15, 2000, p. 12.

★ 1670 ★
Banking (SIC 6020)

Largest Online Banking Vendors

Banks are ranked by assets in billions of dollars.

Commerce Bancorp.	$ 8.3
UMB Financial Corp.	7.9
Cullen/Frost Bankers	7.7
Santander BanCorp.	7.6
Wilmington Trust Corp.	7.3
Trustmark Corp.	6.9
Fulton Financial Corp.	6.6
Valley National Bancorp.	6.4
Whitney Holding Corp.	6.2
Community First Bancshares	6.1

Source: *US Banker*, May 2001, p. 29.

★ 1671 ★
Banking (SIC 6020)

Largest U.S. Banks, 2000

Banks are ranked by assets in billions of dollars as of October 4, 2000.

Citigroup Inc.	$ 791.3
Bank of America Corp.	679.5
Chase Manhattan Corp.	662.4
Bank One Corp.	272.7
Wells Fargo & Co.	259.6
First Union Corp.	258.0
FleetBoston Financial Corp.	220.2
U.S. Banorp	160.6
SunTrust Banks Inc.	99.7
KeyCorp.	84.7

Source: *Chicago Tribune*, October 5, 2000, p. 1, from SNL Securities.

★ 1672 ★

Banking (SIC 6020)

Leading Banks in Mexico

Shares are shown by accounts.

Banamex/Citibank	22.0%
BBVA/Bancomer	18.0
Other	60.0

Source: *Wall Street Journal*, May 18, 2001, p. A3.

★ 1673 ★

Banking (SIC 6020)

Online Banking Market Shares

Leading banks are measured by the percentage of active online banking customers identifying the bank as their primary web bank.

Wells Fargo	14.14%
Bank of America	9.55
Citibank	4.82
Bank One	4.01
First Union	2.96
BankBoston	2.53
Washington Mutual	2.29
Wachovia	1.81
Chase Manhattan	1.72
Fleet Financial	1.34
Other	52.45

Source: *Banking Strategies*, March/April 2000, p. 20, from Gomez Advisors.

★ 1674 ★

Banking (SIC 6020)

Small Business Market in Canada

Market shares are shown in percent.

Royal Bank	21.2%
Canadian Imperial Bank of Commerce	13.3
Bank of Montreal	12.6
Scotiabank	11.2
Other	41.7

Source: "CIBC and Royal Bank See Their Market Share Drop." Retrieved September 14, 2000 from the World Wide Web: http://www.northernlight.com, from Canadian Federation of Independent Business.

★ 1675 ★

Banking (SIC 6020)

Top Banks in Atlanta, GA

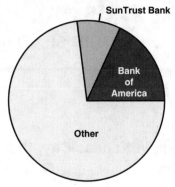

Market shares are shown based on deposits as of June 30, 2000.

Bank of America Corp.	$ 18.2
SunTrust Bank	9.2
Other	72.6

Source: *Atlanta Business Chronicle*, February 9, 2001, p. 1, from Federal Deposit Insurance Corp.

★ 1676 ★

Banking (SIC 6020)

Top Banks in Baltimore, MD

Market shares are shown based on deposits.

Allfirst	18.23%
Bank of America	17.08
Other	64.69

Source: *Baltimore Business Journal*, February 2, 2001, p. 1, from Federal Deposit Insurance Corp.

★ 1677 ★

Banking (SIC 6020)

Top Banks in California

Market shares are shown in percent.

Bank of America	22.7%
Wells Fargo	12.7
Other	64.6

Source: *Contra Costa Times*, March 7, 2001, p. C1.

★ 1678 ★
Banking (SIC 6020)

Top Banks in Canada, 2000

Market shares are shown based on deposits as of October 31, 2000.

Royal Bank of Canada	19.7%
Toronto-Dominion Bank	18.0
CIBC	17.4
Scotiabank	16.9
Bank of Montreal	15.2
Other	12.8

Source: *Marketing Magazine*, June 4, 2001, p. NA.

★ 1679 ★
Banking (SIC 6020)

Top Banks in Colorado

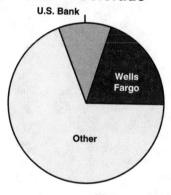

U.S. Bank

Wells Fargo

Other

Market shares are shown in percent.

Wells Fargo	20.0%
U.S. Bank	11.0
Other	69.0

Source: *Milwaukee Journal Sentinel*, October 9, 2000, p. 3.

★ 1680 ★
Banking (SIC 6020)

Top Banks in Columbus, OH

Market shares are shown based on deposits.

Bank One	28.4%
Huntington National Bank	16.6
Fifth Third of Columbus	11.5
Park National Bank	4.5
Other	38.0

Source: *Business First - Greater Columbus Business Authority*, February 23, 2001, p. 1, from Federal Deposit Insurance Corp.

★ 1681 ★
Banking (SIC 6020)

Top Banks in Florida

Shares are shown based on deposits.

Bank of America	21.90%
First Union Corp. of Florida	15.71
SunTrust Banks of Florida	13.24
SouthTrust of Alabama	4.42
Amsouth Bancorp.	2.58
Huntington Bancshares	2.14
Union Planters Holding Corp.	1.91
Ocean Bankshares	1.32
Northern Trust of Florida	1.22
Other	35.56

Source: *Florida Trend*, January 2001, p. 120, from staff research.

★ 1682 ★
Banking (SIC 6020)

Top Banks in Hamilton County, Kentucky

Market shares are shown in percent.

Provident	29.5%
Fifth Third	22.0
Firstar	20.7
PNC	9.7
Key	2.0

Continued on next page.

★ 1682 ★ *Continued*

Banking (SIC 6020)

Top Banks in Hamilton County, Kentucky

Market shares are shown in percent.

Bank One	1.8%
Huntington	1.8
Winton	1.5
Other	11.0

Source: *Business Courier Serving Cincinnati - Northern Kentucky*, February 2, 2001, p. 7, from Federal Deposit Insurance Corp.

★ 1683 ★

Banking (SIC 6020)

Top Banks in Henry County, Georgia

Market shares are shown in percent.

First State	42.0%
Heritage Bank	4.5
First Newton Bank	1.5
Other	52.0

Source: *Atlanta Business Chronicle*, September 29, 2000, p. 1, from T. Stephen Johnson & Associates.

★ 1684 ★

Banking (SIC 6020)

Top Banks in Kansas City, KA

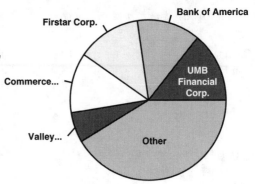

Market shares are shown in percent.

UMB Financial Corp.	13.80%
Bank of America	13.28
Firstar Corp.	13.12
Commerce Bancshares Inc.	11.98
Valley View	6.45
Other	41.37

Source: *Wichita Business Journal*, December 8, 2000, p. 24, from Federal Reserve Bank of Kansas City.

★ 1685 ★

Banking (SIC 6020)

Top Banks in Kentucky

Market shares are shown in percent.

Fifth Third	22.35%
Provident	22.10
Firstar	18.60
PNC	8.20
Bank One	3.10
Huntington	2.90
1st SW	2.70
Key	2.30
Other	22.40

Source: *Business Courier Serving Cincinnati - Northern Kentucky*, February 2, 2001, p. 7, from Federal Deposit Insurance Corp.

★ 1686 ★

Banking (SIC 6020)

Top Banks in Mexico

Market shares are shown in percent as of March 2000.

BBVA-Bancomer	27.0%
Banamex	19.0
Santander-Serfin	16.0
Bital	9.0
Banorte	7.0
Citibank	6.0
Other	16.0

Source: *The Economist*, June 17, 2000, p. 76, from National Banking and Securities Commission.

★ 1687 ★

Banking (SIC 6020)

Top Banks in Minnesota

Shares are shown based on June 1999 deposit data, the most recent available.

Wells Fargo	24.2%
U.S. Bancorp	22.0
TCF Financial Corp.	4.0
Firstar	2.9
Other	47.1

Source: *Star Tribune*, November 26, 2000, p. 1D, from Federal Deposit Insurance Data.

★ 1688 ★

Banking (SIC 6020)

Top Banks in Nashville, TN

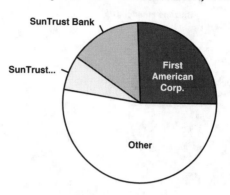

Marekt shares are as of October 1999.

First American Corp.	25.65%
SunTrust Bank	15.11
SunTrust Bank	6.50
Other	52.74

Source: *Nashville Business Journal*, July 24, 2000, p. 1.

★ 1689 ★

Banking (SIC 6020)

Top Banks in Nassau County, FL

Market shares are shown in percent.

Bank of America	20.08%
First Union National Bank	19.32
First Coast Community Bank	18.84
Compass Bank	12.87
Southeastern Bank	11.50
Other	17.39

Source: *Florida Times Union*, April 2, 2001, p. F12, from Florida Bankers Association.

★ 1690 ★

Banking (SIC 6020)

Top Banks in New England

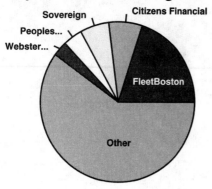

Shares are shown based on deposits.

FleetBoston	19.7%
Citizens Financial	7.1
Sovereign	6.0
Peoples Heritage	4.1
Webster Financial	2.8
Other	60.3

Source: *American Banker*, May 15, 2000, p. 1, from Sheshunoff Information Services Inc.

★ 1691 ★

Banking (SIC 6020)

Top Banks in New Jersey

Market shares are shown in percent.

Summit	14.27%
First Union	11.65
Fleet	8.26
Other	65.82

Source: *Knight-Ridder/Tribune Business News*, February 7, 2001, p. NA.

★ 1692 ★

Banking (SIC 6020)

Top Banks in New York

Market shares are shown in percent.

Chase	47.0%
Deutsche Bank/HSBC/Bank of New York . .	23.0
Citibank	13.0
Other	17.0

Source: *Crain's New York Business*, February 19, 2001, p. 1, from Lehman Brothers.

★ 1693 ★

Banking (SIC 6020)

Top Banks in North Carolina

Market shares are shown based on deposits.

Bank of America	22.0%
BB&T	15.2
Wachovia	13.2
First Union	12.8
Centura Banks	7.0
First Citizens	7.0
National Commerce Bancorp.	5.8
First Charter	1.9
First Bancorp	0.8
Fifelity Bancshares	0.8
Other	13.5

Source: *Business North Carolina*, February 2001, p. 45, from SNL Securities.

★ 1694 ★

Banking (SIC 6020)

Top Banks in Polk County, FL

Market shares are shown based on deposits.

Bank of America	26.6%
First Union	21.0
SunTrust	19.0
Huntington	10.6
Citrus & Chemical	8.6
Other	14.2

Source: *Tampa Bay Business Journal*, January 5, 2001, p. 23, from Florida Bankers Association.

★ 1695 ★

Banking (SIC 6020)

Top Banks in Portland-Vancouver Area

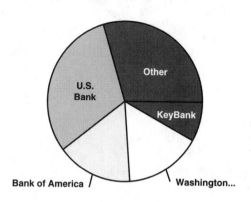

Market shares are shown based on deposits.

Other	29.5%
U.S. Bank	31.0
Bank of America	15.9
Washington Mutual	15.9
KeyBank	7.7

Source: *Business Journal - Portland*, February 23, 2001, p. 1, from Federal Deposit Insurance Corp.

★ 1696 ★

Banking (SIC 6020)

Top Banks in St. Louis, MO

Banks are ranked by deposits, in millions, as of June 30, 2000.

Firstar	$ 8,200
Bank of America	5,300
Commerce	2,600
Union Planters	2,500
First Bank	1,500
Southwest Bank	1,300
First National	679
UMB	675
Allegiant	628
Bank of Edwardville	592

Source: *St. Louis Business Journal*, February 16, 2001, p. 30.

★ 1697 ★

Banking (SIC 6020)

Top Banks in St. Tammany, LA

Market shares are as of June 2000.

Hibernia National Bank	32.0%
Bank One Corp.	24.4
Parish National Bank	11.0
Other	22.6

Source: *New Orleans City Business*, April 2, 2001, p. S15.

★ 1698 ★

Banking (SIC 6020)

Top Banks in Sarasota County, FL

Market shares are shown based on deposits.

Bank of America	32.5%
SunTrust	17.4
First Union	10.8
SouthTrust	9.5
Huntington	7.3
Other	22.5

Source: *Tampa Bay Business Journal*, January 5, 2001, p. 23, from Florida Bankers Association.

★ 1699 ★

Banking (SIC 6020)

Top Banks in South Carolina

Market shares are shown based on deposits as of June 30, 2000.

	($ mil.)	Share
Wachovia	$ 6.02	15.78%
Bank of America	4.84	12.68
BB&T	4.04	10.60
First Citizens	2.26	5.94
Carolina First Bank	2.20	5.78

Source: *The State*, January 30, 2001, p. B6, from Federal Deposit Insurance Corp.

★ 1700 ★

Banking (SIC 6020)

Top Banks in the Bay Area, California for Asians

Figures are based on a survey.

Bank of America	40.0%
Wells Fargo	12.0
Other	48.0

Source: *Contra Costa Times*, March 3, 2001, p. C11.

★ 1701 ★

Banking (SIC 6020)

Top Banks in the New York Area

Area includes five boroughs, plus Putnam, Rockland and Westchester counties. Figures are as of January 24, 2000.

Chase Manhattan	33.3%
Citibank	13.7
HSBC Holdings	7.2
Bank of New York	6.7
First Union	2.7
Green Point	2.6
Dime	2.4
Emigrant Saving	1.7
Astoria Financial	1.6
Other	28.1

Source: *New York Times*, February 6, 2001, p. C1, from J.P. Morgan Chase and SNL Securities.

★ 1702 ★

Banking (SIC 6020)

Top Banks in the Triangle, N.C.

Market shares are shown in percent as of June 30, 2000.

Centura Banks	10.07%
Bank of America	8.92
First Union	8.43
Other	72.58

Source: *Knight-Ridder/Tribune Business News*, February 9, 2001, p. NA, from SNL Securities.

★ 1703 ★

Banking (SIC 6020)

Top Banks in Utah

Companies are ranked by assets in millions of dollars.

American Investment Bank	$ 545.0
Barnes Banking Company	407.2
Bank of Utah	402.0
Bank of American Fork	335.8
Central Bank	312.0
Wells Fargo	272.0
Banc One Utah	269.0
Washington Mutual Bank	194.2

Source: *Utah Business*, April 2001, p. 76.

★ 1704 ★

Banking (SIC 6020)

Top Banks in Virginia

Market shares are shown in percent.

SunTrust Banks Inc.	14.0%
Bank of America	11.0
First Union Corp.	11.0
Wachovia	9.0
Other	55.0

Source: *Knight-Ridder/Tribune Business News*, January 24, 2001, p. NA, from SNL Securities.

★ 1705 ★

Banking (SIC 6020)

Top Banks in Washington D.C.

Market shares are shown in percent.

Bank of America	14.0%
SuNTrust	14.0
Other	72.0

Source: *Washington Times*, February 26, 2001, p. 3.

★ 1706 ★

Banking (SIC 6020)

Top Banks in Wisconsin

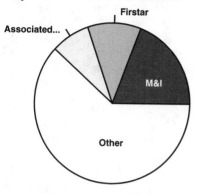

Shares are shown based on deposits.

M&I	19.2%
Firstar	11.4
Associated Banc-corp.	8.1
Other	61.3

Source: *Milwaukee Journal Sentinel*, October 8, 2000, p. 1, from Marshall & Isley Corp.

★ 1707 ★

Banking (SIC 6029)

Top Community Banks in Memphis, TN

Banks are ranked by assets in millions of dollars.

INSOUTH Bank	$ 606.08
Bank of Barlett	403.72
Trust One Bank	339.12
Peoples Bank	333.05
Enterprise National Bank	220.38
BankTennessee	190.83
The Somerville Bank &Trust Co.	175.35

Source: *The Commercial Appeal*, August 27, 2000, p. C1.

★ 1708 ★

Credit Unions (SIC 6060)

Largest Credit Unions, 2000

Firms are ranked by assets in billions of dollars.

Navy FCU	$ 12.41
State Employees	6.58
Pentagon	3.62

Boeing Employees	.$ 3.55
United Airlines Employees	3.10
The Golden 1	3.04
Orange County Teachers	2.73
American Airlines	2.66
Suncoast Schools	2.43
Hughes Aircraft Employees	2.15

Source: *Credit Union Journal*, March 12, 2001, p. 16.

★ 1709 ★

Credit Unions (SIC 6060)

Largest Credit Unions in Sacramento, CA

Companies are ranked by assets in millions, as of December 31, 1999.

The Golden 1 Credit Union	$ 2,564.3
Schools Financial Credit Union	677.9
SAFE Credit Union	648.6
Heritage Community Credit Union	183.1
Sacramento Credit Union	160.3
American River HealthPro Credit Union . .	112.8
First Federal Credit Union	84.6

Source: *Sacramento Business Journal*, April 28, 2000, p. 16.

★ 1710 ★

Credit Unions (SIC 6062)

Largest Credit Unions in Utah

Companies are ranked by assets in millions of dollars.

America First Credit Union	$ 1,766.0
Mountain America Credit Union	800.0
Utah Community Credit Union	285.0
Rocky Mountain Corporate	257.5
University of Utah Credit Union	208.0
Deseret First Credit Union	205.1
Goldenwest Credit Union	177.0
Cyprus Credit Union	136.5

Source: *Utah Business*, April 2001, p. 76.

★ 1711 ★

Money Orders (SIC 6099)

Money Order Market

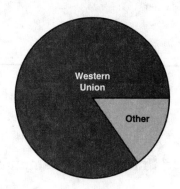

Market shares are shown in percent.

Western Union	85.0%
Other	15.0

Source: *Forbes*, November 13, 2000, p. 224.

SIC 61 - Nondepository Institutions

★ 1712 ★

Credit Cards (SIC 6141)

Credit Card Market

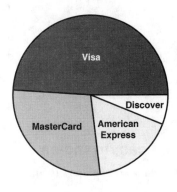

Market shares are shown in percent.

Visa	48.9%
MasterCard	27.7
American Express	17.0
Discover	6.4

Source: *Michigan Retailer*, July/August 2000, p. 1, from Cardweb.com.

★ 1713 ★

Credit Cards (SIC 6141)

Debit Card Market Shares, 2000

Market shares are for the first nine months of the year.

Visa	79.3%
Other	20.7

Source: *CardFax*, January 3, 2001, p. 2.

★ 1714 ★

Credit Cards (SIC 6141)

Largest Credit Card Issuers

Firms are ranked by outstanding debt in billions of dollars.

Citigroup	$ 96.2
MBNA	70.5
First USA	67.0
American Express	50.2
Discover	47.6

Source: *Business Week*, March 19, 2001, p. 91, from Nilson Report.

★ 1715 ★

Credit Cards (SIC 6141)

Largest Credit Card Markets

Credit card spending is shown for Thanksgiving to Christmas on VISA, MasterCard, American Express & Discover. Figures are in billions of dollars.

California	$ 16.30
New York	9.58
Florida	8.16
Texas	6.33
Illinois	5.82

Source: *USA TODAY*, December 18, 2000, p. B1, from www.cardweb.com.

★ 1716 ★

Credit Cards (SIC 6141)

Largest Transaction Acquiring Institutions

The top 10 acquirers account for 76.7% of the $838.5 billion in domestic Visa and Mastercard volume.

Chase Merchant Services	$ 150.5
National Processing Company	115.9

Continued on next page.

★ 1716 ★ *Continued*
Credit Cards (SIC 6141)

Largest Transaction Acquiring Institutions

The top 10 acquirers account for 76.7% of the $838.5 billion in domestic Visa and Mastercard volume.

Paymentech	$ 93.3
Nova Information Systems Inc.	60.0
BA Merchant Services Inc.	50.7
Fifth Third Bank	44.6
Concord EFS/EFS National Bank . . .	37.2
Unified Merchant Services	31.6
Wells Fargo Bank	31.4
U.S. Bancorp.	27.6

Source: *Credit Card News*, July 15, 2000, p. 16.

★ 1717 ★
Credit Cards (SIC 6141)

Leading Credit Card Companies, 1999

Firms are ranked by accounts receivable in billions of dollars as of December 1999.

Citigroup/Associates First	$ 85.9
Bank One	69.4
MBNA	64.3
Discover	38.0
Chase	33.6
Bank of America	19.7

Source: *New York Times*, September 7, 2000, p. C6, from Citigroup.

★ 1718 ★
Credit Cards (SIC 6141)

Offline Debit Card Market

Market shares are shown based on a total of 116.8 million cards.

Bank of America	12.4%
Wells Fargo	7.0
Bank One	3.6
First Union	2.4
FleetBoston	2.2
Other	72.4

Source: *Bank Network News*, September 15, 2000, p. 4.

★ 1719 ★
Loan Arrangers (SIC 6150)

Largest Agricultural Banks

Banks are ranked by total agricultural loans in millions of dollars.

Bank of America NA	$ 2,829.0
Wells Fargo Bank NA	2,390.0
US Bank NA	1,223.8
Sanwa Bank California	928.7
First Union NB	861.0
Keybank NA	798.3
Union Planters NB	682.7
Regions Bank	662.6
First NB of Omaha	390.1
Washington MSB	387.9

Source: *Ag Lender*, July 2000, p. 12.

★ 1720 ★
Loan Arrangers (SIC 6150)

Largest Gross Loan Arrangers

Firms are ranked by millions of dollars in gross loans.

FCS of America	$ 5,118.5
FCS of Mid-America	4,904.5
Northwest FCS	3,054.9
AgStar	1,188.1
First Pioneer Farm Credit	1,185.6
Badgerland FCS	915.2
FCS-AdCountry	906.5
Pacific Country FCS	832.4
Valley PCA/FLCA	742.5
AgGeorgia Farm Credit	627.5

Source: *Ag Lender*, June 2000, p. 10, from Farm Credit System.

★ 1721 ★
Loan Arrangers (SIC 6153)

Small Business Loans

Market shares are shown in percent.

Banks	83.0%
Finance companies	8.0
Other	9.0

Source: *USA TODAY*, January 10, 2001, p. 6B, from National Federation of Independent Business.

★ 1722 ★

Mortgage Loans (SIC 6162)

Largest Mortgage Servicers

Market shares are shown as of June 5, 2000.

Wells Fargo	8.55%
BankAmerica	6.69
Chase Manhattan	6.60
WaMu	5.80
Countrywide	5.37
Other	66.99

Source: *National Mortgage News*, October 9, 2000, p. 1, from *NMN/Mortgage Industry Soourcebook*.

★ 1723 ★

Mortgage Loans (SIC 6162)

Largest Subprime Servicers, 2000

Firms are ranked by value of loans, in millions, for the third quarter.

Advanta Mortgage USA	$ 12,716
Fairbanks Capital Corp.	12,641
Option One Mortgage Group	6,087
CitiFinancial	5,340
Ocwen Financial Corp.	4,665
Mortgage Lenders Network	2,219
Aurora Loan Services	1,752
Wendover Financial Svcs. Corp.	1,650
Countrywide/Full Spectrum	792
Aames Financial Corp.	264

Source: *Mortage Servicing News*, December 2000, p. 17.

★ 1724 ★

Mortgage Loans (SIC 6162)

Mortgage Brokers by State

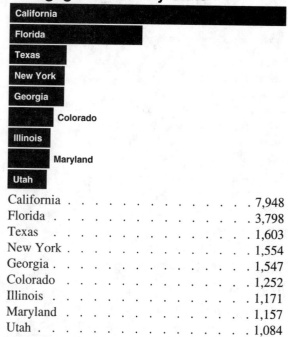

California	7,948
Florida	3,798
Texas	1,603
New York	1,554
Georgia	1,547
Colorado	1,252
Illinois	1,171
Maryland	1,157
Utah	1,084

Source: *Mortgage Banking*, October 2000, p. 96, from Wholesale Access.

★ 1725 ★

Mortgage Loans (SIC 6162)

New Home Loans in Northeast Ohio

Market shares are shown for new homes from January - June 2000.

Third Federal	23.0%
Charter One	7.0
Metropolitan Bank & Trust	5.0
National City Bank of Cleveland	4.6
Wells Fargo Home Mortgage of San Francisco	4.5
Other	56.9

Source: *Crain's Cleveland Business*, January 1, 2001, p. 9, from Realty One.

★ 1726 ★

Mortgage Loans (SIC 6162)

Top Mortgage Loan Arrangers in Cleveland, OH

Market shares are shown based on new homes.

Third Federal 23.0%
Charter One 7.0
Metropolitan Bank & Trust 5.0
National City Bank of Cleveland 4.6
Wells Fargo Home Mortgage of San
   Francisco 4.5
Other 45.9

Source: *Crain's Cleveland Business*, January 1, 2001, p. 9.

★ 1727 ★

Mortgage Loans (SIC 6162)

Top Residential Mortgage Originators, 2000

Originations are for the first half of the year.

	($ mil.)	Share
Chase Manhattan Mortgage . .	$ 33,959	7.60%
Wells Fargo Home Mortgage . . .	29,471	6.13
Bank of America Mortgage	27,760	5.77
Countrywide Home Loans Inc. . .	26,990	5.61
Washington Mutual	20,836	4.33
ABN AMRO Mortgage	10,350	2.15
Cendant Mortgage	9,763	2.03
National City Mortgage	9,472	1.97
CitiMortgage Inc.	9,437	1.96
Golden West Financial Corp. . . .	9,275	1.84

Source: *American Banker*, October 23, 2000, p. 12A.

★ 1728 ★

Loan Arrangers (SIC 6163)

Leveraged Syndicated Loaning Market

Market shares are shown for the third quarter of the year.

Banc of America Securities LLC 21.9%
Chase Manhattan Corp. 17.9
Credit Suisse First Boston 7.3
Morgan Stanley Dean Witter 4.1
Deutsche Bank AG 3.9
Merrill Lynch & Co. Inc. 3.6

FleetBoston Financial Corp. 3.4%
Bank One Corp. 2.6
First Union Corp. 2.2
BMO Nesbitt Burns Inc. 1.9
Other 31.2

Source: *American Banker*, October 3, 2000, p. 2, from Securities Data.

★ 1729 ★

Loan Arrangers (SIC 6163)

Syndicated Loan Arrangers

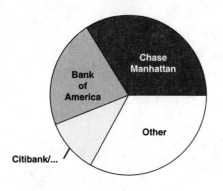

Market shares are shown in percent.

Chase Manhattan 34.0%
Bank of America 21.7
Citibank/SSB 11.0
Other 33.3

Source: *Bank Loan Report*, January 8, 2001, p. 1.

★ 1730 ★

Loan Arrangers (SIC 6163)

Top Lenders in Los Angeles-Long Beach, CA

Market shares are shown in percent.

Washington Mutual Bank 8.48%
Countrywide Home Loans 5.68
Bank of America 5.55
Chase Manhattan Mtg Corp. 4.80
First Nationwide Mtg Corp. 4.49
California Federal Bank 2.82

Continued on next page.

★ **1730** ★ *Continued*

Loan Arrangers (SIC 6163)

Top Lenders in Los Angeles-Long Beach, CA

Market shares are shown in percent.

PNC Mortgage Securities	2.43%
World Savings Bank	2.30
Downey S&L Assoc.	2.30
Other	61.15

Source: *Origination News*, January 2001, p. 9.

★ 1731 ★

Loan Arrangers (SIC 6163)

Top Loan Arrangers in Orlando, FL

Market shares are shown for 1999.

Suntrust Bank	7.42%
Countrywide Home Loans	5.13
Chase Manhattan Mortgage	5.05
Bank of America N.A.	4.06
Suntrust Mortgage Inc.	3.95
FT Mortgage Cos.	3.67
Irwin Mortgage Corp.	3.13
Norwest Mortgage Inc.	2.67
First Union National Bank	2.64
CTX Mortgage Co.	1.80
Other	60.48

Source: *Origination News*, January 2001, p. 9.

SIC 62 - Security and Commodity Brokers

★ 1732 ★

Investment Banking (SIC 6211)

Asset Backed Debt Industry

Market shares are shown in percent.

Salomon Smith Barney	19.5%
Credit Suisse First Boston	14.5
J.P. Morgan	11.6
Morgan Stanley Dean Witter	9.0
Deutsche Bank AG	8.9
Lehman Brothers	8.6
Banc of America Securities	5.9
Merrill Lynch & Co.	5.3
Goldman Sachs & Co.	4.6
Other	12.1

Source: *American Banker*, January 8, 2001, p. 1.

★ 1733 ★

Investment Banking (SIC 6211)

ECN Market Shares, 2000

Shares are shown for July 2000, based on dollar volume traded on the Nasdaq. ECN stands for electronic communication networks.

Instinet	14.3%
Island	8.5
Redi-Book	3.3
B-Trade	1.6
Brut	1.5
Archipelago	1.1
Other	69.7

Source: *Wall Street Letter*, September 25, 2000, p. S18.

★ 1734 ★

Investment Banking (SIC 6211)

Equities Market in Mexico

Market shares are shown in percent.

Accival	9.91%
Vector	8.88
Merrill Lynch	8.47
GBM	7.72
Inbursa	7.68
Santander	6.89
BBV Probursa	6.84
Banorte	6.82
Inverlat	6.30
Goldman Sachs	5.50
Other	24.99

Source: *MB*, November 2000, p. 16, from Bolsa Mexicana de Valores.

★ 1735 ★

Investment Banking (SIC 6211)

Largest Investment Financers in Canada

In 1999, gross revenues reached $8.8 billion, with 70% by large full-service firms. Market shares are shown in percent.

RBC Dominion Securities	15.5%
BMO Nesbitt Burns	13.8
BIBC World Markets	12.7
Scotia Capital	10.2
TD Securities	9.7
Merrill Lynch	6.8
Other	31.3

Source: ''The Canadian Securities Industry.'' Retrieved June 5, 2001 from the World Wide Web: http://www.fin.gc.ca, from *Globe and Mail*.

★ 1736 ★

Investment Banking (SIC 6211)

Largest Money Managers in Detroit, MI

Firms are ranked by assets under management with discretion.

Munder Capital Management	$ 41,073.0
Comerica Bank Private Banking	11,145.6
Loomis Sayles & Co L.P., Value Equity Management Group	3,880.2
Michigan National Corp.	2,579.0
Wilson, Kemp & Associates	1,729.3
Advance Capital Management Inc. . . .	692.0
Flexible Plan Investments Ltd.	682.4
Jay A. Fishman Ltd.	670.2
NorthePointe Capital L.L.C.	650.0
Beacon Investment Co.	474.8

Source: *Crain's Detroit Business*, February 26, 2001, p. 22.

★ 1737 ★

Investment Banking (SIC 6211)

Largest Mutual Fund Groups in Canada

Firms are ranked by assets in billions of dollars.

Investors Group	$ 43.6
Royal Mutual Funds	33.9
Fidelity Investments Canada	32.9
Mackenzie Financial	32.7
TD Asset Management	29.1

Source: *Canadian Business*, October 2, 2000, p. 17, from Investment Funds Institute of Canada.

★ 1738 ★

Investment Banking (SIC 6211)

Largest Online Brokers

Firms are ranked by assets of online customers.

Schwab Online	$ 413.5
Fidelity Online	326.2
TWE Online	113.0
E*Trade	56.7
Ameritrade	34.8
DLJdirect	24.8
Datek	14.3
Fleet Online	13.0
NDB	9.9
Scottrade Online	5.8

Source: *Business Week*, November 20, 2000, p. E102, from Salomon Smith Barney and company reports.

★ 1739 ★

Investment Banking (SIC 6211)

Leading High Tech M&A Advisers

Firms are ranked by value of deals for 1996-2001. Credit is given to target & acquiring advisers.

	($ bil.)	Share
Goldman Sachs & Co.	$ 858.9	41.3%
Credit Suisse First Boston . . .	668.8	32.2
Merrill Lynch & Co.	596.9	28.7
Morgan Stanley	562.9	27.1
Salomon Smith Barney	406.3	19.6
Lehman Brothers	350.3	16.9
J.P. Morgan	315.1	15.2
Bear, Stearns & Co.	253.9	12.2

Continued on next page.

★ 1739 ★ *Continued*

Investment Banking (SIC 6211)

Leading High Tech M&A Advisers

Firms are ranked by value of deals for 1996-2001.
Credit is given to target & acquiring advisers.

	($ bil.)	Share
Lazard	$ 171.8	8.3%
UBS Warburg	87.5	4.2

Source: *Upside*, June 2001, p. 116, from Thomson Financial Securities Data.

★ 1740 ★

Investment Banking (SIC 6211)

Leading Investment Banks in Canada, 2000

Firms are ranked by value of underwriting deals, in billions of dollars.

RBC Dominion	$ 15.5
TD Securities	11.9
Scotia Capital	8.0
SMO Nesbitt Burns	7.9
CIBC World Markets	6.9
Merrill Lynch	6.4
Credit Suisse First Boston	3.2
Salomon Smith Barney	3.1
Goldman Sachs	2.2
Morgan Stanley Dean Witter	2.0

Source: *Maclean's*, May 14, 2001, p. 46, from FP Data Group.

★ 1741 ★

Investment Banking (SIC 6211)

Leading IPO Managers, 2000

Market shares are shown in percent.

Goldman Sachs	24.2%
Morgan Stanley Dean Witter	15.5
Credit Suisse First Boston	15.3
Salomon Smith Barney	12.1
Merrill Lynch	9.2
Deutsche Bank	4.2
J.P. Morgan	3.5

Lehman Brothers	3.4%
FleetBoston Financial	2.9
China International Capital	1.8
Other	7.9

Source: *Wall Street Journal*, January 2, 2001, p. R19.

★ 1742 ★

Investment Banking (SIC 6211)

Leading Loan Book Managers, 2000

Market shares are shown in percent.

J.P. Morgan	34.0%
Banc of Am. Sec.	21.7
Salomon S.B.	11.0
Bank One	4.9
Credit Suisse F.B.	3.9
FleetBoston	2.9
Deutsche Bank	2.7
First Union	1.9
Goldman Sachs	1.6
Societe Generale	1.2
Other	14.1

Source: *Wall Street Journal*, January 2, 2001, p. R19.

★ 1743 ★

Investment Banking (SIC 6211)

RMBS League Market Shares

RMBS stands for residential mortgage backed securities.

CS First Boston/DLJ	17.1%
Lehman Brothers	15.0
Bear, Stearns & Co.	13.0
Other	54.9

Source: *Asset Sales Report*, January 8, 2001, p. 1, from Thomson Financial Securities Data.

★ 1744 ★

Investment Banking (SIC 6211)

Tech Equity Industry

Technology companies raised more than $146 billion in the first nine months of the year. Market shares are shown in percent.

Goldman Sachs	20.5%
Morgan Stanley Dean Witter	16.7

Continued on next page.

★ 1744 ★ *Continued*

Investment Banking (SIC 6211)

Tech Equity Industry

Technology companies raised more than $146 billion in the first nine months of the year. Market shares are shown in percent.

Salomon Smith Barney	12.0%
Credit Suisse First Boston	11.6
Merrill Lynch	11.1
Lehman Brothers	4.3
Deutsche Bank	3.8
Other	20.0

Source: *Infoworld*, October 16, 2000, p. 16, from Thomson Financial Securities Data.

★ 1745 ★

Investment Banking (SIC 6211)

Top Bank Merger Advisers

Firms are ranked by value of announced deals in millions of dollars.

	($ mil.)	Share
Credit Suisse First Boston Corp.	$ 7,313.7	27.18%
J.P. Morgan & Co.	5,150.9	19.14
Merrill Lynch & Co.	2,710.0	10.07
Goldman, Sachs & Co.	2,618.6	9.73
Morgan Stanley Dean Witter & Co.	1,916.6	7.12
Sandler O'Neill & Partners L.P.	1,446.7	5.38
Keefe, Bruyette & Woods Inc.	1,276.1	4.74
Salomon Smith Barney	759.5	2.82
Stifel, Nicolaus & Co.	536.0	1.99
Other	3,178.9	11.81

Source: *U.S. Banker*, September 2000, p. 66, from Sheshunoff Information Services Inc.

★ 1746 ★

Investment Banking (SIC 6211)

Top Managers of Municipal Finance Deals

Market shares are shown in percent.

Salomon Smith	14.0%
PaineWebber	10.8
Other	75.2

Source: *Bond Buyer*, July 5, 2000, p. 37.

★ 1747 ★

Investment Banking (SIC 6211)

Top Mutual Fund Managers in Canada, 2001

Market shares are shown based on total assets as of March 31, 2001.

Investors Group	10.6%
Royal Mutual Funds	8.2
AIM Funds Management	8.0
Fidelity Investments Canada	7.8
Mackenzie Financial	7.6
TD Asset Management	7.2
AGF Management	7.0
CIBC Securities	5.8
CI Mutual Funds	5.3
Franklin Templeton Investments	5.0
Other	27.5

Source: *Marketing Magazine*, June 4, 2001, p. NA, from Investment Funds Institute of Canada.

★ 1748 ★

Investment Banking (SIC 6211)

Who Manages 401(K) Plans

The nation now has $1.7 trillion in 401(k) assets.

Third-party administrators	26.1%
Banks	14.3
Mutual funds	13.2
Insurance companies	12.2
Internal staff	8.1

Continued on next page.

Investment Banking (SIC 6211)

Who Manages 401(K) Plans

The nation now has $1.7 trillion in 401(k) assets.

Consulting firms	5.6%
Brokerage firms	3.1
Investment advisers	1.8
Others	15.6

Source: *New York Times*, November 17, 2000, p. C1, from Profit Sharing/401 (K) Council of America.

★ 1749 ★
Underwriting (SIC 6211)

Corporate Securities Underwriting

Market shares are shown in percent.

Merrill Lynch	15.1%
Salomon Smith Barney	13.1
Morgan Stanley Dean Witter	9.8
Goldman, Sachs	9.4
Credit Suisse First Boston	9.1
Chase Manhattan	6.6
Lehman Brothers	6.5
Banc of America Securities	5.1
J.P. Morgan	4.6
Deutsche Bank	3.9
Other	16.8

Source: *New York Times*, September 13, 2000, p. C14, from Thomson Financial Securities Data.

★ 1750 ★
Underwriting (SIC 6211)

Largest Debt and Equity Underwriting

Market shares are based on proceeds for the year to date.

Merrill Lynch	14.9%
Salomon Smith Barney	12.6
Morgan Stanley Dean Witter	10.2
Goldman Sachs	9.4
Credit Suisse First Boston	9.3
Lehman Brothers	7.0
Chase Manhattan	6.9
Banc of America Securities	5.1
Other	24.6

Source: *Wall Street Journal*, July 13, 2000, p. A18, from Thomson Financial Securities Data.

★ 1751 ★
Underwriting (SIC 6211)

Largest Healthcare Underwriters, 2001

Data are for tax-exempt healthcare issues, January-March 2001.

Merrill Lynch & Co.	27.3%
Bear, Stearns & Co.	20.9
Salomon Smith Barney	12.2
J.P. Morgan Securities	6.6
Morgan Stanley	4.2
Other	28.8

Source: *Modern Healthcare*, April 16, 2001, p. 36, from Thomson Financial Securities Data.

★ 1752 ★
Underwriting (SIC 6211)

Leading Bond Underwriters in Arkansas

Market shares are shown in percent.

Morgan Keegan	18.0%
Salomon Smith Barney	16.0
Stephens Inc.	16.0
Williams & Anderson	10.0
Other	40.0

Source: *Arkansas Democrat-Gazette*, February 1, 2001, p. 1.

★ 1753 ★
Underwriting (SIC 6211)

Top Corporate Security Underwriters

Shares are for the third quarter of the year.

Merrill Lynch	15.9%
Salomon Smith Barney	12.9
Goldman, Sachs	10.1
Morgan Stanlay Dean Witter	9.4
Credit Suisse First Boston	7.2
Deutsche Bank	6.1
Chase Manhattan	5.9
Lehman Brothers	5.7
Banc of America Securities	5.2
J.P. Morgan	4.6
Other	17.0

Source: *New York Times*, October 2, 2000, p. C2, from Thomson Financial Securities Data.

★ 1754 ★

Underwriting (SIC 6211)

Top Equity Underwriters

Market shares are shown in percent.

Goldman Sachs	22.1%
Morgan Stanley Dean Witter	14.7
Merrill Lynch	11.2
Credit Suisse First Boston	11.1
Salomon Smith Barney	10.3
J.P. Morgan	4.9
Lehman Bros.	4.2
FleetBoston Financial	3.4
Other	18.1

Source: *New York Times*, August 30, 2000, p. C19, from company reports and Thompson Financial Securities Data.

★ 1755 ★

Securities Exchanges (SIC 6231)

ECN Trading on the Nasdaq

ECN stands for electronic communication networks. Data are for March 2000. Shares are based on dollar volume.

Instinet	14.2%
Island	6.4
Redi-Book	1.8
B-Trade	1.5
Archipelago	1.0
Brut	1.0
Strike	0.1

Source: *The Economist*, May 20, 2000, p. 50, from Nasdaq.

★ 1756 ★

Financial Information (SIC 6282)

Leading Financial Information Providers

Providers are ranked by revenue in billions of dollars.

Bloomberg	$ 2.4
Reuters	2.3
Bridge Information Systems	1.6

Source: *Business Week*, April 23, 2001, p. 76, from Risk Waters Group.

SIC 63 - Insurance Carriers

★ 1757 ★
Insurance (SIC 6300)

Largest Insurers in Canada

Sun Life Financial Services	
Manulife Financial	
	Great-West Lifeco
	Canada Life Financial
	Clarica Life Insurance

Firms are ranked by assets under management in billions of dollars.

Sun Life Financial Services	$ 206.40
Manulife Financial	81.05
Great-West Lifeco	61.02
Canada Life Financial	40.82
Clarica Life Insurance	29.89

Source: *Wall Street Journal*, May 4, 2001, p. A11, from Tradeline.com.

★ 1758 ★
Insurance (SIC 6300)

Largest Vermont Captives, 1999

Firms are ranked by gross premium volume in millions of dollars.

Marsh Management Services Inc. . . .	$ 1,450.6
IRMG/American Risk Management Corp. .	589.1
Aon Insurance Managers Inc.	483.8
Yankee Captive Management Inc. . . .	374.4
Becher & Carlson Cos.	338.0
AIG Insurance Management Services Inc. .	251.2
Willis Management (Vermont) Ltd. . . .	176.1
Vermont Insurance Management Inc. . . .	167.4

Source: *Business Insurance*, May 1, 2000, p. 20.

★ 1759 ★
Insurance (SIC 6300)

Online Insurance Market

Spending is estimated in billions of dollars.

	2000	2003	Share
Auto	$ 1.2	$ 9.1	86.67%
Home	0.5	0.9	8.57
Term life	0.2	0.4	3.81
Renters	0.1	0.1	0.95

Source: *Grok*, February-March 2001, p. 105, from Forrester Research.

★ 1760 ★
Auto Insurance (SIC 6321)

Largest Auto Insurers, 1999

Firms are ranked by earned premiums in billions of dollars.

State Farm Mutual Auto	$ 22.8
Allstate Insurance Company	14.5
Nationwide Mutual Insurance	4.7
Government Employees Insurance	3.6
Farmers Insurance Exchange	3.2
Progressive Casualty Insurance Co.	2.7
American Family Mutual	2.3
United Services Auto	2.2
Liberty Mutual Insurance Co.	1.7
Usaa Casualty Insurance	1.4

Source: *National Underwriter*, August 21, 2000, p. 1.

★ 1761 ★

Auto Insurance (SIC 6321)

Largest Auto Insurers in Arkansas

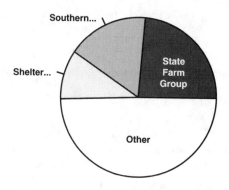

Market shares are shown in percent. Figures are for private auto insurance.

State Farm Group	23.67%
Southern Farm Bureau Group	16.94
Shelter Insurance Cos.	9.76
Other	49.63

Source: *A.M. Best Newswire*, April 13, 2001, p. NA, from A.M.Best & Co.

★ 1762 ★

Auto Insurance (SIC 6321)

Largest Auto Insurers in California

Market shares are shown in percent.

State Farm Group	13.9%
Farmers Insurance	13.4
California State Auto Group	10.2
Allstate Insurance Group	9.1
Automobile Club of Southern California . . .	8.5
Other	44.9

Source: *A.M. Best Newswire*, May 3, 2001, p. NA.

★ 1763 ★

Auto Insurance (SIC 6321)

Largest Auto Insurers in Florida

The auto insurance industry generated $7 billion a year in premiums. Market shares are shown in percent.

State Farm Mutual	21.1%
Allstate	10.7
Progressive Express	9.2

GEICO	7.6%
Allstate Indemnity	6.2
Nationwide Mutual	3.1
USAA	2.5
Hartford of the Midwest	1.7
Other	37.9

Source: *St. Petersburg Times*, June 6, 2000, p. 1E, from Florida Department of Insurance.

★ 1764 ★

Auto Insurance (SIC 6321)

Largest Auto Insurers in Ohio, 1999

Companies are ranked by premiums written in millions of dollars. Market shares are shown in percent.

	($ mil.)	Share
Cincinnati Fin.	$ 59.1	8.4%
Westfield	50.0	6.8
CNA Insurance	43.4	6.1
Liberty Mutual	35.9	5.1
Nationwide	27.8	3.9

Source: *Business Courier Serving Cincinnati-Northern Kentucky*, April 13, 2001, p. 3, from A.M. Best & Co.

★ 1765 ★

Auto Insurance (SIC 6321)

Largest Auto Insurers in Pennsylvania

Market shares are shown in percent. Figures are for private auto insurance.

State Farm Group	18.9%
Allstate Insurance Group	14.8
Other	66.3

Source: *A.M. Best Newswire*, January 2, 2001, p. NA, from A.M. Best.

★ 1766 ★

Auto Insurance (SIC 6321)

Top Auto Insurers

Shares refer to private-passenger market.

State Farm Group	18.9%
Allstate	12.2
Farmers	5.7
Progressive	4.8
Nationwide	4.4

Continued on next page.

★ 1766 ★ *Continued*

Auto Insurance (SIC 6321)

Top Auto Insurers

Shares refer to private-passenger market.

Berkshire Hathaway	4.1%
USAA Group	3.1
Liberty Mutual	2.2
American Family	2.0
Travelers	2.0
Other	36.6

Source: *Best's Review*, October 2000, p. 34, from A.M. Best & Co.

★ 1767 ★

Auto Insurance (SIC 6321)

Top Auto Insurers in Canada, 2000

Market shares are shown based on total premium sales.

ING Canada	10.5%
CGU Group Canada	9.2
Royal & Sunalliance	6.6
Economical Insurance	5.8
Co-operators General	5.7
State Farm Insurance	5.2
AXA Canada	4.3
Groupe Desjardins	4.0
Other	48.7

Source: *Marketing Magazine*, June 4, 2001, p. NA, from *Canadian Insurance*.

★ 1768 ★

Case Management (SIC 6321)

Top Case Management Providers

Firms are ranked by gross revenues in millions of dollars.

Intracorp.	$ 313.0
Concentra Managed Care	142.0
CorVel Corp.	110.0
GENEX Services Inc.	96.4
Crawford & Co.	72.0
National Healthcare Resources Inc.	46.0
Private Healthcare Systems	26.2
Horizon Behavioral Services	23.2

Source: *Business Insurance*, January 22, 2001, p. 3.

★ 1769 ★

Health Insurance (SIC 6321)

Individual Health Insurance Industry

Shares are shown based on value of written policies.

American Community Mutual Insurance Co.	34.68%
Fortis Insurance Co.	18.41
American Republic Insurance Co.	15.60
National Travelers Life Co.	9.00
Golden Rule Insurance Co.	6.18
Other	16.13

Source: "Press Release." Retrieved December 28, 2000 from the World wWide Web: http://www.businesswire.com.

★ 1770 ★

Health Insurance (SIC 6321)

Leading Long-Term Care Insurance Writers, 1998

Market shares are shown in percent.

Metropolitan Life	33.65%
General Electric Capital Assurance	16.21
Aetna Life	8.58
John Hancock Mutual Life	7.15
Unum Life of America	6.30

Continued on next page.

★ 1770 ★ *Continued*
Health Insurance (SIC 6321)

Leading Long-Term Care Insurance Writers, 1998

Market shares are shown in percent.

American Travellers (Conesco Sr. Health) . . 4.36%
PFL Life 2.80
Pioneer Life 2.80
Other 18.15

Source: *Best's Review*, March 2000, p. 105, from A.M. Best.

★ 1771 ★
Dental Plans (SIC 6324)

Leading Dental HMOs in Texas

Prudential Dental Maintenance Org.
Cigna Dental Health of Texas Inc.
Protective DentalCare
Safeguard Health Plans Inc.
Spectra Dental Inc.
Denticare Inc. of Sugar Land
Alpha Dental Programs Inc.

Total enrollment is as of September 2000.

	Members	% of Group
Prudential Dental Maintenance Org.	532,026	32.55%
Cigna Dental Health of Texas Inc.	312,794	19.14
Protective DentalCare	261,564	16.00
Safeguard Health Plans Inc. . .	191,360	11.71
Spectra Dental Inc.	147,608	9.03
Denticare Inc. of Sugar Land . .	136,399	8.34
Alpha Dental Programs Inc. . .	52,821	3.23

Source: *San Antonio Business Journal*, March 2, 2001, p. 14B.

★ 1772 ★
Health Plans (SIC 6324)

Largest Health Plans in Sacramento, CA

Data show enrollment in a four county area.

	Members	Share
Kaiser Permanents	569,359	50.70%
Health Net	175,695	15.65
Blue Cross	121,848	10.85
PacifiCare	106,000	9.44
Other	150,000	13.36

Source: *Sacramento Business Journal*, April 27, 2001, p. 28.

★ 1773 ★
Health Plans (SIC 6324)

Largest HMOs in Michigan

Market shares are shown in percent.

Blue Care Network 23.0%
Health Alliance Plan 16.9
Priority Health 9.2
M-Care 6.9
Other 44.0

Source: *Detroit Free Press*, May 8, 2001, p. 3F, from company filings to Michigan Insurance Bureau.

★ 1774 ★
Health Plans (SIC 6324)

Leading Health Programs in Philadelphia, PA

Market shares are shown in percent. Figures are estimated.

Jefferson Health System 21.0%
Tenet Healthcare Corp. 11.0
Temple University Health System 11.0
University of Pennsylvania Health System . . 11.0
Other 46.0

Source: *Knight-Ridder/Tribune Business News*, May 2, 2001, p. NA.

★ 1775 ★
Health Plans (SIC 6324)

Top Health Care Firms in Hawaii

Kaiser Permanente	
The Queens Health Systems	
Kapi'Olani Health	
Straub Clinic & Hospital Inc.	
Hawaii Health Systems Corp.	
St. Francis Healthcare System of Hawaii	
Kuakini Health System	
Castle Medical Center	

Firms are ranked by sales in millions of dollars.

Kaiser Permanente	$ 520.5
The Queens Health Systems	450.6
Kapi'Olani Health	374.0
Straub Clinic & Hospital Inc.	358.7
Hawaii Health Systems Corp.	240.0
St. Francis Healthcare System of Hawaii . .	226.5
Kuakini Health System	188.0
Castle Medical Center	109.1

Source: *Hawaii Business*, March 1, 2001, p. 73.

★ 1776 ★
Health Plans (SIC 6324)

Top Health Plans in Massachusetts, 1999

Market shares are shown in percent.

Harvard Pilgrim Health Plan	30.5%
Tufts Association HMO	23.6
HMO Blue	21.4
Fallon Community Health Plan	8.1
Other	16.4

Source: *Modern Physician*, August 2000, p. 8, from Massachusetts Division of Insurance.

★ 1777 ★
Disaster Insurance (SIC 6331)

Top Federal Flood Writers, 1999

Market shares are shown in percent.

State Farm Group	20.4%
Bankers Ins. Group Inc.	13.6
Allstate Ins Group	12.0
Mutual of Omaha Group	8.1

Travelers PC Group	7.1%
Assurant Group	6.6
Nationwide Group	4.5
Harford Ins Group	4.0
USAA Group	3.5
Other	20.2

Source: *Best's Review*, November 2000, p. 40, from A.M. Best & Co.

★ 1778 ★
Disaster Insurance (SIC 6331)

Top Fire/Allied Line Insurance Writers, 1999

Allied lines include fire, earthquake, water damage and vandalism.

Allianz of America	5.6%
ACE INA Group	5.3
FM Global Group	4.3
Zurich US Group	4.2
State Farm Group	3.8
Travelers PC Group	3.5
Centurion Ins Group	3.4
St. Paul Cos.	3.0
Amer Intern Group	2.9
Allstate Ins Group	2.6
Other	56.4

Source: *Best's Review*, December 2000, p. 66.

★ 1779 ★
Homeowners Insurance (SIC 6331)

Homeowners Insurance Industry in California

California is the largest market.

State Farm Group	23.2%
Farmers Ins Group	18.8
Other	42.0

Source: *Best's Review*, August 2000, p. 55, from A.M. Best & Co.

★ 1780 ★

Homeowners Insurance (SIC 6331)

Homeowners Insurance Industry in Georgia

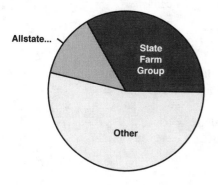

Georgia is the tenth largest market.

State Farm Group	33.5%
Allstate Ins Group	12.5
Other	54.0

Source: *Best's Review*, August 2000, p. 54, from A.M. Best & Co.

★ 1781 ★

Homeowners Insurance (SIC 6331)

Homeowners Insurance Industry in Pennsylvania

Pennsylvania is the fifth largest market.

State Farm Group	18.2%
Erie Ins Group	12.4
Other	69.4

Source: *Best's Review*, August 2000, p. 55, from A.M. Best & Co.

★ 1782 ★

Liability Insurance (SIC 6331)

Leading D&O Insurance Writers

Market shares are shown in percent. D&O stands for Directors & Officers.

AIG	32.7%
Chubb	19.1
Lloyd's	12.5
Aegis	4.5
Hartford	3.1

Genesis (PRMS)	3.1%
Great American	2.6
Special Program Management	2.4
Admiral	2.4
CAN	2.3
Other	15.3

Source: *Best's Review*, May 2001, p. 58, from Tillinghast-Towers Perrin.

★ 1783 ★

Multiple Peril Insurance (SIC 6331)

Commercial Multiple Peril Industry in California

The market includes property, boiler and machinery, crime and general liability coverages. California is the largest market.

Allianz of America	10.7%
Farmers Ins. Group	9.3
Other	80.0

Source: *Best's Review*, August 2000, p. 54, from A.M. Best & Co.

★ 1784 ★

Multiple Peril Insurance (SIC 6331)

Commercial Multiple Peril Industry in New York

The market includes property, boiler and machinery, crime and general liability coverages. New York is the second largest market.

Travelers PC Group	11.7%
CGU Group	7.7
Other	80.6

Source: *Best's Review*, August 2000, p. 54, from A.M. Best & Co.

★ 1785 ★

Property Insurance (SIC 6331)

Largest Homeowners Insurance Writers

Market shares are shown in percent.

State Farm Group	22.6%
Allstate Ins Group	11.5
Farmers Ins Group	6.9

Continued on next page.

★ 1785 ★ *Continued*
Property Insurance (SIC 6331)

Largest Homeowners Insurance Writers

Market shares are shown in percent.

Nationwide Group	4.5%
Travelers PC Group	3.6
USAA Group	3.5
Safeco Ins Cos.	2.3
Chubb Group of Ins Cos.	2.3
Amer Family Ins Group	2.1
Liberty Mutual Ins Cos.	2.0
Other	38.7

Source: *Best's Review*, July 2000, p. 56.

★ 1786 ★
Property Insurance (SIC 6331)

Largest Mobile Home Insurers in Nevada

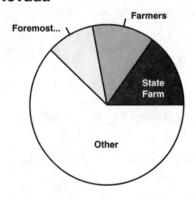

Market shares are shown in percent.

State Farm	15.0%
Farmers	13.0
Foremost Insurance	10.0
Other	62.0

Source: *Knight-Ridder/Tribune Business News*, June 12, 2001, p. NA.

★ 1787 ★
Property Insurance (SIC 6331)

Top Inland Marine Writers, 1999

Insurance covers property damage or loss from fire, weather, theft or traffic accidents.

Amer Intern Group	12.6%
Assurant Group	5.9
State Farm Group	5.5
Travelers PC Group	4.6
Chubb Group of Ins Cos.	4.0
Zurich US Group	3.6
Hartford Ins. Group	3.0
Allianz of America	2.9
CAN Ins Cos.	2.7
St. Paul Cos.	2.7
Other	52.5

Source: *Best's Review*, December 2000, p. 63.

★ 1788 ★
Property Insurance (SIC 6331)

Top Property/Casualty Insurers in Canada, 2000

Market shares are shown based on total premium sales of $21.4 billion.

ING Canada	9.6%
CGU Group	8.5
Co-operators Group	6.8
Royal & Sunalliance	6.2
Economical Insurance	5.0
AXA Canada	4.4
State Farm Insurance	3.5
Wawanesa Mutual Insurance	3.2
Groups Desjardins	3.1
Lloyd's Underwriters	2.5
Other	46.6

Source: *Marketing Magazine*, June 4, 2001, p. NA, from *Canadian Insurance*.

★ 1789 ★
Surplus Line Insurance (SIC 6331)

Surplus Line Market Shares, 1999

Domestic professionals are companies that write more than one-half of their total direct premiums on a nonadmitted basis. Domestic specialty writers are companies with direct nonadmitted premiumn writings of less than 50%.

Domestic professional	68.0%
Lloyd's	18.0
Regulated alien	11.0
Domestic specialty	3.0

Source: *Best's Review*, November 2000, p. 77.

★ 1790 ★
Home Warranties (SIC 6351)

Home Warranty Market in California

Market shares are shown in percent. There were 404,567 sold in 2000.

HWAC	81.3%
Other	18.7

Source: "Press Releases." Retrieved April 9, 2001 from the World Wide Web: http://www.businesswire.com, from Dataquick Products.

★ 1791 ★
Marine Insurance (SIC 6351)

Top Marine Insurers

Market shares are shown in percent.

CNA Ins Cos.	13.8%
Amer Intern Group	10.1
Royal & SunAlliance	6.3
St. Paul Cos.	5.9
CGU Group	5.1
Ace INA Group	5.0
Allianz of America	4.4
Zurich US Group	4.2
Chubb Group Ins Cos.	4.1
Reliance Ins Group	3.2
Other	37.9

Source: *Best's Review*, January 2001, p. 1.

★ 1792 ★
Medical Malpractice Insurance (SIC 6351)

Medical Malpractice Industry in Illinois

Illinois is the fourth largest market.

Illinois St. Medical	47.1%
St Paul Companies	6.4
Other	46.5

Source: *Best's Review*, August 2000, p. 55, from A.M. Best & Co.

★ 1793 ★
Medical Malpractice Insurance (SIC 6351)

Medical Malpractice Industry in North Carolina

North Carolina is the thirteenth largest market.

Medical Mutual Group	31.5%
St. Paul Companies	16.3
Other	52.2

Source: *Best's Review*, August 2000, p. 55, from A.M. Best & Co.

★ 1794 ★
Medical Malpractice Insurance (SIC 6351)

Medical Malpractice Industry in Oregon

Oregon is the thirty second largest market.

CAN Ins Companies	27.5%
Northwest Phys Mutual	27.0
Other	45.5

Source: *Best's Review*, August 2000, p. 55, from A.M. Best & Co.

★ 1795 ★
Medical Malpractice Insurance (SIC 6351)

Medical Malpractice Industry in West Virginia

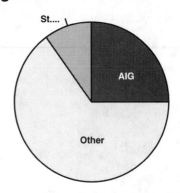

Market shares are shown in percent.

AIG	25.0%
St. Paul Fire and Marine Insurance Co.	10.0
Other	65.0

Source: *Knight-Ridder/Tribune Business News*, February 26, 2001, p. NA.

★ 1796 ★
Medical Malpractice Insurance (SIC 6351)

Top Medical Malpractice Writers, 1999

Market shares are shown in percent.

St Paul Companies	6.8%
MLMIC Group	6.2
Employers Re US Group	4.4
Health Care Indemn	4.2
CAN Ins Companies	4.2
MIIX Group	4.0
Phico Group	3.5
Doctor's Co Ins Group	3.3
Amer Continental Ins	3.1
Other	60.3

Source: *Best's Review*, August 2000, p. 46, from A.M. Best & Co.

★ 1797 ★
Product Liability Insurance (SIC 6351)

Product Liability Industry in Kansas

Kansas is the twenty third largest market.

Travel Air Ins Co	35.0%
St. Paul Companies	12.1
Other	52.9

Source: *Best's Review*, August 2000, p. 57, from A.M. Best & Co.

★ 1798 ★
Product Liability Insurance (SIC 6351)

Product Liability Industry in Maine

Maine is the smallest market.

Liberty Mutual Ins Cos.	19.2%
Royal & SunAlliance	8.7
Other	72.1

Source: *Best's Review*, August 2000, p. 57, from A.M. Best & Co.

★ 1799 ★
Product Liability Insurance (SIC 6351)

Product Liability Industry in Michigan

Michigan is the second largest market.

Dorinco Reins Co.	39.7%
DaimlerChrysler Group	38.0
Other	22.3

Source: *Best's Review*, August 2000, p. 57, from A.M. Best & Co.

★ 1800 ★
Product Liability Insurance (SIC 6351)

Product Liability Industry in New Jersey

New Jersey is the sixth largest market.

Chubb Group of Ins Cos	13.0%
Selective Ins Group Inc.	9.1
Other	77.9

Source: *Best's Review*, August 2000, p. 57, from A.M. Best & Co.

★ 1801 ★

Surety Insurance (SIC 6351)

Fidelity/Surety Industry in South Dakota

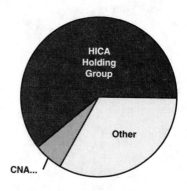

South Dakota is the fourtieth largest market.

HICA Holding Group 60.7%
CNA Ins Companies 6.4
Other 32.9

Source: *Best's Review*, August 2000, p. 59, from A.M. Best & Co.

★ 1802 ★

Surety Insurance (SIC 6351)

Fidelity/Surety Industry in Texas

Texas is the fourth largest market.

CNA Ins Companies 12.4%
St. Paul Companies 8.4
Other 79.2

Source: *Best's Review*, August 2000, p. 59, from A.M. Best & Co.

★ 1803 ★

Workers Comp Insurance (SIC 6351)

Largest Workers Comp Firms in California

California has 19.2% of total U.S. premiums.

State Compensation Insurance Fund of
  California 21.47%
Fremont General Group 8.98
Liberty Mutual Insurance Cos. 7.99
Other 61.56

Source: "A Closer Look." Retrieved April 6, 2001 from the World Wide Web: http://www.bestwire.com, from A.M. Best.

★ 1804 ★

Workers Comp Insurance (SIC 6351)

Largest Workers Comp Insurance Writers, 1999

Market shares are shown in percent.

Liberty Mutual Ins Cos. 9.5%
CNA Ins Companies 5.7
Travelers PC Group 4.2
State Comp Fund California 4.1
Fremont General Group 3.8
Amer Intern Group 3.8
Reliance Ins Group 3.7
Hartford Ins Group 3.5
Kemper Ins Group 3.5
Royal & SunAlliance 3.2
Other 55.0

Source: *Best's Review*, July 2000, p. 56.

★ 1805 ★

Title Insurance (SIC 6361)

Leading Title Insurers

Market shares are shown in percent.

Fidelity National Title 13.69%
First American Title 13.25
Chicago Title Co. 11.14
Stewart Title 5.51
Southland Title Co. 5.49
Commonwealth Land Title Co. 5.31
Equity Title Co. 5.14
Lawyers Title 4.77

Continued on next page.

★ 1805 ★ *Continued*

Title Insurance (SIC 6361)

Leading Title Insurers

Market shares are shown in percent.

American Title Co.	4.56%
Other	31.14

Source: *Los Angeles Business Journal*, March 19, 2001, p. 24.

SIC 64 - Insurance Agents, Brokers, and Service

★ 1806 ★

Insurance Brokers (SIC 6411)

Largest Insurance Brokers

The largest brokers of U.S. business are ranked by revenue in millions of dollars.

Marsh & McLennan Cos. Inc.	$ 3,540.3
Aon Corp.	2,544.0
Willis Group Ltd.	669.2
Arthur J. Gallagher & Co.	539.1
Acordia Inc.	334.5
USI Insurance Services Corp.	320.5
Hilb, Rogal & Hamilton Co.	221.6
Wells Fargo Insurnace Inc.	190.2
Brown & Brown Inc.	172.8
Lockton Cos. Inc.	147.3

Source: *Business Insurance*, December 25, 2000, p. C4.

SIC 65 - Real Estate

★ 1807 ★
Planned Communities (SIC 6510)

Largest Master Planned Communities

| Summerlin, Las Vegas |
| Irvine Ranch, Orange County, CA |
| The Villages, Orlando-Ocala, FL |
| Weston, Fort Lauderdale, FL |
| The Woodlands, Houston |

Figures show number of units.

Summerlin, Las Vegas 3,173
Irvine Ranch, Orange County, CA 2,377
The Villages, Orlando-Ocala, FL 1,849
Weston, Fort Lauderdale, FL 1,728
The Woodlands, Houston 1,679

Source: *Christian Science Monitor*, March 1, 2001, p. 2, from Robert Charles Lessor & Co.

★ 1808 ★
Shopping Centers (SIC 6512)

Largest Shopping Center Managers

Firms are ranked by gross leasable area, in millions of square feet.

Simon Property Group 176.0
Jones Lang LaSalle-Jones Lang LaSalle
  Retail 78.5
Kimco Realty Corp. 66.0
Westfield Corp. Inc. 64.2
Urban Shopping Centers Inc. 60.8
Developers Diversified Realty Corp. 54.2
Trammell Crow Co. 52.0
The Macerich Co. 43.2
The Richard E. Jacobs Group Inc. 41.4
The Rosue Co. 40.7

Source: *Shopping Center World*, March 2001, p. 32.

★ 1809 ★
Shopping Centers (SIC 6512)

Largest Shopping Centers

Centers are ranked by size in millions of square feet.

Mall of America (MN) 4.2
Del Amo Fashion Center (CA) 3.0
King of Prussia Plaza (PA) 2.8
Aventura Mall (FL) 2.7
Woodfield Mall (IL) 2.3

Source: *Shopping Center World*, September 2000, p. u.

★ 1810 ★
Apartment Buildings (SIC 6513)

Leading Apartment Building Owners, 2001

Companies are ranked by number of apartments with ownership interest.

Apartment Investment and Management
  Company 240,540
Equity Residential Properties Trust 228,504
Related Capital Company 148,080
Lend Lease Real Estate Investments Inc. . . 126,357
Boston Capital 106,000
Sunamerica Affordable Housing Partners
  Inc. 95,000
Whitehall Funds 84,000
United Dominion Realty Trust Inc. 79,065
Casden Properties Inc. 71,826
Lefrak Organization Inc. 69,000

Source: *National Real Estate Investor*, March 2001, p. 2.

★ 1811 ★
Real Estate (SIC 6531)

Commercial Property Market in South Florida

Data show the main sources of investment for foreign buyers. During the first three months in $49.1 million was invested in Miami-Dade County, $33.9 million in Broward County and $205.2 million in Palm-Beach County.

Apartment buildings	18.2%
Shopping centers	16.5
Warehouses/industrial buildings	15.9
Offices	12.4
Hotels and motels	9.4

Source: *Broward Daily Business Review*, November 3, 2000, p. A4.

★ 1812 ★
Real Estate (SIC 6531)

Largest Leasing Brokers, 2000

Firms are ranked by lease square footage activity.

CB Richard Ellis	127.51
Cushman & Wakefield Inc.	71.48
Grubb & Ellis	62.82
Insignia/ESG	40.00
Trammell Crow Company	35.24
Adler First Commercial	30.19
Julien J. Studley	25.60
LEE & Associates	22.25
Colliers Seeley	16.02
Cornish & Carey Commercial	14.86

Source: *New York Times*, January 18, 2001, p. C4, from CoStar Group Inc.

★ 1813 ★
Real Estate (SIC 6531)

Largest Real Estate Firms

Firms are ranked by revenues in millions of dollars.

Equity Office Properties	$ 2,264
Del Webb	2,040
Equity Res. Properties	2,030
Simon Property Group	2,021

Source: *Fortune*, April 16, 2001, p. F61.

★ 1814 ★
Real Estate (SIC 6531)

Largest Real Estate Firms in Oahu, Hawaii

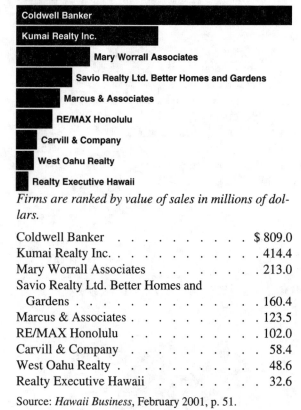

Firms are ranked by value of sales in millions of dollars.

Coldwell Banker	$ 809.0
Kumai Realty Inc.	414.4
Mary Worrall Associates	213.0
Savio Realty Ltd. Better Homes and Gardens	160.4
Marcus & Associates	123.5
RE/MAX Honolulu	102.0
Carvill & Company	58.4
West Oahu Realty	48.6
Realty Executive Hawaii	32.6

Source: *Hawaii Business*, February 2001, p. 51.

★ 1815 ★
Real Estate (SIC 6531)

Largest Real Estate Firms in Pulaski-Saline County, Arkansas

Market shares are shown in percent.

Janet Jones Co.	9.8%
McKay & Co.	8.0
Rainey	6.3
North Little Rock's Real Estate Central	6.2
Other	69.7

Source: *Arkansas Business*, August 28, 2000, p. 1.

★ 1816 ★

Real Estate (SIC 6531)

Largest Realty Firms, 1999

Firms are ranked by transaction sides closed.

NRT Inc. 362,368
HomeServices.com 93,593
Weichart Realtors 77,100
Long & Foster Real Estate Inc. 64,189
Windermere Real Estate 37,641
Prudential California/Americana/John
   Aaroe/Realtors 36,103
Prudential Fox & Roach 34,528
Arvida Realty Services 34,526
Realty Executives of Phoenix 28,000
The DeWolfe Cos. Inc. 25,654

Source: *Realtor Magazine*, July 2000, p. 44.

★ 1817 ★

Real Estate (SIC 6531)

Top Real Estate Firms in New Mexico, 2000

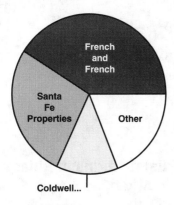

Shares are for the first nine months.

French and French 41.0%
Santa Fe Properties 27.0
Coldwell Banker Trails West Realty 13.0
Other 19.0

Source: *Knight-Ridder/Tribune Business News*, October 20, 2000, p. NA.

SIC 67 - Holding and Other Investment Offices

★ 1818 ★

Bank Holding Companies (SIC 6712)

Largest Bank Holding Companies

Market shares of banking assets.

Bank of America Corp.	9.34%
J.P. Morgan Chase & Co.	9.23
Citigroup Inc.	6.90
Bank One Corp.	4.70
Wells Fargo & Co.	4.35
First Union Corp.	3.69
FleetBoston Financial Corp.	2.64
SunTrust Banks Inc.	1.53
National City Corp.	1.47
U.S. Bancorp.	1.31
Other	54.84

Source: *American Banker*, May 4, 2001, p. 20.

★ 1819 ★

Bank Holding Companies (SIC 6712)

Top Bank Holding Companies, 2000

Figures are in millions of dollars as of June 30, 2000.

Bank of Waunakee	$ 44.3
Union NB&TC	36.6
Kirkwood B&TC	36.1
Capital BK&TC	34.4
California Pacific	33.7
Mitchell Bank	33.4
Quantum NB	33.2
Western St. Bank	31.9
State Bank of Chilton	31.9
Sun West Bank	30.6

Source: *Small Business Banker*, March 2001, p. 16.

★ 1820 ★

Hotels (SIC 7011)

Largest Hotel Firms

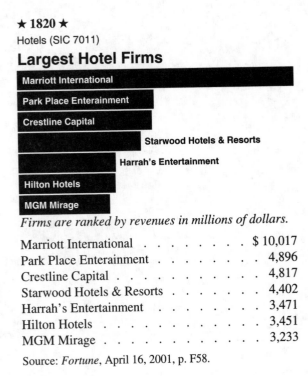

Firms are ranked by revenues in millions of dollars.

Marriott International	$ 10,017
Park Place Enterainment	4,896
Crestline Capital	4,817
Starwood Hotels & Resorts	4,402
Harrah's Entertainment	3,471
Hilton Hotels	3,451
MGM Mirage	3,233

Source: *Fortune*, April 16, 2001, p. F58.

★ 1821 ★

Tax Preparation (SIC 7291)

Electronic Tax Filing

Data show the estimated millions of filers by type.

	1999	2003	2006
Accountant online filing . . .	21.2	31.0	36.0
Telephone filing	5.7	6.5	7.0
Personal online filing	2.2	7.0	9.4

Source: *Grok*, February-March 2001, p. 105, from Internal Revenue Service.

SIC 73 - Business Services

★ 1822 ★
Advertising (SIC 7311)

Largest Advertisers, 2000

Companies are ranked by total measured ad spending in millions of dollars. Figures are for the first six months.

General Motors Corp.	$ 1,401.6
Philip Morris Cos.	889.3
DaimlerChrysler	783.3
Procter & Gamble	642.0
Ford Motor Co.	617.6
Time Warner	543.5
Walt Disney Co.	520.0
Johnson & Johnson	441.9
Pfizer	405.9
Unilever	395.5

Source: *Advertising Age*, November 13, 2000, p. 64.

★ 1823 ★
Advertising (SIC 7311)

Top Ad Agencies, 2000

Firms are ranked by gross income in millions of dollars.

Grey Worldwide	$ 610.0
J. Walter Thompson Co.	574.5
McCann-Erickson Worldwide	507.1
FCB Worldwide	502.2
Y&R Advertising	452.8
Leo Burnett Worldwide	428.1

Source: *Advertising Age*, April 24, 2001, p. S2.

★ 1824 ★
Advertising (SIC 7311)

Top Ad Markets, 2000

Cities are ranked by local shop billings in millions of dollars.

New York City, NY	$ 57,237.6
Chicago, IL	15,212.7
Detroit, MI	8,336.8
Los Angeles, CA	8,225.9
San Francisco, CA	5,855.3
Boston, MA	4,156.1
Minneapolis, MN	3,630.5
Dallas, TX	2,457.0
St. Louis, MO	1,651.0

Source: *Advertising Age*, April 24, 2001, p. S2.

★ 1825 ★
Advertising (SIC 7312)

Top Outdoor Advertising Firms

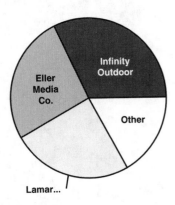

Market shares are shown in percent.

Infinity Outdoor	32.0%
Eller Media Co.	26.0
Lamar Advertising Co.	25.0
Other	17.0

Source: *St. Petersburg Times*, November 26, 2000, p. 1H.

★ 1826 ★
Advertising (SIC 7312)

Top Outdoor Advertising Markets

Market shares are shown in percent.

Local services	11.1%
Retail outlets	10.8
Public transportation, hotels	9.1
Media and advertising	8.3
Restaurants	7.5
Auto dealers	6.6
Auto accessories	5.5
Insurance and real estate	4.9
Financial	4.5
Merchandise	3.8
Other	27.9

Source: *Signs of the Times*, October 2000, p. 82.

★ 1827 ★
Advertising (SIC 7319)

Computer Ad Leaders

Titles are ranked by ad revenue in millions of dollars.

The Wall Street Journal	$ 434.79
Business Week	215.95
Informationweek	157.34
PC Magazine	152.98
Fortune	141.89
Time	121.07
Industry Standard	112.89
Forbes	111.77
USA Today	109.28

Source: *Media Industry Newsletter*, March 12, 2001, p. NA, from Ad Scope.

★ 1828 ★
Advertising (SIC 7319)

Largest B-to-B Interactive Advertisers, 2000

Companies are ranked by online ad spending in millions of dollars. Date are for September 1999 - August 2000.

Network Solutions	$ 45.0
Microsoft	32.4
SkyDesk	13.0
Verio	11.0

Marden-Kane	$ 11.0
NorthPoint Communications	9.2
MatchLogic	9.1
Zixit	8.7
IBM	8.5
Sun Microsystems	7.2

Source: *BtoB*, October 23, 2000, p. 36.

★ 1829 ★
Advertising (SIC 7319)

Largest Brand Advertisers in Newspapers, 1999

Ad revenues are shown in billions of dollars.

Sears	$ 498,639.1
Circuit City Stores	409,397.3
Macys	367,199.1
Kmart	332,619.5
Valassis Coupons	301,305.1
J.C. Penney	299,318.9
News America FSI	282,670.7
Best Buy	250,522.2
Dillards	195,776.1
Alltel Cellular	179,569.8

Source: *Editor & Publisher*, June 19, 2000, p. 62.

★ 1830 ★
Advertising (SIC 7319)

Largest Cable TV Advertisers

Firms are ranked by spending in millions of dollars.

General Motors Corp.	$ 276.7
Procter & Gamble Co.	259.7
Philip Morris Cos.	182.7
MCI Worldcom	163.0
Sony Corp.	132.6
Pfizer	117.6
Johnson & Johnson	117.2
AOL Time Warner	114.6

Source: *Electronic Media*, April 2, 2001, p. 16.

★ 1831 ★
Advertising (SIC 7319)

Largest Grocery Store Advertisers, 2000

Chains are ranked by ad spending in millions of dollars for July 1999 - June 2000.

Albertson's	$ 70.9
Kroger	42.0
Safeway	34.1
Giant Food Stores	33.7
Publix	25.7
Winn-Dixie	24.6
7-Eleven	21.0
Vons	20.5
Ralphs	18.9
Shoprite	17.3

Source: *Supermarket Business*, October 15, 2000, p. 43, from Competitive Media Reporting.

★ 1832 ★
Advertising (SIC 7319)

Largest Hispanic Advertisers, 2000

Spending is shown in millions of dollars for the first seven months of the year.

Procter & Gamble	$ 64.2
AT&T	41.3
WorldCom	40.0
US Government	34.2
General Motors	22.6

Source: *Wall Street Journal*, October 13, 2000, p. B1, from Competitive Media Reporting.

★ 1833 ★
Advertising (SIC 7319)

Largest Network TV Advertisers

Firms are ranked by spending in millions of dollars.

General Motors Corp.	$ 961.8
Procter & Gamble Co.	495.7
Johnson & Johnson	406.6

Philip Morris Cos.	$ 400.0
Pfizer	364.8
Walt Disney Co.	317.1
Unilever	313.4
Tricon Global Restaurants	310.3

Source: *Electronic Media*, April 2, 2001, p. 16.

★ 1834 ★
Advertising (SIC 7319)

Largest Syndicated TV Advertisers

Firms are ranked by spending in millions of dollars.

Procter & Gamble Co.	$ 130.2
General Motors Corp.	114.8
Unilever	95.0
Philip Morris Cos.	89.7
Berkshire Hathaway	80.7
Diageo PLC	77.0
AOL Time Warner	76.7
Johnson & Johnson	75.0

Source: *Electronic Media*, April 2, 2001, p. 16.

★ 1835 ★
Advertising (SIC 7319)

Leading Food Advertisers

Firms are ranked by ad spending on cable television, in thousands of dollars.

Philip Morris	$ 51,020.9
General Mills	25,443.0
PepsiCo.	17,737.2
Kellogg's	14,585.5
Diageo	12,974.6

Source: *Cablevision*, October 30, 2000, p. 56, from Nielsen Media Research.

★ 1836 ★
Advertising (SIC 7319)

Newspaper Advertising by Year

Spending is shown by segment.

	2000 ($ mil.)	2003 ($ mil.)	Share
Retail	$ 21,771	$ 24,880	41.28%
Classified	20,650	25,824	42.85
National	7,355	9,561	15.86

Source: *Editor & Publisher*, August 7, 2000, p. 27, from Veronis & Suhler, The Publishing & Media Group, and Newspaper Association of America.

★ 1837 ★
Advertising (SIC 7319)

Newspaper Industry Revenues, 1999

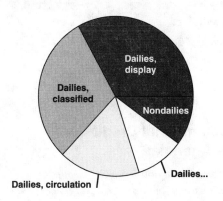

The $63 billion market is estimated. Strong growth is predicted for the industry.

Dailies, display	33.0%
Dailies, classified	30.0
Dailies, circulation	17.0
Dailies, inserts	10.0
Nondailies	10.0

Source: *American Ink Maker*, November 2000, p. 16, from Veronis, Suhler & Associates, Newspaper Association of America, and Kubas Consultants.

★ 1838 ★
Advertising (SIC 7319)

Online Advertising Market, 2000

Shares are for the first quarter of 2000.

Banners	52.0%
Sponsorships	27.0
Classified	4.0
E-mail	3.0
Interstitials	3.0
Other	11.0

Source: *Industry Standard*, August 28, 2000, p. 162, from Internet Advertising Bureau and PricewaterhouseCoopers.

★ 1839 ★
Advertising (SIC 7319)

Online Advertising Market by Segment, 2000

The $2.1 billion market is shown in percent. Data are for the second quarter of 2000.

Search engines/portals	36.0%
Business/financial	15.0
Classified	12.0
Technology	11.0
News/information	10.0
Entertainment	4.0
Sports	2.0
Women	1.0
Other	9.0

Source: *Wall Street Journal*, October 12, 2000, p. B14, from Internet Advertising Bureau and PriceWaterhouseCoopers.

★ 1840 ★
Advertising (SIC 7319)

Projected Ad Spending, 2005

Spending is shown in billions of dollars.

Newspapers	$ 58.9
Broadcast TV	52.3
Radio	23.9
Online	16.5

Continued on next page.

★ 1840 ★ *Continued*
Advertising (SIC 7319)

Projected Ad Spending, 2005

Spending is shown in billions of dollars.

Yellow pages	$ 16.0
Magazines	13.2
Cable TV	12.7
Outdoor	2.2

Source: *Investor's Business Daily*, November 27, 2000, p. A6.

★ 1841 ★
Advertising (SIC 7319)

Spanish Language Advertising

The number of Hispanic Americans has grown 58 percent over the last decade, over four times the rate of the total population. Marketers have begun to respond to this new market. Ad spending is in millions of dollars.

Television	$ 1,200
Radio	557
Newspapers	198
Magazine	55

Source: *U.S. News & World Report*, June 4, 2001, p. 42, from Association of Hispanic Advertising Agencies.

★ 1842 ★
Advertising (SIC 7319)

Top Magazine Advertising Categories, 2000

Spending is shown in billions of dollars.

Technology	$ 1.94
Automotive	1.75
Apparel/accessories	1.31
Toiletries/cosmetics	1.27
Home furnishings/supplies	1.23
Media/advertising	1.21
Financial/insurance/real estate	1.19
Food/food products	1.16

Drugs/remedies	$ 1.13
Retail	1.07

Source: *Media Industry Newsletter*, January 15, 2001, p. NA.

★ 1843 ★
Collection Agencies (SIC 7322)

Largest Collection Agencies, 1999

Firms are ranked by revenue in millions of dollars.

Outsourcing Solutions	$ 503.1
NCO Group Inc.	492.4
Vengroff, Williams & Associates	270.8
IntelliRisk	250.0
GC Service LP	202.0
Equifax Inc.	191.7
Risk Management Alternatives Inc.	191.0
Dun & Bradstreet	150.0
Nationwide Credit Inc.	112.6

Source: *Collections & Credit Risk*, December 2000, p. 28.

★ 1844 ★
Collection Agencies (SIC 7322)

Largest Commercial Credit Card Collection Agencies

Figures are in million of dollars. NCO Group, Outsourcing Solutions Inc. and other major agencies did not report figures.

Verngroff, Williams & Associates	$ 166.2
United Recovery Systems Inc.	82.5
Great Lakes Collection Bureau Inc.	46.7
Williams & Williams Commercial Collections	28.2
Trackers Inc.	18.2
Phillips & Cohen Associates Ltd.	17.5
NCB Management	12.0
Sky Asset Management Services	9.4
Northern California Collection Services Inc.	7.6

Source: *Credit Card Management*, December 2000, p. 58, from *Credit Collections Directory, 2001*.

★ 1845 ★

Collection Agencies (SIC 7322)

Largest Consumer Credit Card Collection Agencies

Figures are in million of dollars. NCO Group, Outsourcing Solutions Inc. and other major agencies did not report figures.

Great Lakes Collection Bureau Inc. . . .	$ 2,421.9
Equifax Inc.	2,402.5
Plaza Associates	1,740.0
Academy Collection Service	1,691.0
First Performance Corp.	1,575.0
Northland Group Inc.	1,000.0
United Recovery Systems Inc.	910.8
Associated Creditors Exchange Inc. . . .	840.0
Viking Collection Service Inc.	800.0

Source: *Credit Card Management*, December 2000, p. 58, from *Credit Collections Directory, 2001*.

★ 1846 ★

Collection Agencies (SIC 7322)

Leading Collections Law Firms, 1999

Firms are ranked by revenues in millions of dollars. Some data are estimated.

Weltman, Weinberg & Reis Co. LPA . . .	$ 35.0
Schreiber & Associates	9.2
Upton, Cohen & Slamowitz	8.9
Mapother and Mapother PSC	8.5
Paris and Paris	8.0
Batzar, Weinberg, Mullooly, Jeffey, Rooney & Flynn	7.0
Wexler & Wexler	6.7
Zwicker & Associates	5.6

Source: *Credit & Collections News*, October 27, 2000, p. 1.

★ 1847 ★

Credit Information (SIC 7323)

Credit Information Market

Market shares are shown in percent.

Dun & Bradstreet	90.0%
Other	10.0

Source: *Electronic Information Report*, November 3, 2000, p. NA.

★ 1848 ★

Direct Marketing (SIC 7331)

B-to-B Direct Marketing Sales

Spending on alternative media, like online, will grow twice as fast (26.1%) as any other sector. Sales are shown in billions of dollars. B-to-B stands for business-to-business.

	1995	2000	2005
Telephone marketing . .	$ 200.2	$ 354.7	$ 566.3
Direct mail	121.5	201.9	335.3
Newspapers	50.7	85.3	137.3
Television	26.4	47.7	77.1
Magazines	25.8	43.8	68.6
Other	16.7	37.2	118.5

Source: *BtoB*, October 9, 2000, p. 42, from Direct Marketing Association.

★ 1849 ★

Direct Marketing (SIC 7331)

Largest Sales Promotion Agencies, 2000

Firms are ranked by sales promotion revenue in millions of dollars.

Carlson Marketing Group	$ 228.1
Bounty SCA Worldwide	190.1
Jack Morton Worldwide	139.2
CommonHealth	131.7
Alcone Marketing Group	117.8
Gary M. Reynolds & Associates	111.8
SPAR Group	104.7
Aspen Marketing Group	102.5
Momentum Worldwide	96.7
Frankel	94.6

Source: *Advertising Age*, May 21, 2001, p. 22.

★ 1850 ★

Pest Control (SIC 7342)

Pest Control Industry

The $4.5 billion market is shown in percent.

Terminix/Orkin	20.0%
Other	80.0

Source: *Pest Control*, January 2000, p. 6.

★ 1851 ★

Heavy Equipment Rental (SIC 7353)

Largest Equipment Renters

Prime Service Inc. and Rental Service Corp.	
Hertz Equipment Rental Corp.	
NationsRent	
	National Equipment Services

Data show number of outlets.

Prime Service Inc. and Rental Service Corp. . . 550
Hertz Equipment Rental Corp. 289
NationsRent 190
National Equipment Services 181

Source: *Underground Construction*, October 2000, p. 64.

★ 1852 ★

Staffing Industry (SIC 7363)

Staffing Industry Revenues

The U.S. staffing industry is expected to hit revenues of over $140 billion in 2000. This is due largely to the tight labor market forcing employers to seek other methods to find workers.

Office/clerical niche . . . . $ 20.0
Temp workers with professional skill sets . . . 14.4
Fees for contingency searches 8.6

Source: "Press Release." Retrieved November 17, 2000 from the World Wide Web: http://www.sireport.com/pressrelease, from Staffing Industry Analysts.

★ 1853 ★

Software (SIC 7372)

Browser Market Shares

Shares are for June 2000.

Microsoft Explorer 86.10%
Netscape Navigator 13.90
Other 0.02

Source: *Infoworld*, July 10, 2000, p. 16, from Statmarket.

★ 1854 ★

Software (SIC 7372)

Client/Server Messaging Installed Base, 1999

Market shares are shown in percent.

Lotus Notes 39.0%
Microsoft Exchange 31.0
GroupWise 15.0
HP OpenMail 10.0
SoftArc 3.0
Other 1.0

Source: *Network World*, August 21, 2000, p. 10, from Managing Online.

★ 1855 ★

Software (SIC 7372)

Collaborative Software Users

Market shares are shown in percent. The market size grew from $2.1 billion in 1998 to $2.4 billion in 1999.

Lotus 52.0%
Microsoft 34.0
Other 14.0

Source: *Wall Street Journal*, September 26, 2000, p. B15, from International Data Corp.

★ 1856 ★

Software (SIC 7372)

Computer Game Software Leaders, 2000

Shares are shown based on units for July 2000.

Havas 12.0%
Electronic Arts 10.4
Mattel 9.7
Hasbro 9.2
Inforgames 7.7
Other 51.0

Source: *New York Times*, August 21, 2000, p. C1, from NPD Group.

★ 1857 ★
Software (SIC 7372)

Computer System Management

Market shares are shown in percent.

Computer Associates	28.4%
IBM	17.4
BMC Software	5.9
Hewlett-Packard	5.5
Veritas Software	3.5
Others	39.3

Source: *Investor's Business Daily*, May 5, 2000, p. A6, from International Data Corp.

★ 1858 ★
Software (SIC 7372)

Content Management Industry, 1999

Shares are estimated.

QRS	40.0%
Ventro	10.0
VerticalNet	7.0
Commerce One	5.0
Aspect Development	5.0
Other	33.0

Source: *Investor's Business Daily*, June 28, 2000, p. A6, from Granada Research.

★ 1859 ★
Software (SIC 7372)

Desktop Operating Market Shares, 1999

Windows	87.0%
Macintosh	5.0
Linux	4.0
Others	4.0

Source: *Wall Street Journal*, November 28, 2000, p. A3, from International Data Corp.

★ 1860 ★
Software (SIC 7372)

Digital Content Security

Macrovision is the leader in the media protection industry, controlling the DVD, CD-ROM, digital pay-per-view and digital delivery market.

Macrovision	99.0%
Other	1.0

Source: "Leader in Digital Contenet Security." Retrieved July 5, 2000 from the World Wide Web: http://www.123jump.com.

★ 1861 ★
Software (SIC 7372)

E-Commerce Software, 2000

Market shares are shown in percent.

Ariba	9.0%
Open Market	6.0
Oracle	6.0
I2 Technologies	5.0
InterWorld	5.0
Sterling Commerce	5.0
GE Information Service	4.0
Vignette	4.0
Other	56.0

Source: *Investor's Business Daily*, October 30, 2000, p. A6, from AMR Research Inc.

★ 1862 ★
Software (SIC 7372)

E-CRM Market Shares

Market shares are shown in percent. CRM stands for customer relationship management.

Broad-Vision	6.8%
Vifnette	6.2
Art Technology Group	2.5
Epiphany	2.0
Others	82.5

Source: *Investor's Business Daily*, December 28, 2000, p. A4, from Yankee Group and Banc of America Securities.

★ 1863 ★

Software (SIC 7372)

EDA Software Market Shares

EDA stands for electronic design automation.

Cadence	23.2%
Synopsys	19.3
Mentor Graphics	11.8
Avant	8.2
Others	37.5

Source: *Investor's Business Daily*, December 20, 2000, p. A8, from Dataquest Inc.

★ 1864 ★

Software (SIC 7372)

Instant Messaging Software

Users are shown, in millions, for August 2000.

AOL Instant Messanger	21.5
Yahoo Messenger	10.6
MSN Messenger	10.3
ICQ Chat	9.1

Source: *USA TODAY*, November 28, 2000, p. B1, from Media Metrix.

★ 1865 ★

Software (SIC 7372)

Largest Application Integration Firms

Market shares are shown in percent.

IBM	14.0%
TIBCO	11.2
NEON	9.0
Vitria	8.8
webMethods	8.6
Mercator	7.0
SeeBeyond	5.7
GXS	5.7
BEA	3.8
iPlanet	3.7
Other	22.5

Source: "Vitria Named Fastes-Growing Application Integration Vendor." Retrieved April 16, 2001 from the World Wide Web: http://www.businesswire.com, from WinterGreen Research.

★ 1866 ★

Software (SIC 7372)

Leading ERP Vendors, 1999

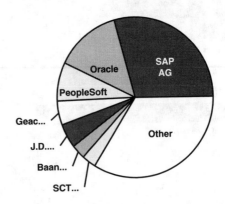

Market shares are shown in percent.

SAP AG	30.0%
Oracle	14.0
PeopleSoft	8.0
Geac SmartEnterprise Solution	5.0
J.D. Edwards & Co.	5.0
Baan Company	3.0
SCT Corporation	3.0
Other	35.0

Source: *Chemical Market Reporter*, September 25, 2000, p. 16, from AMR Research.

★ 1867 ★

Software (SIC 7372)

Media Player Market Shares

Data show millions of downloaded players.

	Users	Share
Real Player	125	45.45%
Windows Media Player	100	36.36
Quicktime Video Player	50	18.18

Source: *Broadcasting & Cable*, June 12, 2000, p. 14, from Digital Technology Consulting.

★ 1868 ★

Software (SIC 7372)

Multimedia Market in Canada

Distribution is based on company revenue. Ontario and Quebec have roughly 68% of the nation's industry.

Business	50.0%
Education	20.0
Home market	13.0
Government	10.0
Other public	4.0

Source: ''Multimedia Industry in Canada.'' Retrieved December 8, 2000 from the World Wide Web: http://www.usatrade.gov.

★ 1869 ★

Software (SIC 7372)

Napster Users by Age

Napster is a popular Internet song swap service that claims to have 30 million users.

34 to 54 year olds	1,636.0%
18 to 34 years	1,607.0
18 years and younger	1,283.0
55 years and older	144.0

Source: *Toronto Star*, October 3, 2000, p. C6, from Media Metrix Inc.

★ 1870 ★

Software (SIC 7372)

Nintendo 64 Game Software Leaders, 2000

Shares are shown based on units for July 2000.

Nintendo	48.8%
Acclaim	8.9
Activision	7.4
Lucasarts	5.8
Electronic Arts	5.0
Other	24.1

Source: *New York Times*, August 21, 2000, p. C1, from NPD Group.

★ 1871 ★

Software (SIC 7372)

Portal Application Software and Services

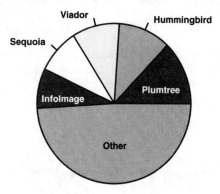

Market shares are shown in percent.

Plumtree	12.8%
Hummingbird	11.4
Viador	9.9
Sequoia	9.0
InfoImage	8.0
Other	48.9

Source: *Investor's Business Daily*, June 21, 2001, p. A6, from Delphi Research and Yankee Group.

★ 1872 ★

Software (SIC 7372)

PPM Market Shares, 1998

The market went from $2.36 billion in 1998 to $3.01 billion in 2000 to $5.14 billion in 2004.

Medic Computer Systems	10.7%
IDX Systems	9.6
Medical Manager	5.6
McKessonHBOC	5.3
Physicians Computer Network	4.5
Infocure	4.2
Other	60.0

Source: *Modern Physician*, March 2000, p. 72, from Frost & Sullivan.

★ 1873 ★

Software (SIC 7372)

Science Software Market

Market shares are shown in percent.

StudyWorks	79.0%
Other	21.0

Source: "StudyWorks Mathmatics Deluxe." Retrieved October 31, 2000 from the World Wide Web: http://www.office.com, from PC Data.

★ 1874 ★

Software (SIC 7372)

Storage Management Vendors, 1999

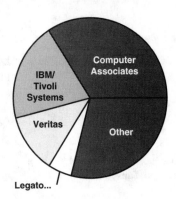

Market shares are shown in percent.

Computer Associates	34.2%
IBM/Tivoli Systems	19.9
Veritas	12.2
Legato Systems Inc.	4.6
Other	29.1

Source: *Investor's Business Daily*, July 18, 2000, p. A12, from International Data Corp. and Dain Rauscher Wessels.

★ 1875 ★

Software (SIC 7372)

Supply Chain Planning Industry

Market shares are shown in percent.

I2 Technologies	30.0%
Manugistics	8.0
Ilog SA	3.0
Logility	2.0
Others	57.0

Source: *Investor's Business Daily*, December 7, 2000, p. A8, from AMR Research Inc.

★ 1876 ★

Software (SIC 7372)

Test Preparation Software Market

Market shares are shown in percent.

Kaplan Software	71.9%
Other	28.1

Source: "Press Releases." Retrieved November 30, 2000 from the World Wide Web: http://www.businesswire.com.

★ 1877 ★

Software (SIC 7372)

Thin Client Market

Market shares are shown in percent.

	2000	2001
Citrix	83.0%	80.0%
Microsoft	8.0	11.0
Tarantella	3.0	5.0
Other	6.0	4.0

Source: *Internetweek*, May 14, 2001, p. 10, from Giga Information Group.

★ 1878 ★

Software (SIC 7372)

Top Value Software Producers

Market shares are shown in percent.

Cosmi	9.7%
Havas Interactive	9.7
Hasbro Interactive	9.6
The Learning Co.	8.7
Electronic Arts	8.0

Continued on next page.

★ 1878 ★ *Continued*
Software (SIC 7372)

Top Value Software Producers

Market shares are shown in percent.

Block Financial	6.2%
Infogrames Entertainment	5.0
Symantec	4.2
ValuSoft	4.2
Activision	4.1
Other	30.6

Source: "Cosmi Ranks Number One in Value Software." Retrieved May 8, 2001 from the World Wide Web: http://www.cosmi.com, from PC Data.

★ 1879 ★
Software (SIC 7372)

VHDL Simulation Market

ModelSim	59.0%
Other	41.0

Source: "Press Release." Retrieved Janaury 30, 2001 from the World Wide Web: http://www.businesswire.com, from Dataquest Inc.

★ 1880 ★
Software (SIC 7372)

Virus Market Share

The virus phenomenon has turned form an IT crisis to a managment problem. Technicians report spending more time fighting rumors than actual computer problems.

VBS/LoveLetter	36.7%
VBS/Kakworm	18.8
W32/Ska-Happy99	3.4
WH97/Market	2.3
WM97/Market-O	1.8
Troj/Mine	1.4
WM97/Melissa	1.4
WM97/Proverb-A	1.4
VBS/Netlog	1.3
Others	25.1

Source: *E Week*, June 26, 2000, p. 69, from Sophos Inc.

★ 1881 ★
Software (SIC 7372)

Web Analytics Market

Market shares are shown in percent.

WebTrends	18.4%
Accrue	14.4
SAS Institute	11.0
NCR	9.0
NetGenesis	8.3
Epiphany	5.4
Microsoft	3.6
Other	29.9

Source: *Investor's Business Daily*, April 2, 2001, p. A6.

★ 1882 ★
Servers (SIC 7373)

Application Server Market

Market shares are shown in percent.

BEA	26.0%
IBM	20.0
ATG	10.0
iPlanet	9.0
Allaire	6.0
Silverstream	6.0
Sybase	6.0
Oracle	2.0
Other	15.0

Source: *Infoworld*, February 19, 2001, p. 12, from Giga Information Group.

★ 1883 ★
Servers (SIC 7373)

Largest Server Producers, 2000

Market shares are shown in percent.

Sun	23.5%
IBM	23.1
Compaq	19.2
Dell	11.6
Hewlett-Packard	10.8
Other	11.9

Source: "Press Release." Retrieved March 8, 2001 from the World Wide Web: http://www.businesswire.com, from Dataquest Inc.

★ 1884 ★

Servers (SIC 7373)

Leading Wintel Server Vendors

Shares are for North America.

Dell	38.3%
Compaq	32.3
IBM	12.5
Hewlett-Packard	7.9
Other	9.0

Source: *Infoworld*, May 7, 2001, p. 16, from Dataquest Inc.

★ 1885 ★

Servers (SIC 7373)

Mid-Range Server Market, 1999

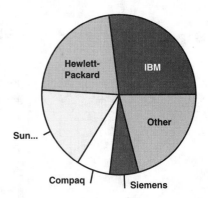

Market shares are shown in percent.

IBM	26.8%
Hewlett-Packard	21.5
Sun Microsystems	17.4
Compaq	6.5
Siemens	6.1
Other	21.1

Source: "Market Share Survey." Retrieved November 20, 2000 from the World Wide Web: http://www.activemedia-guide.com, from International Data Corp.

★ 1886 ★

Servers (SIC 7373)

Rack-Optimized Server Market

Market shares are shown in percent.

Compaq	32.7%
Dell Computer	14.4

Sun Microsystems	13.3%
IBM	8.4
Hewlett-Packard	5.5
VA Linux	3.6
Cobalt	3.2
Other	18.9

Source: *Computer Reseller News*, February 12, 2001, p. 49, from International Data Corp.

★ 1887 ★

Systems Integration (SIC 7373)

Top Systems Integrators for Federal Travelers, 1999

Market shares are shown based on total federal contractors.

Lockheed Martin Corp.	6.43%
Computer Sciences Corp.	5.88
Science Applications Intl. Corp.	5.61
Electronic Data Systems Corp.	4.84
TRW Inc.	3.60
Litton Industries Inc.	3.14
Unisys Corp.	2.93
Northrop Grumman Corp.	2.82
Booz Allen & Hamilton Inc.	2.54
Other	62.21

Source: *Government Executive Procurement Preview*, Annual 2000, p. 69, from General Services Administration.

★ 1888 ★

Computer Services (SIC 7375)

Top Computer Service Contractors, 1999

Market shares are shown based on value of federal contracts.

Lockheed Martin Corp.	6.61%
Computer Sciences Corp.	5.63
Science Applications Intl. Corp.	3.61
Unisys Corp.	2.88
Electronic Data Systems Corp.	2.73
Northrop Grumman Corp.	2.64

Continued on next page.

★ **1888** ★ *Continued*
Computer Services (SIC 7375)

Top Computer Service Contractors, 1999

Market shares are shown based on value of federal contracts.

Raytheon Co.	2.46%
TRW Inc.	2.05
IBM Corp.	1.93
Other	69.46

Source: *Government Executive Procurement Preview*, Annual 2000, p. 66, from General Services Administration.

★ **1889** ★
Information Technology (SIC 7375)

IT Market by Segment

Distributed hardware	24.3%
Software packages	21.8
Mainframe hardware/software	19.9
Telecommunications	10.1
Infrastructure	9.0
Software development	7.8
Consultants	6.6
Other	0.8

Source: *Controllers Update*, April 2001, p. 1.

★ **1890** ★
Information Technology (SIC 7375)

IT Spending by Colleges and Universities

Total spending is $3.1 billion.

Hardware	31.5%
Service and support	20.3
Software	20.0
Communications products and services	15.3
Training	6.5
Other	6.4

Source: *Computer Reseller News*, March 12, 2001, p. 38, from International Data Corp.

★ **1891** ★
Information Technology (SIC 7375)

Largest Healthcare IT Firms, 1999

Firms are ranked by revenue in millions of dollars.

McKesson/HBOC	$ 1,538.0
EDS	1,297.1
SMS Corp.	1,200.0
3Com Corp.	850.0
CSC	521.5
Varian Medical Systems	504.0
SAIC	475.0
NDC Health Information Services	455.6
IDX Systems Corp.	341.0

Source: *Healthcare Informatics*, June 2000, p. 58.

★ **1892** ★
Security Services (SIC 7382)

Largest Security Firms

Firms are ranked by gross revenue in millions of dollars.

ADT Security Services	$ 1,330.0
SecurityLink from Ameritech	482.0
Protection One Inc.	421.1
Brink's Home Security Inc.	203.6
Honeywell Inc. Home & Building Control	200.7
Edison Security Services	90.0
Slomin's Inc.	67.8
Checkpoint Security Systems Group Inc.	55.2
Bay Alarm Co.	50.0

Source: "SDM 100." Retrieved November 4, 1999 from the World Wide Web: http://www.sdmmag.com.

★ **1893** ★
Newswires (SIC 7383)

Newswire Industry Leaders

Data show the market share claimed by each company. Each claims to move about 1,200 news releases a day and challenges the other's claim (no objective measurer of the industry exists).

Business Wire	54.0%
PR Newswire	53.0

Source: *PR Week*, June 5, 2000, p. 19.

★ 1894 ★

Photofinishing (SIC 7384)

Where Film is Processed, 2000

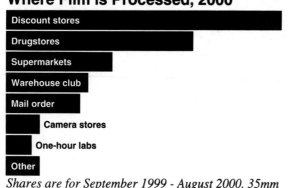

Shares are for September 1999 - August 2000. 35mm had a 73.7% share of film processed, followed by 14.4% for one-time use cameras.

Discount stores	34.4%
Drugstores	23.3
Supermarkets	12.9
Warehouse club	9.9
Mail order	8.8
Camera stores	4.1
One-hour labs	2.8
Other	3.8

Source: "Press Release." Retrieved November 17, 2000 from the World Wide Web: http://www.pmai.org, from Photo Marketing Association.

★ 1895 ★

Conventions (SIC 7389)

Top Sites for Conventions, 2000

Washington D.C.	190
Orlando, FL	163
Chicago, IL	123
San Antonio, TX	105
San Diego, CA	82

Source: *USA TODAY*, March 1, 2000, p. B1, from *Successful Meetings*.

★ 1896 ★

Mergers & Acquisitions (SIC 7389)

Largest Business Media Deals

Most of the firms in business-to-business publishing were involved in some merger or acquisition. Acquirers are in parentheses; price is in millions of dollars.

Harcourt General (Reed Elsevier)	$ 4,500
Primark Corp. (Thomson Corp.)	1,000
Advanstar (Donaldson, Lufkin & Jenrette) . .	900
United News & Media (VNU)	650
Reed Elsevier (Wolters Kluwer)	120

Source: *BtoB*, January 8, 2001, p. 24.

★ 1897 ★

Mergers & Acquisitions (SIC 7389)

Largest Real Estate Mergers

Figures are in billions of dollars.

Chase Securities	$ 8.1
J.P. Morgan	6.1
Banc of America Securities	5.4
Morgan Stanley	4.5

Source: *Real Estate Alert*, January 31, 2001, p. NA.

★ 1898 ★

Mergers & Acquisitions (SIC 7389)

Top Industries for Mergers, 2000

The industry mergers were worth $406.6 billion for the third quarter of the year.

Banking & finance	17.9%
Communications	14.3
Electronics	12.5
Computer software, supplies, and services . .	10.0
Brokerage, investment and consulting	7.5
Other	37.8

Source: *Investor's Business Daily*, October 24, 2000, p. A6, from Mergerstat LP.

★ 1899 ★

Trade Shows (SIC 7389)

Largest Trade Show Organizers, 2000

Reed Exhibition

George Little Management LLC

Miller Freeman Inc.

VNU Expositions

Key3Media Group Inc.

Advanstar Communications Inc.

Society of Manufacturing Engineers

Hall-Erickson

dmg World Media

The trade show industry continued to experience steady growth. Net square feet increased 3.2% and attendance increased 2.8%. Las Vegas was the top trade show site, with 33 shows in the top 200, giving it a 16.4% of the market. Firms are ranked by number of shows organized in the top 200.

	Shows	Share
Reed Exhibition	17	8.4%
George Little Management LLC . .	9	4.5
Miller Freeman Inc.	8	4.0
VNU Expositions	7	3.5
Key3Media Group Inc.	5	2.5
Advanstar Communications Inc. . .	5	2.5
Society of Manufacturing Engineers	4	2.0
Hall-Erickson	4	2.0
dmg World Media	4	2.0

Source: *Tradeshow Week*, April 23, 2001, p. 1.

★ 1900 ★

Trade Shows (SIC 7389)

Leading Industries for Exhibition, 1999

Data show number of shows. A total of 4,503 shows were conducted by 1999, with numbers expected to reach 4,781 in 2000 and 4,867 in 2001. Number of attendees were 102 million in 1999, 112 million in 2000 and 2001.

	No.	Share
Medical and health care	458	10.17%
Computer and computer applications	397	8.82
Home furnishings and interior design	300	6.66
Sporting goods and recreation . . .	278	6.17
Education	264	5.86
Building and construction	238	5.29
Engineering	179	3.98
Landscape and garden supplies . . .	175	3.89
Telecommunications	171	3.80
Other	2,043	45.37

Source: *Industry Standard*, October 23, 2000, p. 218, from *1999 Tradeshow Week Data Book* and Center for Exhibition Industry Research.

★ 1901 ★

Trade Shows (SIC 7389)

Top Sites for Trade Shows

Las Vegas, NV	127
Chicago, IL	124
Orlando, FL	110
New York City, NY	107
Atlanta, GA	92
Dallas, TX	81
New Orleans, LA	80
San Francisco, CA	80
Boston, MA	64

Source: *Christian Science Monitor*, March 16, 2001, p. 2, from *Trade Show Week*.

SIC 75 - Auto Repair, Services, and Parking

★ 1902 ★

Auto Rental (SIC 7514)

Largest Auto Rental Firms, 1999

Companies are ranked by average number of cars in service. Total number of cars is 1,733,392.

	Units	Share
Enterprise	399,941	23.07%
Hertz	280,500	16.18
Avis	210,000	12.11
Alamo	150,000	8.65
Budget	146,000	8.42
National	140,000	8.08
Dollar	70,000	4.04
FRCS (Ford)	48,000	2.77
Thrifty	46,000	2.65
CarTemps USA	38,000	2.19
Other	204,950	11.82

Source: Retrieved September 1, 2000 from the World Wide Web: http://www.autorentalnews.com/00stat3.cfm.

★ 1903 ★

Auto Rental (SIC 7514)

Top Car Rental Firms for Federal Travelers, 1999

Market shares are shown based on total sales.

National	14.6%
Avis	14.5
Dollar	11.0
Budget	10.9
Hertz	10.9
Alamo	10.0
Enterprise	8.6
Thrifty	8.5
Other	10.5

Source: *Government Executive Procurement Preview*, Annual 2000, p. 74, from General Services Administration.

★ 1904 ★

Auto Repair Services (SIC 7530)

Where Installers Buy Supplies

Market shares are shown in percent. The most popular jobber stores used were NAPA and Carquest.

Jobbers	60.0%
Auto retailers	19.0
Warehouse clubs	17.0
Mass merchandisers	4.0

Source: *Aftermarket Business*, October 2000, p. 48.

★ 1905 ★

Equipment Rental (SIC 7530)

Largest Equipment Rental Firms

Firms are ranked by estimated rental revenue in millions of dollars. The industry consists of 15,000-18,000 companies with rental revenues between $15-$20 billion.

United Rentals	$ 2,150
Prime/RSC	1,100
Hertz (HERC)	900
Nation Rent	475
National Equipment Services	450
BET USA	450
Brambles Equipment	190
Neff Corporation	190
AMECO	175
ICM Equipment	165

Source: *Diesel Progress North American Edition*, January 2001, p. 44, from Off-Highway Research.

★ 1906 ★

Retreading Shops (SIC 7531)

Largest Truck Tire Retreaders

Companies are ranked by millions of pounds of rubber used each year. Data refer to medium and heavy truck tire sales.

Goodyear	39.93
Tire Distribution Systems/Bandag	25.50
Treadco Inc.	15.20
Tire Centers L.L.C./Michelin	14.00
Bridgestone/Firestone Inc.	12.00
Les Schwab Tire Centers Inc.	8.41
Premier Bandag Inc.	7.60
Pomp's Tire Service Inc.	6.50
Purcell Tire & Rubber Co.	6.50

Source: *Tire Business*, January 29, 2001, p. 22.

SIC 78 - Motion Pictures

★ 1907 ★

Motion Pictures (SIC 7812)

Box Office Leaders, 2000

Market shares are shown in percent.

Buena Vista	14.8%
Warner Bros.	13.1
Universal	12.2
Paramount	10.1
Fox	8.9
Sony/Columbia	7.7
Other	33.2

Source: *New York Times*, November 6, 2000, p. C20, from Exhibitor relations.

★ 1908 ★

Motion Pictures (SIC 7812)

DVD Sellthrough Market, 2000

Market shares are shown for the year-to-date August 27, 2000. Data are based on consumer purchases from point-of-sale data in more than 16,000 retail locations.

Warner Home Video	27.50%
Buena Vista Home Ent.	14.88
Univ. Studios Home Video	14.13
Columbia TriStar Home Video	9.18

Paramount Home Ent.	7.14%
20th Century Fox Home Ent.	6.26
MGM	6.07
Other	14.84

Source: *Video Week*, September 11, 2000, p. 1.

★ 1909 ★

Motion Pictures (SIC 7812)

Home Video Market in North America

Figures are in millions of units.

	1999	2001
Sell-thru	833	770
Rental	90	80
Premium/promo	90	95
Non-consumer	35	31

Source: "Statistics." Retrieved May 17, 2001 from the World Wide Web: http://www.recordingmedia.org.

★ 1910 ★

Motion Pictures (SIC 7812)

Summer 2000 Market Shares

Summer 2000 is defined as Memorial Day through Labor Day.

Buena Vista	14.7%
Fox	14.7
DreamWorks	14.2
Warner Bros.	13.7
Paramount	12.1
Sony	8.1
Universal	7.6
Other	14.9

Source: *Forbes*, September 16, 2000, p. 68, from *Daily Variety*.

★ 1911 ★
Motion Pictures (SIC 7812)
Top Selling DVD Titles, 2000

Sales are shown in millions of units.

Gladiator	3.4
X-Men	2.2
The Sixth Sense	2.0
The Matrix	1.9
The Patriot	1.8
The Green Mile	1.7
M:1-2	1.7
The Perfect Storm	1.6
Gone in 60 Seconds	1.3
Toy Story/Toy Story 2 set	1.2

Source: *Video Business*, January 15, 2001, p. 19, from *Video Business* research.

★ 1912 ★
Motion Pictures (SIC 7812)
Top Selling VHS Titles, 2000

Sales are shown in millions of units.

Tarzan	11.2
Star Wars: Episode I	9.5
Toy Story 2	8.9
Stuart Little	6.4
Little Mermaid II: Return to Sea	5.2
Pokemon: The First Movie	4.8
X-Men	3.7
Chicken Run	3.7
The Tigger Movie	3.7

Source: *Video Business*, January 15, 2001, p. 19, from *Video Business* research.

★ 1913 ★
Motion Pictures (SIC 7812)
VHS Sellthrough Market, 2000

Market shares are shown for the year-to-date August 27, 2000. Data are based on consumer purchases from point-of-sale data in more than 16,000 retail locations.

Buena Vista	19.05%
Warner Home Video	17.26
Universal Studios Home Video	12.04
Columbia Tristar Home Video	11.40
Fox	10.99
Paramount Home Video	6.77
MGM	3.14
Other	19.35

Source: *Video Week*, September 11, 2000, p. 1.

★ 1914 ★
Film Distribution (SIC 7822)
Large Film Distributors in Canada, 2000

Market shares are shown in percent based on $857 revenue.

Universal	17.1%
Walt Disney	12.9
Warner Bros. Canada	12.4
Sony	12.3
Alliance Atlantis Communications	10.9
Dreamworks	10.5
Paramount Pictures	10.3
Fox	9.7
Other	3.9

Source: *Marketing Magazine*, June 4, 2001, p. NA, from ACNielsen and EDI.

★ 1915 ★

Film Distribution (SIC 7822)

Leading Film Producers, 2000

Market shares are shown based on box office receipts.

Buena Vista	16.4%
Paramount	15.5
Warner Bros.	11.2
Sony Pictures	11.0
Fox	10.7
New/Fine Line	7.8
DreamWorks	6.9
Universal	5.8
Miramax	5.8
Independents	3.2
Other	5.7

Source: *New York Times*, January 22, 2001, p. C12, from Universal Pictures, A.C. Nielsen, and EDI.

★ 1916 ★

Movie Theaters (SIC 7832)

Largest Movie Chains in North America

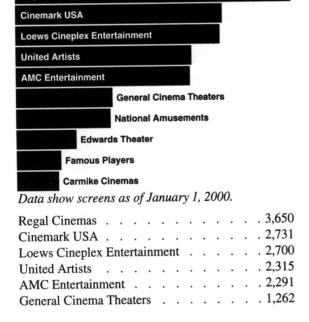

Data show screens as of January 1, 2000.

Regal Cinemas	3,650
Cinemark USA	2,731
Loews Cineplex Entertainment	2,700
United Artists	2,315
AMC Entertainment	2,291
General Cinema Theaters	1,262
National Amusements	1,235
Edwards Theater	775
Famous Players	569
Carmike Cinemas	536

Source: "Box Office Special Report." Retrieved July 24, 2000 from the World Wide Web: http://www.boxoff.com/giantstop.html.

★ 1917 ★

Movie Theaters (SIC 7832)

Movie Theater in San Jose/South Bay, CA

Market shares are shown in percent.

Century Theaters	63.0%
Other	37.0

Source: *San Jose Mercury News*, December 7, 2000, p. 1E, from AC Nielsen-EDI.

★ 1918 ★

Movie Theaters (SIC 7832)

Movie Theater Market in Canada

The data is based on a survey of 624 movie theaters and 68 drive-ins. Larger cinemas have operating revenues of $1 million or over.

Larger cinemas	42.0%
Small and medium-sized cinemas	16.0
Small theaters	1.9
Other	31.1

Source: "Statistics Canada: Movie Theaters and Drive-Ins." Retrieved October 19, 2000 from the World Wide Web: http://www.northernlight.com, from Statistics Canada.

★ 1919 ★

Movie Theaters (SIC 7832)

Movie Theater Market in Mexico

Market shares are shown in percent.

Organizacion Ramirez	35.0%
Cinemex	25.0
Other	40.0

Source: "Mexican Cinema Operators Face Limited Growth Potential." Retrieved September 28, 2000 from the World Wide Web: http://www/office.com.

★ 1920 ★

Movie Theaters (SIC 7832)

Top Movie Chains

Companies are ranked by number of screens. Total screens reached 37,185 in 1999. 1.47 billion people went to the movies during the year, generating $7.45 billion in ticket sales. The industry is suffering from oversupply of megaplexes and lack of a blockbuster film this season.

Regal Cinemas	3,672
Loews Cineplex	2,764
Carmike Cinemas	2,750
AMC	2,644
United Artists Theater	2,210

Source: *Atlanta Journal-Constitution*, October 1, 2000, p. Q1.

★ 1921 ★

Movie Rental (SIC 7841)

DVD Rental Market Shares

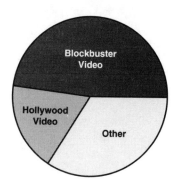

Market shares are shown in percent.

Blockbuster Video	47.9%
Hollywood Video	18.1
Other	34.0

Source: *Video Business*, May 15, 2000, p. 1.

★ 1922 ★

Movie Rental (SIC 7841)

Leading Movie Rental Firms in Canada, 2000

Market shares are shown in percent.

Blockbuster Video Canada	21.6%
Rogers Video	9.8
Superclub Videotron	5.6
Video Update	3.7
Jumbo Video	2.9
Other	56.4

Source: *Marketing Magazine*, June 4, 2001, p. NA, from Video Store Dealers Association.

★ 1923 ★

Movie Rental (SIC 7841)

Movie Rental Spending

More than 12 million U.S. homes have DVD players compared to 88 million homes with VCRs. Spending is shown in millions of dollars.

	1999	2001	Share
VHS rentals	$ 10,000	$ 8,500	78.7%
DVD rentals	110	2,300	21.3

Source: *Investor's Business Daily*, March 21, 2001, p. A8, from Adams Media Research.

★ 1924 ★

Movie Rental (SIC 7841)

Top DVD Firms

Market shares are shown in percent.

Warner	26.0%
Buena Vista	18.7
Universal	16.7
Universal alone	11.7
Fox	9.3
Paramount	8.8
Columbia	8.8
MGM	5.1
DreamWorks	5.0
Artisan	4.4
Other	4.0

Source: *Video Business*, January 15, 2001, p. 19, from Video Business research.

★ 1925 ★

Movie Rental (SIC 7841)

Video Store Market

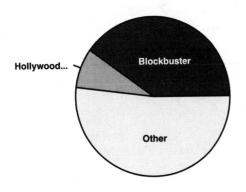

Market shares are estimated in percent.

Blockbuster 40.0%
Hollywood Video 8.0
Other 52.0

Source: *Variety*, November 20, 2000, p. 10.

SIC 79 - Amusement and Recreation Services

★ 1926 ★
Entertainers (SIC 7922)

Top Country Tours, 2000

Tours are ranked by grosses, in millions, for December 13, 1999 - December 4, 2000.

Dixie Chicks	$ 44.3
Tim McGraw & Faith Hill	40.7
George Strait Festival	20.9
Brooks & Dunn	10.7
Alan Jackson	9.0
Shania Twain	9.0
The Judds	8.9
Matina McBride	4.2

Source: *Amusement Business*, December 23, 2000, p. 22, from Amusement Business Boxscore.

★ 1927 ★
Entertainers (SIC 7922)

Top Pop/Rock Tours, 2000

Tours are ranked by grosses, in millions, for December 13, 1999 - December 4, 2000.

'N Sync	$ 59.2
Dave Matthews Band	58.5
Kiss	56.5
Bruce Springsteen	46.7
Crosby, Stills, Nash & Young	42.1
Metallica	40.5
Phish	36.0
Backstreet Boys	31.1

Source: *Amusement Business*, December 23, 2000, p. 22, from Amusement Business Boxscore.

★ 1928 ★
Entertainers (SIC 7922)

Top R&B/Hip Hop/Rap Tours, 2000

Tours are ranked by grosses, in millions, for December 13, 1999 - December 4, 2000.

Tina Turner	$ 108.7
Up In Smoke Tour: Dr. Dre	22.2
Ruff Ryders/Cash Money Tour: DMX	12.3
Mary J. Blige	5.2
D'Angelo	3.3
Luther Vandross	3.0
Soulfest Tour: Maze	2.7
TLC	2.1

Source: *Amusement Business*, December 23, 2000, p. 22, from Amusement Business Boxscore.

★ 1929 ★
Bowling Alleys (SIC 7933)

Bowling Alley Industry

Other refers to small chains and single center operators.

	No.	Share
AMF Bowling	408	7.13%
Brunswick	120	2.10
Other	5,198	90.78

Source: *Wall Street Journal*, December 18, 2000, p. B6, from Bowling Properitor Association of America and AMF Bowling.

★ 1930 ★
Sports (SIC 7941)

Our Favorite Sports

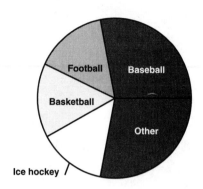

Over 422 million people attended a sporting event in North America in 1999. The top four sports accounted for three-quarters of the total attendance.

Baseball	28.0%
Football	15.0
Basketball	15.0
Ice hockey	14.0
Other	28.0

Source: *Sports Marketing*, November 2000, p. 2.

★ 1931 ★
Health Clubs (SIC 7991)

Health Club Memberships

An estimated 31 million Americans belong to health clubs, a number that should hit 50 million in 2010. Membership will tend to be older. In 1987, 53% of members were 18-34, with 33% of members in this category by 1999. In the 35-54 age range, 30% in 1987 and 38% in 1999. Data show the regions with the highest percentage that belong to a gym.

California	16.7%
Nevada	16.7
Colorado	16.5
Tennessee	16.2
Texas	15.3
Oregon	15.0
Massachusetts	14.9
Alabama	14.7
New Jersey	14.7
New Hampshire	14.5

Source: *DSN Retailing Today*, January 22, 2001, p. 27, from International Health, Racquet & Sportsclub Association.

★ 1932 ★
Slot Machines (SIC 7993)

Slot Machine Industry

74% of all machines are in Nevada.

IGT	72.0%
Other	28.0

Source: *Forbes*, July 3, 2000, p. 74.

★ 1933 ★
Slot Machines (SIC 7993)

Slot Machine Market in Las Vegas' Clark County

Market shares are shown in percent.

International Game Technology	75.0%
WMS	10.0
Other	15.0

Source: *Investor's Business Daily*, September 12, 2000, p. A12.

★ 1934 ★
Video Terminals (SIC 7993)

Video Terminal Market

Video terminals are stealing sales from the old spinning-reel slot machines. Market shares are shown based on shipments.

IGT	48.6%
WMS	27.4
Aristocrat	12.0
Alliance	5.2
CSDS	3.0
Other	3.8

Source: *Investor's Business Daily*, June 5, 2001, p. A10, from company reports and CIBC WorldMarkets.

★ 1935 ★
Amusement Parks (SIC 7996)

Largest Amusement Parks in North America, 2000

Parks are ranked by millions of visitors.

The Magic Kingdom at Walt Disney World	15.4
Disneyland	13.9
Epcot at Walt Disney World	10.6

Continued on next page.

★ 1935 ★ *Continued*

Amusement Parks (SIC 7996)

Largest Amusement Parks in North America, 2000

Parks are ranked by millions of visitors.

Disney-MGM Studios at Walt Disney World	8.9
Disney's Animal Kingdom at Walt Disney World	8.3
Universal Studios at Unviersal Orlando	8.1
Islands of Adventure at Universal Orlando	6.0
Seaworld	5.2
Universal Studios Hollywood	5.2
Busch Gardens Florida	5.0

Source: *Amusement Business*, December 25, 2000, p. 84.

★ 1936 ★

Gambling (SIC 7999)

Riverboat Market Shares in Kansas City, MO

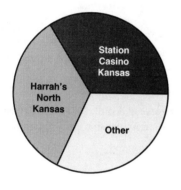

Shares are for September 2000.

Station Casino Kansas City	33.82%
Harrah's North Kansas City Casino	33.77
Other	32.41

Source: *The Kansas City Star*, September 13, 2000, p. 1.

★ 1937 ★

Gambling (SIC 7999)

Top Casinos in St. Louis, MO

Shares are shown based on revenue earned in December 2000. Gamblers at the area's five casinos left behind nearly $684 million last year.

Harrah's	37.0%
Casino Queen	22.0
Ameristar	17.0
Alton Belle	15.0
President	8.0

Source: *St. Louis Post-Dispatch*, January 24, 2001, p. A1, from Missouri Gaming Commission.

SIC 80 - Health Services

Eye Surgery (SIC 8042)

Laser Eye Surgery Market in Cincinnati, OH

The share has been estimated between 50-60%.

LCA Vision	60.0%
Other	40.0

Source: *Business Courier Serving Cincinnati-Northern Kentucky*, July 21, 2000, p. 8.

Eye Surgery (SIC 8042)

Who Performs Eye Laser Surgery

The number of laser eye surgeries have doubled last year to 950,000 procedures. At roughly $1,650 a procedure, Americans will spend $2.43 billion on laser eye surgeries. Shares are for the second quarter of the year.

Corporate chains	48.0%
Independent doctors and medical centers	41.0
Hospitals	10.0

Source: *New York Times*, December 9, 2000, p. B1.

Nursing Homes (SIC 8050)

Largest Nursing Home Chains

Companies are ranked by number of beds at the end of the year.

Beverly Enterprise	62,217
Mariner Post-Acute Network	45,977
Integrated Health Services	45,000
HCR Manor Care	41,347
Sun Healthcare Group	39,867
Genesis Health Ventures	38,506
Vencor	38,336
Life Care Centers of America	27,144
Extendicare Health Centers	20,143
The Evangelical Lutheran Good Samaritan Society	17,026

Source: *Provider*, June 2000, p. 38.

Senior Housing (SIC 8051)

Top Senior Housing Markets

Of the senior housing built since 1997, about 108,500 were assisted living and 54,500 congregate senior housing. Data show units under construction.

Chicago, IL	1,820
Los Angeles, CA	1,745
Detroit, MI	1,562
San Diego, CA	1,380
Baltimore/Washington D.C.	985

Source: *Wall Street Journal*, April 18, 2001, p. B12, from American Seniors Housing Association and Legg Mason Wood Walter Inc.

Hospitals (SIC 8060)

Hospital Market Shares in Tampa Bay, FL

Shares are shown based on number of beds.

	Beds	Share
St. Joseph's Hospitals	883	6.5%
Tampa General Hospital	877	6.5
Lakeland Regional Medical Center	851	6.0
Sarasota Memorial Health Care System	845	6.0
Morton Plant Hospital	687	5.0
Other	9,423	70.0

Source: *Tampa Bay Business Journal*, January 5, 2001, p. 10, from Agency for Health Care Adminsitration.

★ 1943 ★

Hospitals (SIC 8060)

Inpatient Market Shares in the Greensboro, N.C.

Market shares are shown in percent. Data are for 1999.

Moses Cone	89.0%
High Point Regional	3.0
Other	8.0

Source: *Business Journal (North Carolina)*, October 20, 2000, p. 1.

★ 1944 ★

Hospitals (SIC 8060)

Popular Reasons for Hospital Discharges

About 31.8 million inpatients (excluding newborns) were discharged from tha nation's short stay non-Federal hospitals in 1998. The categories shown accounted for more than one million discharges.

Heart disease	4.3%
Delivery	4.0
Psychoses	1.3
Pneumonia	1.3
Malignant neoplasms	1.3
Cerebrovascular disease	1.0
Other	86.8

Source: *Research Alert*, October 6, 2000, p. 9, from National Center for Health Statistics.

★ 1945 ★

Hospitals (SIC 8060)

Top Hospitals in Miami-Dade, FL

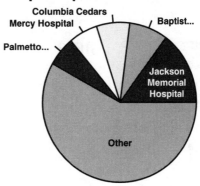

Miami-Dade has a per capita income of $21,000.

Jackson Memorial Hospital	15.1%
Baptist Hospital of Miami	8.4
Columbia Cedars	7.0
Mercy Hospital	5.8
Palmetto General Hospital	5.5
Other	58.2

Source: *South Florida Business Journal*, September 22, 2000, p. 53B.

★ 1946 ★

Hospitals (SIC 8060)

Top Hospitals in Milwaukee, MN

Market shares are shown by admissions.

Aurora Health Care	30.0%
Horizon Healthcare	26.3
Covenant Healthcare	16.0
Prohealthcare	7.3
Other	18.4

Source: *Knight-Ridder/Tribune Business News*, March 31, 2001, p. NA.

★ 1947 ★

Hospitals (SIC 8060)

Top Hospitals in Palm Beach County, FL

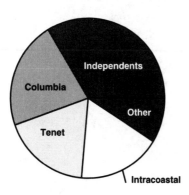

This is the state's richest county with a $36,000 per capita income. It has 12 hospitals with 2,708 beds to serve 576,754 residents. "Independents" represents seven different hospitals.

Independents	37.0%
Columbia	24.0
Tenet	20.0
Intracoastal	19.0
Other	10.0

Source: *South Florida Business Journal*, September 22, 2000, p. 53B.

★ 1948 ★

Surgery (SIC 8060)

Ambulatory Surgery Centers by State, 2000

California	758,365
Florida	700,761
Texas	398,451
Illinois	259,100
Ohio	242,234

Source: *Modern Physician*, April 2001, p. 44, from SMG Marketing Group.

★ 1949 ★

Surgery (SIC 8060)

Leading Plastic Surgeries, 1999

Data show the number of surgeries performed by physicians certified by the American Board of Plastic Surgery.

Tumor removal	521,678
Hand surgery	171,510
Breast reconstruction	82,975
Breast reduction	78,169
Lacerations	69,729

Source: *USA TODAY*, November 12, 2000, p. 8D, from American Board of Plastic Surgery.

★ 1950 ★

Dialysis Centers (SIC 8092)

Dialysis Treatment Industry

Market shares are shown in percent.

Fresenius	24.0%
DaVita	16.0
Gambro	14.0
Renal Care	5.0
Other	41.0

Source: *Nashville Business Journal*, January 19, 2001, p. 1.

SIC 82 - Educational Services

★ 1951 ★
Education (SIC 8200)

Top Destinations for U.S. Students, 1998- 99

The table shows the top destinations for students earning college credit.

United Kingdom	27,720
Spain	12,292
Italy	11,281
France	10,479
Mexico	7,363
Australia	5,368
Germany	4,534
Costa Rica	3,449
Israel	3,302
Ireland	3,073

Source: *USA TODAY*, November 13, 2000, p. 7D, from Open Doors, 2000.

★ 1952 ★
Schools (SIC 8211)

School Classroom Spending

Schools (K-12) spent $285 billion during the 1997-98 year, an average of $6,189 for each student.

Instruction (teachers salaries, textbooks)	61.8%
Support services (maintenance, nurses, library)	33.8
Noninstruction (foodservice, bookstore)	4.4

Source: *Investor's Business Daily*, July 7, 2000, p. A4, from U.S. Department of Education.

★ 1953 ★
Schools (SIC 8211)

Top States in Pre-K Funding

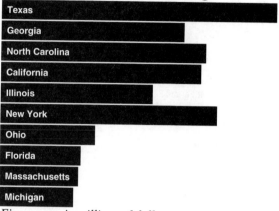

Figures are in millions of dollars.

	1999-2000	2000-2001
Texas	$ 300.0	$ 350.0
Georgia	224.0	232.0
North Carolina	216.0	260.0
California	207.1	253.6
Illinois	179.6	192.4
New York	135.2	275.2
Ohio	114.9	119.2
Florida	101.0	101.0
Massachusetts	93.1	98.1
Michigan	72.3	92.2

Source: *Child Care Information Exchange*, September 2000, p. 82, from Wilson Marketing Group.

★ 1954 ★

Colleges (SIC 8221)

Wealthiest Universities and Colleges, 2000

Companies are ranked by the size of their endowments as of June 30, 2000.

Harvard	$ 18.84
Yale	10.08
U of Texas system	10.01
Stanford	8.65
Princeton	8.40
MIT	6.48
U of Cal. System	5.64
Emory	5.03
Columbia	4.26
Washington U/foundations	4.23

Source: *USA TODAY*, May 8, 2001, p. A1, from National Association of College and University Business Officers.

★ 1955 ★

Libraries (SIC 8231)

Leading Public Libraries

Libraries are ranked by millions of volumes owned.

New York Public Library	10.48
Queens Borough Public Library	9.51
Public Library of Cincinnati and Hamilton County	9.27
Chicago Public Library	9.22
Toronto Public Library	8.71
Free Library of Philadelphia	7.96
Boston Public Library	7.26
County of Los Angeles Public Library . . .	6.88
Carnegie Library of Pittsburgh	6.63

Source: ''Beyond the Book.'' Retrieved June 7, 2001 from the World Wide Web: http://www.ala.org.

SIC 83 - Social Services

★ 1956 ★

Child Care (SIC 8351)

Largest Child Care Organizations

The largest for-profit groups in North America are ranked by capacity.

KinderCare Learning Centers 150,000
La Petite Academy 100,527
Children's World Learning Centers 82,680
Bright Horizons Family Solutions Inc. . . 42,500
Childtime Learning Centers 40,380
Knowledge Learning Corporation 36,126
Nobel Learning Communities 27,500
Childcare Network Inc. 12,832
New Horizons Child Care 12,140
The Sunshine House 10,983

Source: *Child Care Information Exchange*, January 2001, p. 22.

★ 1957 ★

Charities (SIC 8399)

Largest Charities

| Salvation Army |
| YMCA of the USA |
| American Red Cross |
| American Cancer Society |
| Fidelity Investments Charitable Gift Fund |
| Lutheran Services in America |
| United Jewish Communities |
| Habitat for Humanity International |
| Harvard University |

Organizations are ranked by private donations received in millions of dollars.

Salvation Army . . . . $ 1,400.0
YMCA of the USA 693.3
American Red Cross 678.3
American Cancer Society 620.0

Fidelity Investments Charitable Gift Fund . $ 573.4
Lutheran Services in America 559.0
United Jewish Communities 524.3
Habitat for Humanity International 466.7
Harvard University 451.7

Source: *Christian Science Monitor*, October 31, 2000, p. 24, from *Chronicle of Philanthropy*.

★ 1958 ★

Charities (SIC 8399)

Largest Corporate Donors, 1999

Companies are ranked by donations in millions of dollars.

Merck . . . . $ 148.5
DuPont 122.2
Philip Morris 107.8
Wal-Mart 96.0
Bank of America 95.5

Source: *USA TODAY*, December 12, 2000, p. B1, from *Worth* and Council on Economic Priorities.

★ 1959 ★

Charities (SIC 8399)

Where Charitable Dollars Go, 1999

Total contributions reached $190 billion.

Religion 43.0%
Education 14.0
Health 9.0
Human services 9.0
Arts, culture 6.0
Environment 3.0
International affairs 1.0
Other 15.0

Source: *Time*, July 24, 2000, p. 59, from Giving USA and AAFRC Trust for Philanthropy.

★ 1960 ★

Charities (SIC 8399)

Who Gave Charitable Donations, 1999

Distribution is shown in percent.

Individuals 75.6%
Foundations 10.4
Bequests 8.2
Corporations 5.8

Source: *Christian Science Monitor*, December 4, 2000, p. 18, from Giving USA 2000 and AAFRC Trust for Philanthropy.

SIC 84 - Museums, Botanical, Zoological Gardens

★ 1961 ★

Museums (SIC 8412)

Largest Museum Shows

Van Gogh's Van Goghs	
	Egyptian Art in the Age of the Pyramids
	John Singer Sargent Retrospective
Cezanne to Van Gogh	
	Louis Comfort Tiffany at the Met
	Juliao Sarmento at the Hirschhorn
Jackson Pollock	

Data show attendance. The Van Gogh exhibit was held at the Los Angeles County Museum of Art; the Egyptian art exhibit was held at the Metropolitan Museum of Art; the Sargent exhibit was held at the National Gallery of Art; Jackson Pollock exhibit washeld at the Museum of Modern Art.

Van Gogh's Van Goghs	821,004
Egyptian Art in the Age of the Pyramids .	473,234
John Singer Sargent Retrospective	453,937
Cezanne to Van Gogh	429,024
Louis Comfort Tiffany at the Met	371,494
Juliao Sarmento at the Hirschhorn	334,089
Jackson Pollock	329,330

Source: *New York Times*, February 3, 2000, p. B5.

SIC 86 - Membership Organizations

Professional Organizations (SIC 8621)

Leading Utility Trade Associations

Data show number of members.

American Water Works Association 50,000
American Public Power Association 2,000
United States Telecom Association 1,200
Edison Electric Institute 345
American Gas Association 185

Source: *Utility Business*, February 2001, p. 42.

★ 1963 ★

Unions (SIC 8631)

Union Membership, 2000

| Government |
| Manufacturing |
| Services |
| Construction |
| Wholesale, retail trade |
| Transportation |
| Other |

Men make up almost 59% of union membership. By race, 80.5% are white and 15.3% are black.

Government 43.7%
Manufacturing 14.7
Services 11.6
Construction 7.5
Wholesale, retail trade 7.3
Transportation 7.0
Other 5.4

Source: *Christian Science Monitor*, January 29, 2001, p. 15, from U.S. Bureau of Labor Statistics.

★ 1964 ★

Religious Organizations (SIC 8661)

Largest Church Congregations

Data show millions of members in selected churches.

Roman Catholic 62.0
Southern Baptist Convention 15.8
United Methodist Church 8.4
Church of God in Christ 5.5
Church of Jesus Christ of Latter-day Saints . . 4.4
Evangelical Lutheran Church 3.8
Presbyterian Chuch USA 2.6
African Methodist Episcopal (AME) Church . 2.5
Jewish 2.4
Lutheran Church, Missouri Synod 2.0
Islam 2.0

Source: *USA TODAY*, April 26, 2001, p. 7D, from *Yearbook of American and Canadian Churches 2000*, Mosque Study Project 2000, and Institute for Jewish and Community Research.

SIC 87 - Engineering and Management Services

★ 1965 ★

Design Services (SIC 8710)

Largest Design Firms, 2000

Firms are ranked by annual service billings in millions of dollars.

Callison Architecture	$ 40.5
Fitch Worldwide	36.4
Pavlik Design Team	32.9
RTRL Associates Inc.	32.0
Gensler	27.0
MCG Architecture	26.0
Carter & Burgess Inc.	22.5
Little Associates Architects	21.8
Retail Planning Associates	20.5
Perkowitz & Ruth Architects	20.0

Source: *Display & Design Ideas*, April 2001, p. 41.

★ 1966 ★

Design Services (SIC 8711)

Largest Design Building Firms

Firms are ranked by total revenue in billions of dollars.

Bechtel Group Inc.	$ 9.78
Fluor Daniel Inc.	5.69
Foster Wheeler Corp.	2.81
Raytheon Enginners & Constructors	2.06
McDermott International Inc.	1.85
Black & Veatch	1.62
Kellogg Brown & Root	1.55
Peter Kiewit Sons Inc.	1.54
Jacobs Engineering Group Inc.	1.41

Source: *ENR*, June 19, 2000, p. 117.

★ 1967 ★

Engineering Services (SIC 8711)

Largest Engineering Firms in South Florida

Firms are ranked by area gross billings in millions of dollars.

Kimley Horn & Associates	$ 33.6
PBS&J	27.1
Keith & Schners	18.9
Gee & Jenson	11.7
Consul-Tech Engineering	11.4

Source: *South Florida Business Journal*, March 2, 2001, p. 16.

★ 1968 ★

Legal Services (SIC 8711)

Top Law Firms in the Bay Area, CA

Brobeck, Phleger & Harrison
Wilson Sonsini Goodrich & Rosati
Morrison & Foerster
Cooley Godward
Orrick, Herrington & Sutcliffe

Firms are ranked by revenue in millions of dollars.

Brobeck, Phleger & Harrison	$ 476
Wilson Sonsini Goodrich & Rosati	450
Morrison & Foerster	437
Cooley Godward	345
Orrick, Herrington & Sutcliffe	320

Source: *The American Lawyer*, February 2001, p. NA.

★ 1969 ★

Accounting Services (SIC 8721)

Largest Accounting Firms

Firms are ranked by fee income in millions of dollars.

PricewaterhouseCoopers	$ 6,960
Ernst & Young	5,545
Deloitte & Touche	5,300
KPMG	4,700
Arthur Andersen	3,300

Source: *The Accountant*, May 2000, p. 17.

★ 1970 ★

Accounting Services (SIC 8721)

Largest Accounting Firms in Canada

Firms are ranked by fee income in millions of Canadian dollars.

PricewaterhouseCoopers LLP	926.0
Deloitte & Touche	819.0
Ernst & Young	714.6
KPMG LLP	658.0
Grant Thornton Canada	247.8
Arthur Andersen LLP	212.0
BDO Dunwoody LLP	192.0

Source: *International Accounting Bulletin*, February 28, 2001, p. 11.

★ 1971 ★

Accounting Services (SIC 8721)

Largest Accounting Firms in the Midwest, 1999

Firms are ranked by revenue in millions of dollars.

Baird Kurtz & Dobson	$ 106.4
Larson, Allen, Weirshair & Co. LLP	67.0
Eide Bailly	35.2
Rubin, Brown, Gornstein & Co. LLP	20.6
Kennedy & Coe	19.3
Lurie, Besikof, Lapidus & Co. LLP	14.0
Grace & Co.	13.6

Olsen Thielen & Co.	$ 13.1
Boulay, Heutmaker, Zibell & Co.	12.1

Source: *Practical Accountant*, April 2000, p. 42.

★ 1972 ★

Accounting Services (SIC 8721)

Largest Accounting Firms in the North Central U.S., 1999

Firms are ranked by revenue in millions of dollars.

Crowe Chizek & Co.	$ 144.4
Plante & Moran, LLP	117.4
Clifton Gunderson LLC	96.2
Virchow Krause & Co.	62.3
Olive LLP	59.6
Wipfil Ulrich Bertelson	42.1
Thomas Havey LLP	35.0
Hausser & Taylor LLP	30.3

Source: *Practical Accountant*, April 2000, p. 42.

★ 1973 ★

Accounting Services (SIC 8721)

Largest Accounting Firms in the Southeastern U.S., 1999

Firms are ranked by revenue in millions of dollars.

Cherry Bekaert & Holland	$ 33.0
Dixon Odom	28.9
Crisp Hughes Evans	21.4
Goodman & Co.	20.0
Elliott Davis & Co.	19.7
Kaufman Rossin & Co.	18.4
Joseph Decosimo and Company, LLP	17.5
Rachlin Cohen & Holta LLP	16.5

Source: *Practical Accountant*, April 2000, p. 42.

★ 1974 ★

Commercial Research (SIC 8732)

Largest R&D Spenders, 2001

Firms are ranked by spending in billions of dollars.

Ford Motor Company	$ 7.42
Lucent Technologies	7.36
General Motors	5.70
E.I. Du Pont de Nemours	5.30
IBM	5.04

Continued on next page.

★ **1974** ★ *Continued*

Commercial Research (SIC 8732)

Largest R&D Spenders, 2001

Firms are ranked by spending in billions of dollars.

Pfizer	$ 4.70
Intel	4.54
Microsoft	4.28
Motorola	4.14
Cisco Systems	3.43

Source: *R&D Magazine*, January 2001, p. 63.

★ **1975** ★

Management Services (SIC 8741)

Largest Executive Search Firms

Korn/Ferry International
Heidrick & Struggles International
Spencer Stuart
Russell Reynolds Associates
DHR International
Christian & Timbers
Egon Zehnder International
A.T. Kearney Executive Search
Ray & Berndtson
TMP Worldwide Executive Search

Firms are ranked by revenues in millions of dollars.

Korn/Ferry International	$ 385.5
Heidrick & Struggles International	361.7
Spencer Stuart	192.4
Russell Reynolds Associates	160.2
DHR International	61.0
Christian & Timbers	60.7
Egon Zehnder International	57.8
A.T. Kearney Executive Search	45.0
Ray & Berndtson	40.3
TMP Worldwide Executive Search	11.5

Source: "Hunt-Scanlon Report Shows Top Recruiting Firms Grew 31% in 2000." Retrieved April 10, 2001 from the World Wide Web: http://www.businesswire.com, from Hunt Scanlon.

★ **1976** ★

Public Relations Services (SIC 8743)

Leading PR Firms, 2000

Firms are ranked by revenue in thousands of dollars.

Fleishman-Hillard	$ 266,831
Weber Shandwick Worldwide	219,184
Burson-Marsteller	182,259
Hill & Knowlton	177,858
Edelman	168,430
BSMG	147,380
Ketchum	143,779
Porter Novelli	135,888
Ogilvy PR	129,064
Golin/Harris	107,905

Source: *PR Week*, April 23, 2001, p. 1.

★ **1977** ★

Public Relations Services (SIC 8743)

Leading PR Firms in Boston, MA

Firms are ranked by 1999 income in millions of dollars.

Brodeur Worldwide	$ 32.8
Schwartz Communications	16.6
Weber	16.2
Ogilvy	10.0
Cone	9.5
Miller/Shandwick	9.2
Fitzgerald Communications	9.0
Sterling Hager	8.0
Porter Novelli	7.9
GPC International	6.5

Source: *PR Week*, October 23, 2000, p. 35, from *PR Week 2000 Agency Rankings*.

★ **1978** ★

Public Relations Services (SIC 8743)

Leading PR Firms in Florida, 1999

Firms are ranked by income in millions of dollars.

Burson-Marsteller	$ 5.4
Weber	4.3
Fleishman-Hillard	3.4
The Zimmerman Agency	3.3
Wragg & Casas	2.9
The Jeffrey Group	1.9
Edelman	1.9
The Nixon Group	1.9

Continued on next page.

★ 1978 ★ *Continued*
Public Relations Services (SIC 8743)

Leading PR Firms in Florida, 1999

Firms are ranked by income in millions of dollars.

PCI . . . . $ 1.6
The Transmedia Group 1.5

Source: *PR Week*, July 10, 2000, p. 23.

★ 1979 ★
Public Relations Services (SIC 8743)

Leading PR Firms in Kansas, 1999

Firms are ranked by fee income in millions of dollars.

Fleishman-Hillard Inc. . . . . $ 16.13
Corporate Communications Group Inc. . . . 3.40
Barkley Evergreen & Partners Inc. 2.24
Boasberg/Wheeler Communications Inc. . . 1.82
Blades & Associates 1.32

Source: *Kansas City Business Journal*, April 14, 2000, p. 93.

★ 1980 ★
Public Relations Services (SIC 8743)

Leading PR Firms in Los Angeles, CA

Firms are ranked by income in millions of dollars.

Ketchum . . . . $ 15.9
Shandwick 15.4
Hill and Knowlton 13.6
Manning, Selvage & Lee 13.4
Fleishman-Hillard 11.5
Ogilvy 10.9
Golin/Harris 10.8
BSMG 9.3
Burson-Marsteller 8.5

Source: *PR Week*, July 17, 2000, p. 23.

★ 1981 ★
Public Relations Services (SIC 8743)

Leading PR Firms in Minnesota, 1999

Firms are ranked by income in millions of dollars.

Shandwick . . . . $ 18.8
Padilla Speer Beardsley 8.1
Colle & McVoy 7.1

Tunheim Group . . . .$ 5.0
Carmichael Lynch Spong 4.9
Fleishman Hillard 4.3
Karwoski & Courage 2.7
Morgan & Meyers 2.5
Golf & Howard 2.1
LaBreche Murray 1.2

Source: *PR Week*, July 10, 2000, p. 23.

★ 1982 ★
Public Relations Services (SIC 8743)

Leading PR Firms in New York City, NY

Firms are ranked by income in millions of dollars.

Burson-Marsteller . . . . $ 65.6
Ruder Finn 45.9
Edelmann 45.2
Ketchum 32.0
BSMG 31.1
Porter Novelli 28.2
Rowland Worldwide 25.6
Fleishmann-Hillard 24.8
Hill & Knowlton 23.9
Weber 23.1

Source: *PR Week*, June 12, 2000, p. 23.

★ 1983 ★
Public Relations Services (SIC 8743)

Leading PR Firms in San Diego, CA

Firms are ranked by income in millions of dollars.

The Townsend Agency . . . . $ 7,000.3
Stoorza Communications 3,953.7
The Gable Group 2,210.6
Nelson Communications Group 1,867.9
Nuffer Smith Tucker 1,286.7
Cooper Iverson Marketing 1,253.5
Presence EURO RSCG 250.0

Source: *PR Week*, August 14, 2000, p. 49.

★ 1984 ★

Public Relations Services (SIC 8743)

Leading PR Firms in Texas

Firms are ranked by 1999 income in millions of dollars.

Fleishman-Hillard	$ 10.4
Cunningham Comms.	7.3
Springbok Technologies	5.8
Shandwick International	5.0
Vollmer	5.0
BSMG Worldwide	4.5
Edelmann Worldwide	4.2
Publicis Dialog	3.6
TateAustin	3.2
Fogarty Klein monroe	2.5

Source: *PR Week*, July 31, 2000, p. 33, from PRWeek 2000 Agency Rankings.

★ 1985 ★

Public Relations Services (SIC 8743)

Top Sports PR Agencies, 1999

Firms are ranked by income in thousands of dollars.

Ketchum	$ 6,750
Shandwick	4,567
Alan Taylor	4,245
Dan Klores Associates	1,500
Edelman	1,088
Brotman Winter Fried	840
Donnellon Public Relations	819
Jamison Golf Group	562
Tunheim Group	450
The Rasky/Baerlein Group	354

Source: *PR Week*, September 18, 2000, p. 19.

SIC 92 - Justice, Public Order, and Safety

★ 1986 ★

Prisons (SIC 9220)

U.S. Prison Population

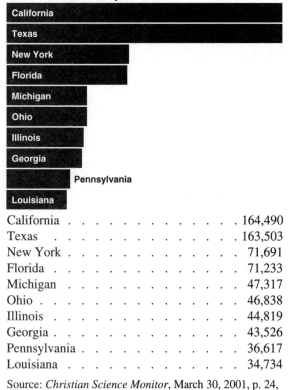

California	
Texas	
New York	
Florida	
Michigan	
Ohio	
Illinois	
Georgia	
Pennsylvania	
Louisiana	

California	164,490
Texas	163,503
New York	71,691
Florida	71,233
Michigan	47,317
Ohio	46,838
Illinois	44,819
Georgia	43,526
Pennsylvania	36,617
Louisiana	34,734

Source: *Christian Science Monitor*, March 30, 2001, p. 24, from Associated Press.

★ 1987 ★

Prisons (SIC 9223)

Private Prison Industry

The table compares the leaders by revenue and number of beds. The two firms have 75% of private prison beds in the industry. The rest are small regional players.

	($ mil.)	Beds
Corrections Corp. of America . .	$ 310.3	61,462
Wackenhut	535.6	39,924

Source: *Wall Street Journal*, May 9, 2001, p. B4, from Thomson Financial/Baseline.

★ 1988 ★

Department of Treasury (SIC 9311)

Top Contractors to the Treasury Department

Market shares are shown based on total contracted purchases.

Goldman Sachs & Co.	12.28%
TRW Inc.	5.82
Crane Co.	3.99
Unisys Corp.	3.83
Morgan Guaranty Trust of New York	3.12
Other	70.96

Source: *Government Executive Procurement Preview*, Annual 2000, p. 101.

SIC 94 - Administration of Human Resources

Taxation (SIC 9411)

Tax Collections By State

Collections are shown in billions of dollars.

California	$ 67.71
New York	36.15
Texas	24.63
Florida	22.51
Michigan	21.69
Pennsylvania	20.63
Illinois	19.77
Ohio	17.64
New Jersey	15.60
North Carolina	13.87

Source: *Investor's Business Daily*, December 8, 2000, p. A26, from The Tax Foundation.

★ 1990 ★

Department of Health and Human Services (SIC 9431)

Top Contractors to the Department of Health/ Human Services

Market shares are shown based on total contracted purchases.

Doug O'Bryan Contracting Inc.	5.15%
Science Applications Intl. Corp.	4.03
Westat Inc.	3.35
TRW Inc.	2.45
Research Triangle Institute	1.63
Other	83.39

Source: *Government Executive Procurement Preview*, Annual 2000, p. 96.

★ 1991 ★

Department of Labor (SIC 9441)

Top Contractors to the Labor Department

Market shares are shown based on total contracted purchases.

Management & Training Corp.	13.74%
Res-Care Inc.	10.56
Texas Educational Foundation	6.19
TRW Inc.	5.98
Career Systems Development Corp.	5.55
Minact Inc.	3.96
Dynamic Education Systems Inc.	3.01
Other	51.01

Source: *Government Executive Procurement Preview*, Annual 2000, p. 101.

★ **1992** ★

Department of Veteran Affairs (SIC 9451)

Top Contractors to the Veteran Affairs Department

Market shares are shown based on total contracted purchases.

Amerisource Distribution Corp.	20.02%
Bindley Western Industries	2.38
Electronic Data Systems Corp.	1.42
Carlyle Group	1.38
Compaq Computer Corp.	1.29
McKesson Corp.	1.23
Other	72.28

Source: *Government Executive Procurement Preview*, Annual 2000, p. 101.

SIC 95 - Environmental Quality and Housing

Environmental Services (SIC 9511)

Largest Environmental Construction/ Remediation Firms

- Bechtel Group Inc.
- The IT Group
- Foster Wheeler Corp.
- Fluor Corp.
- Morrison Knudsen Corp.
- Black & Veatch
- Jacobs Engineering Group Inc.
- URS Corp.
- CH2M Hill Cos. Inc.

Firms are ranked by revenue in millions of dollars.

Bechtel Group Inc.	$ 2,242.0
The IT Group	909.2
Foster Wheeler Corp.	716.9
Fluor Corp.	626.7
Morrison Knudsen Corp.	358.5
Black & Veatch	347.0
Jacobs Engineering Group Inc.	260.0
URS Corp.	253.0
CH2M Hill Cos. Inc.	238.9

Source: *ENR*, July 3, 2000, p. 41.

★ 1994 ★

Environmental Services (SIC 9511)

Largest Environmental Firms

Firms are ranked by revenue in millions of dollars.

U.S. Filter Corp.	$ 5,270.0
Montgomery Watson Inc.	514.3
Camp Dresser & McKee Inc.	482.4
MACTEC Inc.	339.2
Roy F. Weston Inc.	263.7
ENSR Corp.	218.1
Malcolm Pirnie Inc.	173.1

ThermoRetec Corp.	$ 152.5
Ogden Envir. & Energy Svcs. Co. Inc.	145.5

Source: *ENR*, July 3, 2000, p. 41.

★ 1995 ★

Environmental Services (SIC 9511)

Largest Nuclear Waste Firms

Firms are ranked by revenue in millions of dollars.

Fluor Corp.	$ 644.4
Morrison Knudsen Corp.	602.9
Bechtel Group Inc.	567.6
CH2M Hill Cos. Inc.	227.0
Foster Wheeler Corp.	222.5
The IT Group	173.8
Battelle Memorial Institute	111.6
Science Applications Intl. Corp.	88.2
BNFL Inc.	87.4

Source: *ENR*, July 3, 2000, p. 41.

★ 1996 ★

National Parks (SIC 9512)

Most-Visited National Parks

Figures show millions of visitors.

Blue Ridge Parkway	19.0
Golden Gate National Recreation Area	14.5
Great Smokey Mountains National Park	10.1

Source: *USA TODAY*, June 1, 2001, p. A1.

★ **1997** ★

Urban Forestry (SIC 9532)

Urban Forestry in Wisconsin

The table shows the number of street trees and trees pruned annually and trees removed for selected cities.

	Street	Pruned	Removed
Madison, WI	100,000	10,764	1,775
Kenosha, WI	27,000	1,900	363
Appleton, WI . . .	25,000	4,000	300
Waukesha, WI . . .	24,000	3,000	300
Racine, WI	20,000	1,500	287

Source: *American City & County*, April 2001, p. 20, from Park Division of Kenosha, WI.

SIC 96 - Administration of Economic Programs

Department of the Interior (SIC 9611)

Top Contractors to the Department of the Interior

Market shares are shown based on total contracted purchases.

Northrop Grumman Corp.	7.00%
Systems Integration Inc.	3.30
Raytheon Co.	2.10
AMS Operations Corp.	1.60
TRW Inc.	1.25
Other	74.75

Source: *Government Executive Procurement Preview*, Annual 2000, p. 96.

★ 1999 ★

Department of Transportation (SIC 9621)

Top Contractors to the Transportation Department

- IBM Corp.
- Bollinger Shipyards Inc.
- Lockheed Martin Corp.
- Computer Sciences Corp.
- Raytheon Co.
- TRW Inc.
- Marinette Marine Corp.
- Other

Market shares are shown based on total contracted purchases.

IBM Corp.	5.72%
Bollinger Shipyards Inc.	5.32
Lockheed Martin Corp.	5.22
Computer Sciences Corp.	3.06
Raytheon Co.	2.93
TRW Inc.	2.41

Marinette Marine Corp.	2.09%
Other	73.25

Source: *Government Executive Procurement Preview*, Annual 2000, p. 101.

★ 2000 ★

Department of Agriculture (SIC 9641)

Top Contractors to the Agriculture Department

Market shares are shown based on total contracted purchases.

Cargill Inc.	11.33%
Conagra Inc.	8.21
IBM Corp.	5.14
Cal Western Packaging Corp.	3.77
Archer-Daniels-Midland Co.	2.98
United Harvest	2.07
Other	66.50

Source: *Government Executive Procurement Preview*, Annual 2000, p. 96.

SIC 97 - National Security and International Affairs

★ 2001 ★

Defense (SIC 9711)

Top Contractors to the Air Force

Market shares are shown based on total contracted purchases.

Lockheed Martin Corp.	21.91%
Boeing Co.	16.89
Raytheon Co.	5.67
United Technologies Corp.	4.12
Northrop Grumman Corp.	3.80
TRW Inc.	2.42
General Electric Co.	1.40
General Dynamics Corp.	1.20
Honeywell Inc.	1.05
Aerospace Corp.	1.03
Other	40.51

Source: *Government Executive Procurement Preview*, Annual 2000, p. 96.

★ 2002 ★

Defense (SIC 9711)

Where Military/Civilian Personnel Are Stationed

	No.	Share
Germany	69,000	27.27%
Japan	40,000	15.81
South Korea	37,000	14.62
Pacific afloat (SE Asia)	23,000	9.09
Latin America/Caribbean	8,000	3.16
Other	76,000	30.04

Source: *Financial Times*, May 12, 2001, p. 6, from The Military Balance and U.S. Department of Defense.

SOURCE INDEX

This index is divided into *primary sources* and *original sources*. Primary sources are the publications where the market shares were found. Original sources are sources cited in the primary sources. Numbers following the sources are entry numbers, arranged sequentially; the first number refers to the first appearance of the source in *Market Share Reporter*. All told, 1050 organizations are listed.

Primary Sources

20/20 Magazine, 1205, 1207, 1637

"2000 Canadian Consumer Research Result." Retrieved May 5, 2001 from the World Wide Web: http://www.llanda.com, 853, 1630

"2000 Catalog Age 100." Retrieved May 5, 2001 from the World Wide Web: http://www.catalogagemag.com, 1631

"2000 Yearend Statistics." Retrieved June 1, 2001 from the World Wide Web: http://www.riaa.com, 1026

"A Closer Look." Retrieved May 5, 2001 from the World Wide Web: http://www.bestwire.com, 1803

"A Little Company Called Starbucks." Retrieved May 5, 2001 from the World Wide Web: http://www.stuart.iit.edu/StuartBusiness, 909

"A Look Inside the Latin American Endoscopy Market." Retrieved May 5, 2001 from the World Wide Web: http://www.devicelink.com, 1166

ABA Banking Journal, 890

The Accountant, 1969

"Active Apparel Group Inc. to Acquire Everlast." Retrieved May 5, 2001 from the World Wide Web: http://www.fashionall.com, 1249

Adhesive Technology, 802

Advertising Age, 196, 199, 221, 227, 239, 252, 421, 545, 548, 566, 580, 710, 969, 1095, 1285, 1822-1824, 1849

Aftermarket Business, 798, 1106, 1127, 1133-1135, 1520, 1522-1529, 1531-1532, 1904

Ag Lender, 1719-1720

Agri Marketing, 793

Air Cargo World, 1317, 1323-1324

Air Transport World, 1320, 1322

Airline Business, 1309

Akron Beacon Journal, 995, 1593, 1626

"Alcoholic Drinks Market in Canada." Retrieved May 5, 2001 from the World Wide Web: http://www.foodandbeverageamerica.com, 358

"Allergic Rhinitis and Asthma." Retrieved May 5, 2001 from the World Wide Web: http://www.npd.com, 651

"Alternative Delivery Systems for Insulin." Retrieved May 5, 2001 from the World Wide Web: http://www.ahcpub.com, 1186

A.M. Best Newswire, 1761-1762, 1765

American Banker, 1690, 1727-1728, 1732, 1818

American Ceramic Society Bulletin, 88-89

American City & County, 1997

American Drycleaner, 706

American Ink Maker, 806, 1837

American Laboratory, 1167-1174

The American Lawyer, 1968

American Machinist, 903

American Metal Market, 863, 867-868, 872

American Printer, 554

Amusement Business, 1926-1928, 1935

Apparel Industry, 1540, 1545

Appliance, 939, 941, 943, 945, 949, 959, 970-972, 975, 980-983, 986-989, 993-994, 1008-1011, 1019

Appliance Manufacturer, 893-897, 936, 942, 944, 946-948, 950-951, 955-956, 958, 960-963, 966-967, 973-974, 976-977, 984-985, 990-992, 997-999, 1004

Arizona Republic, 1328

Arkansas Business, 1490, 1498, 1815

Arkansas Democrat-Gazette, 1752

Assembly, 874, 1079

Asset Sales Report, 1743

ATI, 613

Atlanta Business Chronicle, 516, 1675, 1683

Atlanta Journal-Constitution, 382, 396, 398, 502, 1920

Audio Week, 1002

Automatic Merchandiser, 1442, 1586, 1607, 1632-1634

Automotive Industries, 1128, 1132

Automotive Manufacturing & Production, 1091

Automotive Marketing, 799, 1521

Automotive News, 818

Automotive News Market Data Book, 1080-1084, 1103, 1107, 1112, 1118-1119

Autoparts Report, 1534

Original Sources

1999 Tradeshow Week Data Book, 1900
AAFRC Trust for Philanthropy, 1959-1960
A.C. Nielsen, 11, 43, 148, 151, 158, 167, 171, 173, 180, 184, 187, 214, 218, 222, 253, 259, 282, 340, 367, 377, 452, 458-459, 466, 533, 539, 549-550, 644, 687-688, 707, 711-712, 730, 734, 739, 741, 773, 969, 978, 1244, 1512-1513, 1622, 1640, 1651, 1914-1915
A.C. Nielsen Convenience Track Major Markets, 1517
A.C. Nielsen-EDI, 1917
A.C. Nielsen MarketTrack, 150, 193, 242, 360, 426, 1488
A.C. Nielsen ScanTrack, 149, 159, 186, 356, 534, 552, 629, 633, 725, 800, 979, 1181, 1282, 1289
Ad Scope, 1827
Adams Handbook, 381
Adams Harkness & Hill, 1067
Adams Media Research, 1923
Adams White Institute, 377
AdRevelance, 1359
Agency for Health Care Administration, 1942
Agricultural Statistics Board, 36
Air Conditioning and Refrigeration Institute, 942
Air Transport Association, 1315
Air Transport Association 2000 Annual Report, 1308
Airborne Express, 1324
Airports Council International, 1323-1324
Albemarle, 646
Allied Business Intelligence, 953
A.M. Best & Co., 1761, 1764-1766, 1770, 1777, 1779-1781, 1783-1784, 1792-1794, 1796-1803
American Association of Motor Vehicle Administrators, 1123-1124
American Board of Plastic Surgery, 1949
American Forest & Paper Association, 525
American Heart Association, 654
American Iron and Steel Institute, 865, 867
American Kennel Club, 64
American Metro/Study Corp., 97, 104, 119
American Seniors Housing Association, 1941
AMF Bowling, 1929
AMR Research Inc., 1861, 1866, 1875
Amusement Business Boxscore, 1926-1928
Arbitron, 34, 1395
Associated Press, 1149, 1986
Association for Manufacturing Technology, 903
Association of American Publishers, 569
Association of American Railroads, 1293-1294
Association of Brewers, 365
Association of Hispanic Advertising Agencies, 1841
Association of Home Appliance Manufacturers, 957
Association with Harvard and Yale Universities, 33

Atofina Chemicals, 603
Audit Bureau of Circulations, 560, 562, 566-567
Autodata Corp., 1093, 1117
Automotive Aftermarket Industries Association, 799
Automotive News, 1095
Automotive News Data Center, 1103, 1112, 1118
Aviation Daily, 1306, 1315
Avon Products, 716, 724, 758
Ball State University Marketing Dept., 14
Banc of America Securities L.L.C., 1193, 1862
Bear, Stearns & Co., 4
The Beer Industry in 2000, 369
Beer Marketers Insights, 372
Beverage Digest, 399, 414
Beverage Digest/Maxwell, 398, 402
Beverage Marketing Corp., 207, 364, 368, 370, 375, 384, 386, 391, 393, 401, 403, 407, 908, 1513-1514, 1607
BIA Financial Network, 1394, 1402
BIA Research, 1393
Bishop Inc., 1068
Bloomberg Financial Markets, 1164-1165
Board-Trac, 1262
Boardwatch, 1378
Bohn & Associates Media, 1397
Bolsa Mexicana de Valores, 1734
Book Industry Study Group, 568
Boston Consulting Group, 1367
Bowling Proprietor Association of America, 1929
BPA International, 567
Bumper Project Group of American Iron and Steel Institute, 1130
Burger King, 1594
Business Communications Co., 2, 27-28, 854, 883-884, 954, 1072, 1074-1075, 1121, 1159, 1161-1162, 1197
Business Travel News, 1332
Cahners Economics, 92, 126
Cahners Instat, 1013, 1047
Canacord Capital Corp., 1224
Canadian Appliance Manufacturers Association, 955
Canadian Energy Research Institute, 79
Canadian Federation of Independent Business, 1674
Canadian Government, 358
Canadian Insurance, 1767, 1788
Canadian Snowboard and Ski Council, 1267
Canwest, 561
CAP Ventures, 553
Carbon Sequestrian Research and Development, 1422
Cardweb.com, 1712
The Carmel Group, 1411, 1420
Carpet Cushion Council, 462
Cattle-Fax, 172
Cellular Telecommunications & Internet Association, 1345
Center for Exhibition Industry Research, 1900

Source Index: Original

PLACE NAMES INDEX

This index shows countries, political entities, states and provinces, regions within countries, parks, airports, and cities. The numbers that follow listings are entry numbers; they are arrangedsequentially so that the first mention of a place is listed first. The index shows references to more than 260 places.

PRODUCTS, SERVICES, NAMES, AND ISSUES INDEX

This index shows, in alphabetical order, references to products, services, personal names, and issues covered in *Market Share Reporter*, 12th Edition. More than 2,350 terms are included. Terms include subjects not readily categorized as products and services, including such subjects as *crime* and *welfare*. The numbers that follow each term refer to entry numbers and are arranged sequentially so that the first mention is listed first.

Products, Services, Names, and Issues Index

Products, Services, Names, and Issues Index

Jelly, 356
Jobbers, 1904
Jock itch products, 1181
Joint compound, 861
Judds, 1926
Juices, 156, 227-232, 234-235, 361
Juices, apple, 235
Juices, blended fruit, 235
Juices, bottled, 361
Juices, bottled and shelf-stable, 10
Juices, chilled, 233
Juices, cranberry, 230
Juices, fruit, 231
Juices, grapefruit, 235
Juices, nutrient-enhanced, 401
Juices, orange, 215, 235
Juices, tomato, 360
Juices, vegetables, excl. tomato juices, 360
Juvenile products, 12
Ketchup, 253
Keyboards, 927
Khakis, 479
Kidney beans, 237
Kiss, 1927
Kitchen dusters, 1271
Kitchen towels, 493
Kitchenware, 17-18
Kitty litter, 29, 1285
Kiwi, 43
Knives, 17
Knives, electric, 985
Knives, paring, 17
Labels, 589, 801
Labels, pressure-sensitive, 589
Laboratory instruments, 1159-1174
Labrador retrievers, 64-65
Lacerations, 1949
Laminates, 1277
Lamp stores, 1557
Lamps, portable, 494
LAN access, 1346
Landscaping, 67-68, 1438
Landscaping and garden supplies, 1900
Lasers, 1065-1066, 1071
Latex, 1194
Lathes, 904
Laundry aids, 691, 706
Laundry detergents, 10, 692-693, 695-696, 1639
Laundry equipment, 965-968
Lawn & garden equipment, 893-897
Lawn & garden industry, 1291, 1451, 1460
Lawn & garden stores, 1450
Lawn and leaf bags, 540

Lawn mowers, 894-895
Laxatives, 640, 642
Layer 3 switches, 1051
Lead, 900
Leaf blowers, 893
Learning services, 1372
Leather, 485, 853
Leather goods stores, 1630
Lecithin, 615
Legal pads, 550
Legal services, 1968
Lemonade, 235
Lens cleaning solutions, 728
Lenses, 1207, 1637
Lettuce, 42
Liability insurance, 1782
Libraries, 1955
Lice remedies, 624
Licensing, 1258, 1542
Licorice, 327-329
Light bulbs, 1000-1001
Light rail, 131
Light trucks, 817, 819
Light vehicles, 1093, 1097
Lighters, 1286
Lighting, 143, 1525
Lighting fixtures, 494, 1459
Lime/rust removers, 705
Limestone, 86, 900
Limo services, 1295-1296
Linerboard, 526, 528
Lingerie, 487-488, 1541
Lip balm, 1658
Lip makeup, 722
Lip medications, 641
Liposomes, 648
Lipstick, 724
Liquid membranes, 1159
Liquor, 359, 361, 378-385, 1470
Lithium, 1074-1075
Livestock, 511
Load balancing industry (for networks), 1056
Loan arrangers, 1719-1721, 1728-1729, 1731
Loans, 1742
Lobsters, 69-70
Local multipoint distribution service (LMDS), 1058
Locks, 1452
Lodging, 1366
Logic devices, 907
Lollipops, 335
Long-distance services, 15, 1349-1351, 1353
Long-term care, 1616
Lotions, 713

Products, Services, Names, and Issues Index

COMPANY INDEX

The more than 3,780 companies and institutions in this book are indexed here in alphabetical order. Numbers following the terms are entry numbers. They are arranged sequentially; the first entry number refers to the first mention of the company in *Market Share Reporter*. Although most organizations appear only once, some entities are referred to under abbreviations in the sources and these have not always been expanded.

A.I. Scientific, 1173
AIG, 1782, 1795
AIG Insurance Management Services Inc., 1758
AIM Funds Management, 1747
Air Canada, 1313
Air Conditioning Co., 134
Air Tran, 1311
Air Wisconsin, 1321
Airborne Express, 1302-1303
Aircelan Systems Inc., 1170
Aiwa, 1006
Ajay Glass & Mirror Co. Inc., 147
AJM Packaging, 538
AK Steel Corp., 863
Akzo Nobel, 788, 790
Alamo, 1902-1903
Alan Taylor, 1985
Alaska Airlines, 1308-1310
Albchem, 603
Alberta Energy, 79
Alberto Culver, 745-746
Albertson's, 1460, 1465, 1484, 1489, 1492, 1495, 1497,
   1502, 1507, 1831
Alcan Aluminum Ltd., 863
Alcatel Alsthom, 1034, 1040, 1043, 1045, 1054
Alcoa Inc., 863
Alcon, 1071
Alcon/Nestle, 729
Alcon/Summit/Autonomous, 1065
Alcone Marketing Group, 1849
Alexandria Moulding, 518
Aliant, 1350
Alkermes Inc., 1440
All Sport, 414
Allaire, 1882
Allegiant, 1696
Allen Canning Co., 225
Allergan, 729
Allfirst, 1676
allhealth.com, 1385
Alliance, 1934
Alliance Atlantis Communications, 1914
Allianz of America, 1778, 1783, 1787, 1791
Allied (ACI), 1064
Allied Domecq, 380, 1603
Allied Domecq Retailing, 1606
Allied Signal, 1138-1139
Allied Signal Burdick & Jackson, 1171
Allied Telesyn, 1052
Allied Waste Industries Inc., 1432
Allstate, 1763, 1766
Allstate Indemnity, 1763
Allstate Insurance Group, 1760, 1762, 1765, 1777-1778,

1780, 1785
Alltel Cellular, 1829
Alltel Corp., 1345
Alltel Publishing, 580
Alpa Lumber, 1454
Alpha Dental Programs Inc., 1771
Altavista Network, 1380
Alteon WebSystems, 1056
Alton Belle, 1937
Altra Energy Techniques, 1365
Alvin W. Vogtle (Southern Nuclear Operating), 1426
Alza Corp., 1440
AM Cosmetics, 717
Amana, 957, 964
Amax Gold Inc., 71
Amazon.com, 1359, 1363, 1380, 1573
AMC, 1068
AMC Entertainment, 1916, 1920
AMD, 1069
AMECO, 1905
Amer Continental Ins, 1796
Amer Family Ins Group, 1785
Amer Intern Group, 1778, 1787, 1791, 1804
America First Credit Union, 1710
America Online, 1389
America Online Canada, 1392
America Online Network, 1380
America Online Time Warner, 1830, 1834
America West, 1306, 1308, 1310, 1316
American Airlines, 950-951, 1306, 1308-1312, 1317, 1320,
   1322, 1708
American Airlines/TWA, 1307
American Battle Monuments Comm., 1358
American Business Forms, 1434
American Camper, 1256
American Cancer Society, 1957
American Color, 585
American Community Mutual Insurance Co., 1769
American Eagle Outfitters, 1540, 1543
American Express, 1332, 1712, 1714
American Family Mutual, 1760, 1766
American Gas Association, 1962
American Greetings, 538, 592
American Heritage Homes, 112
American Home Products, 675
American Homestar Corp., 510
American International Airways, 1318
American Investment Bank, 1703
American Kennel Club, 64
American Licorice Co., 328
American Media Operations, 564
American Public Power Association, 1962
American Recreation, 1256

Company Index

Company Index

Company Index

Company Index

Company Index

Company Index

Wilsonart, 1277
Windermere Real Estate, 1816
Windmere (Black & Decker), 971, 973-974, 985-986, 992
Windows on the World, 1599
Windsor, 1229
The Wine Group, 374
Winn-Dixie, 1484, 1489, 1491, 1497, 1510, 1831
WINS-AM, 1402
Winton, 1682
Wipfil Ulrich Bertelson, 1972
Wise, 436
Wise Business Forms, 591
Wizard Entertainment, 563
WKTY-FM, 1402
WLTW-FM, 1402
WMS, 1933-1934
W.O. Grubb Steel Erection Inc., 146
Wolters Kluwer, 1896
Wolverine World Wide, 849
Wood Dining Services, 1582
Wood-Mode Inc., 507
Woodbridge Labs, 784
Woodfield Mall (IL), 1809
Woodside Homes, 94
World Finer Foods, 442
World Savings Bank, 1730
World Yacht, 1305
WorldCom, 1351-1352, 1377, 1832
Worldcorp. Inc., 1318
Worldtravel BTI, 1332
Worthington Foods, 270, 446
Wragg & Casas, 1978
WRC Media, 575, 579
WSJ.com, 1387
W.W. Norton, 557
WXRK-FM, 1402
X.com, 1384
Xerox, 929-932, 1030, 1215-1217
Y&R Advertising, 1823
Yahoo, 1380
Yahooligans.com, 1383
Yale, 1954
Yamaha, 1010, 1145-1146
Yankee Captive Management Inc., 1758
Yellow, 1300
Yellow Book USA, 580
Yellow Freight System, 1299
YMCA of the USA, 1957
Yokohama, 818
York, 939, 941, 947-948
York Group, 1276
Zaring Homes, 109
Z.B. Industries, 420

Zellers, 1469, 1474
Zimmer, 1199
The Zimmerman Agency, 1978
Zippo, 1286
Zixit, 1828
Zoba, 1024
Zuber Landscape, 68
Zurich US Group, 1778, 1787, 1791
Zwicker & Associates, 1846

BRANDS INDEX

This index shows more than 1,940 brands—including names of periodicals, television programs, popular movies, and other "brand-equivalent" names. Each brand name is followed by one or more numerals; these are entry numbers; they are arranged sequentially, with the first mention of the brand shown first.

Brands Index

Brands Index

Brands Index

Brands Index

Brands Index

Brands Index

APPENDIX I

SIC COVERAGE

This appendix lists the Standard Industrial Classification codes (SICs) included in *Market Share Reporter*. Page numbers are shown following each SIC category; the page shown indicates the first occurrence of an SIC. *NEC* stands for not elsewhere classified.

Agricultural Production - Crops

0115 Corn, p. 9
0116 Soybeans, p. 9
0131 Cotton, p. 9
0160 Vegetables and melons, p. 10
0161 Vegetables and melons, p. 10
0170 Fruits and tree nuts, p. 10
0171 Berry crops, p. 10
0172 Grapes, p. 11
0173 Tree nuts, p. 11
0174 Citrus fruits, p. 12
0175 Deciduous tree fruits, p. 12
0181 Ornamental nursery products, p. 13
0182 Food crops grown under cover, p. 13

Agricultural Production - Livestock

0211 Beef cattle feedlots, p. 14
0214 Sheep and goats, p. 14
0252 Chicken eggs, p. 14
0253 Turkeys and turkey eggs, p. 15
0272 Horses and other equines, p. 15
0279 Animal specialties, nec, p. 15

Agricultural Services

0781 Landscape counseling and planning, p. 17

Fishing, Hunting, and Trapping

0910 Commercial fishing, p. 18

Metal Mining

1041 Gold ores, p. 19
1044 Silver ores, p. 19
1094 Uranium-radium-vanadium ores, p. 19

Coal Mining

1220 Bituminous coal and lignite mining, p. 20

Oil and Gas Extraction

1311 Crude petroleum and natural gas, p. 21
1321 Natural gas liquids, p. 21
1381 Drilling oil and gas wells, p. 22
1382 Oil and gas exploration services, p. 22
1389 Oil and gas field services, nec, p. 22

Nonmetallic Minerals, Except Fuels

1411 Dimension stone, p. 23
1420 Crushed and broken stone, p. 23
1455 Kaolin and ball clay, p. 23
1474 Potash, soda, and borate minerals, p. 24

General Building Contractors

1500 General building contractors, p. 25
1521 Single-family housing construction, p. 25
1531 Operative builders, p. 32
1540 Nonresidential building construction, p. 32
1542 Nonresidential construction, nec, p. 32

Heavy Construction, Except Building

1600 Heavy construction, ex. building, p. 33
1622 Bridge, tunnel, & elevated highway, p. 33
1623 Water, sewer, and utility lines, p. 34

Special Trade Contractors

1711 Plumbing, heating, air-conditioning, p. 35
1721 Painting and paper hanging, p. 35
1731 Electrical work, p. 36
1741 Masonry and other stonework, p. 36
1751 Carpentry work, p. 37
1761 Roofing, siding, and sheet metal work, p. 37

Appendix: SIC Nomenclature

Appendix: SIC Nomenclature

SIC TO NAICS CONVERSION GUIDE

AGRICULTURE, FORESTRY, & FISHING

0111 Wheat
NAICS 11114   Wheat Farming
0112 Rice
NAICS 11116   Rice Farming
0115 Corn
NAICS 11115   Corn Farming
0116 Soybeans
NAICS 11111   Soybean Farming
0119 Cash Grains, nec
NAICS 11113   Dry Pea & Bean Farming
NAICS 11112   Oilseed Farming
NAICS 11115   Corn Farming
NAICS 111191 Oilseed & Grain Combination Farming
NAICS 111199 All Other Grain Farming
0131 Cotton
NAICS 11192   Cotton Farming
0132 Tobacco
NAICS 11191   Tobacco Farming
0133 Sugarcane & Sugar Beets
NAICS 111991 Sugar Beet Farming
NAICS 11193   Sugarcane Farming
0134 Irish Potatoes
NAICS 111211 Potato Farming
0139 Field Crops, Except Cash Grains, nec
NAICS 11194   Hay Farming
NAICS 111992 Peanut Farming
NAICS 111219 Other Vegetable & Melon Farming
NAICS 111998 All Other Miscellaneous Crop Farming
0161 Vegetables & Melons
NAICS 111219 Other Vegetable & Melon Farming
0171 Berry Crops
NAICS 111333 Strawberry Farming
NAICS 111334 Berry Farming
0172 Grapes
NAICS 111332 Grape Vineyards
0173 Tree Nuts
NAICS 111335 Tree Nut Farming
0174 Citrus Fruits
NAICS 11131   Orange Groves
NAICS 11132   Citrus Groves
0175 Deciduous Tree Fruits
NAICS 111331 Apple Orchards
NAICS 111339 Other Noncitrus Fruit Farming
0179 Fruits & Tree Nuts, nec
NAICS 111336 Fruit & Tree Nut Combination Farming
NAICS 111339 Other Noncitrus Fruit Farming
0181 Ornamental Floriculture & Nursery Products
NAICS 111422 Floriculture Production
NAICS 111421 Nursery & Tree Production
0182 Food Crops Grown under Cover
NAICS 111411 Mushroom Production
NAICS 111419 Other Food Crops Grown under Cover
0191 General Farms, Primarily Crop
NAICS 111998 All Other Miscellaneous Crop Farming
0211 Beef Cattle Feedlots
NAICS 112112 Cattle Feedlots
0212 Beef Cattle, Except Feedlots
NAICS 112111 Beef Cattle Ranching & Farming

0213 Hogs
NAICS 11221   Hog & Pig Farming
0214 Sheep & Goats
NAICS 11241   Sheep Farming
NAICS 11242   Goat Farming
0219 General Livestock, Except Dairy & Poultry
NAICS 11299   All Other Animal Production
0241 Dairy Farms
NAICS 112111 Beef Cattle Ranching & Farming
NAICS 11212   Dairy Cattle & Milk Production
0251 Broiler, Fryers, & Roaster Chickens
NAICS 11232   Broilers & Other Meat-type Chicken
                         Production
0252 Chicken Eggs
NAICS 11231   Chicken Egg Production
0253 Turkey & Turkey Eggs
NAICS 11233   Turkey Production
0254 Poultry Hatcheries
NAICS 11234   Poultry Hatcheries
0259 Poultry & Eggs, nec
NAICS 11239   Other Poultry Production
0271 Fur-bearing Animals & Rabbits
NAICS 11293   Fur-bearing Animal & Rabbit Production
0272 Horses & Other Equines
NAICS 11292   Horse & Other Equine Production
0273 Animal Aquaculture
NAICS 112511 Finfish Farming & Fish Hatcheries
NAICS 112512 Shellfish Farming
NAICS 112519 Other Animal Aquaculture
0279 Animal Specialities, nec
NAICS 11291   Apiculture
NAICS 11299   All Other Animal Production
0291 General Farms, Primarily Livestock & Animal Specialties
NAICS 11299   All Other Animal Production
0711 Soil Preparation Services
NAICS 115112 Soil Preparation, Planting & Cultivating
0721 Crop Planting, Cultivating & Protecting
NAICS 48122   Nonscheduled Speciality Air Transportation
NAICS 115112 Soil Preparation, Planting & Cultivating
0722 Crop Harvesting, Primarily by Machine
NAICS 115113 Crop Harvesting, Primarily by Machine
0723 Crop Preparation Services for Market, Except Cotton Ginning
NAICS 115114 Postharvest Crop Activities
0724 Cotton Ginning
NAICS 115111 Cotton Ginning
0741 Veterinary Service for Livestock
NAICS 54194   Veterinary Services
0742 Veterinary Services for Animal Specialties
NAICS 54194   Veterinary Services
0751 Livestock Services, Except Veterinary
NAICS 311611 Animal Slaughtering
NAICS 11521   Support Activities for Animal Production
0752 Animal Specialty Services, Except Veterinary
NAICS 11521   Support Activities for Animal Production
NAICS 81291   Pet Care Services
0761 Farm Labor Contractors & Crew Leaders
NAICS 115115 Farm Labor Contractors & Crew Leaders
0762 Farm Management Services
NAICS 115116 Farm Management Services
0781 Landscape Counseling & Planning
NAICS 54169   Other Scientific & Technical Consulting
                         Services
NAICS 54132   Landscape Architectural Services

0782 Lawn & Garden Services
NAICS 56173   Landscaping Services
0783 Ornamental Shrub & Tree Services
NAICS 56173   Landscaping Services
0811 Timber Tracts
NAICS 111421 Nursery & Tree Production
NAICS 11311   Timber Tract Operations
0831 Forest Nurseries & Gathering of Forest Products
NAICS 111998 All Other Miscellaneous Crop
NAICS 11321   Forest Nurseries & Gathering of Forest
         Products
0851 Forestry Services
NAICS 11531   Support Activities for Forestry
0912 Finfish
NAICS 114111 Finfish Fishing
0913 Shellfish
NAICS 114112 Shellfish Fishing
0919 Miscellaneous Marine Products
NAICS 114119 Other Marine Fishing
NAICS 111998 All Other Miscellaneous Crop Farming
0921 Fish Hatcheries & Preserves
NAICS 112511 Finfish Farming & Fish Hatcheries
NAICS 112512 Shellfish Farming
0971 Hunting, Trapping, & Game Propagation
NAICS 11421   Hunting & Trapping

MINING INDUSTRIES

1011 Iron Ores
NAICS 21221   Iron Ore Mining
1021 Copper Ores
NAICS 212234 Copper Ore & Nickel Ore Mining
1031 Lead & Zinc Ores
NAICS 212231 Lead Ore & Zinc Ore Mining
1041 Gold Ores
NAICS 212221 Gold Ore Mining
1044 Silver Ores
NAICS 212222 Silver Ore Mining
1061 Ferroalloy Ores, Except Vanadium
NAICS 212234 Copper Ore & Nickel Ore Mining
NAICS 212299 Other Metal Ore Mining
1081 Metal Mining Services
NAICS 213115 Support Activities for Metal Mining
NAICS 54136   Geophysical Surveying & Mapping Services
1094 Uranium-radium-vanadium Ores
NAICS 212291 Uranium-radium-vanadium Ore Mining
1099 Miscellaneous Metal Ores, nec
NAICS 212299 Other Metal Ore Mining
1221 Bituminous Coal & Lignite Surface Mining
NAICS 212111 Bituminous Coal & Lignite Surface Mining
1222 Bituminous Coal Underground Mining
NAICS 212112 Bituminous Coal Underground Mining
1231 Anthracite Mining
NAICS 212113 Anthracite Mining
1241 Coal Mining Services
NAICS 213114 Support Activities for Coal Mining
1311 Crude Petroleum & Natural Gas
NAICS 211111 Crude Petroleum & Natural Gas Extraction
1321 Natural Gas Liquids
NAICS 211112 Natural Gas Liquid Extraction
1381 Drilling Oil & Gas Wells
NAICS 213111 Drilling Oil & Gas Wells

1382 Oil & Gas Field Exploration Services
NAICS 48122   Nonscheduled Speciality Air Transportation
NAICS 54136   Geophysical Surveying & Mapping Services
NAICS 213112 Support Activities for Oil & Gas Field
         Operations
1389 Oil & Gas Field Services, nec
NAICS 213113 Other Oil & Gas Field Support Activities
1411 Dimension Stone
NAICS 212311 Dimension Stone Mining & Quarry
1422 Crushed & Broken Limestone
NAICS 212312 Crushed & Broken Limestone Mining &
         Quarrying
1423 Crushed & Broken Granite
NAICS 212313 Crushed & Broken Granite Mining &
         Quarrying
1429 Crushed & Broken Stone, nec
NAICS 212319 Other Crushed & Broken Stone Mining &
         Quarrying
1442 Construction Sand & Gravel
NAICS 212321 Construction Sand & Gravel Mining
1446 Industrial Sand
NAICS 212322 Industrial Sand Mining
1455 Kaolin & Ball Clay
NAICS 212324 Kaolin & Ball Clay Mining
1459 Clay, Ceramic, & Refractory Minerals, nec
NAICS 212325 Clay & Ceramic & Refractory Minerals Mining
1474 Potash, Soda, & Borate Minerals
NAICS 212391 Potash, Soda, & Borate Mineral Mining
1475 Phosphate Rock
NAICS 212392 Phosphate Rock Mining
1479 Chemical & Fertilizer Mineral Mining, nec
NAICS 212393 Other Chemical & Fertilizer Mineral Mining
1481 Nonmetallic Minerals Services Except Fuels
NAICS 213116 Support Activities for Non-metallic Minerals
NAICS 54136   Geophysical Surveying & Mapping Services
1499 Miscellaneous Nonmetallic Minerals, Except Fuels
NAICS 212319 Other Crushed & Broken Stone Mining or
         Quarrying
NAICS 212399 All Other Non-metallic Mineral Mining

CONSTRUCTION INDUSTRIES

1521 General Contractors-single-family Houses
NAICS 23321   Single Family Housing Construction
**1522 General Contractors-residential Buildings, Other than
    Single-family**
NAICS 23332   Commercial & Institutional Building
         Construction
NAICS 23322   Multifamily Housing Construction
1531 Operative Builders
NAICS 23321   Single Family Housing Construction
NAICS 23322   Multifamily Housing Construction
NAICS 23331   Manufacturing & Industrial Building
         Construction
NAICS 23332   Commercial & Institutional Building
         Construction
1541 General Contractors-industrial Buildings & Warehouses
NAICS 23332   Commercial & Institutional Building
         Construction
NAICS 23331   Manufacturing & Industrial Building
         Construction

1542 General Contractors-nonresidential Buildings, Other than Industrial Buildings & Warehouses
NAICS 23332 Commercial & Institutional Building Construction
1611 Highway & Street Construction, Except Elevated Highways
NAICS 23411 Highway & Street Construction
1622 Bridge, Tunnel, & Elevated Highway Construction
NAICS 23412 Bridge & Tunnel Construction
1623 Water, Sewer, Pipeline, & Communications & Power Line Construction
NAICS 23491 Water, Sewer & Pipeline Construction
NAICS 23492 Power & Communication Transmission Line Construction
1629 Heavy Construction, nec
NAICS 23493 Industrial Nonbuilding Structure Construction
NAICS 23499 All Other Heavy Construction
1711 Plumbing, Heating, & Air-conditioning
NAICS 23511 Plumbing, Heating & Air-conditioning Contractors
1721 Painting & Paper Hanging
NAICS 23521 Painting & Wall Covering Contractors
1731 Electrical Work
NAICS 561621 Security Systems Services
NAICS 23531 Electrical Contractors
1741 Masonry, Stone Setting & Other Stone Work
NAICS 23541 Masonry & Stone Contractors
1742 Plastering, Drywall, Acoustical & Insulation Work
NAICS 23542 Drywall, Plastering, Acoustical & Insulation Contractors
1743 Terrazzo, Tile, Marble, & Mosaic Work
NAICS 23542 Drywall, Plastering, Acoustical & Insulation Contractors
NAICS 23543 Tile, Marble, Terrazzo & Mosaic Contractors
1751 Carpentry Work
NAICS 23551 Carpentry Contractors
1752 Floor Laying & Other Floor Work, nec
NAICS 23552 Floor Laying & Other Floor Contractors
1761 Roofing, Siding, & Sheet Metal Work
NAICS 23561 Roofing, Siding, & Sheet Metal Contractors
1771 Concrete Work
NAICS 23542 Drywall, Plastering, Acoustical & Insulation Contractors
NAICS 23571 Concrete Contractors
1781 Water Well Drilling
NAICS 23581 Water Well Drilling Contractors
1791 Structural Steel Erection
NAICS 23591 Structural Steel Erection Contractors
1793 Glass & Glazing Work
NAICS 23592 Glass & Glazing Contractors
1794 Excavation Work
NAICS 23593 Excavation Contractors
1795 Wrecking & Demolition Work
NAICS 23594 Wrecking & Demolition Contractors
1796 Installation or Erection of Building Equipment, nec
NAICS 23595 Building Equipment & Other Machinery Installation Contractors
1799 Special Trade Contractors, nec
NAICS 23521 Painting & Wall Covering Contractors
NAICS 23592 Glass & Glazing Contractors
NAICS 56291 Remediation Services
NAICS 23599 All Other Special Trade Contractors

FOOD & KINDRED PRODUCTS

2011 Meat Packing Plants
NAICS 311611 Animal Slaughtering
2013 Sausages & Other Prepared Meats
NAICS 311612 Meat Processed from Carcasses
2015 Poultry Slaughtering & Processing
NAICS 311615 Poultry Processing
NAICS 311999 All Other Miscellaneous Food Manufacturing
2021 Creamery Butter
NAICS 311512 Creamery Butter Manufacturing
2022 Natural, Processed, & Imitation Cheese
NAICS 311513 Cheese Manufacturing
2023 Dry, Condensed, & Evaporated Dairy Products
NAICS 311514 Dry, Condensed, & Evaporated Milk Manufacturing
2024 Ice Cream & Frozen Desserts
NAICS 31152 Ice Cream & Frozen Dessert Manufacturing
2026 Fluid Milk
NAICS 311511 Fluid Milk Manufacturing
2032 Canned Specialties
NAICS 311422 Specialty Canning
NAICS 311999 All Other Miscellaneous Food Manufacturing
2033 Canned Fruits, Vegetables, Preserves, Jams, & Jellies
NAICS 311421 Fruit & Vegetable Canning
2034 Dried & Dehydrated Fruits, Vegetables, & Soup Mixes
NAICS 311423 Dried & Dehydrated Food Manufacturing
NAICS 311211 Flour Milling
2035 Pickled Fruits & Vegetables, Vegetables Sauces & Seasonings, & Salad Dressings
NAICS 311421 Fruit & Vegetable Canning
NAICS 311941 Mayonnaise, Dressing, & Other Prepared Sauce Manufacturing
2037 Frozen Fruits, Fruit Juices, & Vegetables
NAICS 311411 Frozen Fruit, Juice, & Vegetable Processing
2038 Frozen Specialties, nec
NAICS 311412 Frozen Specialty Food Manufacturing
2041 Flour & Other Grain Mill Products
NAICS 311211 Flour Milling
2043 Cereal Breakfast Foods
NAICS 31192 Coffee & Tea Manufacturing
NAICS 31123 Breakfast Cereal Manufacturing
2044 Rice Milling
NAICS 311212 Rice Milling
2045 Prepared Flour Mixes & Doughs
NAICS 311822 Flour Mixes & Dough Manufacturing from Purchased Flour
2046 Wet Corn Milling
NAICS 311221 Wet Corn Milling
2047 Dog & Cat Food
NAICS 311111 Dog & Cat Food Manufacturing
2048 Prepared Feed & Feed Ingredients for Animals & Fowls, Except Dogs & Cats
NAICS 311611 Animal Slaughtering
NAICS 311119 Other Animal Food Manufacturing
2051 Bread & Other Bakery Products, Except Cookies & Crackers
NAICS 311812 Commercial Bakeries
2052 Cookies & Crackers
NAICS 311821 Cookie & Cracker Manufacturing
NAICS 311919 Other Snack Food Manufacturing
NAICS 311812 Commercial Bakeries

2053 Frozen Bakery Products, Except Bread
NAICS 311813 Frozen Bakery Product Manufacturing
2061 Cane Sugar, Except Refining
NAICS 311311 Sugarcane Mills
2062 Cane Sugar Refining
NAICS 311312 Cane Sugar Refining
2063 Beet Sugar
NAICS 311313 Beet Sugar Manufacturing
2064 Candy & Other Confectionery Products
NAICS 31133 Confectionery Manufacturing from Purchased
Chocolate
NAICS 31134 Non-chocolate Confectionery Manufacturing
2066 Chocolate & Cocoa Products
NAICS 31132 Chocolate & Confectionery Manufacturing from
Cacao Beans
2067 Chewing Gum
NAICS 31134 Non-chocolate Confectionery Manufacturing
2068 Salted & Roasted Nuts & Seeds
NAICS 311911 Roasted Nuts & Peanut Butter Manufacturing
2074 Cottonseed Oil Mills
NAICS 311223 Other Oilseed Processing
NAICS 311225 Fats & Oils Refining & Blending
2075 Soybean Oil Mills
NAICS 311222 Soybean Processing
NAICS 311225 Fats & Oils Refining & Blending
2076 Vegetable Oil Mills, Except Corn, Cottonseed, & Soybeans
NAICS 311223 Other Oilseed Processing
NAICS 311225 Fats & Oils Refining & Blending
2077 Animal & Marine Fats & Oils
NAICS 311613 Rendering & Meat By-product Processing
NAICS 311711 Seafood Canning
NAICS 311712 Fresh & Frozen Seafood Processing
NAICS 311225 Edible Fats & Oils Manufacturing
**2079 Shortening, Table Oils, Margarine, & Other Edible Fats &
Oils, nec**
NAICS 311225 Edible Fats & Oils Manufacturing
NAICS 311222 Soybean Processing
NAICS 311223 Other Oilseed Processing
2082 Malt Beverages
NAICS 31212 Breweries
2083 Malt
NAICS 311213 Malt Manufacturing
2084 Wines, Brandy, & Brandy Spirits
NAICS 31213 Wineries
2085 Distilled & Blended Liquors
NAICS 31214 Distilleries
2086 Bottled & Canned Soft Drinks & Carbonated Waters
NAICS 312111 Soft Drink Manufacturing
NAICS 312112 Bottled Water Manufacturing
2087 Flavoring Extracts & Flavoring Syrups nec
NAICS 31193 Flavoring Syrup & Concentrate Manufacturing
NAICS 311942 Spice & Extract Manufacturing
NAICS 311999 All Other Miscellaneous Food Manufacturing
2091 Canned & Cured Fish & Seafood
NAICS 311711 Seafood Canning
2092 Prepared Fresh or Frozen Fish & Seafoods
NAICS 311712 Fresh & Frozen Seafood Processing
2095 Roasted Coffee
NAICS 31192 Coffee & Tea Manufacturing
NAICS 311942 Spice & Extract Manufacturing
2096 Potato Chips, Corn Chips, & Similar Snacks
NAICS 311919 Other Snack Food Manufacturing

2097 Manufactured Ice
NAICS 312113 Ice Manufacturing
2098 Macaroni, Spaghetti, Vermicelli, & Noodles
NAICS 311823 Pasta Manufacturing
2099 Food Preparations, nec
NAICS 311423 Dried & Dehydrated Food Manufacturing
NAICS 111998 All Other Miscellaneous Crop Farming
NAICS 31134 Non-chocolate Confectionery Manufacturing
NAICS 311911 Roasted Nuts & Peanut Butter Manufacturing
NAICS 311991 Perishable Prepared Food Manufacturing
NAICS 31183 Tortilla Manufacturing
NAICS 31192 Coffee & Tea Manufacturing
NAICS 311941 Mayonnaise, Dressing, & Other Prepared Sauce
Manufacturing
NAICS 311942 Spice & Extract Manufacturing
NAICS 311999 All Other Miscellaneous Food Manufacturing

TOBACCO PRODUCTS

2111 Cigarettes
NAICS 312221 Cigarette Manufacturing
2121 Cigars
NAICS 312229 Other Tobacco Product Manufacturing
2131 Chewing & Smoking Tobacco & Snuff
NAICS 312229 Other Tobacco Product Manufacturing
2141 Tobacco Stemming & Redrying
NAICS 312229 Other Tobacco Product Manufacturing
NAICS 31221 Tobacco Stemming & Redrying

TEXTILE MILL PRODUCTS

2211 Broadwoven Fabric Mills, Cotton
NAICS 31321 Broadwoven Fabric Mills
2221 Broadwoven Fabric Mills, Manmade Fiber & Silk
NAICS 31321 Broadwoven Fabric Mills
2231 Broadwoven Fabric Mills, Wool
NAICS 31321 Broadwoven Fabric Mills
NAICS 313311 Broadwoven Fabric Finishing Mills
NAICS 313312 Textile & Fabric Finishing Mills
**2241 Narrow Fabric & Other Smallware Mills: Cotton, Wool,
Silk, & Manmade Fiber**
NAICS 313221 Narrow Fabric Mills
2251 Women's Full-length & Knee-length Hosiery, Except Socks
NAICS 315111 Sheer Hosiery Mills
2252 Hosiery, nec
NAICS 315111 Sheer Hosiery Mills
NAICS 315119 Other Hosiery & Sock Mills
2253 Knit Outerwear Mills
NAICS 315191 Outerwear Knitting Mills
2254 Knit Underwear & Nightwear Mills
NAICS 315192 Underwear & Nightwear Knitting Mills
2257 Weft Knit Fabric Mills
NAICS 313241 Weft Knit Fabric Mills
NAICS 313312 Textile & Fabric Finishing Mills
2258 Lace & Warp Knit Fabric Mills
NAICS 313249 Other Knit Fabric & Lace Mills
NAICS 313312 Textile & Fabric Finishing Mills
2259 Knitting Mills, nec
NAICS 315191 Outerwear Knitting Mills
NAICS 315192 Underwear & Nightwear Knitting Mills
NAICS 313241 Weft Knit Fabric Mills
NAICS 313249 Other Knit Fabric & Lace Mills

2261 Finishers of Broadwoven Fabrics of Cotton
NAICS 313311 Broadwoven Fabric Finishing Mills
2262 Finishers of Broadwoven Fabrics of Manmade Fiber & Silk
NAICS 313311 Broadwoven Fabric Finishing Mills
2269 Finishers of Textiles, nec
NAICS 313311 Broadwoven Fabric Finishing Mills
NAICS 313312 Textile & Fabric Finishing Mills
2273 Carpets & Rugs
NAICS 31411   Carpet & Rug Mills
2281 Yarn Spinning Mills
NAICS 313111 Yarn Spinning Mills
2282 Yarn Texturizing, Throwing, Twisting, & Winding Mills
NAICS 313112 Yarn Texturing, Throwing & Twisting Mills
NAICS 313312 Textile & Fabric Finishing Mills
2284 Thread Mills
NAICS 313113 Thread Mills
NAICS 313312 Textile & Fabric Finishing Mills
2295 Coated Fabrics, Not Rubberized
NAICS 31332   Fabric Coating Mills
2296 Tire Cord & Fabrics
NAICS 314992 Tire Cord & Tire Fabric Mills
2297 Nonwoven Fabrics
NAICS 31323   Nonwoven Fabric Mills
2298 Cordage & Twine
NAICS 314991 Rope, Cordage & Twine Mills
2299 Textile Goods, nec
NAICS 31321   Broadwoven Fabric Mills
NAICS 31323   Nonwoven Fabric Mills
NAICS 313312 Textile & Fabric Finishing Mills
NAICS 313221 Narrow Fabric Mills
NAICS 313113 Thread Mills
NAICS 313111 Yarn Spinning Mills
NAICS 314999 All Other Miscellaneous Textile Product Mills

APPAREL & OTHER FINISHED PRODUCTS MADE FROM FABRICS & SIMILAR MATERIALS

2311 Men's & Boys' Suits, Coats & Overcoats
NAICS 315211 Men's & Boys' Cut & Sew Apparel Contractors
NAICS 315222 Men's & Boys' Cut & Sew Suit, Coat, & Overcoat Manufacturing
2321 Men's & Boys' Shirts, Except Work Shirts
NAICS 315211 Men's & Boys' Cut & Sew Apparel Contractors
NAICS 315223 Men's & Boys' Cut & Sew Shirt, Manufacturing
2322 Men's & Boys' Underwear & Nightwear
NAICS 315211 Men's & Boys' Cut & Sew Apparel Contractors
NAICS 315221 Men's & Boys' Cut & Sew Underwear & Nightwear Manufacturing
2323 Men's & Boys' Neckwear
NAICS 315993 Men's & Boys' Neckwear Manufacturing
2325 Men's & Boys' Trousers & Slacks
NAICS 315211 Men's & Boys' Cut & Sew Apparel Contractors
NAICS 315224 Men's & Boys' Cut & Sew Trouser, Slack, & Jean Manufacturing
2326 Men's & Boys' Work Clothing
NAICS 315211 Men's & Boys' Cut & Sew Apparel Contractors
NAICS 315225 Men's & Boys' Cut & Sew Work Clothing Manufacturing
2329 Men's & Boys' Clothing, nec
NAICS 315211 Men's & Boys' Cut & Sew Apparel Contractors

NAICS 315228 Men's & Boys' Cut & Sew Other Outerwear Manufacturing
NAICS 315299 All Other Cut & Sew Apparel Manufacturing
2331 Women's, Misses', & Juniors' Blouses & Shirts
NAICS 315212 Women's & Girls' Cut & Sew Apparel Contractors
NAICS 315232 Women's & Girls' Cut & Sew Blouse & Shirt Manufacturing
2335 Women's, Misses' & Junior's Dresses
NAICS 315212 Women's & Girls' Cut & Sew Apparel Contractors
NAICS 315233 Women's & Girls' Cut & Sew Dress Manufacturing
2337 Women's, Misses' & Juniors' Suits, Skirts & Coats
NAICS 315212 Women's & Girls' Cut & Sew Apparel Contractors
NAICS 315234 Women's & Girls' Cut & Sew Suit, Coat, Tailored Jacket, & Skirt Manufacturing
2339 Women's, Misses' & Juniors' Outerwear, nec
NAICS 315999 Other Apparel Accessories & Other Apparel Manufacturing
NAICS 315212 Women's & Girls' Cut & Sew Apparel Contractors
NAICS 315299 All Other Cut & Sew Apparel Manufacturing
NAICS 315238 Women's & Girls' Cut & Sew Other Outerwear Manufacturing
2341 Women's, Misses, Children's, & Infants' Underwear & Nightwear
NAICS 315212 Women's & Girls' Cut & Sew Apparel Contractors
NAICS 315211 Men's & Boys' Cut & Sew Apparel Contractors
NAICS 315231 Women's & Girls' Cut & Sew Lingerie, Loungewear, & Nightwear Manufacturing
NAICS 315221 Men's & Boys' Cut & Sew Underwear & Nightwear Manufacturing
NAICS 315291 Infants' Cut & Sew Apparel Manufacturing
2342 Brassieres, Girdles, & Allied Garments
NAICS 315212 Women's & Girls' Cut & Sew Apparel Contractors
NAICS 315231 Women's & Girls' Cut & Sew Lingerie, Loungewear, & Nightwear Manufacturing
2353 Hats, Caps, & Millinery
NAICS 315991 Hat, Cap, & Millinery Manufacturing
2361 Girls', Children's & Infants' Dresses, Blouses & Shirts
NAICS 315291 Infants' Cut & Sew Apparel Manufacturing
NAICS 315223 Men's & Boys' Cut & Sew Shirt, Manufacturing
NAICS 315211 Men's & Boys' Cut & Sew Apparel Contractors
NAICS 315232 Women's & Girls' Cut & Sew Blouse & Shirt Manufacturing
NAICS 315233 Women's & Girls' Cut & Sew Dress Manufacturing
NAICS 315212 Women's & Girls' Cut & Sew Apparel Contractors
2369 Girls', Children's & Infants' Outerwear, nec
NAICS 315291 Infants' Cut & Sew Apparel Manufacturing
NAICS 315222 Men's & Boys' Cut & Sew Suit, Coat, & Overcoat Manufacturing
NAICS 315224 Men's & Boys' Cut & Sew Trouser, Slack, & Jean Manufacturing
NAICS 315228 Men's & Boys' Cut & Sew Other Outerwear Manufacturing
NAICS 315221 Men's & Boys' Cut & Sew Underwear & Nightwear Manufacturing
NAICS 315211 Men's & Boys' Cut & Sew Apparel Contractors

NAICS 315234 Women's & Girls' Cut & Sew Suit, Coat, Tailored Jacket, & Skirt Manufacturing

NAICS 315238 Women's & Girls' Cut & Sew Other Outerwear Manufacturing

NAICS 315231 Women's & Girls' Cut & Sew Lingerie, Loungewear, & Nightwear Manufacturing

NAICS 315212 Women's & Girls' Cut & Sew Apparel Contractors

2371 Fur Goods

NAICS 315292 Fur & Leather Apparel Manufacturing

2381 Dress & Work Gloves, Except Knit & All-leather

NAICS 315992 Glove & Mitten Manufacturing

2384 Robes & Dressing Gowns

NAICS 315231 Women's & Girls' Cut & Sew Lingerie, Loungewear, & Nightwear Manufacturing

NAICS 315221 Men's & Boys' Cut & Sew Underwear & Nightwear Manufacturing

NAICS 315211 Men's & Boys' Cut & Sew Apparel Contractors

NAICS 315212 Women's & Girls' Cut & Sew Apparel Contractors

2385 Waterproof Outerwear

NAICS 315222 Men's & Boys' Cut & Sew Suit, Coat, & Overcoat Manufacturing

NAICS 315234 Women's & Girls' Cut & Sew Suit, Coat, Tailored Jacket, & Skirt Manufacturing

NAICS 315228 Men's & Boys' Cut & Sew Other Outerwear Manufacturing

NAICS 315238 Women's & Girls' Cut & Sew Other Outerwear Manufacturing

NAICS 315291 Infants' Cut & Sew Apparel Manufacturing

NAICS 315999 Other Apparel Accessories & Other Apparel Manufacturing

NAICS 315211 Men's & Boys' Cut & Sew Apparel Contractors

NAICS 315212 Women's & Girls' Cut & Sew Apparel Contractors

2386 Leather & Sheep-lined Clothing

NAICS 315292 Fur & Leather Apparel Manufacturing

2387 Apparel Belts

NAICS 315999 Other Apparel Accessories & Other Apparel Manufacturing

2389 Apparel & Accessories, nec

NAICS 315999 Other Apparel Accessories & Other Apparel Manufacturing

NAICS 315299 All Other Cut & Sew Apparel Manufacturing

NAICS 315231 Women's & Girls' Cut & Sew Lingerie, Loungewear, & Nightwear Manufacturing

NAICS 315212 Women's & Girls' Cut & Sew Apparel Contractors

NAICS 315211 Mens' & Boys' Cut & Sew Apparel Contractors

2391 Curtains & Draperies

NAICS 314121 Curtain & Drapery Mills

2392 Housefurnishings, Except Curtains & Draperies

NAICS 314911 Textile Bag Mills

NAICS 339994 Broom, Brush & Mop Manufacturing

NAICS 314129 Other Household Textile Product Mills

2393 Textile Bags

NAICS 314911 Textile Bag Mills

2394 Canvas & Related Products

NAICS 314912 Canvas & Related Product Mills

2395 Pleating, Decorative & Novelty Stitching, & Tucking for the Trade

NAICS 314999 All Other Miscellaneous Textile Product Mills

NAICS 315211 Mens' & Boys' Cut & Sew Apparel Contractors

NAICS 315212 Women's & Girls' Cut & Sew Apparel Contractors

2396 Automotive Trimmings, Apparel Findings, & Related Products

NAICS 33636 Motor Vehicle Fabric Accessories & Seat Manufacturing

NAICS 315999 Other Apparel Accessories, & Other Apparel Manufacturing

NAICS 323113 Commercial Screen Printing

NAICS 314999 All Other Miscellaneous Textile Product Mills

2397 Schiffli Machine Embroideries

NAICS 313222 Schiffli Machine Embroidery

2399 Fabricated Textile Products, nec

NAICS 33636 Motor Vehicle Fabric Accessories & Seat Manufacturing

NAICS 315999 Other Apparel Accessories & Other Apparel Manufacturing

NAICS 314999 All Other Miscellaneous Textile Product Mills

LUMBER & WOOD PRODUCTS, EXCEPT FURNITURE

2411 Logging

NAICS 11331 Logging

2421 Sawmills & Planing Mills, General

NAICS 321913 Softwood Cut Stock, Resawing Lumber, & Planing

NAICS 321113 Sawmills

NAICS 321914 Other Millwork

NAICS 321999 All Other Miscellaneous Wood Product Manufacturing

2426 Hardwood Dimension & Flooring Mills

NAICS 321914 Other Millwork

NAICS 321999 All Other Miscellaneous Wood Product Manufacturing

NAICS 337139 Other Wood Furniture Manufacturing

NAICS 321912 Hardwood Dimension Mills

2429 Special Product Sawmills, nec

NAICS 321113 Sawmills

NAICS 321913 Softwood Cut Stock, Resawing Lumber, & Planing

NAICS 321999 All Other Miscellaneous Wood Product Manufacturing

2431 Millwork

NAICS 321911 Wood Window & Door Manufacturing

NAICS 321914 Other Millwork

2434 Wood Kitchen Cabinets

NAICS 337131 Wood Kitchen Cabinet & Counter Top Manufacturing

2435 Hardwood Veneer & Plywood

NAICS 321211 Hardwood Veneer & Plywood Manufacturing

2436 Softwood Veneer & Plywood

NAICS 321212 Softwood Veneer & Plywood Manufacturing

2439 Structural Wood Members, nec

NAICS 321913 Softwood Cut Stock, Resawing Lumber, & Planing

NAICS 321214 Truss Manufacturing

NAICS 321213 Engineered Wood Member Manufacturing

2441 Nailed & Lock Corner Wood Boxes & Shook

NAICS 32192 Wood Container & Pallet Manufacturing

2448 Wood Pallets & Skids

NAICS 32192 Wood Container & Pallet Manufacturing

2449 Wood Containers, nec
NAICS 32192　Wood Container & Pallet Manufacturing
2451 Mobile Homes
NAICS 321991 Manufactured Home Manufacturing
2452 Prefabricated Wood Buildings & Components
NAICS 321992 Prefabricated Wood Building Manufacturing
2491 Wood Preserving
NAICS 321114 Wood Preservation
2493 Reconstituted Wood Products
NAICS 321219 Reconstituted Wood Product Manufacturing
2499 Wood Products, nec
NAICS 339999 All Other Miscellaneous Manufacturing
NAICS 337139 Other Wood Furniture Manufacturing
NAICS 337148 Other Nonwood Furniture Manufacturing
NAICS 32192　Wood Container & Pallet Manufacturing
NAICS 321999 All Other Miscellaneous Wood Product
　　　　　Manufacturing

FURNITURE & FIXTURES

2511 Wood Household Furniture, Except Upholstered
NAICS 337122 Wood Household Furniture Manufacturing
2512 Wood Household Furniture, Upholstered
NAICS 337121 Upholstered Household Furniture
　　　　　Manufacturing
2514 Metal Household Furniture
NAICS 337124 Metal Household Furniture Manufacturing
2515 Mattresses, Foundations, & Convertible Beds
NAICS 33791　Mattress Manufacturing
NAICS 337132 Upholstered Wood Household Furniture
　　　　　Manufacturing
2517 Wood Television, Radio, Phonograph & Sewing Machine Cabinets
NAICS 337139 Other Wood Furniture Manufacturing
2519 Household Furniture, nec
NAICS 337143 Household Furniture (except Wood & Metal)
　　　　　Manufacturing
2521 Wood Office Furniture
NAICS 337134 Wood Office Furniture Manufacturing
2522 Office Furniture, Except Wood
NAICS 337141 Nonwood Office Furniture Manufacturing
2531 Public Building & Related Furniture
NAICS 33636　Motor Vehicle Fabric Accessories & Seat
　　　　　Manufacturing
NAICS 337139 Other Wood Furniture Manufacturing
NAICS 337148 Other Nonwood Furniture Manufacturing
NAICS 339942 Lead Pencil & Art Good Manufacturing
2541 Wood Office & Store Fixtures, Partitions, Shelving, & Lockers
NAICS 337131 Wood Kitchen Cabinet & Counter Top
　　　　　Manufacturing
NAICS 337135 Custom Architectural Woodwork, Millwork, &
　　　　　Fixtures
NAICS 337139 Other Wood Furniture Manufacturing
2542 Office & Store Fixtures, Partitions Shelving, & Lockers, Except Wood
NAICS 337145 Nonwood Showcase, Partition, Shelving, &
　　　　　Locker Manufacturing
2591 Drapery Hardware & Window Blinds & Shades
NAICS 33792　Blind & Shade Manufacturing
2599 Furniture & Fixtures, nec
NAICS 339113 Surgical Appliance & Supplies Manufacturing
NAICS 337139 Other Wood Furniture Manufacturing

NAICS 337148 Other Nonwood Furniture Manufacturing

PAPER & ALLIED PRODUCTS

2611 Pulp Mills
NAICS 32211　Pulp Mills
NAICS 322121 Paper Mills
NAICS 32213　Paperboard Mills
2621 Paper Mills
NAICS 322121 Paper Mills
NAICS 322122 Newsprint Mills
2631 Paperboard Mills
NAICS 32213　Paperboard Mills
2652 Setup Paperboard Boxes
NAICS 322213 Setup Paperboard Box Manufacturing
2653 Corrugated & Solid Fiber Boxes
NAICS 322211 Corrugated & Solid Fiber Box Manufacturing
2655 Fiber Cans, Tubes, Drums, & Similar Products
NAICS 322214 Fiber Can, Tube, Drum, & Similar Products
　　　　　Manufacturing
2656 Sanitary Food Containers, Except Folding
NAICS 322215 Non-folding Sanitary Food Container
　　　　　Manufacturing
2657 Folding Paperboard Boxes, Including Sanitary
NAICS 322212 Folding Paperboard Box Manufacturing
2671 Packaging Paper & Plastics Film, Coated & Laminated
NAICS 322221 Coated & Laminated Packaging Paper &
　　　　　Plastics Film Manufacturing
NAICS 326112 Unsupported Plastics Packaging Film & Sheet
　　　　　Manufacturing
2672 Coated & Laminated Paper, nec
NAICS 322222 Coated & Laminated Paper Manufacturing
2673 Plastics, Foil, & Coated Paper Bags
NAICS 322223 Plastics, Foil, & Coated Paper Bag
　　　　　Manufacturing
NAICS 326111 Unsupported Plastics Bag Manufacturing
2674 Uncoated Paper & Multiwall Bags
NAICS 322224 Uncoated Paper & Multiwall Bag
　　　　　Manufacturing
2675 Die-cut Paper & Paperboard & Cardboard
NAICS 322231 Die-cut Paper & Paperboard Office Supplies
　　　　　Manufacturing
NAICS 322292 Surface-coated Paperboard Manufacturing
NAICS 322298 All Other Converted Paper Product
　　　　　Manufacturing
2676 Sanitary Paper Products
NAICS 322291 Sanitary Paper Product Manufacturing
2677 Envelopes
NAICS 322232 Envelope Manufacturing
2678 Stationery, Tablets, & Related Products
NAICS 322233 Stationery, Tablet, & Related Product
　　　　　Manufacturing
2679 Converted Paper & Paperboard Products, nec
NAICS 322215 Non-folding Sanitary Food Container
　　　　　Manufacturing
NAICS 322222 Coated & Laminated Paper Manufacturing
NAICS 322231 Die-cut Paper & Paperboard Office Supplies
　　　　　Manufacturing
NAICS 322298 All Other Converted Paper Product
　　　　　Manufacturing

Appendix: SIC/NAICS Conversion

PRINTING, PUBLISHING, & ALLIED INDUSTRIES

2711 Newspapers: Publishing, or Publishing & Printing
NAICS 51111   Newspaper Publishers
2721 Periodicals: Publishing, or Publishing & Printing
NAICS 51112   Periodical Publishers
2731 Books: Publishing, or Publishing & Printing
NAICS 51223   Music Publishers
NAICS 51113   Book Publishers
2732 Book Printing
NAICS 323117 Book Printing
2741 Miscellaneous Publishing
NAICS 51114   Database & Directory Publishers
NAICS 51223   Music Publishers
NAICS 511199 All Other Publishers
2752 Commercial Printing, Lithographic
NAICS 323114 Quick Printing
NAICS 323110 Commercial Lithographic Printing
2754 Commercial Printing, Gravure
NAICS 323111 Commercial Gravure Printing
2759 Commercial Printing, nec
NAICS 323113 Commercial Screen Printing
NAICS 323112 Commercial Flexographic Printing
NAICS 323114 Quick Printing
NAICS 323115 Digital Printing
NAICS 323119 Other Commercial Printing
2761 Manifold Business Forms
NAICS 323116 Manifold Business Form Printing
2771 Greeting Cards
NAICS 323110 Commercial Lithographic Printing
NAICS 323111 Commercial Gravure Printing
NAICS 323112 Commercial Flexographic Printing
NAICS 323113 Commercial Screen Printing
NAICS 323119 Other Commercial Printing
NAICS 511191 Greeting Card Publishers
2782 Blankbooks, Loose-leaf Binders & Devices
NAICS 323110 Commercial Lithographic Printing
NAICS 323111 Commercial Gravure Printing
NAICS 323112 Commercial Flexographic Printing
NAICS 323113 Commercial Screen Printing
NAICS 323119 Other Commercial Printing
NAICS 323118 Blankbook, Loose-leaf Binder & Device
   Manufacturing
2789 Bookbinding & Related Work
NAICS 323121 Tradebinding & Related Work
2791 Typesetting
NAICS 323122 Prepress Services
2796 Platemaking & Related Services
NAICS 323122 Prepress Services

CHEMICALS & ALLIED PRODUCTS

2812 Alkalies & Chlorine
NAICS 325181 Alkalies & Chlorine Manufacturing
2813 Industrial Gases
NAICS 32512   Industrial Gas Manufacturing
2816 Inorganic Pigments
NAICS 325131 Inorganic Dye & Pigment Manufacturing
NAICS 325182 Carbon Black Manufacturing
2819 Industrial Inorganic Chemicals, nec
NAICS 325998 All Other Miscellaneous Chemical Product
   Manufacturing

NAICS 331311 Alumina Refining
NAICS 325131 Inorganic Dye & Pigment Manufacturing
NAICS 325188 All Other Basic Inorganic Chemical
   Manufacturing
2821 Plastics Material Synthetic Resins, & Nonvulcanizable Elastomers
NAICS 325211 Plastics Material & Resin Manufacturing
2822 Synthetic Rubber
NAICS 325212 Synthetic Rubber Manufacturing
2823 Cellulosic Manmade Fibers
NAICS 325221 Cellulosic Manmade Fiber Manufacturing
2824 Manmade Organic Fibers, Except Cellulosic
NAICS 325222 Noncellulosic Organic Fiber Manufacturing
2833 Medicinal Chemicals & Botanical Products
NAICS 325411 Medicinal & Botanical Manufacturing
2834 Pharmaceutical Preparations
NAICS 325412 Pharmaceutical Preparation Manufacturing
2835 In Vitro & in Vivo Diagnostic Substances
NAICS 325412 Pharmaceutical Preparation Manufacturing
NAICS 325413 In-vitro Diagnostic Substance Manufacturing
2836 Biological Products, Except Diagnostic Substances
NAICS 325414 Biological Product Manufacturing
2841 Soaps & Other Detergents, Except Speciality Cleaners
NAICS 325611 Soap & Other Detergent Manufacturing
2842 Speciality Cleaning, Polishing, & Sanitary Preparations
NAICS 325612 Polish & Other Sanitation Good Manufacturing
2843 Surface Active Agents, Finishing Agents, Sulfonated Oils, & Assistants
NAICS 325613 Surface Active Agent Manufacturing
2844 Perfumes, Cosmetics, & Other Toilet Preparations
NAICS 32562   Toilet Preparation Manufacturing
NAICS 325611 Soap & Other Detergent Manufacturing
2851 Paints, Varnishes, Lacquers, Enamels, & Allied Products
NAICS 32551   Paint & Coating Manufacturing
2861 Gum & Wood Chemicals
NAICS 325191 Gum & Wood Chemical Manufacturing
2865 Cyclic Organic Crudes & Intermediates, & Organic Dyes & Pigments
NAICS 32511   Petrochemical Manufacturing
NAICS 325132 Organic Dye & Pigment Manufacturing
NAICS 325192 Cyclic Crude & Intermediate Manufacturing
2869 Industrial Organic Chemicals, nec
NAICS 32511   Petrochemical Manufacturing
NAICS 325188 All Other Inorganic Chemical Manufacturing
NAICS 325193 Ethyl Alcohol Manufacturing
NAICS 32512   Industrial Gas Manufacturing
NAICS 325199 All Other Basic Organic Chemical
   Manufacturing
2873 Nitrogenous Fertilizers
NAICS 325311 Nitrogenous Fertilizer Manufacturing
2874 Phosphatic Fertilizers
NAICS 325312 Phosphatic Fertilizer Manufacturing
2875 Fertilizers, Mixing Only
NAICS 325314 Fertilizer Manufacturing
2879 Pesticides & Agricultural Chemicals, nec
NAICS 32532   Pesticide & Other Agricultural Chemical
   Manufacturing
2891 Adhesives & Sealants
NAICS 32552   Adhesive & Sealant Manufacturing
2892 Explosives
NAICS 32592   Explosives Manufacturing
2893 Printing Ink
NAICS 32591   Printing Ink Manufacturing

2895 Carbon Black
NAICS 325182 Carbon Black Manufacturing
2899 Chemicals & Chemical Preparations, nec
NAICS 32551 Paint & Coating Manufacturing
NAICS 311942 Spice & Extract Manufacturing
NAICS 325199 All Other Basic Organic Chemical
            Manufacturing
NAICS 325998 All Other Miscellaneous Chemical Product
            Manufacturing

PETROLEUM REFINING & RELATED INDUSTRIES

2911 Petroleum Refining
NAICS 32411 Petroleum Refineries
2951 Asphalt Paving Mixtures & Blocks
NAICS 324121 Asphalt Paving Mixture & Block Manufacturing
2952 Asphalt Felts & Coatings
NAICS 324122 Asphalt Shingle & Coating Materials
            Manufacturing
2992 Lubricating Oils & Greases
NAICS 324191 Petroleum Lubricating Oil & Grease
            Manufacturing 2999

RUBBER & MISCELLANEOUS PLASTICS PRODUCTS

3011 Tires & Inner Tubes
NAICS 326211 Tire Manufacturing
3021 Rubber & Plastics Footwear
NAICS 316211 Rubber & Plastics Footwear Manufacturing
3052 Rubber & Plastics Hose & Belting
NAICS 32622 Rubber & Plastics Hoses & Belting
            Manufacturing
3053 Gaskets, Packing, & Sealing Devices
NAICS 339991 Gasket, Packing, & Sealing Device
            Manufacturing
**3061 Molded, Extruded, & Lathe-cut Mechanical Rubber
     Products**
NAICS 326291 Rubber Product Manufacturing for Mechanical
            Use
3069 Fabricated Rubber Products, nec
NAICS 31332 Fabric Coating Mills
NAICS 326192 Resilient Floor Covering Manufacturing
NAICS 326299 All Other Rubber Product Manufacturing
3081 Unsupported Plastics Film & Sheet
NAICS 326113 Unsupported Plastics Film & Sheet
            Manufacturing
3082 Unsupported Plastics Profile Shapes
NAICS 326121 Unsupported Plastics Profile Shape
            Manufacturing
3083 Laminated Plastics Plate, Sheet, & Profile Shapes
NAICS 32613 Laminated Plastics Plate, Sheet, & Shape
            Manufacturing
3084 Plastic Pipe
NAICS 326122 Plastic Pipe & Pipe Fitting Manufacturing
3085 Plastics Bottles
NAICS 32616 Plastics Bottle Manufacturing
3086 Plastics Foam Products
NAICS 32615 Urethane & Other Foam Product
            Manufacturing
NAICS 32614 Polystyrene Foam Product Manufacturing

3087 Custom Compounding of Purchased Plastics Resins
NAICS 325991 Custom Compounding of Purchased Resin
3088 Plastics Plumbing Fixtures
NAICS 326191 Plastics Plumbing Fixtures Manufacturing
3089 Plastics Products, nec
NAICS 326122 Plastics Pipe & Pipe Fitting Manufacturing
NAICS 326121 Unsupported Plastics Profile Shape
            Manufacturing
NAICS 326199 All Other Plastics Product Manufacturing

LEATHER & LEATHER PRODUCTS

3111 Leather Tanning & Finishing
NAICS 31611 Leather & Hide Tanning & Finishing
3131 Boot & Shoe Cut Stock & Findings
NAICS 321999 All Other Miscellaneous Wood Product
            Manufacturing
NAICS 339993 Fastener, Button, Needle, & Pin Manufacturing
NAICS 316999 All Other Leather Good Manufacturing
3142 House Slippers
NAICS 316212 House Slipper Manufacturing
3143 Men's Footwear, Except Athletic
NAICS 316213 Men's Footwear Manufacturing
3144 Women's Footwear, Except Athletic
NAICS 316214 Women's Footwear Manufacturing
3149 Footwear, Except Rubber, nec
NAICS 316219 Other Footwear Manufacturing
3151 Leather Gloves & Mittens
NAICS 315992 Glove & Mitten Manufacturing
3161 Luggage
NAICS 316991 Luggage Manufacturing
3171 Women's Handbags & Purses
NAICS 316992 Women's Handbag & Purse Manufacturing
**3172 Personal Leather Goods, Except Women's Handbags &
     Purses**
NAICS 316993 Personal Leather Good Manufacturing
3199 Leather Goods, nec
NAICS 316999 All Other Leather Good Manufacturing

STONE, CLAY, GLASS, & CONCRETE PRODUCTS

3211 Flat Glass
NAICS 327211 Flat Glass Manufacturing
3221 Glass Containers
NAICS 327213 Glass Container Manufacturing
3229 Pressed & Blown Glass & Glassware, nec
NAICS 327212 Other Pressed & Blown Glass & Glassware
            Manufacturing
3231 Glass Products, Made of Purchased Glass
NAICS 327215 Glass Product Manufacturing Made of
            Purchased Glass
3241 Cement, Hydraulic
NAICS 32731 Hydraulic Cement Manufacturing
3251 Brick & Structural Clay Tile
NAICS 327121 Brick & Structural Clay Tile Manufacturing
3253 Ceramic Wall & Floor Tile
NAICS 327122 Ceramic Wall & Floor Tile Manufacturing
3255 Clay Refractories
NAICS 327124 Clay Refractory Manufacturing

Appendix: SIC/NAICS Conversion

3259 Structural Clay Products, nec
NAICS 327123 Other Structural Clay Product Manufacturing

3261 Vitreous China Plumbing Fixtures & China & Earthenware Fittings & Bathroom Accessories
NAICS 327111 Vitreous China Plumbing Fixture & China & Earthenware Fittings & Bathroom Accessories Manufacturing

3262 Vitreous China Table & Kitchen Articles
NAICS 327112 Vitreous China, Fine Earthenware & Other Pottery Product Manufacturing

3263 Fine Earthenware Table & Kitchen Articles
NAICS 327112 Vitreous China, Fine Earthenware & Other Pottery Product Manufacturing

3264 Porcelain Electrical Supplies
NAICS 327113 Porcelain Electrical Supply Manufacturing

3269 Pottery Products, nec
NAICS 327112 Vitreous China, Fine Earthenware, & Other Pottery Product Manufacturing

3271 Concrete Block & Brick
NAICS 327331 Concrete Block & Brick Manufacturing

3272 Concrete Products, Except Block & Brick
NAICS 327999 All Other Miscellaneous Nonmetallic Mineral Product Manufacturing
NAICS 327332 Concrete Pipe Manufacturing
NAICS 32739 Other Concrete Product Manufacturing

3273 Ready-mixed Concrete
NAICS 32732 Ready-mix Concrete Manufacturing

3274 Lime
NAICS 32741 Lime Manufacturing

3275 Gypsum Products
NAICS 32742 Gypsum & Gypsum Product Manufacturing

3281 Cut Stone & Stone Products
NAICS 327991 Cut Stone & Stone Product Manufacturing

3291 Abrasive Products
NAICS 332999 All Other Miscellaneous Fabricated Metal Product Manufacturing
NAICS 32791 Abrasive Product Manufacturing

3292 Asbestos Products
NAICS 33634 Motor Vehicle Brake System Manufacturing
NAICS 327999 All Other Miscellaneous Nonmetallic Mineral Product Manufacturing

3295 Minerals & Earths, Ground or Otherwise Treated
NAICS 327992 Ground or Treated Mineral & Earth Manufacturing

3296 Mineral Wool
NAICS 327993 Mineral Wool Manufacturing

3297 Nonclay Refractories
NAICS 327125 Nonclay Refractory Manufacturing

3299 Nonmetallic Mineral Products, nec
NAICS 32742 Gypsum & Gypsum Product Manufacturing
NAICS 327999 All Other Miscellaneous Nonmetallic Mineral Product Manufacturing

PRIMARY METALS INDUSTRIES

3312 Steel Works, Blast Furnaces , & Rolling Mills
NAICS 324199 All Other Petroleum & Coal Products Manufacturing
NAICS 331111 Iron & Steel Mills

3313 Electrometallurgical Products, Except Steel
NAICS 331112 Electrometallurgical Ferroalloy Product Manufacturing

NAICS 331492 Secondary Smelting, Refining, & Alloying of Nonferrous Metals

3315 Steel Wiredrawing & Steel Nails & Spikes
NAICS 331222 Steel Wire Drawing
NAICS 332618 Other Fabricated Wire Product Manufacturing

3316 Cold-rolled Steel Sheet, Strip, & Bars
NAICS 331221 Cold-rolled Steel Shape Manufacturing

3317 Steel Pipe & Tubes
NAICS 33121 Iron & Steel Pipes & Tubes Manufacturing from Purchased Steel

3321 Gray & Ductile Iron Foundries
NAICS 331511 Iron Foundries

3322 Malleable Iron Foundries
NAICS 331511 Iron Foundries

3324 Steel Investment Foundries
NAICS 331512 Steel Investment Foundries

3325 Steel Foundries, nec
NAICS 331513 Steel Foundries

3331 Primary Smelting & Refining of Copper
NAICS 331411 Primary Smelting & Refining of Copper

3334 Primary Production of Aluminum
NAICS 331312 Primary Aluminum Production

3339 Primary Smelting & Refining of Nonferrous Metals, Except Copper & Aluminum
NAICS 331419 Primary Smelting & Refining of Nonferrous Metals

3341 Secondary Smelting & Refining of Nonferrous Metals
NAICS 331314 Secondary Smelting & Alloying of Aluminum
NAICS 331423 Secondary Smelting, Refining, & Alloying of Copper
NAICS 331492 Secondary Smelting, Refining, & Alloying of Nonferrous Metals

3351 Rolling, Drawing, & Extruding of Copper
NAICS 331421 Copper Rolling, Drawing, & Extruding

3353 Aluminum Sheet, Plate, & Foil
NAICS 331315 Aluminum Sheet, Plate, & Foil Manufacturing

3354 Aluminum Extruded Products
NAICS 331316 Aluminum Extruded Product Manufacturing

3355 Aluminum Rolling & Drawing, nec
NAICS 331319 Other Aluminum Rolling & Drawing,

3356 Rolling, Drawing, & Extruding of Nonferrous Metals, Except Copper & Aluminum
NAICS 331491 Nonferrous Metal Rolling. Drawing, & Extruding

3357 Drawing & Insulating of Nonferrous Wire
NAICS 331319 Other Aluminum Rolling & Drawing
NAICS 331422 Copper Wire Drawing
NAICS 331491 Nonferrous Metal Rolling, Drawing, & Extruding
NAICS 335921 Fiber Optic Cable Manufacturing
NAICS 335929 Other Communication & Energy Wire Manufacturing

3363 Aluminum Die-castings
NAICS 331521 Aluminum Die-castings

3364 Nonferrous Die-castings, Except Aluminum
NAICS 331522 Nonferrous Die-castings

3365 Aluminum Foundries
NAICS 331524 Aluminum Foundries

3366 Copper Foundries
NAICS 331525 Copper Foundries

3369 Nonferrous Foundries, Except Aluminum & Copper
NAICS 331528 Other Nonferrous Foundries

3398 Metal Heat Treating
NAICS 332811 Metal Heat Treating
3399 Primary Metal Products, nec
NAICS 331111 Iron & Steel Mills
NAICS 331314 Secondary Smelting & Alloying of Aluminum
NAICS 331423 Secondary Smelting, Refining & Alloying of Copper
NAICS 331492 Secondary Smelting, Refining, & Alloying of Nonferrous Metals
NAICS 332618 Other Fabricated Wire Product Manufacturing
NAICS 332813 Electroplating, Plating, Polishing, Anodizing, & Coloring

FABRICATED METAL PRODUCTS, EXCEPT MACHINERY & TRANSPORTATION EQUIPMENT

3411 Metal Cans
NAICS 332431 Metal Can Manufacturing
3412 Metal Shipping Barrels, Drums, Kegs & Pails
NAICS 332439 Other Metal Container Manufacturing
3421 Cutlery
NAICS 332211 Cutlery & Flatware Manufacturing
3423 Hand & Edge Tools, Except Machine Tools & Handsaws
NAICS 332212 Hand & Edge Tool Manufacturing
3425 Saw Blades & Handsaws
NAICS 332213 Saw Blade & Handsaw Manufacturing
3429 Hardware, nec
NAICS 332439 Other Metal Container Manufacturing
NAICS 332919 Other Metal Valve & Pipe Fitting Manufacturing
NAICS 33251 Hardware Manufacturing
3431 Enameled Iron & Metal Sanitary Ware
NAICS 332998 Enameled Iron & Metal Sanitary Ware Manufacturing
3432 Plumbing Fixture Fittings & Trim
NAICS 332913 Plumbing Fixture Fitting & Trim Manufacturing
NAICS 332999 All Other Miscellaneous Fabricated Metal Product Manufacturing
3433 Heating Equipment, Except Electric & Warm Air Furnaces
NAICS 333414 Heating Equipment Manufacturing
3441 Fabricated Structural Metal
NAICS 332312 Fabricated Structural Metal Manufacturing
3442 Metal Doors, Sash, Frames, Molding, & Trim Manufacturing
NAICS 332321 Metal Window & Door Manufacturing
3443 Fabricated Plate Work
NAICS 332313 Plate Work Manufacturing
NAICS 33241 Power Boiler & Heat Exchanger Manufacturing
NAICS 33242 Metal Tank Manufacturing
NAICS 333415 Air-conditioning & Warm Air Heating Equipment & Commercial & Industrial Refrigeration Equipment Manufacturing
3444 Sheet Metal Work
NAICS 332322 Sheet Metal Work Manufacturing
NAICS 332439 Other Metal Container Manufacturing
3446 Architectural & Ornamental Metal Work
NAICS 332323 Ornamental & Architectural Metal Work Manufacturing
3448 Prefabricated Metal Buildings & Components
NAICS 332311 Prefabricated Metal Building & Component Manufacturing

3449 Miscellaneous Structural Metal Work
NAICS 332114 Custom Roll Forming
NAICS 332312 Fabricated Structural Metal Manufacturing
NAICS 332321 Metal Window & Door Manufacturing
NAICS 332323 Ornamental & Architectural Metal Work Manufacturing
3451 Screw Machine Products
NAICS 332721 Precision Turned Product Manufacturing
3452 Bolts, Nuts, Screws, Rivets, & Washers
NAICS 332722 Bolt, Nut, Screw, Rivet, & Washer Manufacturing
3462 Iron & Steel Forgings
NAICS 332111 Iron & Steel Forging
3463 Nonferrous Forgings
NAICS 332112 Nonferrous Forging
3465 Automotive Stamping
NAICS 33637 Motor Vehicle Metal Stamping
3466 Crowns & Closures
NAICS 332115 Crown & Closure Manufacturing
3469 Metal Stamping, nec
NAICS 339911 Jewelry Manufacturing
NAICS 332116 Metal Stamping
NAICS 332214 Kitchen Utensil, Pot & Pan Manufacturing
3471 Electroplating, Plating, Polishing, Anodizing, & Coloring
NAICS 332813 Electroplating, Plating, Polishing, Anodizing, & Coloring
3479 Coating, Engraving, & Allied Services, nec
NAICS 339914 Costume Jewelry & Novelty Manufacturing
NAICS 339911 Jewelry Manufacturing
NAICS 339912 Silverware & Plated Ware Manufacturing
NAICS 332812 Metal Coating, Engraving , & Allied Services to Manufacturers
3482 Small Arms Ammunition
NAICS 332992 Small Arms Ammunition Manufacturing
3483 Ammunition, Except for Small Arms
NAICS 332993 Ammunition Manufacturing
3484 Small Arms
NAICS 332994 Small Arms Manufacturing
3489 Ordnance & Accessories, nec
NAICS 332995 Other Ordnance & Accessories Manufacturing 3491
3492 Fluid Power Valves & Hose Fittings
NAICS 332912 Fluid Power Valve & Hose Fitting Manufacturing
3493 Steel Springs, Except Wire
NAICS 332611 Steel Spring Manufacturing
3494 Valves & Pipe Fittings, nec
NAICS 332919 Other Metal Valve & Pipe Fitting Manufacturing
NAICS 332999 All Other Miscellaneous Fabricated Metal Product Manufacturing
3495 Wire Springs
NAICS 332612 Wire Spring Manufacturing
NAICS 334518 Watch, Clock, & Part Manufacturing
3496 Miscellaneous Fabricated Wire Products
NAICS 332618 Other Fabricated Wire Product Manufacturing
3497 Metal Foil & Leaf
NAICS 322225 Laminated Aluminum Foil Manufacturing for Flexible Packaging Uses
NAICS 332999 All Other Miscellaneous Fabricated Metal Product Manufacturing
3498 Fabricated Pipe & Pipe Fittings
NAICS 332996 Fabricated Pipe & Pipe Fitting Manufacturing

3499 Fabricated Metal Products, nec
NAICS 337148 Other Nonwood Furniture Manufacturing
NAICS 332117 Powder Metallurgy Part Manufacturing
NAICS 332439 Other Metal Container Manufacturing
NAICS 33251   Hardware Manufacturing
NAICS 332919 Other Metal Valve & Pipe Fitting
    Manufacturing
NAICS 339914 Costume Jewelry & Novelty Manufacturing
NAICS 332999 All Other Miscellaneous Fabricated Metal
    Product Manufacturing

INDUSTRIAL & COMMERCIAL MACHINERY & COMPUTER EQUIPMENT

3511 Steam, Gas, & Hydraulic Turbines, & Turbine Generator Set Units
NAICS 333611 Turbine & Turbine Generator Set Unit
    Manufacturing
3519 Internal Combustion Engines, nec
NAICS 336399 All Other Motor Vehicle Parts Manufacturing
NAICS 333618 Other Engine Equipment Manufacturing
3523 Farm Machinery & Equipment
NAICS 333111 Farm Machinery & Equipment Manufacturing
NAICS 332323 Ornamental & Architectural Metal Work
    Manufacturing
NAICS 332212 Hand & Edge Tool Manufacturing
NAICS 333922 Conveyor & Conveying Equipment
    Manufacturing
3524 Lawn & Garden Tractors & Home Lawn & Garden Equipment
NAICS 333112 Lawn & Garden Tractor & Home Lawn &
    Garden Equipment Manufacturing
NAICS 332212 Hand & Edge Tool Manufacturing
3531 Construction Machinery & Equipment
NAICS 33651   Railroad Rolling Stock Manufacturing
NAICS 333923 Overhead Traveling Crane, Hoist, & Monorail
    System Manufacturing
NAICS 33312   Construction Machinery Manufacturing
3532 Mining Machinery & Equipment, Except Oil & Gas Field Machinery & Equipment
NAICS 333131 Mining Machinery & Equipment Manufacturing
3533 Oil & Gas Field Machinery & Equipment
NAICS 333132 Oil & Gas Field Machinery & Equipment
    Manufacturing
3534 Elevators & Moving Stairways
NAICS 333921 Elevator & Moving Stairway Manufacturing
3535 Conveyors & Conveying Equipment
NAICS 333922 Conveyor & Conveying Equipment
    Manufacturing
3536 Overhead Traveling Cranes, Hoists & Monorail Systems
NAICS 333923 Overhead Traveling Crane, Hoist & Monorail
    System Manufacturing
3537 Industrial Trucks, Tractors, Trailers, & Stackers
NAICS 333924 Industrial Truck, Tractor, Trailer, & Stacker
    Machinery Manufacturing
NAICS 332999 All Other Miscellaneous Fabricated Metal
    Product Manufacturing
NAICS 332439 Other Metal Container Manufacturing
3541 Machine Tools, Metal Cutting Type
NAICS 333512 Machine Tool Manufacturing
3542 Machine Tools, Metal Forming Type
NAICS 333513 Machine Tool Manufacturing

3543 Industrial Patterns
NAICS 332997 Industrial Pattern Manufacturing
3544 Special Dies & Tools, Die Sets, Jigs & Fixtures, & Industrial Molds
NAICS 333514 Special Die & Tool, Die Set, Jig, & Fixture
    Manufacturing
NAICS 333511 Industrial Mold Manufacturing
3545 Cutting Tools, Machine Tool Accessories, & Machinists' Precision Measuring Devices
NAICS 333515 Cutting Tool & Machine Tool Accessory
    Manufacturing
NAICS 332212 Hand & Edge Tool Manufacturing
3546 Power-driven Handtools
NAICS 333991 Power-driven Hand Tool Manufacturing
3547 Rolling Mill Machinery & Equipment
NAICS 333516 Rolling Mill Machinery & Equipment
    Manufacturing
3548 Electric & Gas Welding & Soldering Equipment
NAICS 333992 Welding & Soldering Equipment Manufacturing
NAICS 335311 Power, Distribution, & Specialty Transformer
    Manufacturing
3549 Metalworking Machinery, nec
NAICS 333518 Other Metalworking Machinery Manufacturing
    3552
3553 Woodworking Machinery
NAICS 33321   Sawmill & Woodworking Machinery
    Manufacturing
3554 Paper Industries Machinery
NAICS 333291 Paper Industry Machinery Manufacturing
3555 Printing Trades Machinery & Equipment
NAICS 333293 Printing Machinery & Equipment
    Manufacturing
3556 Food Products Machinery
NAICS 333294 Food Product Machinery Manufacturing
3559 Special Industry Machinery, nec
NAICS 33322   Rubber & Plastics Industry Machinery
    Manufacturing
NAICS 333319 Other Commercial & Service Industry
    Machinery Manufacturing
NAICS 333295 Semiconductor Manufacturing Machinery
NAICS 333298 All Other Industrial Machinery Manufacturing
3561 Pumps & Pumping Equipment
NAICS 333911 Pump & Pumping Equipment Manufacturing
3562 Ball & Roller Bearings
NAICS 332991 Ball & Roller Bearing Manufacturing
3563 Air & Gas Compressors
NAICS 333912 Air & Gas Compressor Manufacturing
3564 Industrial & Commercial Fans & Blowers & Air Purification Equipment
NAICS 333411 Air Purification Equipment Manufacturing
NAICS 333412 Industrial & Commercial Fan & Blower
    Manufacturing
3565 Packaging Machinery
NAICS 333993 Packaging Machinery Manufacturing
3566 Speed Changers, Industrial High-speed Drives, & Gears
NAICS 333612 Speed Changer, Industrial High-speed Drive, &
    Gear Manufacturing
3567 Industrial Process Furnaces & Ovens
NAICS 333994 Industrial Process Furnace & Oven
    Manufacturing
3568 Mechanical Power Transmission Equipment, nec
NAICS 333613 Mechanical Power Transmission Equipment
    Manufacturing

3569 General Industrial Machinery & Equipment, nec
NAICS 333999 All Other General Purpose Machinery
Manufacturing
3571 Electronic Computers
NAICS 334111 Electronic Computer Manufacturing
3572 Computer Storage Devices
NAICS 334112 Computer Storage Device Manufacturing
3575 Computer Terminals
NAICS 334113 Computer Terminal Manufacturing
3577 Computer Peripheral Equipment, nec
NAICS 334119 Other Computer Peripheral Equipment
Manufacturing
**3578 Calculating & Accounting Machines, Except Electronic
Computers**
NAICS 334119 Other Computer Peripheral Equipment
Manufacturing
NAICS 333313 Office Machinery Manufacturing
3579 Office Machines, nec
NAICS 339942 Lead Pencil & Art Good Manufacturing
NAICS 334518 Watch, Clock, & Part Manufacturing
NAICS 333313 Office Machinery Manufacturing
3581 Automatic Vending Machines
NAICS 333311 Automatic Vending Machine Manufacturing
3582 Commercial Laundry, Drycleaning, & Pressing Machines
NAICS 333312 Commercial Laundry, Drycleaning, & Pressing
Machine Manufacturing
**3585 Air-conditioning & Warm Air Heating Equipment &
Commercial & Industrial Refrigeration Equipment**
NAICS 336391 Motor Vehicle Air Conditioning Manufacturing
NAICS 333415 Air Conditioning & Warm Air Heating
Equipment & Commercial & Industrial
Refrigeration Equipment Manufacturing
3586 Measuring & Dispensing Pumps
NAICS 333913 Measuring & Dispensing Pump Manufacturing
3589 Service Industry Machinery, nec
NAICS 333319 Other Commercial and Service Industry
Machinery Manufacturing
3592 Carburetors, Pistons, Piston Rings & Valves
NAICS 336311 Carburetor, Piston, Piston Ring & Valve
Manufacturing
3593 Fluid Power Cylinders & Actuators
NAICS 333995 Fluid Power Cylinder & Actuator
Manufacturing
3594 Fluid Power Pumps & Motors
NAICS 333996 Fluid Power Pump & Motor Manufacturing
3596 Scales & Balances, Except Laboratory
NAICS 333997 Scale & Balance Manufacturing
3599 Industrial & Commercial Machinery & Equipment, nec
NAICS 336399 All Other Motor Vehicle Part Manufacturing
NAICS 332999 All Other Miscellaneous Fabricated Metal
Product Manufacturing
NAICS 333319 Other Commercial & Service Industry
Machinery Manufacturing
NAICS 33271 Machine Shops
NAICS 333999 All Other General Purpose Machinery
Manufacturing

ELECTRONIC & OTHER ELECTRICAL EQUIPMENT & COMPONENTS, EXCEPT COMPUTER EQUIPMENT

3612 Power, Distribution, & Specialty Transformers
NAICS 335311 Power, Distribution, & Specialty Transformer
Manufacturing
3613 Switchgear & Switchboard Apparatus
NAICS 335313 Switchgear & Switchboard Apparatus
Manufacturing
3621 Motors & Generators
NAICS 335312 Motor & Generator Manufacturing
3624 Carbon & Graphite Products
NAICS 335991 Carbon & Graphite Product Manufacturing
3625 Relays & Industrial Controls
NAICS 335314 Relay & Industrial Control Manufacturing
3629 Electrical Industrial Apparatus, nec
NAICS 335999 All Other Miscellaneous Electrical Equipment
& Component Manufacturing
3631 Household Cooking Equipment
NAICS 335221 Household Cooking Appliance Manufacturing
3632 Household Refrigerators & Home & Farm Freezers
NAICS 335222 Household Refrigerator & Home Freezer
Manufacturing
3633 Household Laundry Equipment
NAICS 335224 Household Laundry Equipment Manufacturing
3634 Electric Housewares & Fans
NAICS 335211 Electric Housewares & Fan Manufacturing
3635 Household Vacuum Cleaners
NAICS 335212 Household Vacuum Cleaner Manufacturing
3639 Household Appliances, nec
NAICS 335212 Household Vacuum Cleaner Manufacturing
NAICS 333298 All Other Industrial Machinery Manufacturing
NAICS 335228 Other Household Appliance Manufacturing
3641 Electric Lamp Bulbs & Tubes
NAICS 33511 Electric Lamp Bulb & Part Manufacturing
3643 Current-carrying Wiring Devices
NAICS 335931 Current-carrying Wiring Device Manufacturing
3644 Noncurrent-carrying Wiring Devices
NAICS 335932 Noncurrent-carrying Wiring Device
Manufacturing
3645 Residential Electric Lighting Fixtures
NAICS 335121 Residential Electric Lighting Fixture
Manufacturing
**3646 Commercial, Industrial, & Institutional Electric Lighting
Fixtures**
NAICS 335122 Commercial, Industrial, & Institutional Electric
Lighting Fixture Manufacturing
3647 Vehicular Lighting Equipment
NAICS 336321 Vehicular Lighting Equipment Manufacturing
3648 Lighting Equipment, nec
NAICS 335129 Other Lighting Equipment Manufacturing
3651 Household Audio & Video Equipment
NAICS 33431 Audio & Video Equipment Manufacturing 3652
NAICS 51222 Integrated Record Production/distribution
3661 Telephone & Telegraph Apparatus
NAICS 33421 Telephone Apparatus Manufacturing
NAICS 334416 Electronic Coil, Transformer, & Other Inductor
Manufacturing
NAICS 334418 Printed Circuit/electronics Assembly
Manufacturing

Appendix: SIC/NAICS Conversion

3663 Radio & Television Broadcasting & Communication Equipment
NAICS 33422   Radio & Television Broadcasting & Wireless Communications Equipment Manufacturing

3669 Communications Equipment, nec
NAICS 33429   Other Communication Equipment Manufacturing

3671 Electron Tubes
NAICS 334411 Electron Tube Manufacturing

3672 Printed Circuit Boards
NAICS 334412 Printed Circuit Board Manufacturing

3674 Semiconductors & Related Devices
NAICS 334413 Semiconductor & Related Device Manufacturing

3675 Electronic Capacitors
NAICS 334414 Electronic Capacitor Manufacturing

3676 Electronic Resistors
NAICS 334415 Electronic Resistor Manufacturing

3677 Electronic Coils, Transformers, & Other Inductors
NAICS 334416 Electronic Coil, Transformer, & Other Inductor Manufacturing

3678 Electronic ConNECtors
NAICS 334417 Electronic ConNECtor Manufacturing

3679 Electronic Components, nec
NAICS 33422   Radio & Television Broadcasting & Wireless Communications Equipment Manufacturing
NAICS 334418 Printed Circuit/electronics Assembly Manufacturing
NAICS 336322 Other Motor Vehicle Electrical & Electronic Equipment Manufacturing
NAICS 334419 Other Electronic Component Manufacturing

3691 Storage Batteries
NAICS 335911 Storage Battery Manufacturing

3692 Primary Batteries, Dry & Wet
NAICS 335912 Dry & Wet Primary Battery Manufacturing

3694 Electrical Equipment for Internal Combustion Engines
NAICS 336322 Other Motor Vehicle Electrical & Electronic Equipment Manufacturing

3695 Magnetic & Optical Recording Media
NAICS 334613 Magnetic & Optical Recording Media Manufacturing

3699 Electrical Machinery, Equipment, & Supplies, nec
NAICS 333319 Other Commercial & Service Industry Machinery Manufacturing
NAICS 333618 Other Engine Equipment Manufacturing
NAICS 334119 Other Computer Peripheral Equipment Manufacturing Classify According to Function
NAICS 335129 Other Lighting Equipment Manufacturing
NAICS 335999 All Other Miscellaneous Electrical Equipment & Component Manufacturing

TRANSPORTATION EQUIPMENT

3711 Motor Vehicles & Passenger Car Bodies
NAICS 336111 Automobile Manufacturing
NAICS 336112 Light Truck & Utility Vehicle Manufacturing
NAICS 33612   Heavy Duty Truck Manufacturing
NAICS 336211 Motor Vehicle Body Manufacturing
NAICS 336992 Military Armored Vehicle, Tank, & Tank Component Manufacturing

3713 Truck & Bus Bodies
NAICS 336211 Motor Vehicle Body Manufacturing

3714 Motor Vehicle Parts & Accessories
NAICS 336211 Motor Vehicle Body Manufacturing
NAICS 336312 Gasoline Engine & Engine Parts Manufacturing
NAICS 336322 Other Motor Vehicle Electrical & Electronic Equipment Manufacturing
NAICS 33633   Motor Vehicle Steering & Suspension Components Manufacturing
NAICS 33634   Motor Vehicle Brake System Manufacturing
NAICS 33635   Motor Vehicle Transmission & Power Train Parts Manufacturing
NAICS 336399 All Other Motor Vehicle Parts Manufacturing

3715 Truck Trailers
NAICS 336212 Truck Trailer Manufacturing

3716 Motor Homes
NAICS 336213 Motor Home Manufacturing

3721 Aircraft
NAICS 336411 Aircraft Manufacturing

3724 Aircraft Engines & Engine Parts
NAICS 336412 Aircraft Engine & Engine Parts Manufacturing
                3728
NAICS 336413 Other Aircraft Part & Auxiliary Equipment Manufacturing

3731 Ship Building & Repairing
NAICS 336611 Ship Building & Repairing

3732 Boat Building & Repairing
NAICS 81149   Other Personal & Household Goods Repair & Maintenance
NAICS 336612 Boat Building

3743 Railroad Equipment
NAICS 333911 Pump & Pumping Equipment Manufacturing
NAICS 33651   Railroad Rolling Stock Manufacturing

3751 Motorcycles, Bicycles, & Parts
NAICS 336991 Motorcycle, Bicycle, & Parts Manufacturing

3761 Guided Missiles & Space Vehicles
NAICS 336414 Guided Missile & Space Vehicle Manufacturing
                3764

3769 Guided Missile Space Vehicle Parts & Auxiliary Equipment, nec
NAICS 336419 Other Guided Missile & Space Vehicle Parts & Auxiliary Equipment Manufacturing

3792 Travel Trailers & Campers
NAICS 336214 Travel Trailer & Camper Manufacturing

3795 Tanks & Tank Components
NAICS 336992 Military Armored Vehicle, Tank, & Tank Component Manufacturing

3799 Transportation Equipment, nec
NAICS 336214 Travel Trailer & Camper Manufacturing
NAICS 332212 Hand & Edge Tool Manufacturing
NAICS 336999 All Other Transportation Equipment Manufacturing

MEASURING, ANALYZING, & CONTROLLING INSTRUMENTS

3812 Search, Detection, Navigation, Guidance, Aeronautical, & Nautical Systems & Instruments
NAICS 334511 Search, Detection, Navigation, Guidance, Aeronautical, & Nautical System & Instrument Manufacturing

3821 Laboratory Apparatus & Furniture
NAICS 339111 Laboratory Apparatus & Furniture Manufacturing

3822 Automatic Controls for Regulating Residential & Commercial Environments & Appliances
NAICS 334512 Automatic Environmental Control Manufacturing for Regulating Residential, Commercial, & Appliance Use
3823 Industrial Instruments for Measurement, Display, & Control of Process Variables & Related Products
NAICS 334513 Instruments & Related Product Manufacturing for Measuring Displaying, & Controlling Industrial Process Variables
3824 Totalizing Fluid Meters & Counting Devices
NAICS 334514 Totalizing Fluid Meter & Counting Device Manufacturing
3825 Instruments for Measuring & Testing of Electricity & Electrical Signals
NAICS 334416 Electronic Coil, Transformer, & Other Inductor Manufacturing
NAICS 334515 Instrument Manufacturing for Measuring & Testing Electricity & Electrical Signals
3826 Laboratory Analytical Instruments
NAICS 334516 Analytical Laboratory Instrument Manufacturing
3827 Optical Instruments & Lenses
NAICS 333314 Optical Instrument & Lens Manufacturing
3829 Measuring & Controlling Devices, nec
NAICS 339112 Surgical & Medical Instrument Manufacturing
NAICS 334519 Other Measuring & Controlling Device Manufacturing
3841 Surgical & Medical Instruments & Apparatus
NAICS 339112 Surgical & Medical Instrument Manufacturing
3842 Orthopedic, Prosthetic, & Surgical Appliances & Supplies
NAICS 339113 Surgical Appliance & Supplies Manufacturing
NAICS 334510 Electromedical & Electrotherapeutic Apparatus Manufacturing
3843 Dental Equipment & Supplies
NAICS 339114 Dental Equipment & Supplies Manufacturing
3844 X-ray Apparatus & Tubes & Related Irradiation Apparatus
NAICS 334517 Irradiation Apparatus Manufacturing
3845 Electromedical & Electrotherapeutic Apparatus
NAICS 334517 Irradiation Apparatus Manufacturing
NAICS 334510 Electromedical & Electrotherapeutic Apparatus Manufacturing
3851 Ophthalmic Goods
NAICS 339115 Ophthalmic Goods Manufacturing
3861 Photographic Equipment & Supplies
NAICS 333315 Photographic & Photocopying Equipment Manufacturing
NAICS 325992 Photographic Film, Paper, Plate & Chemical Manufacturing
3873 Watches, Clocks, Clockwork Operated Devices & Parts
NAICS 334518 Watch, Clock, & Part Manufacturing

MISCELLANEOUS MANUFACTURING INDUSTRIES

3911 Jewelry, Precious Metal
NAICS 339911 Jewelry Manufacturing
3914 Silverware, Plated Ware, & Stainless Steel Ware
NAICS 332211 Cutlery & Flatware Manufacturing
NAICS 339912 Silverware & Plated Ware Manufacturing
3915 Jewelers' Findings & Materials, & Lapidary Work
NAICS 339913 Jewelers' Material & Lapidary Work Manufacturing

3931 Musical Instruments
NAICS 339992 Musical Instrument Manufacturing
3942 Dolls & Stuffed Toys
NAICS 339931 Doll & Stuffed Toy Manufacturing
3944 Games, Toys, & Children's Vehicles, Except Dolls & Bicycles
NAICS 336991 Motorcycle, Bicycle & Parts Manufacturing
NAICS 339932 Game, Toy, & Children's Vehicle Manufacturing
3949 Sporting & Athletic Goods, nec
NAICS 33992 Sporting & Athletic Good Manufacturing
3951 Pens, Mechanical Pencils & Parts
NAICS 339941 Pen & Mechanical Pencil Manufacturing
3952 Lead Pencils, Crayons, & Artist's Materials
NAICS 337139 Other Wood Furniture Manufacturing
NAICS 337139 Other Wood Furniture Manufacturing
NAICS 325998 All Other Miscellaneous Chemical Manufacturing
NAICS 339942 Lead Pencil & Art Good Manufacturing
3953 Marking Devices
NAICS 339943 Marking Device Manufacturing
3955 Carbon Paper & Inked Ribbons
NAICS 339944 Carbon Paper & Inked Ribbon Manufacturing
3961 Costume Jewelry & Costume Novelties, Except Precious Metals
NAICS 339914 Costume Jewelry & Novelty Manufacturing
3965 Fasteners, Buttons, Needles, & Pins
NAICS 339993 Fastener, Button, Needle & Pin Manufacturing
3991 Brooms & Brushes
NAICS 339994 Broom, Brush & Mop Manufacturing
3993 Signs & Advertising Specialties
NAICS 33995 Sign Manufacturing
3995 Burial Caskets
NAICS 339995 Burial Casket Manufacturing
3996 Linoleum, Asphalted-felt-base, & Other Hard Surface Floor Coverings, nec
NAICS 326192 Resilient Floor Covering Manufacturing
3999 Manufacturing Industries, nec
NAICS 337148 Other Nonwood Furniture Manufacturing
NAICS 321999 All Other Miscellaneous Wood Product Manufacturing
NAICS 31611 Leather & Hide Tanning & Finishing
NAICS 335121 Residential Electric Lighting Fixture Manufacturing
NAICS 325998 All Other Miscellaneous Chemical Product Manufacturing
NAICS 332999 All Other Miscellaneous Fabricated Metal Product Manufacturing
NAICS 326199 All Other Plastics Product Manufacturing
NAICS 323112 Commercial Flexographic Printing
NAICS 323111 Commercial Gravure Printing
NAICS 323110 Commercial Lithographic Printing
NAICS 323113 Commercial Screen Printing
NAICS 323119 Other Commercial Printing
NAICS 332212 Hand & Edge Tool Manufacturing
NAICS 339999 All Other Miscellaneous Manufacturing

TRANSPORTATION, COMMUNICATIONS, ELECTRIC, GAS, & SANITARY SERVICES

4011 Railroads, Line-haul Operating
NAICS 482111 Line-haul Railroads
4013 Railroad Switching & Terminal Establishments
NAICS 482112 Short Line Railroads
NAICS 48821 Support Activities for Rail Transportation
4111 Local & Suburban Transit
NAICS 485111 Mixed Mode Transit Systems
NAICS 485112 Commuter Rail Systems
NAICS 485113 Bus & Motor Vehicle Transit Systems
NAICS 485119 Other Urban Transit Systems
NAICS 485999 All Other Transit & Ground Passenger
        Transportation
4119 Local Passenger Transportation, nec
NAICS 62191 Ambulance Service
NAICS 48541 School & Employee Bus Transportation
NAICS 48711 Scenic & Sightseeing Transportation , Land
NAICS 485991 Special Needs Transportation
NAICS 485999 All Other Transit & Ground Passenger
        Transportation
NAICS 48532 Limousine Service
4121 Taxicabs
NAICS 48531 Taxi Service
4131 Intercity & Rural Bus Transportation
NAICS 48521 Interurban & Rural Bus Transportation
4141 Local Bus Charter Service
NAICS 48551 Charter Bus Industry
4142 Bus Charter Service, Except Local
NAICS 48551 Charter Bus Industry
4151 School Buses
NAICS 48541 School & Employee Bus Transportation
4173 Terminal & Service Facilities for Motor Vehicle Passenger Transportation
NAICS 48849 Other Support Activities for Road
        Transportation
4212 Local Trucking Without Storage
NAICS 562111 Solid Waste Collection
NAICS 562112 Hazardous Waste Collection
NAICS 562119 Other Waste Collection
NAICS 48411 General Freight Trucking, Local
NAICS 48421 Used Household & Office Goods Moving
NAICS 48422 Specialized Freight Trucking, Local
4213 Trucking, Except Local
NAICS 484121 General Freight Trucking, Long-distance,
        Truckload
NAICS 484122 General Freight Trucking, Long-distance, less
        than Truckload
NAICS 48421 Used Household & Office Goods Moving
NAICS 48423 Specialized Freight Trucking, Long-distance
4214 Local Trucking with Storage
NAICS 48411 General Freight Trucking, Local
NAICS 48421 Used Household & Office Goods Moving
NAICS 48422 Specialized Freight Trucking, Local
4215 Couriers Services Except by Air
NAICS 49211 Couriers
NAICS 49221 Local Messengers & Local Delivery
4221 Farm Product Warehousing & Storage
NAICS 49313 Farm Product Storage Facilities
4222 Refrigerated Warehousing & Storage
NAICS 49312 Refrigerated Storage Facilities

4225 General Warehousing & Storage
NAICS 49311 General Warehousing & Storage Facilities
NAICS 53113 Lessors of Miniwarehouses & Self Storage
        Units
4226 Special Warehousing & Storage, nec
NAICS 49312 Refrigerated Warehousing & Storage Facilities
NAICS 49311 General Warehousing & Storage Facilities
NAICS 49319 Other Warehousing & Storage Facilities
4231 Terminal & Joint Terminal Maintenance Facilities for Motor Freight Transportation
NAICS 48849 Other Support Activities for Road
        Transportation
4311 United States Postal Service
NAICS 49111 Postal Service
4412 Deep Sea Foreign Transportation of Freight
NAICS 483111 Deep Sea Freight Transportation
4424 Deep Sea Domestic Transportation of Freight
NAICS 483113 Coastal & Great Lakes Freight Transportation
4432 Freight Transportation on the Great Lakes - St. Lawrence Seaway
NAICS 483113 Coastal & Great Lakes Freight Transportation
4449 Water Transportation of Freight, nec
NAICS 483211 Inland Water Freight Transportation
4481 Deep Sea Transportation of Passengers, Except by Ferry
NAICS 483112 Deep Sea Passenger Transportation
NAICS 483114 Coastal & Great Lakes Passenger
        Transportation
4482 Ferries
NAICS 483114 Coastal & Great Lakes Passenger
        Transportation
NAICS 483212 Inland Water Passenger Transportation
4489 Water Transportation of Passengers, nec
NAICS 483212 Inland Water Passenger Transportation
NAICS 48721 Scenic & Sightseeing Transportation, Water
4491 Marine Cargo Handling
NAICS 48831 Port & Harbor Operations
NAICS 48832 Marine Cargo Handling
4492 Towing & Tugboat Services
NAICS 483113 Coastal & Great Lakes Freight Transportation
NAICS 483211 Inland Water Freight Transportation
NAICS 48833 Navigational Services to Shipping
4493 Marinas
NAICS 71393 Marinas
4499 Water Transportation Services, nec
NAICS 532411 Commercial Air, Rail, & Water Transportation
        Equipment Rental & Leasing
NAICS 48831 Port & Harbor Operations
NAICS 48833 Navigational Services to Shipping
NAICS 48839 Other Support Activities for Water
        Transportation
4512 Air Transportation, Scheduled
NAICS 481111 Scheduled Passenger Air Transportation
NAICS 481112 Scheduled Freight Air Transportation
4513 Air Courier Services
NAICS 49211 Couriers
4522 Air Transportation, Nonscheduled
NAICS 62191 Ambulance Services
NAICS 481212 Nonscheduled Chartered Freight Air
        Transportation
NAICS 481211 Nonscheduled Chartered Passenger Air
        Transportation
NAICS 48122 Nonscheduled Speciality Air Transportation
NAICS 48799 Scenic & Sightseeing Transportation , Other

4581 Airports, Flying Fields, & Airport Terminal Services
NAICS 488111 Air Traffic Control
NAICS 488112 Airport Operations, Except Air Traffic Control
NAICS 56172 Janitorial Services
NAICS 48819 Other Support Activities for Air Transportation

4612 Crude Petroleum Pipelines
NAICS 48611 Pipeline Transportation of Crude Oil

4613 Refined Petroleum Pipelines
NAICS 48691 Pipeline Transportation of Refined Petroleum Products

4619 Pipelines, nec
NAICS 48699 All Other Pipeline Transportation

4724 Travel Agencies
NAICS 56151 Travel Agencies

4725 Tour Operators
NAICS 56152 Tour Operators

4729 Arrangement of Passenger Transportation, nec
NAICS 488999 All Other Support Activities for Transportation
NAICS 561599 All Other Travel Arrangement & Reservation Services

4731 Arrangement of Transportation of Freight & Cargo
NAICS 541618 Other Management Consulting Services
NAICS 48851 Freight Transportation Arrangement

4741 Rental of Railroad Cars
NAICS 532411 Commercial Air, Rail, & Water Transportation Equipment Rental & Leasing
NAICS 48821 Support Activities for Rail Transportation

4783 Packing & Crating
NAICS 488991 Packing & Crating

4785 Fixed Facilities & Inspection & Weighing Services for Motor Vehicle Transportation
NAICS 48839 Other Support Activities for Water Transportation
NAICS 48849 Other Support Activities for Road Transportation

4789 Transportation Services, nec
NAICS 488999 All Other Support Activities for Transportation
NAICS 48711 Scenic & Sightseeing Transportation, Land
NAICS 48821 Support Activities for Rail Transportation

4812 Radiotelephone Communications
NAICS 513321 Paging
NAICS 513322 Cellular & Other Wireless Telecommunications
NAICS 51333 Telecommunications Resellers

4813 Telephone Communications, Except Radiotelephone
NAICS 51331 Wired Telecommunications Carriers
NAICS 51333 Telecommunications Resellers

4822 Telegraph & Other Message Communications
NAICS 51331 Wired Telecommunications Carriers

4832 Radio Broadcasting Stations
NAICS 513111 Radio Networks
NAICS 513112 Radio Stations

4833 Television Broadcasting Stations
NAICS 51312 Television Broadcasting

4841 Cable & Other Pay Television Services
NAICS 51321 Cable Networks
NAICS 51322 Cable & Other Program Distribution

4899 Communications Services, nec
NAICS 513322 Cellular & Other Wireless Telecommunications
NAICS 51334 Satellite Telecommunications
NAICS 51339 Other Telecommunications

4911 Electric Services
NAICS 221111 Hydroelectric Power Generation
NAICS 221112 Fossil Fuel Electric Power Generation
NAICS 221113 Nuclear Electric Power Generation

NAICS 221119 Other Electric Power Generation
NAICS 221121 Electric Bulk Power Transmission & Control
NAICS 221122 Electric Power Distribution

4922 Natural Gas Transmission
NAICS 48621 Pipeline Transportation of Natural Gas

4923 Natural Gas Transmission & Distribution
NAICS 22121 Natural Gas Distribution
NAICS 48621 Pipeline Transportation of Natural Gas

4924 Natural Gas Distribution
NAICS 22121 Natural Gas Distribution

4925 Mixed, Manufactured, or Liquefied Petroleum Gas Production And/or Distribution
NAICS 22121 Natural Gas Distribution

4931 Electric & Other Services Combined
NAICS 221111 Hydroelectric Power Generation
NAICS 221112 Fossil Fuel Electric Power Generation
NAICS 221113 Nuclear Electric Power Generation
NAICS 221119 Other Electric Power Generation
NAICS 221121 Electric Bulk Power Transmission & Control
NAICS 221122 Electric Power Distribution
NAICS 22121 Natural Gas Distribution

4932 Gas & Other Services Combined
NAICS 22121 Natural Gas Distribution

4939 Combination Utilities, nec
NAICS 221111 Hydroelectric Power Generation
NAICS 221112 Fossil Fuel Electric Power Generation
NAICS 221113 Nuclear Electric Power Generation
NAICS 221119 Other Electric Power Generation
NAICS 221121 Electric Bulk Power Transmission & Control
NAICS 221122 Electric Power Distribution
NAICS 22121 Natural Gas Distribution

4941 Water Supply
NAICS 22131 Water Supply & Irrigation Systems

4952 Sewerage Systems
NAICS 22132 Sewage Treatment Facilities

4953 Refuse Systems
NAICS 562111 Solid Waste Collection
NAICS 562112 Hazardous Waste Collection
NAICS 56292 Materials Recovery Facilities
NAICS 562119 Other Waste Collection
NAICS 562211 Hazardous Waste Treatment & Disposal
NAICS 562212 Solid Waste Landfills
NAICS 562213 Solid Waste Combustors & Incinerators
NAICS 562219 Other Nonhazardous Waste Treatment & Disposal

4959 Sanitary Services, nec
NAICS 488112 Airport Operations, Except Air Traffic Control
NAICS 56291 Remediation Services
NAICS 56171 Exterminating & Pest Control Services
NAICS 562998 All Other Miscellaneous Waste Management Services

4961 Steam & Air-conditioning Supply
NAICS 22133 Steam & Air-conditioning Supply

4971 Irrigation Systems
NAICS 22131 Water Supply & Irrigation Systems

WHOLESALE TRADE

5012 Automobiles & Other Motor Vehicles
NAICS 42111 Automobile & Other Motor Vehicle Wholesalers

5013 Motor Vehicle Supplies & New Parts
NAICS 44131 Automotive Parts & Accessories Stores - Retail
NAICS 42112 Motor Vehicle Supplies & New Part Wholesalers

5014 Tires & Tubes
NAICS 44132 Tire Dealers - Retail
NAICS 42113 Tire & Tube Wholesalers

5015 Motor Vehicle Parts, Used
NAICS 42114 Motor Vehicle Part Wholesalers

5021 Furniture
NAICS 44211 Furniture Stores
NAICS 42121 Furniture Wholesalers

5023 Home Furnishings
NAICS 44221 Floor Covering Stores
NAICS 42122 Home Furnishing Wholesalers

5031 Lumber, Plywood, Millwork, & Wood Panels
NAICS 44419 Other Building Material Dealers
NAICS 42131 Lumber, Plywood, Millwork, & Wood Panel Wholesalers

5032 Brick, Stone & Related Construction Materials
NAICS 44419 Other Building Material Dealers
NAICS 42132 Brick, Stone & Related Construction Material Wholesalers

5033 Roofing, Siding, & Insulation Materials
NAICS 42133 Roofing, Siding, & Insulation Material Wholesalers

5039 Construction Materials, nec
NAICS 44419 Other Building Material Dealers
NAICS 42139 Other Construction Material Wholesalers

5043 Photographic Equipment & Supplies
NAICS 42141 Photographic Equipment & Supplies Wholesalers

5044 Office Equipment
NAICS 42142 Office Equipment Wholesalers

5045 Computers & Computer Peripheral Equipment & Software
NAICS 42143 Computer & Computer Peripheral Equipment & Software Wholesalers
NAICS 44312 Computer & Software Stores - Retail

5046 Commercial Equipment, nec
NAICS 42144 Other Commercial Equipment Wholesalers

5047 Medical, Dental, & Hospital Equipment & Supplies
NAICS 42145 Medical, Dental & Hospital Equipment & Supplies Wholesalers
NAICS 446199 All Other Health & Personal Care Stores - Retail

5048 Ophthalmic Goods
NAICS 42146 Ophthalmic Goods Wholesalers

5049 Professional Equipment & Supplies, nec
NAICS 42149 Other Professional Equipment & Supplies Wholesalers
NAICS 45321 Office Supplies & Stationery Stores - Retail

5051 Metals Service Centers & Offices
NAICS 42151 Metals Service Centers & Offices

5052 Coal & Other Minerals & Ores
NAICS 42152 Coal & Other Mineral & Ore Wholesalers

5063 Electrical Apparatus & Equipment Wiring Supplies, & Construction Materials
NAICS 44419 Other Building Material Dealers
NAICS 42161 Electrical Apparatus & Equipment, Wiring Supplies & Construction Material Wholesalers

5064 Electrical Appliances, Television & Radio Sets
NAICS 42162 Electrical Appliance, Television & Radio Set Wholesalers

5065 Electronic Parts & Equipment, Not Elsewhere Classified
NAICS 42169 Other Electronic Parts & Equipment Wholesalers

5072 Hardware
NAICS 42171 Hardware Wholesalers

5074 Plumbing & Heating Equipment & Supplies
NAICS 44419 Other Building Material Dealers
NAICS 42172 Plumbing & Heating Equipment & Supplies Wholesalers

5075 Warm Air Heating & Air-conditioning Equipment & Supplies
NAICS 42173 Warm Air Heating & Air-conditioning Equipment & Supplies Wholesalers

5078 Refrigeration Equipment & Supplies
NAICS 42174 Refrigeration Equipment & Supplies Wholesalers

5082 Construction & Mining Machinery & Equipment
NAICS 42181 Construction & Mining Machinery & Equipment Wholesalers

5083 Farm & Garden Machinery & Equipment
NAICS 42182 Farm & Garden Machinery & Equipment Wholesalers
NAICS 44421 Outdoor Power Equipment Stores - Retail

5084 Industrial Machinery & Equipment
NAICS 42183 Industrial Machinery & Equipment Wholesalers

5085 Industrial Supplies
NAICS 42183 Industrial Machinery & Equipment Wholesalers
NAICS 42184 Industrial Supplies Wholesalers
NAICS 81131 Commercial & Industrial Machinery & Equipment Repair & Maintenance

5087 Service Establishment Equipment & Supplies
NAICS 42185 Service Establishment Equipment & Supplies Wholesalers
NAICS 44612 Cosmetics, Beauty Supplies, & Perfume Stores

5088 Transportation Equipment & Supplies, Except Motor Vehicles
NAICS 42186 Transportation Equipment & Supplies Wholesalers

5091 Sporting & Recreational Goods & Supplies
NAICS 42191 Sporting & Recreational Goods & Supplies Wholesalers

5092 Toys & Hobby Goods & Supplies
NAICS 42192 Toy & Hobby Goods & Supplies Wholesalers

5093 Scrap & Waste Materials
NAICS 42193 Recyclable Material Wholesalers

5094 Jewelry, Watches, Precious Stones, & Precious Metals
NAICS 42194 Jewelry, Watch , Precious Stone, & Precious Metal Wholesalers

5099 Durable Goods, nec
NAICS 42199 Other Miscellaneous Durable Goods Wholesalers

5111 Printing & Writing Paper
NAICS 42211 Printing & Writing Paper Wholesalers

5112 Stationery & Office Supplies
NAICS 45321 Office Supplies & Stationery Stores
NAICS 42212 Stationery & Office Supplies Wholesalers

5113 Industrial & Personal Service Paper
NAICS 42213 Industrial & Personal Service Paper Wholesalers

5122 Drugs, Drug Proprietaries, & Druggists' Sundries
NAICS 42221 Drugs, Drug Proprietaries, & Druggists' Sundries Wholesalers

5131 Piece Goods, Notions, & Other Dry Goods
NAICS 313311 Broadwoven Fabric Finishing Mills
NAICS 313312 Textile & Fabric Finishing Mills
NAICS 42231 Piece Goods, Notions, & Other Dry Goods
   Wholesalers
5136 Men's & Boys' Clothing & Furnishings
NAICS 42232 Men's & Boys' Clothing & Furnishings
   Wholesalers
5137 Women's Children's & Infants' Clothing & Accessories
NAICS 42233 Women's, Children's, & Infants' Clothing &
   Accessories Wholesalers
5139 Footwear
NAICS 42234 Footwear Wholesalers
5141 Groceries, General Line
NAICS 42241 General Line Grocery Wholesalers
5142 Packaged Frozen Foods
NAICS 42242 Packaged Frozen Food Wholesalers
5143 Dairy Products, Except Dried or Canned
NAICS 42243 Dairy Products Wholesalers
5144 Poultry & Poultry Products
NAICS 42244 Poultry & Poultry Product Wholesalers
5145 Confectionery
NAICS 42245 Confectionery Wholesalers
5146 Fish & Seafoods
NAICS 42246 Fish & Seafood Wholesalers
5147 Meats & Meat Products
NAICS 311612 Meat Processed from Carcasses
NAICS 42247 Meat & Meat Product Wholesalers
5148 Fresh Fruits & Vegetables
NAICS 42248 Fresh Fruit & Vegetable Wholesalers
5149 Groceries & Related Products, nec
NAICS 42249 Other Grocery & Related Product Wholesalers
5153 Grain & Field Beans
NAICS 42251 Grain & Field Bean Wholesalers
5154 Livestock
NAICS 42252 Livestock Wholesalers
5159 Farm-product Raw Materials, nec
NAICS 42259 Other Farm Product Raw Material Wholesalers
5162 Plastics Materials & Basic Forms & Shapes
NAICS 42261 Plastics Materials & Basic Forms & Shapes
   Wholesalers
5169 Chemicals & Allied Products, nec
NAICS 42269 Other Chemical & Allied Products Wholesalers
5171 Petroleum Bulk Stations & Terminals
NAICS 454311 Heating Oil Dealers
NAICS 454312 Liquefied Petroleum Gas Dealers
NAICS 42271 Petroleum Bulk Stations & Terminals
5172 Petroleum & Petroleum Products Wholesalers, Except Bulk Stations & Terminals
NAICS 42272 Petroleum & Petroleum Products Wholesalers
5181 Beer & Ale
NAICS 42281 Beer & Ale Wholesalers
5182 Wine & Distilled Alcoholic Beverages
NAICS 42282 Wine & Distilled Alcoholic Beverage
   Wholesalers
5191 Farm Supplies
NAICS 44422 Nursery & Garden Centers - Retail
NAICS 42291 Farm Supplies Wholesalers
5192 Books, Periodicals, & Newspapers
NAICS 42292 Book, Periodical & Newspaper Wholesalers
5193 Flowers, Nursery Stock, & Florists' Supplies
NAICS 42293 Flower, Nursery Stock & Florists' Supplies
   Wholesalers
NAICS 44422 Nursery & Garden Centers - Retail

5194 Tobacco & Tobacco Products
NAICS 42294 Tobacco & Tobacco Product Wholesalers
5198 Paint, Varnishes, & Supplies
NAICS 42295 Paint, Varnish & Supplies Wholesalers
NAICS 44412 Paint & Wallpaper Stores
5199 Nondurable Goods, nec
NAICS 54189 Other Services Related to Advertising
NAICS 42299 Other Miscellaneous Nondurable Goods
   Wholesalers

RETAIL TRADE

5211 Lumber & Other Building Materials Dealers
NAICS 44411 Home Centers
NAICS 42131 Lumber, Plywood, Millwork & Wood Panel
   Wholesalers
NAICS 44419 Other Building Material Dealers
5231 Paint, Glass, & Wallpaper Stores
NAICS 42295 Paint, Varnish & Supplies Wholesalers
NAICS 44419 Other Building Material Dealers
NAICS 44412 Paint & Wallpaper Stores
5251 Hardware Stores
NAICS 44413 Hardware Stores
5261 Retail Nurseries, Lawn & Garden Supply Stores
NAICS 44422 Nursery & Garden Centers
NAICS 453998 All Other Miscellaneous Store Retailers
NAICS 44421 Outdoor Power Equipment Stores
5271 Mobile Home Dealers
NAICS 45393 Manufactured Home Dealers
5311 Department Stores
NAICS 45211 Department Stores
5331 Variety Stores
NAICS 45299 All Other General Merchandise Stores
5399 Miscellaneous General Merchandise Stores
NAICS 45291 Warehouse Clubs & Superstores
NAICS 45299 All Other General Merchandise Stores
5411 Grocery Stores
NAICS 44711 Gasoline Stations with Convenience Stores
NAICS 44511 Supermarkets & Other Grocery Stores
NAICS 45291 Warehouse Clubs & Superstores
NAICS 44512 Convenience Stores
5421 Meat & Fish Markets, Including Freezer Provisioners
NAICS 45439 Other Direct Selling Establishments
NAICS 44521 Meat Markets
NAICS 44522 Fish & Seafood Markets
5431 Fruit & Vegetable Markets
NAICS 44523 Fruit & Vegetable Markets
5441 Candy, Nut, & Confectionery Stores
NAICS 445292 Confectionery & Nut Stores
5451 Dairy Products Stores
NAICS 445299 All Other Specialty Food Stores
5461 Retail Bakeries
NAICS 722213 Snack & Nonalcoholic Beverage Bars
NAICS 311811 Retail Bakeries
NAICS 445291 Baked Goods Stores
5499 Miscellaneous Food Stores
NAICS 44521 Meat Markets
NAICS 722211 Limited-service Restaurants
NAICS 446191 Food Supplement Stores
NAICS 445299 All Other Specialty Food Stores
5511 Motor Vehicle Dealers
NAICS 44111 New Car Dealers

5521 Motor Vehicle Dealers
NAICS 44112   Used Car Dealers
5531 Auto & Home Supply Stores
NAICS 44132   Tire Dealers
NAICS 44131   Automotive Parts & Accessories Stores
5541 Gasoline Service Stations
NAICS 44711   Gasoline Stations with Convenience Store
NAICS 44719   Other Gasoline Stations
5551 Boat Dealers
NAICS 441222 Boat Dealers
5561 Recreational Vehicle Dealers
NAICS 44121   Recreational Vehicle Dealers
5571 Motorcycle Dealers
NAICS 441221 Motorcycle Dealers
5599 Automotive Dealers, nec
NAICS 441229 All Other Motor Vehicle Dealers
5611 Men's & Boys' Clothing & Accessory Stores
NAICS 44811   Men's Clothing Stores
NAICS 44815   Clothing Accessories Stores
5621 Women's Clothing Stores
NAICS 44812   Women's Clothing Stores
5632 Women's Accessory & Specialty Stores
NAICS 44819   Other Clothing Stores
NAICS 44815   Clothing Accessories Stores
5641 Children's & Infants' Wear Stores
NAICS 44813   Children's & Infants' Clothing Stores
5651 Family Clothing Stores
NAICS 44814   Family Clothing Stores
5661 Shoe Stores
NAICS 44821   Shoe Stores
5699 Miscellaneous Apparel & Accessory Stores
NAICS 315   Included in Apparel Manufacturing Subsector
                   Based on Type of Garment Produced
NAICS 44819   Other Clothing Stores
NAICS 44815   Clothing Accessories Stores
5712 Furniture Stores
NAICS 337133 Wood Household Furniture, Except
                   Upholstered, Manufacturing
NAICS 337131 Wood Kitchen Cabinet & Counter Top
                   Manufacturing
NAICS 337132 Upholstered Household Furniture
                   Manufacturing
NAICS 44211   Furniture Stores
5713 Floor Covering Stores
NAICS 44221   Floor Covering Stores
5714 Drapery, Curtain, & Upholstery Stores
NAICS 442291 Window Treatment Stores
NAICS 45113   Sewing, Needlework & Piece Goods Stores
NAICS 314121 Curtain & Drapery Mills
5719 Miscellaneous Homefurnishings Stores
NAICS 442291 Window Treatment Stores
NAICS 442299 All Other Home Furnishings Stores
5722 Household Appliance Stores
NAICS 443111 Household Appliance Stores
5731 Radio, Television, & Consumer Electronics Stores
NAICS 443112 Radio, Television, & Other Electronics Stores
NAICS 44131   Automotive Parts & Accessories Stores
5734 Computer & Computer Software Stores
NAICS 44312   Computer & Software Stores
5735 Record & Prerecorded Tape Stores
NAICS 45122   Prerecorded Tape, Compact Disc & Record
                   Stores

5736 Musical Instrument Stores
NAICS 45114   Musical Instrument & Supplies Stores
5812 Eating & Drinking Places
NAICS 72211   Full-service Restaurants
NAICS 722211 Limited-service Restaurants
NAICS 722212 Cafeterias
NAICS 722213 Snack & Nonalcoholic Beverage Bars
NAICS 72231   Foodservice Contractors
NAICS 72232   Caterers
NAICS 71111   Theater Companies & Dinner Theaters
5813 Drinking Places
NAICS 72241   Drinking Places
5912 Drug Stores & Proprietary Stores
NAICS 44611   Pharmacies & Drug Stores
5921 Liquor Stores
NAICS 44531   Beer, Wine & Liquor Stores
5932 Used Merchandise Stores
NAICS 522298 All Other Non-depository Credit
                   Intermediation
NAICS 45331   Used Merchandise Stores
5941 Sporting Goods Stores & Bicycle Shops
NAICS 45111   Sporting Goods Stores
5942 Book Stores
NAICS 451211 Book Stores
5943 Stationery Stores
NAICS 45321   Office Supplies & Stationery Stores
5944 Jewelry Stores
NAICS 44831   Jewelry Stores
5945 Hobby, Toy, & Game Shops
NAICS 45112   Hobby, Toy & Game Stores
5946 Camera & Photographic Supply Stores
NAICS 44313   Camera & Photographic Supplies Stores
5947 Gift, Novelty, & Souvenir Shops
NAICS 45322   Gift, Novelty & Souvenir Stores
5948 Luggage & Leather Goods Stores
NAICS 44832   Luggage & Leather Goods Stores
5949 Sewing, Needlework, & Piece Goods Stores
NAICS 45113   Sewing, Needlework & Piece Goods Stores
5961 Catalog & Mail-order Houses
NAICS 45411   Electronic Shopping & Mail-order Houses
5962 Automatic Merchandising Machine Operator
NAICS 45421   Vending Machine Operators
5963 Direct Selling Establishments
NAICS 72233   Mobile Caterers
NAICS 45439   Other Direct Selling Establishments
5983 Fuel Oil Dealers
NAICS 454311 Heating Oil Dealers
5984 Liquefied Petroleum Gas Dealers
NAICS 454312 Liquefied Petroleum Gas Dealers
5989 Fuel Dealers, nec
NAICS 454319 Other Fuel Dealers
5992 Florists
NAICS 45311   Florists
5993 Tobacco Stores & Stands
NAICS 453991 Tobacco Stores
5994 News Dealers & Newsstands
NAICS 451212 News Dealers & Newsstands
5995 Optical Goods Stores
NAICS 339117 Eyeglass & Contact Lens Manufacturing
NAICS 44613   Optical Goods Stores
5999 Miscellaneous Retail Stores, nec
NAICS 44612   Cosmetics, Beauty Supplies & Perfume Stores
NAICS 446199 All Other Health & Personal Care Stores
NAICS 45391   Pet & Pet Supplies Stores

NAICS 45392   Art Dealers
NAICS 443111 Household Appliance Stores
NAICS 443112 Radio, Television & Other Electronics Stores
NAICS 44831   Jewelry Stores
NAICS 453999 All Other Miscellaneous Store Retailers

FINANCE, INSURANCE, & REAL ESTATE

6011 Federal Reserve Banks
NAICS 52111   Monetary Authorities-central Banks
6019 Central Reserve Depository Institutions, nec
NAICS 52232   Financial Transactions Processing, Reserve, & Clearing House Activities
6021 National Commercial Banks
NAICS 52211   Commercial Banking
NAICS 52221   Credit Card Issuing
NAICS 523991 Trust, Fiduciary & Custody Activities
6022 State Commercial Banks
NAICS 52211   Commercial Banking
NAICS 52221   Credit Card Issuing
NAICS 52219   Other Depository Intermediation
NAICS 523991 Trust, Fiduciary & Custody Activities
6029 Commercial Banks, nec
NAICS 52211   Commercial Banking
6035 Savings Institutions, Federally Chartered
NAICS 52212   Savings Institutions
6036 Savings Institutions, Not Federally Chartered
NAICS 52212   Savings Institutions
6061 Credit Unions, Federally Chartered
NAICS 52213   Credit Unions
6062 Credit Unions, Not Federally Chartered
NAICS 52213   Credit Unions
6081 Branches & Agencies of Foreign Banks
NAICS 522293 International Trade Financing
NAICS 52211   Commercial Banking
NAICS 522298 All Other Non-depository Credit Intermediation
6082 Foreign Trade & International Banking Institutions
NAICS 522293 International Trade Financing
6091 Nondeposit Trust Facilities
NAICS 523991 Trust, Fiduciary, & Custody Activities
6099 Functions Related to Deposit Banking, nec
NAICS 52232   Financial Transactions Processing, Reserve, & Clearing House Activities
NAICS 52313   Commodity Contracts Dealing
NAICS 523991 Trust, Fiduciary, & Custody Activities
NAICS 523999 Miscellaneous Financial Investment Activities
NAICS 52239   Other Activities Related to Credit Intermediation
6111 Federal & Federally Sponsored Credit Agencies
NAICS 522293 International Trade Financing
NAICS 522294 Secondary Market Financing
NAICS 522298 All Other Non-depository Credit Intermediation
6141 Personal Credit Institutions
NAICS 52221   Credit Card Issuing
NAICS 52222   Sales Financing
NAICS 522291 Consumer Lending
6153 Short-term Business Credit Institutions, Except Agricultural
NAICS 52222   Sales Financing
NAICS 52232   Financial Transactions Processing, Reserve, & Clearing House Activities

NAICS 522298 All Other Non-depository Credit Intermediation
6159 Miscellaneous Business Credit Institutions
NAICS 52222   Sales Financing
NAICS 532   Included in Rental & Leasing Services Subsector by Type of Equipment & Method of Operation
NAICS 522293 International Trade Financing
NAICS 522298 All Other Non-depository Credit Intermediation
6162 Mortgage Bankers & Loan Correspondents
NAICS 522292 Real Estate Credit
NAICS 52239   Other Activities Related to Credit Intermediation
6163 Loan Brokers
NAICS 52231   Mortgage & Other Loan Brokers
6211 Security Brokers, Dealers, & Flotation Companies
NAICS 52311   Investment Banking & Securities Dealing
NAICS 52312   Securities Brokerage
NAICS 52391   Miscellaneous Intermediation
NAICS 523999 Miscellaneous Financial Investment Activities
6221 Commodity Contracts Brokers & Dealers
NAICS 52313   Commodity Contracts Dealing
NAICS 52314   Commodity Brokerage
6231 Security & Commodity Exchanges
NAICS 52321   Securities & Commodity Exchanges
6282 Investment Advice
NAICS 52392   Portfolio Management
NAICS 52393   Investment Advice
6289 Services Allied with the Exchange of Securities or Commodities, nec
NAICS 523991 Trust, Fiduciary, & Custody Activities
NAICS 523999 Miscellaneous Financial Investment Activities
6311 Life Insurance
NAICS 524113 Direct Life Insurance Carriers
NAICS 52413   Reinsurance Carriers
6321 Accident & Health Insurance
NAICS 524114 Direct Health & Medical Insurance Carriers
NAICS 52519   Other Insurance Funds
NAICS 52413   Reinsurance Carriers
6324 Hospital & Medical Service Plans
NAICS 524114 Direct Health & Medical Insurance Carriers
NAICS 52519   Other Insurance Funds
NAICS 52413   Reinsurance Carriers
6331 Fire, Marine, & Casualty Insurance
NAICS 524126 Direct Property & Casualty Insurance Carriers
NAICS 52519   Other Insurance Funds
NAICS 52413   Reinsurance Carriers
6351 Surety Insurance
NAICS 524126 Direct Property & Casualty Insurance Carriers
NAICS 52413   Reinsurance Carriers
6361 Title Insurance
NAICS 524127 Direct Title Insurance Carriers
NAICS 52413   Reinsurance Carriers
6371 Pension, Health, & Welfare Funds
NAICS 52392   Portfolio Management
NAICS 524292 Third Party Administration for Insurance & Pension Funds
NAICS 52511   Pension Funds
NAICS 52512   Health & Welfare Funds
6399 Insurance Carriers, nec
NAICS 524128 Other Direct Insurance Carriers

6411 Insurance Agents, Brokers, & Service
NAICS 52421   Insurance Agencies & Brokerages
NAICS 524291 Claims Adjusters
NAICS 524292 Third Party Administrators for Insurance &
  Pension Funds
NAICS 524298 All Other Insurance Related Activities
6512 Operators of Nonresidential Buildings
NAICS 71131   Promoters of Performing Arts, Sports & Similar
  Events with Facilities
NAICS 53112   Lessors of Nonresidential Buildings
6513 Operators of Apartment Buildings
NAICS 53111   Lessors of Residential Buildings & Dwellings
6514 Operators of Dwellings Other than Apartment Buildings
NAICS 53111   Lessors of Residential Buildings & Dwellings
6515 Operators of Residential Mobile Home Sites
NAICS 53119   Lessors of Other Real Estate Property
6517 Lessors of Railroad Property
NAICS 53119   Lessors of Other Real Estate Property
6519 Lessors of Real Property, nec
NAICS 53119   Lessors of Other Real Estate Property
6531 Real Estate Agents & Managers
NAICS 53121   Offices of Real Estate Agents & Brokers
NAICS 81399   Other Similar Organizations
NAICS 531311 Residential Property Managers
NAICS 531312 Nonresidential Property Managers
NAICS 53132   Offices of Real Estate Appraisers
NAICS 81222   Cemeteries & Crematories
NAICS 531399 All Other Activities Related to Real Estate
6541 Title Abstract Offices
NAICS 541191 Title Abstract & Settlement Offices
6552 Land Subdividers & Developers, Except Cemeteries
NAICS 23311   Land Subdivision & Land Development
6553 Cemetery Subdividers & Developers
NAICS 81222   Cemeteries & Crematories
6712 Offices of Bank Holding Companies
NAICS 551111 Offices of Bank Holding Companies
6719 Offices of Holding Companies, nec
NAICS 551112 Offices of Other Holding Companies
6722 Management Investment Offices, Open-end
NAICS 52591   Open-end Investment Funds
**6726 Unit Investment Trusts, Face-amount Certificate Offices, &
  Closed-end Management Investment Offices**
NAICS 52599   Other Financial Vehicles
6732 Education, Religious, & Charitable Trusts
NAICS 813211 Grantmaking Foundations
6733 Trusts, Except Educational, Religious, & Charitable
NAICS 52392   Portfolio Management
NAICS 523991 Trust, Fiduciary, & Custody Services
NAICS 52519   Other Insurance Funds
NAICS 52592   Trusts, Estates, & Agency Accounts
6792 Oil Royalty Traders
NAICS 523999 Miscellaneous Financial Investment Activities
NAICS 53311   Owners & Lessors of Other Non-financial
  Assets
6794 Patent Owners & Lessors
NAICS 53311   Owners & Lessors of Other Non-financial
  Assets
6798 Real Estate Investment Trusts
NAICS 52593   Real Estate Investment Trusts
6799 Investors, nec
NAICS 52391   Miscellaneous Intermediation
NAICS 52392   Portfolio Management
NAICS 52313   Commodity Contracts Dealing
NAICS 523999 Miscellaneous Financial Investment Activities

SERVICE INDUSTRIES

7011 Hotels & Motels
NAICS 72111   Hotels & Motels
NAICS 72112   Casino Hotels
NAICS 721191 Bed & Breakfast Inns
NAICS 721199 All Other Traveler Accommodation
7021 Rooming & Boarding Houses
NAICS 72131   Rooming & Boarding Houses
7032 Sporting & Recreational Camps
NAICS 721214 Recreational & Vacation Camps
7033 Recreational Vehicle Parks & Campsites
NAICS 721211 Rv & Campgrounds
**7041 Organization Hotels & Lodging Houses, on Membership
  Basis**
NAICS 72111   Hotels & Motels
NAICS 72131   Rooming & Boarding Houses
7211 Power Laundries, Family & Commercial
NAICS 812321 Laundries, Family & Commercial
7212 Garment Pressing, & Agents for Laundries
NAICS 812391 Garment Pressing & Agents for Laundries
7213 Linen Supply
NAICS 812331 Linen Supply
7215 Coin-operated Laundry & Drycleaning
NAICS 81231   Coin-operated Laundries & Drycleaners
7216 Drycleaning Plants, Except Rug Cleaning
NAICS 812322 Drycleaning Plants
7217 Carpet & Upholstery Cleaning
NAICS 56174   Carpet & Upholstery Cleaning Services
7218 Industrial Launderers
NAICS 812332 Industrial Launderers
7219 Laundry & Garment Services, nec
NAICS 812331 Linen Supply
NAICS 81149   Other Personal & Household Goods Repair &
  Maintenance
NAICS 812399 All Other Laundry Services
7221 Photographic Studios, Portrait
NAICS 541921 Photographic Studios, Portrait
7231 Beauty Shops
NAICS 812112 Beauty Salons
NAICS 812113 Nail Salons
NAICS 611511 Cosmetology & Barber Schools
7241 Barber Shops
NAICS 812111 Barber Shops
NAICS 611511 Cosmetology & Barber Schools
7251 Shoe Repair Shops & Shoeshine Parlors
NAICS 81143   Footwear & Leather Goods Repair
7261 Funeral Services & Crematories
NAICS 81221   Funeral Homes
NAICS 81222   Cemeteries & Crematories
7291 Tax Return Preparation Services
NAICS 541213 Tax Preparation Services
7299 Miscellaneous Personal Services, nec
NAICS 62441   Child Day Care Services
NAICS 812191 Diet & Weight Reducing Centers
NAICS 53222   Formal Wear & Costume Rental
NAICS 812199 Other Personal Care Services
NAICS 81299   All Other Personal Services
7311 Advertising Agencies
NAICS 54181   Advertising Agencies
7312 Outdoor Advertising Services
NAICS 54185   Display Advertising

7313 Radio, Television, & Publishers' Advertising Representatives
NAICS 54184   Media Representatives
7319 Advertising, nec
NAICS 481219 Other Nonscheduled Air Transportation
NAICS 54183   Media Buying Agencies
NAICS 54185   Display Advertising
NAICS 54187   Advertising Material Distribution Services
NAICS 54189   Other Services Related to Advertising
7322 Adjustment & Collection Services
NAICS 56144   Collection Agencies
NAICS 561491 Repossession Services
7323 Credit Reporting Services
NAICS 56145   Credit Bureaus
7331 Direct Mail Advertising Services
NAICS 54186   Direct Mail Advertising
7334 Photocopying & Duplicating Services
NAICS 561431 Photocopying & Duplicating Services
7335 Commercial Photography
NAICS 48122   Nonscheduled Speciality Air Transportation
NAICS 541922 Commercial Photography
7336 Commercial Art & Graphic Design
NAICS 54143   Commercial Art & Graphic Design Services
7338 Secretarial & Court Reporting Services
NAICS 56141   Document Preparation Services
NAICS 561492 Court Reporting & Stenotype Services
7342 Disinfecting & Pest Control Services
NAICS 56172   Janitorial Services
NAICS 56171   Exterminating & Pest Control Services
7349 Building Cleaning & Maintenance Services, nec
NAICS 56172   Janitorial Services
7352 Medical Equipment Rental & Leasing
NAICS 532291 Home Health Equipment Rental
NAICS 53249   Other Commercial & Industrial Machinery & Equipment Rental & Leasing
7353 Heavy Construction Equipment Rental & Leasing
NAICS 23499   All Other Heavy Construction
NAICS 532412 Construction, Mining & Forestry Machinery & Equipment Rental & Leasing
7359 Equipment Rental & Leasing, nec
NAICS 53221   Consumer Electronics & Appliances Rental
NAICS 53231   General Rental Centers
NAICS 532299 All Other Consumer Goods Rental
NAICS 532412 Construction, Mining & Forestry Machinery & Equipment Rental & Leasing
NAICS 532411 Commercial Air, Rail, & Water Transportation Equipment Rental & Leasing
NAICS 562991 Septic Tank & Related Services
NAICS 53242   Office Machinery & Equipment Rental & Leasing
NAICS 53249   Other Commercial & Industrial Machinery & Equipment Rental & Leasing
7361 Employment Agencies
NAICS 541612 Human Resources & Executive Search Consulting Services
NAICS 56131   Employment Placement Agencies
7363 Help Supply Services
NAICS 56132   Temporary Help Services
NAICS 56133   Employee Leasing Services
7371 Computer Programming Services
NAICS 541511 Custom Computer Programming Services
7372 Prepackaged Software
NAICS 51121   Software Publishers
NAICS 334611 Software Reproducing

7373 Computer Integrated Systems Design
NAICS 541512 Computer Systems Design Services
7374 Computer Processing & Data Preparation & Processing Services
NAICS 51421   Data Processing Services
7375 Information Retrieval Services
NAICS 514191 On-line Information Services
7376 Computer Facilities Management Services
NAICS 541513 Computer Facilities Management Services
7377 Computer Rental & Leasing
NAICS 53242   Office Machinery & Equipment Rental & Leasing
7378 Computer Maintenance & Repair
NAICS 44312   Computer & Software Stores
NAICS 811212 Computer & Office Machine Repair & Maintenance
7379 Computer Related Services, nec
NAICS 541512 Computer Systems Design Services
NAICS 541519 Other Computer Related Services
7381 Detective, Guard, & Armored Car Services
NAICS 561611 Investigation Services
NAICS 561612 Security Guards & Patrol Services
NAICS 561613 Armored Car Services
7382 Security Systems Services
NAICS 561621 Security Systems Services
7383 News Syndicates
NAICS 51411   New Syndicates
7384 Photofinishing Laboratories
NAICS 812921 Photo Finishing Laboratories
NAICS 812922 One-hour Photo Finishing
7389 Business Services, nec
NAICS 51224   Sound Recording Studios
NAICS 51229   Other Sound Recording Industries
NAICS 541199 All Other Legal Services
NAICS 81299   All Other Personal Services
NAICS 54137   Surveying & Mapping Services
NAICS 54141   Interior Design Services
NAICS 54142   Industrial Design Services
NAICS 54134   Drafting Services
NAICS 54149   Other Specialized Design Services
NAICS 54189   Other Services Related to Advertising
NAICS 54193   Translation & Interpretation Services
NAICS 54135   Building Inspection Services
NAICS 54199   All Other Professional, Scientific & Technical Services
NAICS 71141   Agents & Managers for Artists, Athletes, Entertainers & Other Public Figures
NAICS 561422 Telemarketing Bureaus
NAICS 561432 Private Mail Centers
NAICS 561439 Other Business Service Centers
NAICS 561491 Repossession Services
NAICS 56191   Packaging & Labeling Services
NAICS 56179   Other Services to Buildings & Dwellings
NAICS 561599 All Other Travel Arrangement & Reservation Services
NAICS 56192   Convention & Trade Show Organizers
NAICS 561591 Convention & Visitors Bureaus
NAICS 52232   Financial Transactions, Processing, Reserve & Clearing House Activities
NAICS 561499 All Other Business Support Services
NAICS 56199   All Other Support Services
7513 Truck Rental & Leasing, Without Drivers
NAICS 53212   Truck, Utility Trailer & Rv Rental & Leasing

7514 Passenger Car Rental
NAICS 532111 Passenger Cars Rental
7515 Passenger Car Leasing
NAICS 532112 Passenger Cars Leasing
7519 Utility Trailer & Recreational Vehicle Rental
NAICS 53212   Truck, Utility Trailer & Rv Rental & Leasing
7521 Automobile Parking
NAICS 81293   Parking Lots & Garages
7532 Top, Body, & Upholstery Repair Shops & Paint Shops
NAICS 811121 Automotive Body, Paint, & Upholstery Repair & Maintenance
7533 Automotive Exhaust System Repair Shops
NAICS 811112 Automotive Exhaust System Repair
7534 Tire Retreading & Repair Shops
NAICS 326212 Tire Retreading
NAICS 811198 All Other Automotive Repair & Maintenance
7536 Automotive Glass Replacement Shops
NAICS 811122 Automotive Glass Replacement Shops
7537 Automotive Transmission Repair Shops
NAICS 811113 Automotive Transmission Repair
7538 General Automotive Repair Shops
NAICS 811111 General Automotive Repair
7539 Automotive Repair Shops, nec
NAICS 811118 Other Automotive Mechanical & Electrical Repair & Maintenance
7542 Carwashes
NAICS 811192 Car Washes
7549 Automotive Services, Except Repair & Carwashes
NAICS 811191 Automotive Oil Change & Lubrication Shops
NAICS 48841   Motor Vehicle Towing
NAICS 811198 All Other Automotive Repair & Maintenance
7622 Radio & Television Repair Shops
NAICS 811211 Consumer Electronics Repair & Maintenance
NAICS 443112 Radio, Television & Other Electronics Stores
7623 Refrigeration & Air-conditioning Services & Repair Shops
NAICS 443111 Household Appliance Stores
NAICS 81131   Commercial & Industrial Machinery & Equipment Repair & Maintenance
NAICS 811412 Appliance Repair & Maintenance
7629 Electrical & Electronic Repair Shops, nec
NAICS 443111 Household Appliance Stores
NAICS 811212 Computer & Office Machine Repair & Maintenance
NAICS 811213 Communication Equipment Repair & Maintenance
NAICS 811219 Other Electronic & Precision Equipment Repair & Maintenance
NAICS 811412 Appliance Repair & Maintenance
NAICS 811211 Consumer Electronics Repair & Maintenance
7631 Watch, Clock, & Jewelry Repair
NAICS 81149   Other Personal & Household Goods Repair & Maintenance
7641 Reupholster & Furniture Repair
NAICS 81142   Reupholstery & Furniture Repair
7692 Welding Repair
NAICS 81149   Other Personal & Household Goods Repair & Maintenance
7694 Armature Rewinding Shops
NAICS 81131   Commercial & Industrial Machinery & Equipment Repair & Maintenance
NAICS 335312 Motor & Generator Manufacturing
7699 Repair Shops & Related Services, nec
NAICS 561622 Locksmiths
NAICS 562991 Septic Tank & Related Services

NAICS 56179   Other Services to Buildings & Dwellings
NAICS 48839   Other Supporting Activities for Water Transportation
NAICS 45111   Sporting Goods Stores
NAICS 81131   Commercial & Industrial Machinery & Equipment Repair & Maintenance
NAICS 11521   Support Activities for Animal Production
NAICS 811212 Computer & Office Machine Repair & Maintenance
NAICS 811219 Other Electronic & Precision Equipment Repair & Maintenance
NAICS 811411 Home & Garden Equipment Repair & Maintenance
NAICS 811412 Appliance Repair & Maintenance
NAICS 81143   Footwear & Leather Goods Repair
NAICS 81149   Other Personal & Household Goods Repair & Maintenance
7812 Motion Picture & Video Tape Production
NAICS 51211   Motion Picture & Video Production
7819 Services Allied to Motion Picture Production
NAICS 512191 Teleproduction & Other Post-production Services
NAICS 56131   Employment Placement Agencies
NAICS 53222   Formal Wear & Costumes Rental
NAICS 53249   Other Commercial & Industrial Machinery & Equipment Rental & Leasing
NAICS 541214 Payroll Services
NAICS 71151   Independent Artists, Writers, & Performers
NAICS 334612 Prerecorded Compact Disc , Tape, & Record Manufacturing
NAICS 512199 Other Motion Picture & Video Industries
7822 Motion Picture & Video Tape Distribution
NAICS 42199   Other Miscellaneous Durable Goods Wholesalers
NAICS 51212   Motion Picture & Video Distribution
7829 Services Allied to Motion Picture Distribution
NAICS 512199 Other Motion Picture & Video Industries
NAICS 51212   Motion Picture & Video Distribution
7832 Motion Picture Theaters, Except Drive-ins.
NAICS 512131 Motion Picture Theaters, Except Drive-in
7833 Drive-in Motion Picture Theaters
NAICS 512132 Drive-in Motion Picture Theaters
7841 Video Tape Rental
NAICS 53223   Video Tapes & Disc Rental
7911 Dance Studios, Schools, & Halls
NAICS 71399   All Other Amusement & Recreation Industries
NAICS 61161   Fine Arts Schools
7922 Theatrical Producers & Miscellaneous Theatrical Services
NAICS 56131   Employment Placement Agencies
NAICS 71111   Theater Companies & Dinner Theaters
NAICS 71141   Agents & Managers for Artists, Athletes, Entertainers & Other Public Figures
NAICS 71112   Dance Companies
NAICS 71131   Promoters of Performing Arts, Sports, & Similar Events with Facilities
NAICS 71132   Promoters of Performing Arts, Sports, & Similar Events Without Facilities
NAICS 51229   Other Sound Recording Industries
NAICS 53249   Other Commercial & Industrial Machinery & Equipment Rental & Leasing
7929 Bands, Orchestras, Actors, & Other Entertainers & Entertainment Groups
NAICS 71113   Musical Groups & Artists
NAICS 71151   Independent Artists, Writers, & Performers

NAICS 71119　Other Performing Arts Companies

7933 Bowling Centers
NAICS 71395　Bowling Centers

7941 Professional Sports Clubs & Promoters
NAICS 711211 Sports Teams & Clubs
NAICS 71141　Agents & Managers for Artists, Athletes, Entertainers , & Other Public Figures
NAICS 71132　Promoters of Arts, Sports & Similar Events Without Facilities
NAICS 71131　Promoters of Arts, Sports, & Similar Events with Facilities
NAICS 711219 Other Spectator Sports

7948 Racing, Including Track Operations
NAICS 711212 Race Tracks
NAICS 711219 Other Spectator Sports

7991 Physical Fitness Facilities
NAICS 71394　Fitness & Recreational Sports Centers

7992 Public Golf Courses
NAICS 71391　Golf Courses & Country Clubs

7993 Coin Operated Amusement Devices
NAICS 71312　Amusement Arcades
NAICS 71329　Other Gambling Industries
NAICS 71399　All Other Amusement & Recreation Industries

7996 Amusement Parks
NAICS 71311　Amusement & Theme Parks

7997 Membership Sports & Recreation Clubs
NAICS 48122　Nonscheduled Speciality Air Transportation
NAICS 71391　Golf Courses & Country Clubs
NAICS 71394　Fitness & Recreational Sports Centers
NAICS 71399　All Other Amusement & Recreation Industries

7999 Amusement & Recreation Services, nec
NAICS 561599 All Other Travel Arrangement & Reservation Services
NAICS 48799　Scenic & Sightseeing Transportation, Other
NAICS 71119　Other Performing Arts Companies
NAICS 711219 Other Spectator Sports
NAICS 71392　Skiing Facilities
NAICS 71394　Fitness & Recreational Sports Centers
NAICS 71321　Casinos
NAICS 71329　Other Gambling Industries
NAICS 71219　Nature Parks & Other Similar Institutions
NAICS 61162　Sports & Recreation Instruction
NAICS 532292 Recreational Goods Rental
NAICS 48711　Scenic & Sightseeing Transportation, Land
NAICS 48721　Scenic & Sightseeing Transportation, Water
NAICS 71399　All Other Amusement & Recreation Industries

8011 Offices & Clinics of Doctors of Medicine
NAICS 621493 Freestanding Ambulatory Surgical & Emergency Centers
NAICS 621491 Hmo Medical Centers
NAICS 621112 Offices of Physicians, Mental Health Specialists
NAICS 621111 Offices of Physicians

8021 Offices & Clinics of Dentists
NAICS 62121　Offices of Dentists

8031 Offices & Clinics of Doctors of Osteopathy
NAICS 621111 Offices of Physicians
NAICS 621112 Offices of Physicians, Mental Health Specialists

8041 Offices & Clinics of Chiropractors
NAICS 62131　Offices of Chiropractors

8042 Offices & Clinics of Optometrists
NAICS 62132　Offices of Optometrists

8043 Offices & Clinics of Podiatrists
NAICS 621391 Offices of Podiatrists

8049 Offices & Clinics of Health Practitioners, nec
NAICS 62133　Offices of Mental Health Practitioners
NAICS 62134　Offices of Physical, Occupational, & Speech Therapists & Audiologists
NAICS 621399 Offices of All Other Miscellaneous Health Practitioners

8051 Skilled Nursing Care Facilities
NAICS 623311 Continuing Care Retirement Communities
NAICS 62311　Nursing Care Facilities

8052 Intermediate Care Facilities
NAICS 623311 Continuing Care Retirement Communities
NAICS 62321　Residential Mental Retardation Facilities
NAICS 62311　Nursing Care Facilities

8059 Nursing & Personal Care Facilities, nec
NAICS 623311 Continuing Care Retirement Communities
NAICS 62311　Nursing Care Facilities

8062 General Medical & Surgical Hospitals
NAICS 62211　General Medical & Surgical Hospitals

8063 Psychiatric Hospitals
NAICS 62221　Psychiatric & Substance Abuse Hospitals

8069 Specialty Hospitals, Except Psychiatric
NAICS 62211　General Medical & Surgical Hospitals
NAICS 62221　Psychiatric & Substance Abuse Hospitals
NAICS 62231　Specialty Hospitals

8071 Medical Laboratories
NAICS 621512 Diagnostic Imaging Centers
NAICS 621511 Medical Laboratories

8072 Dental Laboratories
NAICS 339116 Dental Laboratories

8082 Home Health Care Services
NAICS 62161　Home Health Care Services

8092 Kidney Dialysis Centers
NAICS 621492 Kidney Dialysis Centers

8093 Specialty Outpatient Facilities, nec
NAICS 62141　Family Planning Centers
NAICS 62142　Outpatient Mental Health & Substance Abuse Centers
NAICS 621498 All Other Outpatient Care Facilities

8099 Health & Allied Services, nec
NAICS 621991 Blood & Organ Banks
NAICS 54143　Graphic Design Services
NAICS 541922 Commercial Photography
NAICS 62141　Family Planning Centers
NAICS 621999 All Other Miscellaneous Ambulatory Health Care Services

8111 Legal Services
NAICS 54111　Offices of Lawyers

8211 Elementary & Secondary Schools
NAICS 61111　Elementary & Secondary Schools

8221 Colleges, Universities, & Professional Schools
NAICS 61131　Colleges, Universities & Professional Schools

8222 Junior Colleges & Technical Institutes
NAICS 61121　Junior Colleges

8231 Libraries
NAICS 51412　Libraries & Archives

8243 Data Processing Schools
NAICS 611519 Other Technical & Trade Schools
NAICS 61142　Computer Training

8244 Business & Secretarial Schools
NAICS 61141　Business & Secretarial Schools

8249 Vocational Schools, nec
NAICS 611513 Apprenticeship Training
NAICS 611512 Flight Training
NAICS 611519 Other Technical & Trade Schools

8299 Schools & Educational Services, nec
NAICS 48122   Nonscheduled speciality Air Transportation
NAICS 611512 Flight Training
NAICS 611692 Automobile Driving Schools
NAICS 61171   Educational Support Services
NAICS 611691 Exam Preparation & Tutoring
NAICS 61161   Fine Arts Schools
NAICS 61163   Language Schools
NAICS 61143   Professional & Management Development
              Training Schools
NAICS 611699 All Other Miscellaneous Schools & Instruction

8322 Individual & Family Social Services
NAICS 62411   Child & Youth Services
NAICS 62421   Community Food Services
NAICS 624229 Other Community Housing Services
NAICS 62423   Emergency & Other Relief Services
NAICS 62412   Services for the Elderly & Persons with
              Disabilities
NAICS 624221 Temporary Shelters
NAICS 92215   Parole Offices & Probation Offices
NAICS 62419   Other Individual & Family Services

8331 Job Training & Vocational Rehabilitation Services
NAICS 62431   Vocational Rehabilitation Services

8351 Child Day Care Services
NAICS 62441   Child Day Care Services

8361 Residential Care
NAICS 623312 Homes for the Elderly
NAICS 62322   Residential Mental Health & Substance Abuse
              Facilities
NAICS 62399   Other Residential Care Facilities

8399 Social Services, nec
NAICS 813212 Voluntary Health Organizations
NAICS 813219 Other Grantmaking & Giving Services
NAICS 813311 Human Rights Organizations
NAICS 813312 Environment, Conservation & Wildlife
              Organizations
NAICS 813319 Other Social Advocacy Organizations

8412 Museums & Art Galleries
NAICS 71211   Museums
NAICS 71212   Historical Sites

8422 Arboreta & Botanical or Zoological Gardens
NAICS 71213   Zoos & Botanical Gardens
NAICS 71219   Nature Parks & Other Similar Institutions

8611 Business Associations
NAICS 81391   Business Associations

8621 Professional Membership Organizations
NAICS 81392   Professional Organizations

8631 Labor Unions & Similar Labor Organizations
NAICS 81393   Labor Unions & Similar Labor Organizations

8641 Civic, Social, & Fraternal Associations
NAICS 81341   Civic & Social Organizations
NAICS 81399   Other Similar Organizations
NAICS 92115   American Indian & Alaska Native Tribal
              Governments
NAICS 62411   Child & Youth Services

8651 Political Organizations
NAICS 81394   Political Organizations

8661 Religious Organizations
NAICS 81311   Religious Organizations

8699 Membership Organizations, nec
NAICS 81341   Civic & Social Organizations
NAICS 81391   Business Associations
NAICS 813312 Environment, Conservation, & Wildlife
              Organizations

NAICS 561599 All Other Travel Arrangement & Reservation
              Services
NAICS 81399   Other Similar Organizations

8711 Engineering Services
NAICS 54133   Engineering Services

8712 Architectural Services
NAICS 54131   Architectural Services

8713 Surveying Services
NAICS 48122   Nonscheduled Air Speciality Transportation
NAICS 54136   Geophysical Surveying & Mapping Services
NAICS 54137   Surveying & Mapping Services

8721 Accounting, Auditing, & Bookkeeping Services
NAICS 541211 Offices of Certified Public Accountants
NAICS 541214 Payroll Services
NAICS 541219 Other Accounting Services

8731 Commercial Physical & Biological Research
NAICS 54171   Research & Development in the Physical
              Sciences & Engineering Sciences
NAICS 54172   Research & Development in the Life Sciences

**8732 Commercial Economic, Sociological, & Educational
     Research**
NAICS 54173   Research & Development in the Social Sciences
              & Humanities
NAICS 54191   Marketing Research & Public Opinion Polling

8733 Noncommercial Research Organizations
NAICS 54171   Research & Development in the Physical
              Sciences & Engineering Sciences
NAICS 54172   Research & Development in the Life Sciences
NAICS 54173   Research & Development in the Social Sciences
              & Humanities

8734 Testing Laboratories
NAICS 54194   Veterinary Services
NAICS 54138   Testing Laboratories

8741 Management Services
NAICS 56111   Office Administrative Services
NAICS 23   Included in Construction Sector by Type of
              Construction

8742 Management Consulting Services
NAICS 541611 Administrative Management & General
              Management Consulting Services
NAICS 541612 Human Resources & Executive Search Services
NAICS 541613 Marketing Consulting Services
NAICS 541614 Process, Physical, Distribution & Logistics
              Consulting Services

8743 Public Relations Services
NAICS 54182   Public Relations Agencies

8744 Facilities Support Management Services
NAICS 56121   Facilities Support Services

8748 Business Consulting Services, nec
NAICS 61171   Educational Support Services
NAICS 541618 Other Management Consulting Services
NAICS 54169   Other Scientific & Technical Consulting
              Services

8811 Private Households
NAICS 81411   Private Households

8999 Services, nec
NAICS 71151   Independent Artists, Writers, & Performers
NAICS 51221   Record Production
NAICS 54169   Other Scientific & Technical Consulting
              Services
NAICS 51223   Music Publishers
NAICS 541612 Human Resources & Executive Search
              Consulting Services
NAICS 514199 All Other Information Services

NAICS 54162   Environmental Consulting Services

PUBLIC ADMINISTRATION

9111 Executive Offices
NAICS 92111   Executive Offices
9121 Legislative Bodies
NAICS 92112   Legislative Bodies
9131 Executive & Legislative Offices, Combined
NAICS 92114   Executive & Legislative Offices, Combined
9199 General Government, nec
NAICS 92119   All Other General Government
9211 Courts
NAICS 92211   Courts
9221 Police Protection
NAICS 92212   Police Protection
9222 Legal Counsel & Prosecution
NAICS 92213   Legal Counsel & Prosecution
9223 Correctional Institutions
NAICS 92214   Correctional Institutions
9224 Fire Protection
NAICS 92216   Fire Protection
9229 Public Order & Safety, nec
NAICS 92219   All Other Justice, Public Order, & Safety
9311 Public Finance, Taxation, & Monetary Policy
NAICS 92113   Public Finance
9411 Administration of Educational Programs
NAICS 92311   Administration of Education Programs
9431 Administration of Public Health Programs
NAICS 92312   Administration of Public Health Programs
9441 Administration of Social, Human Resource & Income Maintenance Programs
NAICS 92313   Administration of Social, Human Resource & Income Maintenance Programs
9451 Administration of Veteran's Affairs, Except Health Insurance
NAICS 92314   Administration of Veteran's Affairs
9511 Air & Water Resource & Solid Waste Management
NAICS 92411   Air & Water Resource & Solid Waste Management
9512 Land, Mineral, Wildlife, & Forest Conservation
NAICS 92412   Land, Mineral, Wildlife, & Forest Conservation
9531 Administration of Housing Programs
NAICS 92511   Administration of Housing Programs
9532 Administration of Urban Planning & Community & Rural Development
NAICS 92512   Administration of Urban Planning & Community & Rural Development
9611 Administration of General Economic Programs
NAICS 92611   Administration of General Economic Programs
9621 Regulations & Administration of Transportation Programs
NAICS 488111 Air Traffic Control
NAICS 92612   Regulation & Administration of Transportation Programs
9631 Regulation & Administration of Communications, Electric, Gas, & Other Utilities
NAICS 92613   Regulation & Administration of Communications, Electric, Gas, & Other Utilities
9641 Regulation of Agricultural Marketing & Commodity
NAICS 92614   Regulation of Agricultural Marketing & Commodity

9651 Regulation, Licensing, & Inspection of Miscellaneous Commercial Sectors
NAICS 92615   Regulation, Licensing, & Inspection of Miscellaneous Commercial Sectors
9661 Space Research & Technology
NAICS 92711   Space Research & Technology
9711 National Security
NAICS 92811   National Security
9721 International Affairs
NAICS 92812   International Affairs
9999 Nonclassifiable Establishments
NAICS 99999   Unclassified Establishments

NAICS TO SIC CONVERSION GUIDE

AGRICULTURE, FORESTRY, FISHING, & HUNTING

11111 Soybean Farming
SIC 0116 Soybeans
11112 Oilseed Farming
SIC 0119 Cash Grains, nec
11113 Dry Pea & Bean Farming
SIC 0119 Cash Grains, nec
11114 Wheat Farming
SIC 0111 Wheat
11115 Corn Farming
SIC 0115 Corn
SIC 0119 Cash Grains, nec
11116 Rice Farming
SIC 0112 Rice
111191 Oilseed & Grain Combination Farming
SIC 0119 Cash Grains, nec
111199 All Other Grain Farming
SIC 0119 Cash Grains, nec
111211 Potato Farming
SIC 0134 Irish Potatoes
111219 Other Vegetable & Melon Farming
SIC 0161 Vegetables & Melons
SIC 0139 Field Crops Except Cash Grains
11131 Orange Groves
SIC 0174 Citrus Fruits
11132 Citrus Groves
SIC 0174 Citrus Fruits
111331 Apple Orchards
SIC 0175 Deciduous Tree Fruits
111332 Grape Vineyards
SIC 0172 Grapes
111333 Strawberry Farming
SIC 0171 Berry Crops
111334 Berry Farming
SIC 0171 Berry Crops
111335 Tree Nut Farming
SIC 0173 Tree Nuts
111336 Fruit & Tree Nut Combination Farming
SIC 0179 Fruits & Tree Nuts, nec
111339 Other Noncitrus Fruit Farming
SIC 0175 Deciduous Tree Fruits
SIC 0179 Fruit & Tree Nuts, nec
111411 Mushroom Production
SIC 0182 Food Crops Grown Under Cover
111419 Other Food Crops Grown Under Cover
SIC 0182 Food Crops Grown Under Cover
111421 Nursery & Tree Production
SIC 0181 Ornamental Floriculture & Nursery Products
SIC 0811 Timber Tracts
111422 Floriculture Production
SIC 0181 Ornamental Floriculture & Nursery Products
11191 Tobacco Farming
SIC 0132 Tobacco
11192 Cotton Farming
SIC 0131 Cotton
11193 Sugarcane Farming
SIC 0133 Sugarcane & Sugar Beets

11194 Hay Farming
SIC 0139 Field Crops, Except Cash Grains, nec
111991 Sugar Beet Farming
SIC 0133 Sugarcane & Sugar Beets
111992 Peanut Farming
SIC 0139 Field Crops, Except Cash Grains, nec
111998 All Other Miscellaneous Crop Farming
SIC 0139 Field Crops, Except Cash Grains, nec
SIC 0191 General Farms, Primarily Crop
SIC 0831 Forest Products
SIC 0919 Miscellaneous Marine Products
SIC 2099 Food Preparations, nec
112111 Beef Cattle Ranching & Farming
SIC 0212 Beef Cattle, Except Feedlots
SIC 0241 Dairy Farms
112112 Cattle Feedlots
SIC 0211 Beef Cattle Feedlots
11212 Dairy Cattle & Milk Production
SIC 0241 Dairy Farms
11213 Dual Purpose Cattle Ranching & Farming
No SIC equivalent
11221 Hog & Pig Farming
SIC 0213 Hogs
11231 Chicken Egg Production
SIC 0252 Chicken Eggs
11232 Broilers & Other Meat Type Chicken Production
SIC 0251 Broiler, Fryers, & Roaster Chickens
11233 Turkey Production
SIC 0253 Turkey & Turkey Eggs
11234 Poultry Hatcheries
SIC 0254 Poultry Hatcheries
11239 Other Poultry Production
SIC 0259 Poultry & Eggs, nec
11241 Sheep Farming
SIC 0214 Sheep & Goats
11242 Goat Farming
SIC 0214 Sheep & Goats
112511 Finfish Farming & Fish Hatcheries
SIC 0273 Animal Aquaculture
SIC 0921 Fish Hatcheries & Preserves
112512 Shellfish Farming
SIC 0273 Animal Aquaculture
SIC 0921 Fish Hatcheries & Preserves
112519 Other Animal Aquaculture
SIC 0273 Animal Aquaculture
11291 Apiculture
SIC 0279 Animal Specialties, nec
11292 Horse & Other Equine Production
SIC 0272 Horses & Other Equines
11293 Fur-Bearing Animal & Rabbit Production
SIC 0271 Fur-Bearing Animals & Rabbits
11299 All Other Animal Production
SIC 0219 General Livestock, Except Dairy & Poultry
SIC 0279 Animal Specialties, nec
SIC 0291 General Farms, Primarily Livestock & Animal
   Specialties;
11311 Timber Tract Operations
SIC 0811 Timber Tracts
11321 Forest Nurseries & Gathering of Forest Products
SIC 0831 Forest Nurseries & Gathering of Forest Products
11331 Logging
SIC 2411 Logging

114111 Finfish Fishing
SIC 0912 Finfish
114112 Shellfish Fishing
SIC 0913 Shellfish
114119 Other Marine Fishing
SIC 0919 Miscellaneous Marine Products
11421 Hunting & Trapping
SIC 0971 Hunting & Trapping, & Game Propagation;
115111 Cotton Ginning
SIC 0724 Cotton Ginning
115112 Soil Preparation, Planting, & Cultivating
SIC 0711 Soil Preparation Services
SIC 0721 Crop Planting, Cultivating, & Protecting
115113 Crop Harvesting, Primarily by Machine
SIC 0722 Crop Harvesting, Primarily by Machine
115114 Other Postharvest Crop Activities
SIC 0723 Crop Preparation Services For Market, Except Cotton
    Ginning
115115 Farm Labor Contractors & Crew Leaders
SIC 0761 Farm Labor Contractors & Crew Leaders
115116 Farm Management Services
SIC 0762 Farm Management Services
11521 Support Activities for Animal Production
SIC 0751 Livestock Services, Except Veterinary
SIC 0752 Animal Specialty Services, Except Veterinary
SIC 7699 Repair Services, nec
11531 Support Activities for Forestry
SIC 0851 Forestry Services

MINING

211111 Crude Petroleum & Natural Gas Extraction
SIC 1311 Crude Petroleum & Natural Gas
211112 Natural Gas Liquid Extraction
SIC 1321 Natural Gas Liquids
212111 Bituminous Coal & Lignite Surface Mining
SIC 1221 Bituminous Coal & Lignite Surface Mining
212112 Bituminous Coal Underground Mining
SIC 1222 Bituminous Coal Underground Mining
212113 Anthracite Mining
SIC 1231 Anthracite Mining
21221 Iron Ore Mining
SIC 1011 Iron Ores
212221 Gold Ore Mining
SIC 1041 Gold Ores
212222 Silver Ore Mining
SIC 1044 Silver Ores
212231 Lead Ore & Zinc Ore Mining
SIC 1031 Lead & Zinc Ores
212234 Copper Ore & Nickel Ore Mining
SIC 1021 Copper Ores
212291 Uranium-Radium-Vanadium Ore Mining
SIC 1094 Uranium-Radium-Vanadium Ores
212299 All Other Metal Ore Mining
SIC 1061 Ferroalloy Ores, Except Vanadium
SIC 1099 Miscellaneous Metal Ores, nec
212311 Dimension Stone Mining & Quarrying
SIC 1411 Dimension Stone
212312 Crushed & Broken Limestone Mining & Quarrying
SIC 1422 Crushed & Broken Limestone
212313 Crushed & Broken Granite Mining & Quarrying
SIC 1423 Crushed & Broken Granite

212319 Other Crushed & Broken Stone Mining & Quarrying
SIC 1429 Crushed & Broken Stone, nec
SIC 1499 Miscellaneous Nonmetallic Minerals, Except Fuels
212321 Construction Sand & Gravel Mining
SIC 1442 Construction Sand & Gravel
212322 Industrial Sand Mining
SIC 1446 Industrial Sand
212324 Kaolin & Ball Clay Mining
SIC 1455 Kaolin & Ball Clay
212325 Clay & Ceramic & Refractory Minerals Mining
SIC 1459 Clay, Ceramic, & Refractory Minerals, nec
212391 Potash, Soda, & Borate Mineral Mining
SIC 1474 Potash, Soda, & Borate Minerals
212392 Phosphate Rock Mining
SIC 1475 Phosphate Rock
212393 Other Chemical & Fertilizer Mineral Mining
SIC 1479 Chemical & Fertilizer Mineral Mining, nec
212399 All Other Nonmetallic Mineral Mining
SIC 1499 Miscellaneous Nonmetallic Minerals, Except Fuels
213111 Drilling Oil & Gas Wells
SIC 1381 Drilling Oil & Gas Wells
213112 Support Activities for Oil & Gas Operations
SIC 1382 Oil & Gas Field Exploration Services
SIC 1389 Oil & Gas Field Services, nec
213113 Other Gas & Field Support Activities
SIC 1389 Oil & Gas Field Services, nec
213114 Support Activities for Coal Mining
SIC 1241 Coal Mining Services
213115 Support Activities for Metal Mining
SIC 1081 Metal Mining Services
213116 Support Activities for Nonmetallic Minerals, Except Fuels
SIC 1481 Nonmetallic Minerals Services, Except Fuels

UTILITIES

221111 Hydroelectric Power Generation
SIC 4911 Electric Services
SIC 4931 Electric & Other Services Combined
SIC 4939 Combination Utilities, nec
221112 Fossil Fuel Electric Power Generation
SIC 4911 Electric Services
SIC 4931 Electric & Other Services Combined
SIC 4939 Combination Utilities, nec
221113 Nuclear Electric Power Generation
SIC 4911 Electric Services
SIC 4931 Electric & Other Services Combined
SIC 4939 Combination Utilities, nec
221119 Other Electric Power Generation
SIC 4911 Electric Services
SIC 4931 Electric & Other Services Combined
SIC 4939 Combination Utilities, nec
221121 Electric Bulk Power Transmission & Control
SIC 4911 Electric Services
SIC 4931 Electric & Other Services Combined
SIC 4939 Combination Utilities, NEC
221122 Electric Power Distribution
SIC 4911 Electric Services
SIC 4931 Electric & Other Services Combined
SIC 4939 Combination Utilities, nec
22121 Natural Gas Distribution
SIC 4923 Natural Gas Transmission & Distribution
SIC 4924 Natural Gas Distribution

SIC 4925 Mixed, Manufactured, or Liquefied Petroleum Gas
    Production and/or Distribution
SIC 4931 Electronic & Other Services Combined
SIC 4932 Gas & Other Services Combined
SIC 4939 Combination Utilities, nec

22131 Water Supply & Irrigation Systems
SIC 4941 Water Supply
SIC 4971 Irrigation Systems

22132 Sewage Treatment Facilities
SIC 4952 Sewerage Systems

22133 Steam & Air-Conditioning Supply
SIC 4961 Steam & Air-Conditioning Supply

CONSTRUCTION

23311 Land Subdivision & Land Development
SIC 6552 Land Subdividers & Developers, Except Cemeteries

23321 Single Family Housing Construction
SIC 1521 General contractors-Single-Family Houses
SIC 1531 Operative Builders

23322 Multifamily Housing Construction
SIC 1522 General Contractors-Residential Building, Other
    Than Single-Family
SIC 1531 Operative Builders

23331 Manufacturing & Industrial Building Construction
SIC 1531 Operative Builders
SIC 1541 General Contractors-Industrial Buildings &
    Warehouses

23332 Commercial & Institutional Building Construction
SIC 1522 General Contractors-Residential Building Other than
    Single-Family
SIC 1531 Operative Builders
SIC 1541 General Contractors-Industrial Buildings &
    Warehouses
SIC 1542 General Contractor-Nonresidential Buildings, Other
    than Industrial Buildings & Warehouses

23411 Highway & Street Construction
SIC 1611 Highway & Street Construction, Except Elevated
    Highways

23412 Bridge & Tunnel Construction
SIC 1622 Bridge, Tunnel, & Elevated Highway Construction

2349   Other Heavy Construction

23491 Water, Sewer, & Pipeline Construction
SIC 1623 Water, Sewer, Pipeline, & Communications & Power
    Line Construction

**23492 Power & Communication Transmission Line
    Construction**
SIC 1623 Water, Sewer, Pipelines, & Communications & Power
    Line Construction

23493 Industrial Nonbuilding Structure Construction
SIC 1629 Heavy Construction, nec

23499 All Other Heavy Construction
SIC 1629 Heavy Construction, nec
SIC 7353 Construction Equipment Rental & Leasing

23511 Plumbing, Heating & Air-Conditioning Contractors
SIC 1711 Plumbing, Heating & Air-Conditioning

23521 Painting & Wall Covering Contractors
SIC 1721 Painting & Paper Hanging
SIC 1799 Special Trade Contractors, nec

23531 Electrical Contractors
SIC 1731 Electrical Work

23541 Masonry & Stone Contractors
SIC 1741 Masonry, Stone Setting & Other Stone Work

23542 Drywall, Plastering, Acoustical & Insulation Contractors
SIC 1742 Plastering, Drywall, Acoustical, & Insulation Work
SIC 1743 Terrazzo, Tile, Marble & Mosaic work
SIC 1771 Concrete Work

23543 Tile, Marble, Terrazzo & Mosaic Contractors
SIC 1743 Terrazzo, Tile, Marble, & Mosaic Work

23551 Carpentry Contractors
SIC 1751 Carpentry Work

23552 Floor Laying & Other Floor Contractors
SIC 1752 Floor Laying & Other Floor Work, nec

23561 Roofing, Siding & Sheet Metal Contractors
SIC 1761 Roofing, Siding, & Sheet Metal Work

23571 Concrete Contractors
SIC 1771 Concrete Work

23581 Water Well Drilling Contractors
SIC 1781 Water Well Drilling

23591 Structural Steel Erection Contractors
SIC 1791 Structural Steel Erection

23592 Glass & Glazing Contractors
SIC 1793 Glass & Glazing Work
SIC 1799 Specialty Trade Contractors, nec

23593 Excavation Contractors
SIC 1794 Excavation Work

23594 Wrecking & Demolition Contractors
SIC 1795 Wrecking & Demolition Work

**23595 Building Equipment & Other Machinery Installation
    Contractors**
SIC 1796 Installation of Erection of Building Equipment, nec

23599 All Other Special Trade Contractors
SIC 1799 Special Trade Contractors, nec

FOOD MANUFACTURING

311111 Dog & Cat Food Manufacturing
SIC 2047 Dog & Cat Food

311119 Other Animal Food Manufacturing
SIC 2048 Prepared Feeds & Feed Ingredients for Animals &
    Fowls, Except Dogs & Cats

311211 Flour Milling
SIC 2034 Dehydrated Fruits, Vegetables & Soup Mixes
SIC 2041 Flour & Other Grain Mill Products

311212 Rice Milling
SIC 2044 Rice Milling

311213 Malt Manufacturing
SIC 2083 Malt

311221 Wet Corn Milling
SIC 2046 Wet Corn Milling

311222 Soybean Processing
SIC 2075 Soybean Oil Mills
SIC 2079 Shortening, Table Oils, Margarine, & Other Edible
    Fats & Oils, nec

311223 Other Oilseed Processing
SIC 2074 Cottonseed Oil Mills
SIC 2079 Shortening, Table Oils, Margarine & Other Edible
    Fats & Oils, nec
SIC 2076 Vegetable Oil Mills, Except Corn, Cottonseed, &
    Soybean

311225 Edible Fats & Oils Manufacturing
SIC 2077 Animal & Marine Fats & Oil, nec
SIC 2074 Cottonseed Oil Mills
SIC 2075 Soybean Oil Mills

SIC 2076 Vegetable Oil Mills, Except Corn, Cottonseed, &
      Soybean
SIC 2079 Shortening, Table Oils, Margarine, & Other Edible
      Fats & Oils, nec

31123   Breakfast Cereal Manufacturing
SIC 2043 Cereal Breakfast Foods

311311 Sugarcane Mills
SIC 2061 Cane Sugar, Except Refining

311312 Cane Sugar Refining
SIC 2062 Cane Sugar Refining

311313 Beet Sugar Manufacturing
SIC 2063 Beet Sugar

**31132   Chocolate & Confectionery Manufacturing from Cacao
      Beans**
SIC 2066 Chocolate & Cocoa Products

31133   Confectionery Manufacturing from Purchased Chocolate
SIC 2064 Candy & Other Confectionery Products

31134   Non-Chocolate Confectionery Manufacturing
SIC 2064 Candy & Other Confectionery Products
SIC 2067 Chewing Gum
SIC 2099 Food Preparations, nec

311411 Frozen Fruit, Juice & Vegetable Processing
SIC 2037 Frozen Fruits, Fruit Juices, & Vegetables

311412 Frozen Specialty Food Manufacturing
SIC 2038 Frozen Specialties, NEC

311421 Fruit & Vegetable Canning
SIC 2033 Canned Fruits, Vegetables, Preserves, Jams, & Jellies
SIC 2035 Pickled Fruits & Vegetables, Vegetable Sauces, &
      Seasonings & Salad Dressings

311422 Specialty Canning
SIC 2032 Canned Specialties

311423 Dried & Dehydrated Food Manufacturing
SIC 2034 Dried & Dehydrated Fruits, Vegetables & Soup
      Mixes
SIC 2099 Food Preparation, nec

311511 Fluid Milk Manufacturing
SIC 2026 Fluid Milk

311512 Creamery Butter Manufacturing
SIC 2021 Creamery Butter

311513 Cheese Manufacturing
SIC 2022 Natural, Processed, & Imitation Cheese

311514 Dry, Condensed, & Evaporated Milk Manufacturing
SIC 2023 Dry, Condensed & Evaporated Dairy Products

31152   Ice Cream & Frozen Dessert Manufacturing
SIC 2024 Ice Cream & Frozen Desserts

311611 Animal Slaughtering
SIC 0751 Livestock Services, Except Veterinary
SIC 2011 Meat Packing Plants
SIC 2048 Prepared Feeds & Feed Ingredients for Animals &
      Fowls, Except Dogs & Cats

311612 Meat Processed from Carcasses
SIC 2013 Sausages & Other Prepared Meats
SIC 5147 Meat & Meat Products

311613 Rendering & Meat By-product Processing
SIC 2077 Animal & Marine Fats & Oils

311615 Poultry Processing
SIC 2015 Poultry Slaughtering & Processing

311711 Seafood Canning
SIC 2077 Animal & Marine Fats & Oils
SIC 2091 Canned & Cured Fish & Seafood

311712 Fresh & Frozen Seafood Processing
SIC 2077 Animal & Marine Fats & Oils
SIC 2092 Prepared Fresh or Frozen Fish & Seafood

311811 Retail Bakeries
SIC 5461 Retail Bakeries

311812 Commercial Bakeries
SIC 2051 Bread & Other Bakery Products, Except Cookies &
      Crackers
SIC 2052 Cookies & Crackers

311813 Frozen Bakery Product Manufacturing
SIC 2053 Frozen Bakery Products, Except Bread

311821 Cookie & Cracker Manufacturing
SIC 2052 Cookies & Crackers

**311822 Flour Mixes & Dough Manufacturing from Purchased
      Flour**
SIC 2045 Prepared Flour Mixes & Doughs

311823 Pasta Manufacturing
SIC 2098 Macaroni, Spaghetti, Vermicelli & Noodles

31183   Tortilla Manufacturing
SIC 2099 Food Preparations, nec

311911 Roasted Nuts & Peanut Butter Manufacturing
SIC 2068 Salted & Roasted Nuts & Seeds
SIC 2099 Food Preparations, nec

311919 Other Snack Food Manufacturing
SIC 2052 Cookies & Crackers
SIC 2096 Potato Chips, Corn Chips, & Similar Snacks

31192   Coffee & Tea Manufacturing
SIC 2043 Cereal Breakfast Foods
SIC 2095 Roasted Coffee
SIC 2099 Food Preparations, nec

31193   Flavoring Syrup & Concentrate Manufacturing
SIC 2087 Flavoring Extracts & Flavoring Syrups

**311941 Mayonnaise, Dressing & Other Prepared Sauce
      Manufacturing**
SIC 2035 Pickled Fruits & Vegetables, Vegetable Seasonings, &
      Sauces & Salad Dressings
SIC 2099 Food Preparations, nec

311942 Spice & Extract Manufacturing
SIC 2087 Flavoring Extracts & Flavoring Syrups
SIC 2095 Roasted Coffee
SIC 2099 Food Preparations, nec
SIC 2899 Chemical Preparations, nec

311991 Perishable Prepared Food Manufacturing
SIC 2099 Food Preparations, nec

311999 All Other Miscellaneous Food Manufacturing
SIC 2015 Poultry Slaughtering & Processing
SIC 2032 Canned Specialties
SIC 2087 Flavoring Extracts & Flavoring Syrups
SIC 2099 Food Preparations, nec

BEVERAGE & TOBACCO PRODUCT MANUFACTURING

312111 Soft Drink Manufacturing
SIC 2086 Bottled & Canned Soft Drinks & Carbonated Water

312112 Bottled Water Manufacturing
SIC 2086 Bottled & Canned Soft Drinks & Carbonated Water

312113 Ice Manufacturing
SIC 2097 Manufactured Ice

31212   Breweries
SIC 2082 Malt Beverages

31213   Wineries
SIC 2084 Wines, Brandy, & Brandy Spirits

31214   Distilleries
SIC 2085 Distilled & Blended Liquors

31221 Tobacco Stemming & Redrying
SIC 2141 Tobacco Stemming & Redrying
312221 Cigarette Manufacturing
SIC 2111 Cigarettes
312229 Other Tobacco Product Manufacturing
SIC 2121 Cigars
SIC 2131 Chewing & Smoking Tobacco & Snuff
SIC 2141 Tobacco Stemming & Redrying

TEXTILE MILLS

313111 Yarn Spinning Mills
SIC 2281 Yarn Spinning Mills
SIC 2299 Textile Goods, nec
313112 Yarn Texturing, Throwing & Twisting Mills
SIC 2282 Yarn Texturing, Throwing, Winding Mills
313113 Thread Mills
SIC 2284 Thread Mills
SIC 2299 Textile Goods, NEC
31321 Broadwoven Fabric Mills
SIC 2211 Broadwoven Fabric Mills, Cotton
SIC 2221 Broadwoven Fabric Mills, Manmade Fiber & Silk
SIC 2231 Broadwoven Fabric Mills, Wool
SIC 2299 Textile Goods, nec
313221 Narrow Fabric Mills
SIC 2241 Narrow Fabric & Other Smallware Mills: Cotton, Wool, Silk & Manmade Fiber
SIC 2299 Textile Goods, nec
313222 Schiffli Machine Embroidery
SIC 2397 Schiffli Machine Embroideries
31323 Nonwoven Fabric Mills
SIC 2297 Nonwoven Fabrics
SIC 2299 Textile Goods, nec
313241 Weft Knit Fabric Mills
SIC 2257 Weft Knit Fabric Mills
SIC 2259 Knitting Mills nec
313249 Other Knit Fabric & Lace Mills
SIC 2258 Lace & Warp Knit Fabric Mills
SIC 2259 Knitting Mills nec
313311 Broadwoven Fabric Finishing Mills
SIC 2231 Broadwoven Fabric Mills, Wool
SIC 2261 Finishers of Broadwoven Fabrics of Cotton
SIC 2262 Finishers of Broadwoven Fabrics of Manmade Fiber & Silk
SIC 2269 Finishers of Textiles, nec
SIC 5131 Piece Goods & Notions
313312 Textile & Fabric Finishing Mills
SIC 2231 Broadwoven Fabric Mills, Wool
SIC 2257 Weft Knit Fabric Mills
SIC 2258 Lace & Warp Knit Fabric Mills
SIC 2269 Finishers of Textiles, nec
SIC 2282 Yarn Texturizing, Throwing, Twisting, & Winding Mills
SIC 2284 Thread Mills
SIC 2299 Textile Goods, nec
SIC 5131 Piece Goods & Notions
31332 Fabric Coating Mills
SIC 2295 Coated Fabrics, Not Rubberized
SIC 3069 Fabricated Rubber Products, nec

TEXTILE PRODUCT MILLS

31411 Carpet & Rug Mills
SIC 2273 Carpets & Rugs
314121 Curtain & Drapery Mills
SIC 2391 Curtains & Draperies
SIC 5714 Drapery, Curtain, & Upholstery Stores
314129 Other Household Textile Product Mills
SIC 2392 Housefurnishings, Except Curtains & Draperies
314911 Textile Bag Mills
SIC 2392 Housefurnishings, Except Curtains & Draperies
SIC 2393 Textile Bags
314912 Canvas & Related Product Mills
SIC 2394 Canvas & Related Products
314991 Rope, Cordage & Twine Mills
SIC 2298 Cordage & Twine
314992 Tire Cord & Tire Fabric Mills
SIC 2296 Tire Cord & Fabrics
314999 All Other Miscellaneous Textile Product Mills
SIC 2299 Textile Goods, nec
SIC 2395 Pleating, Decorative & Novelty Stitching, & Tucking for the Trade
SIC 2396 Automotive Trimmings, Apparel Findings, & Related Products
SIC 2399 Fabricated Textile Products, nec

APPAREL MANUFACTURING

315111 Sheer Hosiery Mills
SIC 2251 Women's Full-Length & Knee-Length Hosiery, Except socks
SIC 2252 Hosiery, nec
315119 Other Hosiery & Sock Mills
SIC 2252 Hosiery, nec
315191 Outerwear Knitting Mills
SIC 2253 Knit Outerwear Mills
SIC 2259 Knitting Mills, nec
315192 Underwear & Nightwear Knitting Mills
SIC 2254 Knit Underwear & Nightwear Mills
SIC 2259 Knitting Mills, nec
315211 Men's & Boys' Cut & Sew Apparel Contractors
SIC 2311 Men's & Boys' Suits, Coats, & Overcoats
SIC 2321 Men's & Boys' Shirts, Except Work Shirts
SIC 2322 Men's & Boys' Underwear & Nightwear
SIC 2325 Men's & Boys' Trousers & Slacks
SIC 2326 Men's & Boys' Work Clothing
SIC 2329 Men's & Boys' Clothing, nec
SIC 2341 Women's, Misses', Children's, & Infants' Underwear & Nightwear
SIC 2361 Girls', Children's, & Infants' Dresses, Blouses & Shirts
SIC 2369 Girls', Children's, & Infants' Outerwear, nec
SIC 2384 Robes & Dressing Gowns
SIC 2385 Waterproof Outerwear
SIC 2389 Apparel & Accessories, nec
SIC 2395 Pleating, Decorative & Novelty Stitching, & Tucking for the Trade
315212 Women's & Girls' Cut & Sew Apparel Contractors
SIC 2331 Women's, Misses', & Juniors' Blouses & Shirts
SIC 2335 Women's, Misses' & Juniors' Dresses
SIC 2337 Women's, Misses', & Juniors' Suits, Skirts, & Coats
SIC 2339 Women's, Misses', & Juniors' Outerwear, nec

SIC 2341 Women's, Misses', Children's, & Infants' Underwear
& Nightwear
SIC 2342 Brassieres, Girdles, & Allied Garments
SIC 2361 Girls', Children's, & Infants' Dresses, Blouses, &
Shirts
SIC 2369 Girls', Children's, & Infants' Outerwear, nec
SIC 2384 Robes & Dressing Gowns
SIC 2385 Waterproof Outerwear
SIC 2389 Apparel & Accessories, nec
SIC 2395 Pleating, Decorative & Novelty Stitching, & Tucking
for the Trade
**315221 Men's & Boys' Cut & Sew Underwear & Nightwear
Manufacturing**
SIC 2322 Men's & Boys' Underwear & Nightwear
SIC 2341 Women's, Misses', Children's, & Infants' Underwear
& Nightwear
SIC 2369 Girls', Children's, & Infants' Outerwear, nec
SIC 2384 Robes & Dressing Gowns
**315222 Men's & Boys' Cut & Sew Suit, Coat & Overcoat
Manufacturing**
SIC 2311 Men's & Boys' Suits, Coats, & Overcoats
SIC 2369 Girls', Children's, & Infants' Outerwear, nec
SIC 2385 Waterproof Outerwear
315223 Men's & Boys' Cut & Sew Shirt Manufacturing
SIC 2321 Men's & Boys' Shirts, Except Work Shirts
SIC 2361 Girls', Children's, & Infants' Dresses, Blouses, &
Shirts
**315224 Men's & Boys' Cut & Sew Trouser, Slack & Jean
Manufacturing**
SIC 2325 Men's & Boys' Trousers & Slacks
SIC 2369 Girls', Children's, & Infants' Outerwear, NEC
315225 Men's & Boys' Cut & Sew Work Clothing Manufacturing
SIC 2326 Men's & Boys' Work Clothing
**315228 Men's & Boys' Cut & Sew Other Outerwear
Manufacturing**
SIC 2329 Men's & Boys' Clothing, nec
SIC 2369 Girls', Children's, & Infants' Outerwear, nec
SIC 2385 Waterproof Outerwear
**315231 Women's & Girls' Cut & Sew Lingerie, Loungewear &
Nightwear Manufacturing**
SIC 2341 Women's, Misses', Children's, & Infants' Underwear
& Nightwear
SIC 2342 Brassieres, Girdles, & Allied Garments
SIC 2369 Girls', Children's, & Infants' Outerwear, nec
SIC 2384 Robes & Dressing Gowns
SIC 2389 Apparel & Accessories, NEC
**315232 Women's & Girls' Cut & Sew Blouse & Shirt
Manufacturing**
SIC 2331 Women's, Misses', & Juniors' Blouses & Shirts
SIC 2361 Girls', Children's, & Infants' Dresses, Blouses &
Shirts
315233 Women's & Girls' Cut & Sew Dress Manufacturing
SIC 2335 Women's, Misses', & Juniors' Dresses
SIC 2361 Girls', Children's, & Infants' Dresses, Blouses &
Shirts
**315234 Women's & Girls' Cut & Sew Suit, Coat, Tailored Jacket
& Skirt Manufacturing**
SIC 2337 Women's, Misses', & Juniors' Suits, Skirts, & Coats
SIC 2369 Girls', Children's, & Infants' Outerwear, nec
SIC 2385 Waterproof Outerwear
**315238 Women's & Girls' Cut & Sew Other Outerwear
Manufacturing**
SIC 2339 Women's, Misses', & Juniors' Outerwear, nec
SIC 2369 Girls', Children's, & Infants' Outerwear, nec

SIC 2385 Waterproof Outerwear
315291 Infants' Cut & Sew Apparel Manufacturing
SIC 2341 Women's, Misses', Children's, & Infants' Underwear
& Nightwear
SIC 2361 Girls', Children's, & Infants' Dresses, Blouses, &
Shirts
SIC 2369 Girls', Children's, & Infants' Outerwear, nec
SIC 2385 Waterproof Outerwear
315292 Fur & Leather Apparel Manufacturing
SIC 2371 Fur Goods
SIC 2386 Leather & Sheep-lined Clothing
315299 All Other Cut & Sew Apparel Manufacturing
SIC 2329 Men's & Boys' Outerwear, nec
SIC 2339 Women's, Misses', & Juniors' Outerwear, nec
SIC 2389 Apparel & Accessories, nec
315991 Hat, Cap & Millinery Manufacturing
SIC 2353 Hats, Caps, & Millinery
315992 Glove & Mitten Manufacturing
SIC 2381 Dress & Work Gloves, Except Knit & All-Leather
SIC 3151 Leather Gloves & Mittens
315993 Men's & Boys' Neckwear Manufacturing
SIC 2323 Men's & Boys' Neckwear
**315999 Other Apparel Accessories & Other Apparel
Manufacturing**
SIC 2339 Women's, Misses', & Juniors' Outerwear, nec
SIC 2385 Waterproof Outerwear
SIC 2387 Apparel Belts
SIC 2389 Apparel & Accessories, nec
SIC 2396 Automotive Trimmings, Apparel Findings, & Related
Products
SIC 2399 Fabricated Textile Products, nec

LEATHER & ALLIED PRODUCT MANUFACTURING

31611   Leather & Hide Tanning & Finishing
SIC 3111 Leather Tanning & Finishing
SIC 3999 Manufacturing Industries, nec
316211 Rubber & Plastics Footwear Manufacturing
SIC 3021 Rubber & Plastics Footwear
316212 House Slipper Manufacturing
SIC 3142 House Slippers
316213 Men's Footwear Manufacturing
SIC 3143 Men's Footwear, Except Athletic
316214 Women's Footwear Manufacturing
SIC 3144 Women's Footwear, Except Athletic
316219 Other Footwear Manufacturing
SIC 3149 Footwear Except Rubber, NEC
316991 Luggage Manufacturing
SIC 3161 Luggage
316992 Women's Handbag & Purse Manufacturing
SIC 3171 Women's Handbags & Purses
316993 Personal Leather Good Manufacturing
SIC 3172 Personal Leather Goods, Except Women's Handbags
& Purses
316999 All Other Leather Good Manufacturing
SIC 3131 Boot & Shoe Cut Stock & Findings
SIC 3199 Leather Goods, nec

WOOD PRODUCT MANUFACTURING

321113 Sawmills
SIC 2421 Sawmills & Planing Mills, General
SIC 2429 Special Product Sawmills, nec

321114 Wood Preservation
SIC 2491 Wood Preserving

321211 Hardwood Veneer & Plywood Manufacturing
SIC 2435 Hardwood Veneer & Plywood

321212 Softwood Veneer & Plywood Manufacturing
SIC 2436 Softwood Veneer & Plywood

321213 Engineered Wood Member Manufacturing
SIC 2439 Structural Wood Members, nec

321214 Truss Manufacturing
SIC 2439 Structural Wood Members, nec

321219 Reconstituted Wood Product Manufacturing
SIC 2493 Reconstituted Wood Products

321911 Wood Window & Door Manufacturing
SIC 2431 Millwork

321912 Hardwood Dimension Mills
SIC 2426 Hardwood Dimension & Flooring Mills

321913 Softwood Cut Stock, Resawing Lumber, & Planing
SIC 2421 Sawmills & Planing Mills, General
SIC 2429 Special Product Sawmills, nec
SIC 2439 Structural Wood Members, nec

321914 Other Millwork
SIC 2421 Sawmills & Planing Mills, General
SIC 2426 Hardwood Dimension & Flooring Mills
SIC 2431 Millwork

32192 Wood Container & Pallet Manufacturing
SIC 2441 Nailed & Lock Corner Wood Boxes & Shook
SIC 2448 Wood Pallets & Skids
SIC 2449 Wood Containers, NEC
SIC 2499 Wood Products, nec

321991 Manufactured Home Manufacturing
SIC 2451 Mobile Homes

321992 Prefabricated Wood Building Manufacturing
SIC 2452 Prefabricated Wood Buildings & Components

321999 All Other Miscellaneous Wood Product Manufacturing
SIC 2426 Hardwood Dimension & Flooring Mills
SIC 2499 Wood Products, nec
SIC 3131 Boot & Shoe Cut Stock & Findings
SIC 3999 Manufacturing Industries, nec
SIC 2421 Sawmills & Planing Mills, General
SIC 2429 Special Product Sawmills, nec

PAPER MANUFACTURING

32211 Pulp Mills
SIC 2611 Pulp Mills

322121 Paper Mills
SIC 2611 Pulp Mills
SIC 2621 Paper Mills

322122 Newsprint Mills
SIC 2621 Paper Mills

32213 Paperboard Mills
SIC 2611 Pulp Mills
SIC 2631 Paperboard Mills

322211 Corrugated & Solid Fiber Box Manufacturing
SIC 2653 Corrugated & Solid Fiber Boxes

322212 Folding Paperboard Box Manufacturing
SIC 2657 Folding Paperboard Boxes, Including Sanitary

322213 Setup Paperboard Box Manufacturing
SIC 2652 Setup Paperboard Boxes

322214 Fiber Can, Tube, Drum, & Similar Products Manufacturing
SIC 2655 Fiber Cans, Tubes, Drums, & Similar Products

322215 Non-Folding Sanitary Food Container Manufacturing
SIC 2656 Sanitary Food Containers, Except Folding
SIC 2679 Converted Paper & Paperboard Products, NEC

322221 Coated & Laminated Packaging Paper & Plastics Film Manufacturing
SIC 2671 Packaging Paper & Plastics Film, Coated & Laminated

322222 Coated & Laminated Paper Manufacturing
SIC 2672 Coated & Laminated Paper, nec
SIC 2679 Converted Paper & Paperboard Products, nec

322223 Plastics, Foil, & Coated Paper Bag Manufacturing
SIC 2673 Plastics, Foil, & Coated Paper Bags

322224 Uncoated Paper & Multiwall Bag Manufacturing
SIC 2674 Uncoated Paper & Multiwall Bags

322225 Laminated Aluminum Foil Manufacturing for Flexible Packaging Uses
SIC 3497 Metal Foil & Leaf

322231 Die-Cut Paper & Paperboard Office Supplies Manufacturing
SIC 2675 Die-Cut Paper & Paperboard & Cardboard
SIC 2679 Converted Paper & Paperboard Products, nec

322232 Envelope Manufacturing
SIC 2677 Envelopes

322233 Stationery, Tablet, & Related Product Manufacturing
SIC 2678 Stationery, Tablets, & Related Products

322291 Sanitary Paper Product Manufacturing
SIC 2676 Sanitary Paper Products

322292 Surface-Coated Paperboard Manufacturing
SIC 2675 Die-Cut Paper & Paperboard & Cardboard

322298 All Other Converted Paper Product Manufacturing
SIC 2675 Die-Cut Paper & Paperboard & Cardboard
SIC 2679 Converted Paper & Paperboard Products, NEC

PRINTING & RELATED SUPPORT ACTIVITIES

323110 Commercial Lithographic Printing
SIC 2752 Commercial Printing, Lithographic
SIC 2771 Greeting Cards
SIC 2782 Blankbooks, Loose-leaf Binders & Devices
SIC 3999 Manufacturing Industries, nec

323111 Commercial Gravure Printing
SIC 2754 Commercial Printing, Gravure
SIC 2771 Greeting Cards
SIC 2782 Blankbooks, Loose-leaf Binders & Devices
SIC 3999 Manufacturing Industries, nec

323112 Commercial Flexographic Printing
SIC 2759 Commercial Printing, NEC
SIC 2771 Greeting Cards
SIC 2782 Blankbooks, Loose-leaf Binders & Devices
SIC 3999 Manufacturing Industries, nec

323113 Commercial Screen Printing
SIC 2396 Automotive Trimmings, Apparel Findings, & Related Products
SIC 2759 Commercial Printing, nec
SIC 2771 Greeting Cards
SIC 2782 Blankbooks, Loose-leaf Binders & Devices
SIC 3999 Manufacturing Industries, nec

323114 Quick Printing
SIC 2752 Commercial Printing, Lithographic
SIC 2759 Commercial Printing, nec
323115 Digital Printing
SIC 2759 Commercial Printing, nec
323116 Manifold Business Form Printing
SIC 2761 Manifold Business Forms
323117 Book Printing
SIC 2732 Book Printing
323118 Blankbook, Loose-leaf Binder & Device Manufacturing
SIC 2782 Blankbooks, Loose-leaf Binders & Devices
323119 Other Commercial Printing
SIC 2759 Commercial Printing, nec
SIC 2771 Greeting Cards
SIC 2782 Blankbooks, Loose-leaf Binders & Devices
SIC 3999 Manufacturing Industries, nec
323121 Tradebinding & Related Work
SIC 2789 Bookbinding & Related Work
323122 Prepress Services
SIC 2791 Typesetting
SIC 2796 Platemaking & Related Services

PETROLEUM & COAL PRODUCTS MANUFACTURING

32411 Petroleum Refineries
SIC 2911 Petroleum Refining
324121 Asphalt Paving Mixture & Block Manufacturing
SIC 2951 Asphalt Paving Mixtures & Blocks
324122 Asphalt Shingle & Coating Materials Manufacturing
SIC 2952 Asphalt Felts & Coatings
324191 Petroleum Lubricating Oil & Grease Manufacturing
SIC 2992 Lubricating Oils & Greases
324199 All Other Petroleum & Coal Products Manufacturing
SIC 2999 Products of Petroleum & Coal, nec
SIC 3312 Blast Furnaces & Steel Mills

CHEMICAL MANUFACTURING

32511 Petrochemical Manufacturing
SIC 2865 Cyclic Organic Crudes & Intermediates, & Organic
Dyes & Pigments
SIC 2869 Industrial Organic Chemicals, nec
32512 Industrial Gas Manufacturing
SIC 2813 Industrial Gases
SIC 2869 Industrial Organic Chemicals, nec
325131 Inorganic Dye & Pigment Manufacturing
SIC 2816 Inorganic Pigments
SIC 2819 Industrial Inorganic Chemicals, nec
325132 Organic Dye & Pigment Manufacturing
SIC 2865 Cyclic Organic Crudes & Intermediates, & Organic
Dyes & Pigments
325181 Alkalies & Chlorine Manufacturing
SIC 2812 Alkalies & Chlorine
325182 Carbon Black Manufacturing
SIC 2816 Inorganic pigments
SIC 2895 Carbon Black
325188 All Other Basic Inorganic Chemical Manufacturing
SIC 2819 Industrial Inorganic Chemicals, nec
SIC 2869 Industrial Organic Chemicals, nec

325191 Gum & Wood Chemical Manufacturing
SIC 2861 Gum & Wood Chemicals
325192 Cyclic Crude & Intermediate Manufacturing
SIC 2865 Cyclic Organic Crudes & Intermediates & Organic
Dyes & Pigments
325193 Ethyl Alcohol Manufacturing
SIC 2869 Industrial Organic Chemicals
325199 All Other Basic Organic Chemical Manufacturing
SIC 2869 Industrial Organic Chemicals, nec
SIC 2899 Chemical & Chemical Preparations, nec
325211 Plastics Material & Resin Manufacturing
SIC 2821 Plastics Materials, Synthetic & Resins, &
Nonvulcanizable Elastomers
325212 Synthetic Rubber Manufacturing
SIC 2822 Synthetic Rubber
325221 Cellulosic Manmade Fiber Manufacturing
SIC 2823 Cellulosic Manmade Fibers
325222 Noncellulosic Organic Fiber Manufacturing
SIC 2824 Manmade Organic Fibers, Except Cellulosic
325311 Nitrogenous Fertilizer Manufacturing
SIC 2873 Nitrogenous Fertilizers
325312 Phosphatic Fertilizer Manufacturing
SIC 2874 Phosphatic Fertilizers
325314 Fertilizer Manufacturing
SIC 2875 Fertilizers, Mixing Only
32532   Pesticide & Other Agricultural Chemical Manufacturing
SIC 2879 Pesticides & Agricultural Chemicals, nec
325411 Medicinal & Botanical Manufacturing
SIC 2833 Medicinal Chemicals & Botanical Products
325412 Pharmaceutical Preparation Manufacturing
SIC 2834 Pharmaceutical Preparations
SIC 2835 In-Vitro & In-Vivo Diagnostic Substances
325413 In-Vitro Diagnostic Substance Manufacturing
SIC 2835 In-Vitro & In-Vivo Diagnostic Substances
325414 Biological Product Manufacturing
SIC 2836 Biological Products, Except Diagnostic Substance
32551   Paint & Coating Manufacturing
SIC 2851 Paints, Varnishes, Lacquers, Enamels & Allied
Products
SIC 2899 Chemicals & Chemical Preparations, nec
32552   Adhesive & Sealant Manufacturing
SIC 2891 Adhesives & Sealants
325611 Soap & Other Detergent Manufacturing
SIC 2841 Soaps & Other Detergents, Except Specialty Cleaners
SIC 2844 Toilet Preparations
325612 Polish & Other Sanitation Good Manufacturing
SIC 2842 Specialty Cleaning, Polishing, & Sanitary Preparations
325613 Surface Active Agent Manufacturing
SIC 2843 Surface Active Agents, Finishing Agents, Sulfonated
Oils, & Assistants
32562   Toilet Preparation Manufacturing
SIC 2844 Perfumes, Cosmetics, & Other Toilet Preparations
32591   Printing Ink Manufacturing
SIC 2893 Printing Ink
32592   Explosives Manufacturing
SIC 2892 Explosives
325991 Custom Compounding of Purchased Resin
SIC 3087 Custom Compounding of Purchased Plastics Resin
**325992 Photographic Film, Paper, Plate & Chemical
Manufacturing**
SIC 3861 Photographic Equipment & Supplies

325998 All Other Miscellaneous Chemical Product Manufacturing
SIC 2819 Industrial Inorganic Chemicals, nec
SIC 2899 Chemicals & Chemical Preparations, nec
SIC 3952 Lead Pencils & Art Goods
SIC 3999 Manufacturing Industries, nec

PLASTICS & RUBBER PRODUCTS MANUFACTURING

326111 Unsupported Plastics Bag Manufacturing
SIC 2673 Plastics, Foil, & Coated Paper Bags
326112 Unsupported Plastics Packaging Film & Sheet Manufacturing
SIC 2671 Packaging Paper & Plastics Film, Coated, & Laminated
326113 Unsupported Plastics Film & Sheet Manufacturing
SIC 3081 Unsupported Plastics Film & Sheets
326121 Unsupported Plastics Profile Shape Manufacturing
SIC 3082 Unsupported Plastics Profile Shapes
SIC 3089 Plastics Product, nec
326122 Plastics Pipe & Pipe Fitting Manufacturing
SIC 3084 Plastics Pipe
SIC 3089 Plastics Products, nec
32613 Laminated Plastics Plate, Sheet & Shape Manufacturing
SIC 3083 Laminated Plastics Plate, Sheet & Profile Shapes
32614 Polystyrene Foam Product Manufacturing
SIC 3086 Plastics Foam Products
32615 Urethane & Other Foam Product Manufacturing
SIC 3086 Plastics Foam Products
32616 Plastics Bottle Manufacturing
SIC 3085 Plastics Bottles
326191 Plastics Plumbing Fixture Manufacturing
SIC 3088 Plastics Plumbing Fixtures
326192 Resilient Floor Covering Manufacturing
SIC 3069 Fabricated Rubber Products, nec
SIC 3996 Linoleum, Asphalted-Felt-Base, & Other Hard Surface Floor Coverings, nec
326199 All Other Plastics Product Manufacturing
SIC 3089 Plastics Products, nec
SIC 3999 Manufacturing Industries, nec
326211 Tire Manufacturing
SIC 3011 Tires & Inner Tubes
326212 Tire Retreading
SIC 7534 Tire Retreading & Repair Shops
32622 Rubber & Plastics Hoses & Belting Manufacturing
SIC 3052 Rubber & Plastics Hose & Belting
326291 Rubber Product Manufacturing for Mechanical Use
SIC 3061 Molded, Extruded, & Lathe-Cut Mechanical Rubber Goods
326299 All Other Rubber Product Manufacturing
SIC 3069 Fabricated Rubber Products, nec

NONMETALLIC MINERAL PRODUCT MANUFACTURING

327111 Vitreous China Plumbing Fixture & China & Earthenware Fittings & Bathroom Accessories Manufacturing
SIC 3261 Vitreous China Plumbing Fixtures & China & Earthenware Fittings & Bathroom Accessories

327112 Vitreous China, Fine Earthenware & Other Pottery Product Manufacturing
SIC 3262 Vitreous China Table & Kitchen Articles
SIC 3263 Fine Earthenware Table & Kitchen Articles
SIC 3269 Pottery Products, nec
327113 Porcelain Electrical Supply Manufacturing
SIC 3264 Porcelain Electrical Supplies
327121 Brick & Structural Clay Tile Manufacturing
SIC 3251 Brick & Structural Clay Tile
327122 Ceramic Wall & Floor Tile Manufacturing
SIC 3253 Ceramic Wall & Floor Tile
327123 Other Structural Clay Product Manufacturing
SIC 3259 Structural Clay Products, nec
327124 Clay Refractory Manufacturing
SIC 3255 Clay Refractories
327125 Nonclay Refractory Manufacturing
SIC 3297 Nonclay Refractories
327211 Flat Glass Manufacturing
SIC 3211 Flat Glass
327212 Other Pressed & Blown Glass & Glassware Manufacturing
SIC 3229 Pressed & Blown Glass & Glassware, nec
327213 Glass Container Manufacturing
SIC 3221 Glass Containers
327215 Glass Product Manufacturing Made of Purchased Glass
SIC 3231 Glass Products Made of Purchased Glass
32731 Hydraulic Cement Manufacturing
SIC 3241 Cement, Hydraulic
32732 Ready-Mix Concrete Manufacturing
SIC 3273 Ready-Mixed Concrete
327331 Concrete Block & Brick Manufacturing
SIC 3271 Concrete Block & Brick
327332 Concrete Pipe Manufacturing
SIC 3272 Concrete Products, Except Block & Brick
32739 Other Concrete Product Manufacturing
SIC 3272 Concrete Products, Except Block & Brick
32741 Lime Manufacturing
SIC 3274 Lime
32742 Gypsum & Gypsum Product Manufacturing
SIC 3275 Gypsum Products
SIC 3299 Nonmetallic Mineral Products, nec
32791 Abrasive Product Manufacturing
SIC 3291 Abrasive Products
327991 Cut Stone & Stone Product Manufacturing
SIC 3281 Cut Stone & Stone Products
327992 Ground or Treated Mineral & Earth Manufacturing
SIC 3295 Minerals & Earths, Ground or Otherwise Treated
327993 Mineral Wool Manufacturing
SIC 3296 Mineral Wool
327999 All Other Miscellaneous Nonmetallic Mineral Product Manufacturing
SIC 3272 Concrete Products, Except Block & Brick
SIC 3292 Asbestos Products
SIC 3299 Nonmetallic Mineral Products, nec

PRIMARY METAL MANUFACTURING

331111 Iron & Steel Mills
SIC 3312 Steel Works, Blast Furnaces , & Rolling Mills
SIC 3399 Primary Metal Products, nec
331112 Electrometallurgical Ferroalloy Product Manufacturing
SIC 3313 Electrometallurgical Products, Except Steel

33121 Iron & Steel Pipes & Tubes Manufacturing from Purchased Steel
SIC 3317 Steel Pipe & Tubes

331221 Cold-Rolled Steel Shape Manufacturing
SIC 3316 Cold-Rolled Steel Sheet, Strip & Bars

331222 Steel Wire Drawing
SIC 3315 Steel Wiredrawing & Steel Nails & Spikes

331311 Alumina Refining
SIC 2819 Industrial Inorganic Chemicals, nec

331312 Primary Aluminum Production
SIC 3334 Primary Production of Aluminum

331314 Secondary Smelting & Alloying of Aluminum
SIC 3341 Secondary Smelting & Refining of Nonferrous Metals
SIC 3399 Primary Metal Products, nec

331315 Aluminum Sheet, Plate & Foil Manufacturing
SIC 3353 Aluminum Sheet, Plate, & Foil

331316 Aluminum Extruded Product Manufacturing
SIC 3354 Aluminum Extruded Products

331319 Other Aluminum Rolling & Drawing
SIC 3355 Aluminum Rolling & Drawing, nec
SIC 3357 Drawing & Insulating of Nonferrous Wire

331411 Primary Smelting & Refining of Copper
SIC 3331 Primary Smelting & Refining of Copper

331419 Primary Smelting & Refining of Nonferrous Metal
SIC 3339 Primary Smelting & Refining of Nonferrous Metals, Except Copper & Aluminum

331421 Copper Rolling, Drawing & Extruding
SIC 3351 Rolling, Drawing, & Extruding of Copper

331422 Copper Wire Drawing
SIC 3357 Drawing & Insulating of Nonferrous Wire

331423 Secondary Smelting, Refining, & Alloying of Copper
SIC 3341 Secondary Smelting & Refining of Nonferrous Metals
SIC 3399 Primary Metal Products, nec

331491 Nonferrous Metal Rolling, Drawing & Extruding
SIC 3356 Rolling, Drawing & Extruding of Nonferrous Metals, Except Copper & Aluminum
SIC 3357 Drawing & Insulating of Nonferrous Wire

331492 Secondary Smelting, Refining, & Alloying of Nonferrous Metal
SIC 3313 Electrometallurgical Products, Except Steel
SIC 3341 Secondary Smelting & Reining of Nonferrous Metals
SIC 3399 Primary Metal Products, nec

331511 Iron Foundries
SIC 3321 Gray & Ductile Iron Foundries
SIC 3322 Malleable Iron Foundries

331512 Steel Investment Foundries
SIC 3324 Steel Investment Foundries

331513 Steel Foundries,
SIC 3325 Steel Foundries, nec

331521 Aluminum Die-Castings
SIC 3363 Aluminum Die-Castings

331522 Nonferrous Die-Castings
SIC 3364 Nonferrous Die-Castings, Except Aluminum

331524 Aluminum Foundries
SIC 3365 Aluminum Foundries

331525 Copper Foundries
SIC 3366 Copper Foundries

331528 Other Nonferrous Foundries
SIC 3369 Nonferrous Foundries, Except Aluminum & Copper

FABRICATED METAL PRODUCT MANUFACTURING

332111 Iron & Steel Forging
SIC 3462 Iron & Steel Forgings

332112 Nonferrous Forging
SIC 3463 Nonferrous Forgings

332114 Custom Roll Forming
SIC 3449 Miscellaneous Structural Metal Work

332115 Crown & Closure Manufacturing
SIC 3466 Crowns & Closures

332116 Metal Stamping
SIC 3469 Metal Stampings, nec

332117 Powder Metallurgy Part Manufacturing
SIC 3499 Fabricated Metal Products, nec

332211 Cutlery & Flatware Manufacturing
SIC 3421 Cutlery
SIC 3914 Silverware, Plated Ware, & Stainless Steel Ware

332212 Hand & Edge Tool Manufacturing
SIC 3423 Hand & Edge Tools, Except Machine Tools & Handsaws
SIC 3523 Farm Machinery & Equipment
SIC 3524 Lawn & Garden Tractors & Home Lawn & Garden Equipment
SIC 3545 Cutting Tools, Machine Tools Accessories, & Machinist Precision Measuring Devices
SIC 3799 Transportation Equipment, nec
SIC 3999 Manufacturing Industries, nec

332213 Saw Blade & Handsaw Manufacturing
SIC 3425 Saw Blades & Handsaws

332214 Kitchen Utensil, Pot & Pan Manufacturing
SIC 3469 Metal Stampings, nec

332311 Prefabricated Metal Building & Component Manufacturing
SIC 3448 Prefabricated Metal Buildings & Components

332312 Fabricated Structural Metal Manufacturing
SIC 3441 Fabricated Structural Metal
SIC 3449 Miscellaneous Structural Metal Work

332313 Plate Work Manufacturing
SIC 3443 Fabricated Plate Work

332321 Metal Window & Door Manufacturing
SIC 3442 Metal Doors, Sash, Frames, Molding & Trim
SIC 3449 Miscellaneous Structural Metal Work

332322 Sheet Metal Work Manufacturing
SIC 3444 Sheet Metal Work

332323 Ornamental & Architectural Metal Work Manufacturing
SIC 3446 Architectural & Ornamental Metal Work
SIC 3449 Miscellaneous Structural Metal Work
SIC 3523 Farm Machinery & Equipment

33241 Power Boiler & Heat Exchanger Manufacturing
SIC 3443 Fabricated Plate Work

33242 Metal Tank Manufacturing
SIC 3443 Fabricated Plate Work

332431 Metal Can Manufacturing
SIC 3411 Metal Cans

332439 Other Metal Container Manufacturing
SIC 3412 Metal Shipping Barrels, Drums, Kegs, & Pails
SIC 3429 Hardware, nec
SIC 3444 Sheet Metal Work
SIC 3499 Fabricated Metal Products, nec
SIC 3537 Industrial Trucks, Tractors, Trailers, & Stackers

33251 Hardware Manufacturing
SIC 3429 Hardware, nec
SIC 3499 Fabricated Metal Products, nec

332611 Steel Spring Manufacturing
SIC 3493 Steel Springs, Except Wire

332612 Wire Spring Manufacturing
SIC 3495 Wire Springs

332618 Other Fabricated Wire Product Manufacturing
SIC 3315 Steel Wiredrawing & Steel Nails & Spikes
SIC 3399 Primary Metal Products, nec
SIC 3496 Miscellaneous Fabricated Wire Products

33271 Machine Shops
SIC 3599 Industrial & Commercial Machinery & Equipment, nec

332721 Precision Turned Product Manufacturing
SIC 3451 Screw Machine Products

332722 Bolt, Nut, Screw, Rivet & Washer Manufacturing
SIC 3452 Bolts, Nuts, Screws, Rivets, & Washers

332811 Metal Heat Treating
SIC 3398 Metal Heat Treating

332812 Metal Coating, Engraving , & Allied Services to Manufacturers
SIC 3479 Coating, Engraving, & Allied Services, nec

332813 Electroplating, Plating, Polishing, Anodizing & Coloring
SIC 3399 Primary Metal Products, nec
SIC 3471 Electroplating, Plating, Polishing, Anodizing, & Coloring

332911 Industrial Valve Manufacturing
SIC 3491 Industrial Valves

332912 Fluid Power Valve & Hose Fitting Manufacturing
SIC 3492 Fluid Power Valves & Hose Fittings
SIC 3728 Aircraft Parts & Auxiliary Equipment, nec

332913 Plumbing Fixture Fitting & Trim Manufacturing
SIC 3432 Plumbing Fixture Fittings & Trim

332919 Other Metal Valve & Pipe Fitting Manufacturing
SIC 3429 Hardware, nec
SIC 3494 Valves & Pipe Fittings, nec
SIC 3499 Fabricated Metal Products, nec

332991 Ball & Roller Bearing Manufacturing
SIC 3562 Ball & Roller Bearings

332992 Small Arms Ammunition Manufacturing
SIC 3482 Small Arms Ammunition

332993 Ammunition Manufacturing
SIC 3483 Ammunition, Except for Small Arms

332994 Small Arms Manufacturing
SIC 3484 Small Arms

332995 Other Ordnance & Accessories Manufacturing
SIC 3489 Ordnance & Accessories, nec

332996 Fabricated Pipe & Pipe Fitting Manufacturing
SIC 3498 Fabricated Pipe & Pipe Fittings

332997 Industrial Pattern Manufacturing
SIC 3543 Industrial Patterns

332998 Enameled Iron & Metal Sanitary Ware Manufacturing
SIC 3431 Enameled Iron & Metal Sanitary Ware

332999 All Other Miscellaneous Fabricated Metal Product Manufacturing
SIC 3291 Abrasive Products
SIC 3432 Plumbing Fixture Fittings & Trim
SIC 3494 Valves & Pipe Fittings, nec
SIC 3497 Metal Foil & Leaf
SIC 3499 Fabricated Metal Products, NEC
SIC 3537 Industrial Trucks, Tractors, Trailers, & Stackers
SIC 3599 Industrial & Commercial Machinery & Equipment, nec
SIC 3999 Manufacturing Industries, nec

MACHINERY MANUFACTURING

333111 Farm Machinery & Equipment Manufacturing
SIC 3523 Farm Machinery & Equipment

333112 Lawn & Garden Tractor & Home Lawn & Garden Equipment Manufacturing
SIC 3524 Lawn & Garden Tractors & Home Lawn & Garden Equipment

33312 Construction Machinery Manufacturing
SIC 3531 Construction Machinery & Equipment

333131 Mining Machinery & Equipment Manufacturing
SIC 3532 Mining Machinery & Equipment, Except Oil & Gas Field Machinery & Equipment

333132 Oil & Gas Field Machinery & Equipment Manufacturing
SIC 3533 Oil & Gas Field Machinery & Equipment

33321 Sawmill & Woodworking Machinery Manufacturing
SIC 3553 Woodworking Machinery

33322 Rubber & Plastics Industry Machinery Manufacturing
SIC 3559 Special Industry Machinery, nec

333291 Paper Industry Machinery Manufacturing
SIC 3554 Paper Industries Machinery

333292 Textile Machinery Manufacturing
SIC 3552 Textile Machinery

333293 Printing Machinery & Equipment Manufacturing
SIC 3555 Printing Trades Machinery & Equipment

333294 Food Product Machinery Manufacturing
SIC 3556 Food Products Machinery

333295 Semiconductor Machinery Manufacturing
SIC 3559 Special Industry Machinery, nec

333298 All Other Industrial Machinery Manufacturing
SIC 3559 Special Industry Machinery, nec
SIC 3639 Household Appliances, nec

333311 Automatic Vending Machine Manufacturing
SIC 3581 Automatic Vending Machines

333312 Commercial Laundry, Drycleaning & Pressing Machine Manufacturing
SIC 3582 Commercial Laundry, Drycleaning & Pressing Machines

333313 Office Machinery Manufacturing
SIC 3578 Calculating & Accounting Machinery, Except Electronic Computers
SIC 3579 Office Machines, nec

333314 Optical Instrument & Lens Manufacturing
SIC 3827 Optical Instruments & Lenses

333315 Photographic & Photocopying Equipment Manufacturing
SIC 3861 Photographic Equipment & Supplies

333319 Other Commercial & Service Industry Machinery Manufacturing
SIC 3559 Special Industry Machinery, nec
SIC 3589 Service Industry Machinery, nec
SIC 3599 Industrial & Commercial Machinery & Equipment, nec
SIC 3699 Electrical Machinery, Equipment & Supplies, nec

333411 Air Purification Equipment Manufacturing
SIC 3564 Industrial & Commercial Fans & Blowers & Air Purification Equipment

333412 Industrial & Commercial Fan & Blower Manufacturing
SIC 3564 Industrial & Commercial Fans & Blowers & Air Purification Equipment

333414 Heating Equipment Manufacturing
SIC 3433 Heating Equipment, Except Electric & Warm Air Furnaces

SIC 3634 Electric Housewares & Fans

333415 Air-Conditioning & Warm Air Heating Equipment & Commercial & Industrial Refrigeration Equipment Manufacturing

SIC 3443 Fabricated Plate Work

SIC 3585 Air-Conditioning & Warm Air Heating Equipment & Commercial & Industrial Refrigeration Equipment

333511 Industrial Mold Manufacturing

SIC 3544 Special Dies & Tools, Die Sets, Jigs & Fixtures, & Industrial Molds

333512 Machine Tool Manufacturing

SIC 3541 Machine Tools, Metal Cutting Type

333513 Machine Tool Manufacturing

SIC 3542 Machine Tools, Metal Forming Type

333514 Special Die & Tool, Die Set, Jig & Fixture Manufacturing

SIC 3544 Special Dies & Tools, Die Sets, Jigs & Fixtures, & Industrial Molds

333515 Cutting Tool & Machine Tool Accessory Manufacturing

SIC 3545 Cutting Tools, Machine Tool Accessories, & Machinists' Precision Measuring Devices

333516 Rolling Mill Machinery & Equipment Manufacturing

SIC 3547 Rolling Mill Machinery & Equipment

333518 Other Metalworking Machinery Manufacturing

SIC 3549 Metalworking Machinery, nec

333611 Turbine & Turbine Generator Set Unit Manufacturing

SIC 3511 Steam, Gas, & Hydraulic Turbines, & Turbine Generator Set Units

333612 Speed Changer, Industrial High-Speed Drive & Gear Manufacturing

SIC 3566 Speed Changers, Industrial High-Speed Drives, & Gears

333613 Mechanical Power Transmission Equipment Manufacturing

SIC 3568 Mechanical Power Transmission Equipment, nec

333618 Other Engine Equipment Manufacturing

SIC 3519 Internal Combustion Engines, nec

SIC 3699 Electrical Machinery, Equipment & Supplies, nec

333911 Pump & Pumping Equipment Manufacturing

SIC 3561 Pumps & Pumping Equipment

SIC 3743 Railroad Equipment

333912 Air & Gas Compressor Manufacturing

SIC 3563 Air & Gas Compressors

333913 Measuring & Dispensing Pump Manufacturing

SIC 3586 Measuring & Dispensing Pumps

333921 Elevator & Moving Stairway Manufacturing

SIC 3534 Elevators & Moving Stairways

333922 Conveyor & Conveying Equipment Manufacturing

SIC 3523 Farm Machinery & Equipment

SIC 3535 Conveyors & Conveying Equipment

333923 Overhead Traveling Crane, Hoist & Monorail System Manufacturing

SIC 3536 Overhead Traveling Cranes, Hoists, & Monorail Systems

SIC 3531 Construction Machinery & Equipment

333924 Industrial Truck, Tractor, Trailer & Stacker Machinery Manufacturing

SIC 3537 Industrial Trucks, Tractors, Trailers, & Stackers

333991 Power-Driven Hand Tool Manufacturing

SIC 3546 Power-Driven Handtools

333992 Welding & Soldering Equipment Manufacturing

SIC 3548 Electric & Gas Welding & Soldering Equipment

333993 Packaging Machinery Manufacturing

SIC 3565 Packaging Machinery

333994 Industrial Process Furnace & Oven Manufacturing

SIC 3567 Industrial Process Furnaces & Ovens

333995 Fluid Power Cylinder & Actuator Manufacturing

SIC 3593 Fluid Power Cylinders & Actuators

333996 Fluid Power Pump & Motor Manufacturing

SIC 3594 Fluid Power Pumps & Motors

333997 Scale & Balance Manufacturing

SIC 3596 Scales & Balances, Except Laboratory

333999 All Other General Purpose Machinery Manufacturing

SIC 3599 Industrial & Commercial Machinery & Equipment, nec

SIC 3569 General Industrial Machinery & Equipment, nec

COMPUTER & ELECTRONIC PRODUCT MANUFACTURING

334111 Electronic Computer Manufacturing

SIC 3571 Electronic Computers

334112 Computer Storage Device Manufacturing

SIC 3572 Computer Storage Devices

334113 Computer Terminal Manufacturing

SIC 3575 Computer Terminals

334119 Other Computer Peripheral Equipment Manufacturing

SIC 3577 Computer Peripheral Equipment, nec

SIC 3578 Calculating & Accounting Machines, Except Electronic Computers

SIC 3699 Electrical Machinery, Equipment & Supplies, nec

33421 Telephone Apparatus Manufacturing

SIC 3661 Telephone & Telegraph Apparatus

33422 Radio & Television Broadcasting & Wireless Communications Equipment Manufacturing

SIC 3663 Radio & Television Broadcasting & Communication Equipment

SIC 3679 Electronic Components, nec

33429 Other Communications Equipment Manufacturing

SIC 3669 Communications Equipment, nec

33431 Audio & Video Equipment Manufacturing

SIC 3651 Household Audio & Video Equipment

334411 Electron Tube Manufacturing

SIC 3671 Electron Tubes

334412 Printed Circuit Board Manufacturing

SIC 3672 Printed Circuit Boards

334413 Semiconductor & Related Device Manufacturing

SIC 3674 Semiconductors & Related Devices

334414 Electronic Capacitor Manufacturing

SIC 3675 Electronic Capacitors

334415 Electronic Resistor Manufacturing

SIC 3676 Electronic Resistors

334416 Electronic Coil, Transformer, & Other Inductor Manufacturing

SIC 3661 Telephone & Telegraph Apparatus

SIC 3677 Electronic Coils, Transformers, & Other Inductors

SIC 3825 Instruments for Measuring & Testing of Electricity & Electrical Signals

334417 Electronic Connector Manufacturing

SIC 3678 Electronic Connectors

334418 Printed Circuit/Electronics Assembly Manufacturing

SIC 3679 Electronic Components, nec

SIC 3661 Telephone & Telegraph Apparatus

334419 Other Electronic Component Manufacturing
SIC 3679 Electronic Components, nec
334510 Electromedical & Electrotherapeutic Apparatus Manufacturing
SIC 3842 Orthopedic, Prosthetic & Surgical Appliances & Supplies
SIC 3845 Electromedical & Electrotherapeutic Apparatus
334511 Search, Detection, Navigation, Guidance, Aeronautical, & Nautical System & Instrument Manufacturing
SIC 3812 Search, Detection, Navigation, Guidance, Aeronautical, & Nautical Systems & Instruments
334512 Automatic Environmental Control Manufacturing for Residential, Commercial & Appliance Use
SIC 3822 Automatic Controls for Regulating Residential & Commercial Environments & Appliances
334513 Instruments & Related Products Manufacturing for Measuring, Displaying, & Controlling Industrial Process Variables
SIC 3823 Industrial Instruments for Measurement, Display, & Control of Process Variables; & Related Products
334514 Totalizing Fluid Meter & Counting Device Manufacturing
SIC 3824 Totalizing Fluid Meters & Counting Devices
334515 Instrument Manufacturing for Measuring & Testing Electricity & Electrical Signals
SIC 3825 Instruments for Measuring & Testing of Electricity & Electrical Signals
334516 Analytical Laboratory Instrument Manufacturing
SIC 3826 Laboratory Analytical Instruments
334517 Irradiation Apparatus Manufacturing
SIC 3844 X-Ray Apparatus & Tubes & Related Irradiation Apparatus
SIC 3845 Electromedical & Electrotherapeutic Apparatus
334518 Watch, Clock, & Part Manufacturing
SIC 3495 Wire Springs
SIC 3579 Office Machines, nec
SIC 3873 Watches, Clocks, Clockwork Operated Devices, & Parts
334519 Other Measuring & Controlling Device Manufacturing
SIC 3829 Measuring & Controlling Devices, nec
334611 Software Reproducing
SIC 7372 Prepackaged Software
334612 Prerecorded Compact Disc , Tape, & Record Reproducing
SIC 3652 Phonograph Records & Prerecorded Audio Tapes & Disks
SIC 7819 Services Allied to Motion Picture Production
334613 Magnetic & Optical Recording Media Manufacturing
SIC 3695 Magnetic & Optical Recording Media

ELECTRICAL EQUIPMENT, APPLIANCE, & COMPONENT MANUFACTURING

33511 Electric Lamp Bulb & Part Manufacturing
SIC 3641 Electric Lamp Bulbs & Tubes
335121 Residential Electric Lighting Fixture Manufacturing
SIC 3645 Residential Electric Lighting Fixtures
SIC 3999 Manufacturing Industries, nec
335122 Commercial, Industrial & Institutional Electric Lighting Fixture Manufacturing
SIC 3646 Commercial, Industrial, & Institutional Electric Lighting Fixtures

335129 Other Lighting Equipment Manufacturing
SIC 3648 Lighting Equipment, nec
SIC 3699 Electrical Machinery, Equipment, & Supplies, nec
335211 Electric Housewares & Fan Manufacturing
SIC 3634 Electric Housewares & Fans
335212 Household Vacuum Cleaner Manufacturing
SIC 3635 Household Vacuum Cleaners
SIC 3639 Household Appliances, nec
335221 Household Cooking Appliance Manufacturing
SIC 3631 Household Cooking Equipment
335222 Household Refrigerator & Home Freezer Manufacturing
SIC 3632 Household Refrigerators & Home & Farm Freezers
335224 Household Laundry Equipment Manufacturing
SIC 3633 Household Laundry Equipment
335228 Other Household Appliance Manufacturing
SIC 3639 Household Appliances, nec
335311 Power, Distribution & Specialty Transformer Manufacturing
SIC 3548 Electric & Gas Welding & Soldering Equipment
SIC 3612 Power, Distribution, & Speciality Transformers
335312 Motor & Generator Manufacturing
SIC 3621 Motors & Generators
SIC 7694 Armature Rewinding Shops
335313 Switchgear & Switchboard Apparatus Manufacturing
SIC 3613 Switchgear & Switchboard Apparatus
335314 Relay & Industrial Control Manufacturing
SIC 3625 Relays & Industrial Controls
335911 Storage Battery Manufacturing
SIC 3691 Storage Batteries
335912 Dry & Wet Primary Battery Manufacturing
SIC 3692 Primary Batteries, Dry & Wet
335921 Fiber-Optic Cable Manufacturing
SIC 3357 Drawing & Insulating of Nonferrous Wire
335929 Other Communication & Energy Wire Manufacturing
SIC 3357 Drawing & Insulating of Nonferrous Wire
335931 Current-Carrying Wiring Device Manufacturing
SIC 3643 Current-Carrying Wiring Devices
335932 Noncurrent-Carrying Wiring Device Manufacturing
SIC 3644 Noncurrent-Carrying Wiring Devices
335991 Carbon & Graphite Product Manufacturing
SIC 3624 Carbon & Graphite Products
335999 All Other Miscellaneous Electrical Equipment & Component Manufacturing
SIC 3629 Electrical Industrial Apparatus, nec
SIC 3699 Electrical Machinery, Equipment, & Supplies, nec

TRANSPORTATION EQUIPMENT MANUFACTURING

336111 Automobile Manufacturing
SIC 3711 Motor Vehicles & Passenger Car Bodies
336112 Light Truck & Utility Vehicle Manufacturing
SIC 3711 Motor Vehicles & Passenger Car Bodies
33612 Heavy Duty Truck Manufacturing
SIC 3711 Motor Vehicles & Passenger Car Bodies
336211 Motor Vehicle Body Manufacturing
SIC 3711 Motor Vehicles & Passenger Car Bodies
SIC 3713 Truck & Bus Bodies
SIC 3714 Motor Vehicle Parts & Accessories
336212 Truck Trailer Manufacturing
SIC 3715 Truck Trailers

336213 Motor Home Manufacturing
SIC 3716 Motor Homes
336214 Travel Trailer & Camper Manufacturing
SIC 3792 Travel Trailers & Campers
SIC 3799 Transportation Equipment, nec
336311 Carburetor, Piston, Piston Ring & Valve Manufacturing
SIC 3592 Carburetors, Pistons, Piston Rings, & Valves
336312 Gasoline Engine & Engine Parts Manufacturing
SIC 3714 Motor Vehicle Parts & Accessories
336321 Vehicular Lighting Equipment Manufacturing
SIC 3647 Vehicular Lighting Equipment
336322 Other Motor Vehicle Electrical & Electronic Equipment Manufacturing
SIC 3679 Electronic Components, nec
SIC 3694 Electrical Equipment for Internal Combustion Engines
SIC 3714 Motor Vehicle Parts & Accessories
33633 Motor Vehicle Steering & Suspension Components Manufacturing
SIC 3714 Motor Vehicle Parts & Accessories
33634 Motor Vehicle Brake System Manufacturing
SIC 3292 Asbestos Products
SIC 3714 Motor Vehicle Parts & Accessories
33635 Motor Vehicle Transmission & Power Train Parts Manufacturing
SIC 3714 Motor Vehicle Parts & Accessories
33636 Motor Vehicle Fabric Accessories & Seat Manufacturing
SIC 2396 Automotive Trimmings, Apparel Findings, & Related Products
SIC 2399 Fabricated Textile Products, nec
SIC 2531 Public Building & Related Furniture
33637 Motor Vehicle Metal Stamping
SIC 3465 Automotive Stampings
336391 Motor Vehicle Air-Conditioning Manufacturing
SIC 3585 Air-Conditioning & Warm Air Heating Equipment & Commercial & Industrial Refrigeration Equipment
336399 All Other Motor Vehicle Parts Manufacturing
SIC 3519 Internal Combustion Engines, nec
SIC 3599 Industrial & Commercial Machinery & Equipment, NEC
SIC 3714 Motor Vehicle Parts & Accessories
336411 Aircraft Manufacturing
SIC 3721 Aircraft
336412 Aircraft Engine & Engine Parts Manufacturing
SIC 3724 Aircraft Engines & Engine Parts
336413 Other Aircraft Part & Auxiliary Equipment Manufacturing
SIC 3728 Aircraft Parts & Auxiliary Equipment, nec
336414 Guided Missile & Space Vehicle Manufacturing
SIC 3761 Guided Missiles & Space Vehicles
336415 Guided Missile & Space Vehicle Propulsion Unit & Propulsion Unit Parts Manufacturing
SIC 3764 Guided Missile & Space Vehicle Propulsion Units & Propulsion Unit Parts
336419 Other Guided Missile & Space Vehicle Parts & Auxiliary Equipment Manufacturing
SIC 3769 Guided Missile & Space Vehicle Parts & Auxiliary Equipment
33651 Railroad Rolling Stock Manufacturing
SIC 3531 Construction Machinery & Equipment
SIC 3743 Railroad Equipment
336611 Ship Building & Repairing
SIC 3731 Ship Building & Repairing

336612 Boat Building
SIC 3732 Boat Building & Repairing
336991 Motorcycle, Bicycle, & Parts Manufacturing
SIC 3944 Games, Toys, & Children's Vehicles, Except Dolls & Bicycles
SIC 3751 Motorcycles, Bicycles & Parts
336992 Military Armored Vehicle, Tank & Tank Component Manufacturing
SIC 3711 Motor Vehicles & Passenger Car Bodies
SIC 3795 Tanks & Tank Components
336999 All Other Transportation Equipment Manufacturing
SIC 3799 Transportation Equipment, nec

FURNITURE & RELATED PRODUCT MANUFACTURING

337121 Upholstered Household Furniture Manufacturing
SIC 2512 Wood Household Furniture, Upholstered
SIC 2515 Mattress, Foundations, & Convertible Beds
SIC 5712 Furniture
337122 Nonupholstered Wood Household Furniture Manufacturing
SIC 2511 Wood Household Furniture, Except Upholstered
SIC 5712 Furniture Stores
337124 Metal Household Furniture Manufacturing
SIC 2514 Metal Household Furniture
337125 Household Furniture Manufacturing
SIC 2519 Household Furniture, NEC
337127 Institutional Furniture Manufacturing
SIC 2531 Public Building & Related Furniture
SIC 2599 Furniture & Fixtures, nec
SIC 3952 Lead Pencils, Crayons, & Artist's Materials
SIC 3999 Manufacturing Industries, nec
337129 Wood Television, Radio, & Sewing Machine Cabinet Manufacturing
SIC 2517 Wood Television, Radio, Phonograph, & Sewing Machine Cabinets
337131 Wood Kitchen & Counter Top Manufacturing
SIC 2434 Wood Kitchen Cabinets
SIC 2541 Wood Office & Store Fixtures, Partitions, Shelving, & Lockers
SIC 5712 Furniture Stores
337132 Upholstered Wood Household Furniture Manufacturing
SIC 2515 Mattresses, Foundations, & Convertible Beds
SIC 5712 Furniture Stores
337133 Wood Household Furniture
SIC 5712 Furniture Stores
337134 Wood Office Furniture Manufacturing
SIC 2521 Wood Office Furniture
337135 Custom Architectural Woodwork, Millwork, & Fixtures
SIC 2541 Wood Office & Store Fixtures, Partitions, Shelving, and Lockers
337139 Other Wood Furniture Manufacturing
SIC 2426 Hardwood Dimension & Flooring Mills
SIC 2499 Wood Products, nec
SIC 2517 Wood Television, Radio, Phonograph, & Sewing Machine Cabinets
SIC 2531 Public Building & Related Furniture
SIC 2541 Wood Office & Store Fixtures, Partitions., Shelving, & Lockers
SIC 2599 Furniture & Fixtures, nec
SIC 3952 Lead Pencils, Crayons, & Artist's Materials

337141 Nonwood Office Furniture Manufacturing
SIC 2522 Office Furniture, Except Wood
337143 Household Furniture Manufacturing
SIC 2519 Household Furniture, NEC
337145 Nonwood Showcase, Partition, Shelving, & Locker Manufacturing
SIC 2542 Office & Store Fixtures, Partitions, Shelving, & Lockers, Except Wood
337148 Other Nonwood Furniture Manufacturing
SIC 2499 Wood Products, NEC
SIC 2531 Public Building & Related Furniture
SIC 2599 Furniture & Fixtures, nec
SIC 3499 Fabricated Metal Products, nec
SIC 3952 Lead Pencils, Crayons, & Artist's Materials
SIC 3999 Manufacturing Industries, nec
337212 Custom Architectural Woodwork & Millwork Manufacturing
SIC 2541 Wood Office & Store Fixtures, Partitions, Shelving, & Lockers
337214 Nonwood Office Furniture Manufacturing
SIC 2522 Office Furniture, Except Wood
337215 Showcase, Partition, Shelving, & Locker Manufacturing
SIC 2542 Office & Store Fixtures, Partitions, Shelving, & Lockers, Except Wood
SIC 2541 Wood Office & Store Fixtures, Partitions, Shelving, & Lockers
SIC 2426 Hardwood Dimension & Flooring Mills
SIC 3499 Fabricated Metal Products, nec
33791 Mattress Manufacturing
SIC 2515 Mattresses, Foundations & Convertible Beds
33792 Blind & Shade Manufacturing
SIC 2591 Drapery Hardware & Window Blinds & Shades

MISCELLANEOUS MANUFACTURING

339111 Laboratory Apparatus & Furniture Manufacturing
SIC 3829 Measuring & Controlling Devices, nec
339112 Surgical & Medical Instrument Manufacturing
SIC 3841 Surgical & Medical Instruments & Apparatus
SIC 3829 Measuring & Controlling Devices, nec
339113 Surgical Appliance & Supplies Manufacturing
SIC 2599 Furniture & Fixtures, nec
SIC 3842 Orthopedic, Prosthetic, & Surgical Appliances & Supplies
339114 Dental Equipment & Supplies Manufacturing
SIC 3843 Dental Equipment & Supplies
339115 Ophthalmic Goods Manufacturing
SIC 3851 Opthalmic Goods
SIC 5995 Optical Goods Stores
339116 Dental Laboratories
SIC 8072 Dental Laboratories 339117 Eyeglass & Contact Lens Manufacturing
SIC 5995 Optical Goods Stores
339911 Jewelry Manufacturing
SIC 3469 Metal Stamping, nec
SIC 3479 Coating, Engraving, & Allied Services, nec
SIC 3911 Jewelry, Precious Metal
339912 Silverware & Plated Ware Manufacturing
SIC 3479 Coating, Engraving, & Allied Services, nec
SIC 3914 Silverware, Plated Ware, & Stainless Steel Ware
339913 Jewelers' Material & Lapidary Work Manufacturing
SIC 3915 Jewelers' Findings & Materials, & Lapidary Work

339914 Costume Jewelry & Novelty Manufacturing
SIC 3479 Coating, Engraving, & Allied Services, nec
SIC 3499 Fabricated Metal Products, nec
SIC 3961 Costume Jewelry & Costume Novelties, Except Precious Metal
33992 Sporting & Athletic Goods Manufacturing
SIC 3949 Sporting & Athletic Goods, nec
339931 Doll & Stuffed Toy Manufacturing
SIC 3942 Dolls & Stuffed Toys
339932 Game, Toy, & Children's Vehicle Manufacturing
SIC 3944 Games, Toys, & Children's Vehicles, Except Dolls & Bicycles
339941 Pen & Mechanical Pencil Manufacturing
SIC 3951 Pens, Mechanical Pencils, & Parts
339942 Lead Pencil & Art Good Manufacturing
SIC 2531 Public Buildings & Related Furniture
SIC 3579 Office Machines, nec
SIC 3952 Lead Pencils, Crayons, & Artists' Materials
339943 Marking Device Manufacturing
SIC 3953 Marking Devices
339944 Carbon Paper & Inked Ribbon Manufacturing
SIC 3955 Carbon Paper & Inked Ribbons
33995 Sign Manufacturing
SIC 3993 Signs & Advertising Specialties
339991 Gasket, Packing, & Sealing Device Manufacturing
SIC 3053 Gaskets, Packing, & Sealing Devices
339992 Musical Instrument Manufacturing
SIC 3931 Musical Instruments
339993 Fastener, Button, Needle & Pin Manufacturing
SIC 3965 Fasteners, Buttons, Needles, & Pins
SIC 3131 Boat & Shoe Cut Stock & Findings
339994 Broom, Brush & Mop Manufacturing
SIC 3991 Brooms & Brushes
SIC 2392 Housefurnishings, Except Curtains & Draperies
339995 Burial Casket Manufacturing
SIC 3995 Burial Caskets
339999 All Other Miscellaneous Manufacturing
SIC 2499 Wood Products, NEC
SIC 3999 Manufacturing Industries, nec

WHOLESALE TRADE

42111 Automobile & Other Motor Vehicle Wholesalers
SIC 5012 Automobiles & Other Motor Vehicles
42112 Motor Vehicle Supplies & New Part Wholesalers
SIC 5013 Motor Vehicle Supplies & New Parts
42113 Tire & Tube Wholesalers
SIC 5014 Tires & Tubes
42114 Motor Vehicle Part Wholesalers
SIC 5015 Motor Vehicle Parts, Used
42121 Furniture Wholesalers
SIC 5021 Furniture
42122 Home Furnishing Wholesalers
SIC 5023 Homefurnishings
42131 Lumber, Plywood, Millwork & Wood Panel Wholesalers
SIC 5031 Lumber, Plywood, Millwork, & Wood Panels
SIC 5211 Lumber & Other Building Materials Dealers - Retail
42132 Brick, Stone & Related Construction Material Wholesalers
SIC 5032 Brick, Stone, & Related Construction Materials
42133 Roofing, Siding & Insulation Material Wholesalers
SIC 5033 Roofing, Siding, & Insulation Materials

42139　Other Construction Material Wholesalers
SIC 5039 Construction Materials, nec

42141　Photographic Equipment & Supplies Wholesalers
SIC 5043 Photographic Equipment & Supplies

42142　Office Equipment Wholesalers
SIC 5044 Office Equipment

42143　Computer & Computer Peripheral Equipment & Software Wholesalers
SIC 5045 Computers & Computer Peripherals Equipment & Software

42144　Other Commercial Equipment Wholesalers
SIC 5046 Commercial Equipment, nec

42145　Medical, Dental & Hospital Equipment & Supplies Wholesalers
SIC 5047 Medical, Dental & Hospital Equipment & Supplies

42146　Ophthalmic Goods Wholesalers
SIC 5048 Ophthalmic Goods

42149　Other Professional Equipment & Supplies Wholesalers
SIC 5049 Professional Equipment & Supplies, nec

42151　Metal Service Centers & Offices
SIC 5051 Metals Service Centers & Offices

42152　Coal & Other Mineral & Ore Wholesalers
SIC 5052 Coal & Other Mineral & Ores

42161　Electrical Apparatus & Equipment, Wiring Supplies & Construction Material Wholesalers
SIC 5063 Electrical Apparatus & Equipment, Wiring Supplies & Construction Materials

42162　Electrical Appliance, Television & Radio Set Wholesalers
SIC 5064 Electrical Appliances, Television & Radio Sets

42169　Other Electronic Parts & Equipment Wholesalers
SIC 5065 Electronic Parts & Equipment, nec

42171　Hardware Wholesalers
SIC 5072 Hardware

42172　Plumbing & Heating Equipment & Supplies Wholesalers
SIC 5074 Plumbing & Heating Equipment & Supplies

42173　Warm Air Heating & Air-Conditioning Equipment & Supplies Wholesalers
SIC 5075 Warm Air Heating & Air-Conditioning Equipment & Supplies

42174　Refrigeration Equipment & Supplies Wholesalers
SIC 5078 Refrigeration Equipment & Supplies

42181　Construction & Mining Machinery & Equipment Wholesalers
SIC 5082 Construction & Mining Machinery & Equipment

42182　Farm & Garden Machinery & Equipment Wholesalers
SIC 5083 Farm & Garden Machinery & Equipment

42183　Industrial Machinery & Equipment Wholesalers
SIC 5084 Industrial Machinery & Equipment
SIC 5085 Industrial Supplies

42184　Industrial Supplies Wholesalers
SIC 5085 Industrial Supplies

42185　Service Establishment Equipment & Supplies Wholesalers
SIC 5087 Service Establishment Equipment & Supplies Wholesalers

42186　Transportation Equipment & Supplies Wholesalers
SIC 5088 Transportation Equipment and Supplies, Except Motor Vehicles

42191　Sporting & Recreational Goods & Supplies Wholesalers
SIC 5091 Sporting & Recreational Goods & Supplies

42192　Toy & Hobby Goods & Supplies Wholesalers
SIC 5092 Toys & Hobby Goods & Supplies

42193　Recyclable Material Wholesalers
SIC 5093 Scrap & Waste Materials

42194　Jewelry, Watch, Precious Stone & Precious Metal Wholesalers
SIC 5094 Jewelry, Watches, Precious Stones, & Precious Metals

42199　Other Miscellaneous Durable Goods Wholesalers
SIC 5099 Durable Goods, nec
SIC 7822 Motion Picture & Video Tape Distribution

42211　Printing & Writing Paper Wholesalers
SIC 5111 Printing & Writing Paper

42212　Stationary & Office Supplies Wholesalers
SIC 5112 Stationery & Office Supplies

42213　Industrial & Personal Service Paper Wholesalers
SIC 5113 Industrial & Personal Service Paper

42221　Drug, Drug Proprietaries & Druggists' Sundries Wholesalers
SIC 5122 Drugs, Drug Proprietaries, & Druggists' Sundries

42231　Piece Goods, Notions & Other Dry Goods Wholesalers
SIC 5131 Piece Goods, Notions, & Other Dry Goods

42232　Men's & Boys' Clothing & Furnishings Wholesalers
SIC 5136 Men's & Boys' Clothing & Furnishings

42233　Women's, Children's, & Infants' & Accessories Wholesalers
SIC 5137 Women's, Children's, & Infants' Clothing & Accessories

42234　Footwear Wholesalers
SIC 5139 Footwear

42241　General Line Grocery Wholesalers
SIC 5141 Groceries, General Line

42242　Packaged Frozen Food Wholesalers
SIC 5142 Packaged Frozen Foods

42243　Dairy Product Wholesalers
SIC 5143 Dairy Products, Except Dried or Canned

42244　Poultry & Poultry Product Wholesalers
SIC 5144 Poultry & Poultry Products

42245　Confectionery Wholesalers
SIC 5145 Confectionery

42246　Fish & Seafood Wholesalers
SIC 5146 Fish & Seafoods

42247　Meat & Meat Product Wholesalers
SIC 5147 Meats & Meat Products

42248　Fresh Fruit & Vegetable Wholesalers
SIC 5148 Fresh Fruits & Vegetables

42249　Other Grocery & Related Products Wholesalers
SIC 5149 Groceries & Related Products, nec

42251　Grain & Field Bean Wholesalers
SIC 5153 Grain & Field Beans

42252　Livestock Wholesalers
SIC 5154 Livestock

42259　Other Farm Product Raw Material Wholesalers
SIC 5159 Farm-Product Raw Materials, nec

42261　Plastics Materials & Basic Forms & Shapes Wholesalers
SIC 5162 Plastics Materials & Basic Forms & Shapes

42269　Other Chemical & Allied Products Wholesalers
SIC 5169 Chemicals & Allied Products, nec

42271　Petroleum Bulk Stations & Terminals
SIC 5171 Petroleum Bulk Stations & Terminals

42272　Petroleum & Petroleum Products Wholesalers
SIC 5172 Petroleum & Petroleum Products Wholesalers, Except Bulk Stations & Terminals

42281　Beer & Ale Wholesalers
SIC 5181 Beer & Ale

42282 Wine & Distilled Alcoholic Beverage Wholesalers
SIC 5182 Wine & Distilled Alcoholic Beverages

42291 Farm Supplies Wholesalers
SIC 5191 Farm Supplies

42292 Book, Periodical & Newspaper Wholesalers
SIC 5192 Books, Periodicals, & Newspapers

42293 Flower, Nursery Stock & Florists' Supplies Wholesalers
SIC 5193 Flowers, Nursery Stock, & Florists' Supplies

42294 Tobacco & Tobacco Product Wholesalers
SIC 5194 Tobacco & Tobacco Products

42295 Paint, Varnish & Supplies Wholesalers
SIC 5198 Paints, Varnishes, & Supplies
SIC 5231 Paint, Glass & Wallpaper Stores

42299 Other Miscellaneous Nondurable Goods Wholesalers
SIC 5199 Nondurable Goods, nec

RETAIL TRADE

44111 New Car Dealers
SIC 5511 Motor Vehicle Dealers, New and Used

44112 Used Car Dealers
SIC 5521 Motor Vehicle Dealers, Used Only

44121 Recreational Vehicle Dealers
SIC 5561 Recreational Vehicle Dealers

441221 Motorcycle Dealers
SIC 5571 Motorcycle Dealers

441222 Boat Dealers
SIC 5551 Boat Dealers

441229 All Other Motor Vehicle Dealers
SIC 5599 Automotive Dealers, NEC

44131 Automotive Parts & Accessories Stores
SIC 5013 Motor Vehicle Supplies & New Parts
SIC 5731 Radio, Television, & Consumer Electronics Stores
SIC 5531 Auto & Home Supply Stores

44132 Tire Dealers
SIC 5014 Tires & Tubes
SIC 5531 Auto & Home Supply Stores

44211 Furniture Stores
SIC 5021 Furniture
SIC 5712 Furniture Stores

44221 Floor Covering Stores
SIC 5023 Homefurnishings
SIC 5713 Floor Coverings Stores

442291 Window Treatment Stores
SIC 5714 Drapery, Curtain, & Upholstery Stores
SIC 5719 Miscellaneous Homefurnishings Stores

442299 All Other Home Furnishings Stores
SIC 5719 Miscellaneous Homefurnishings Stores

443111 Household Appliance Stores
SIC 5722 Household Appliance Stores
SIC 5999 Miscellaneous Retail Stores, nec
SIC 7623 Refrigeration & Air-Conditioning Service & Repair Shops
SIC 7629 Electrical & Electronic Repair Shops, nec

443112 Radio, Television & Other Electronics Stores
SIC 5731 Radio, Television, & Consumer Electronics Stores
SIC 5999 Miscellaneous Retail Stores, nec
SIC 7622 Radio & Television Repair Shops

44312 Computer & Software Stores
SIC 5045 Computers & Computer Peripheral Equipment & Software
SIC 7378 Computer Maintenance & Repair '
SIC 5734 Computer & Computer Software Stores

44313 Camera & Photographic Supplies Stores
SIC 5946 Camera & Photographic Supply Stores

44411 Home Centers
SIC 5211 Lumber & Other Building Materials Dealers

44412 Paint & Wallpaper Stores
SIC 5198 Paints, Varnishes, & Supplies
SIC 5231 Paint, Glass, & Wallpaper Stores

44413 Hardware Stores
SIC 5251 Hardware Stores

44419 Other Building Material Dealers
SIC 5031 Lumber, Plywood, Millwork, & Wood Panels
SIC 5032 Brick, Stone, & Related Construction Materials
SIC 5039 Construction Materials, nec
SIC 5063 Electrical Apparatus & Equipment, Wiring Supplies, & Construction Materials
SIC 5074 Plumbing & Heating Equipment & Supplies
SIC 5211 Lumber & Other Building Materials Dealers
SIC 5231 Paint, Glass, & Wallpaper Stores

44421 Outdoor Power Equipment Stores
SIC 5083 Farm & Garden Machinery & Equipment
SIC 5261 Retail Nurseries, Lawn & Garden Supply Stores

44422 Nursery & Garden Centers
SIC 5191 Farm Supplies
SIC 5193 Flowers, Nursery Stock, & Florists' Supplies
SIC 5261 Retail Nurseries, Lawn & Garden Supply Stores

44511 Supermarkets & Other Grocery Stores
SIC 5411 Grocery Stores

44512 Convenience Stores
SIC 5411 Grocery Stores

44521 Meat Markets
SIC 5421 Meat & Fish Markets, Including Freezer Provisioners
SIC 5499 Miscellaneous Food Stores

44522 Fish & Seafood Markets
SIC 5421 Meat & Fish Markets, Including Freezer Provisioners

44523 Fruit & Vegetable Markets
SIC 5431 Fruit & Vegetable Markets

445291 Baked Goods Stores
SIC 5461 Retail Bakeries

445292 Confectionery & Nut Stores
SIC 5441 Candy, Nut & Confectionery Stores

445299 All Other Specialty Food Stores
SIC 5499 Miscellaneous Food Stores
SIC 5451 Dairy Products Stores

44531 Beer, Wine & Liquor Stores
SIC 5921 Liquor Stores

44611 Pharmacies & Drug Stores
SIC 5912 Drug Stores & Proprietary Stores

44612 Cosmetics, Beauty Supplies & Perfume Stores
SIC 5087 Service Establishment Equipment & Supplies
SIC 5999 Miscellaneous Retail Stores, nec

44613 Optical Goods Stores
SIC 5995 Optical Goods Stores

446191 Food Supplement Stores
SIC 5499 Miscellaneous Food Stores

446199 All Other Health & Personal Care Stores
SIC 5047 Medical, Dental, & Hospital Equipment & Supplies
SIC 5999 Miscellaneous Retail Stores, nec

44711 Gasoline Stations with Convenience Stores
SIC 5541 Gasoline Service Station
SIC 5411 Grocery Stores

44719 Other Gasoline Stations
SIC 5541 Gasoline Service Station

44811 Men's Clothing Stores
SIC 5611 Men's & Boys' Clothing & Accessory Stores
44812 Women's Clothing Stores
SIC 5621 Women's Clothing Stores
44813 Children's & Infants' Clothing Stores
SIC 5641 Children's & Infants' Wear Stores
44814 Family Clothing Stores
SIC 5651 Family Clothing Stores
44815 Clothing Accessories Stores
SIC 5611 Men's & Boys' Clothing & Accessory Stores
SIC 5632 Women's Accessory & Specialty Stores
SIC 5699 Miscellaneous Apparel & Accessory Stores
44819 Other Clothing Stores
SIC 5699 Miscellaneous Apparel & Accessory Stores
SIC 5632 Women's Accessory & Specialty Stores
44821 Shoe Stores
SIC 5661 Shoe Stores
44831 Jewelry Stores
SIC 5999 Miscellaneous Retailer, nec
SIC 5944 Jewelry Stores
44832 Luggage & Leather Goods Stores
SIC 5948 Luggage & Leather Goods Stores
45111 Sporting Goods Stores
SIC 7699 Repair Shops & Related Services, NEC
SIC 5941 Sporting Goods Stores & Bicycle Shops
45112 Hobby, Toy & Game Stores
SIC 5945 Hobby, Toy, & Game Stores
45113 Sewing, Needlework & Piece Goods Stores
SIC 5714 Drapery, Curtain, & Upholstery Stores
SIC 5949 Sewing, Needlework, & Piece Goods Stores
45114 Musical Instrument & Supplies Stores
SIC 5736 Musical Instruments Stores
451211 Book Stores
SIC 5942 Book Stores
451212 News Dealers & Newsstands
SIC 5994 News Dealers & Newsstands
45122 Prerecorded Tape, Compact Disc & Record Stores
SIC 5735 Record & Prerecorded Tape Stores
45211 Department Stores
SIC 5311 Department Stores
45291 Warehouse Clubs & Superstores
SIC 5399 Miscellaneous General Merchandise Stores
SIC 5411 Grocery Stores
45299 All Other General Merchandise Stores
SIC 5399 Miscellaneous General Merchandise Stores
SIC 5331 Variety Stores
45311 Florists
SIC 5992 Florists
45321 Office Supplies & Stationery Stores
SIC 5049 Professional Equipment & Supplies, nec
SIC 5112 Stationery & Office Supplies
SIC 5943 Stationery Stores
45322 Gift, Novelty & Souvenir Stores
SIC 5947 Gift, Novelty, & Souvenir Shops
45331 Used Merchandise Stores
SIC 5932 Used Merchandise Stores
45391 Pet & Pet Supplies Stores
SIC 5999 Miscellaneous Retail Stores, NEC
45392 Art Dealers
SIC 5999 Miscellaneous Retail Stores, nec
45393 Manufactured Home Dealers
SIC 5271 Mobile Home Dealers

453991 Tobacco Stores
SIC 5993 Tobacco Stores & Stands
453999 All Other Miscellaneous Store Retailers
SIC 5999 Miscellaneous Retail Stores, nec
SIC 5261 Retail Nurseries, Lawn & Garden Supply Stores
45411 Electronic Shopping & Mail-Order Houses
SIC 5961 Catalog & Mail-Order Houses
45421 Vending Machine Operators
SIC 5962 Automatic Merchandise Machine Operators
454311 Heating Oil Dealers
SIC 5171 Petroleum Bulk Stations & Terminals
SIC 5983 Fuel Oil Dealers
454312 Liquefied Petroleum Gas Dealers
SIC 5171 Petroleum Bulk Stations & Terminals
SIC 5984 Liquefied Petroleum Gas Dealers
454319 Other Fuel Dealers
SIC 5989 Fuel Dealers, nec
45439 Other Direct Selling Establishments
SIC 5421 Meat & Fish Markets, Including Freezer Provisioners
SIC 5963 Direct Selling Establishments

TRANSPORTATION & WAREHOUSING

481111 Scheduled Passenger Air Transportation
SIC 4512 Air Transportation, Scheduled
481112 Scheduled Freight Air Transportation
SIC 4512 Air Transportation, Scheduled
481211 Nonscheduled Chartered Passenger Air Transportation
SIC 4522 Air Transportation, Nonscheduled
481212 Nonscheduled Chartered Freight Air Transportation
SIC 4522 Air Transportation, Nonscheduled
481219 Other Nonscheduled Air Transportation
SIC 7319 Advertising, nec
48122 Nonscheduled Speciality Air Transportation
SIC 0721 Crop Planting, Cultivating, & Protecting
SIC 1382 Oil & Gas Field Exploration Services
SIC 4522 Air Transportation, Nonscheduled
SIC 7335 Commercial Photography
SIC 7997 Membership Sports & Recreation Clubs
SIC 8299 Schools & Educational Services, nec
SIC 8713 Surveying Services
482111 Line-Haul Railroads
SIC 4011 Railroads, Line-Haul Operating
482112 Short Line Railroads
SIC 4013 Railroad Switching & Terminal Establishments
483111 Deep Sea Freight Transportation
SIC 4412 Deep Sea Foreign Transportation of Freight
483112 Deep Sea Passenger Transportation
SIC 4481 Deep Sea Transportation of Passengers, Except by Ferry
483113 Coastal & Great Lakes Freight Transportation
SIC 4424 Deep Sea Domestic Transportation of Freight
SIC 4432 Freight Transportation on the Great Lakes - St. Lawrence Seaway
SIC 4492 Towing & Tugboat Services
483114 Coastal & Great Lakes Passenger Transportation
SIC 4481 Deep Sea Transportation of Passengers, Except by Ferry
SIC 4482 Ferries
483211 Inland Water Freight Transportation
SIC 4449 Water Transportation of Freight, nec
SIC 4492 Towing & Tugboat Services

483212 Inland Water Passenger Transportation
SIC 4482 Ferries
SIC 4489 Water Transportation of Passengers, nec
48411 General Freight Trucking, Local
SIC 4212 Local Trucking without Storage
SIC 4214 Local Trucking with Storage
484121 General Freight Trucking, Long-Distance, Truckload
SIC 4213 Trucking, Except Local
484122 General Freight Trucking, Long-Distance, Less Than Truckload
SIC 4213 Trucking, Except Local
48421 Used Household & Office Goods Moving
SIC 4212 Local Trucking Without Storage
SIC 4213 Trucking, Except Local
SIC 4214 Local Trucking With Storage
48422 Specialized Freight Trucking, Local
SIC 4212 Local Trucking without Storage
SIC 4214 Local Trucking with Storage
48423 Specialized Freight Trucking, Long-Distance
SIC 4213 Trucking, Except Local
485111 Mixed Mode Transit Systems
SIC 4111 Local & Suburban Transit
485112 Commuter Rail Systems
SIC 4111 Local & Suburban Transit
485113 Bus & Motor Vehicle Transit Systems
SIC 4111 Local & Suburban Transit
485119 Other Urban Transit Systems
SIC 4111 Local & Suburban Transit
48521 Interurban & Rural Bus Transportation
SIC 4131 Intercity & Rural Bus Transportation
48531 Taxi Service
SIC 4121 Taxicabs
48532 Limousine Service
SIC 4119 Local Passenger Transportation, nec
48541 School & Employee Bus Transportation
SIC 4151 School Buses
SIC 4119 Local Passenger Transportation, nec
48551 Charter Bus Industry
SIC 4141 Local Charter Bus Service
SIC 4142 Bus Charter Services, Except Local
485991 Special Needs Transportation
SIC 4119 Local Passenger Transportation, nec
485999 All Other Transit & Ground Passenger Transportation
SIC 4111 Local & Suburban Transit
SIC 4119 Local Passenger Transportation, nec
48611 Pipeline Transportation of Crude Oil
SIC 4612 Crude Petroleum Pipelines
48621 Pipeline Transportation of Natural Gas
SIC 4922 Natural Gas Transmission
SIC 4923 Natural Gas Transmission & Distribution
48691 Pipeline Transportation of Refined Petroleum Products
SIC 4613 Refined Petroleum Pipelines
48699 All Other Pipeline Transportation
SIC 4619 Pipelines, nec
48711 Scenic & Sightseeing Transportation, Land
SIC 4119 Local Passenger Transportation, nec
SIC 4789 Transportation Services, nec
SIC 7999 Amusement & Recreation Services, nec
48721 Scenic & Sightseeing Transportation, Water
SIC 4489 Water Transportation of Passengers, nec
SIC 7999 Amusement & Recreation Services, nec
48799 Scenic & Sightseeing Transportation, Other
SIC 4522 Air Transportation, Nonscheduled
SIC 7999 Amusement & Recreation Services, nec

488111 Air Traffic Control
SIC 4581 Airports, Flying Fields, & Airport Terminal Services
SIC 9621 Regulation & Administration of Transportation Programs
488112 Airport Operations, except Air Traffic Control
SIC 4581 Airports, Flying Fields, & Airport Terminal Services
SIC 4959 Sanitary Services, nec
488119 Other Airport Operations
SIC 4581 Airports, Flying Fields, & Airport Terminal Services
SIC 4959 Sanitary Services, nec
48819 Other Support Activities for Air Transportation
SIC 4581 Airports, Flying Fields, & Airport Terminal Services
48821 Support Activities for Rail Transportation
SIC 4013 Railroad Switching & Terminal Establishments
SIC 4741 Rental of Railroad Cars
SIC 4789 Transportation Services, nec
48831 Port & Harbor Operations
SIC 4491 Marine Cargo Handling
SIC 4499 Water Transportation Services, nec
48832 Marine Cargo Handling
SIC 4491 Marine Cargo Handling
48833 Navigational Services to Shipping
SIC 4492 Towing & Tugboat Services
SIC 4499 Water Transportation Services, nec
48839 Other Support Activities for Water Transportation
SIC 4499 Water Transportation Services, nec
SIC 4785 Fixed Facilities & Inspection & Weighing Services for Motor Vehicle Transportation
SIC 7699 Repair Shops & Related Services, nec
48841 Motor Vehicle Towing
SIC 7549 Automotive Services, Except Repair & Carwashes
48849 Other Support Activities for Road Transportation
SIC 4173 Terminal & Service Facilities for Motor Vehicle Passenger Transportation
SIC 4231 Terminal & Joint Terminal Maintenance Facilities for Motor Freight Transportation
SIC 4785 Fixed Facilities & Inspection & Weighing Services for Motor Vehicle Transportation
48851 Freight Transportation Arrangement
SIC 4731 Arrangement of Transportation of Freight & Cargo
488991 Packing & Crating
SIC 4783 Packing & Crating
488999 All Other Support Activities for Transportation
SIC 4729 Arrangement of Passenger Transportation, nec
SIC 4789 Transportation Services, nec
49111 Postal Service
SIC 4311 United States Postal Service
49211 Couriers
SIC 4215 Courier Services, Except by Air
SIC 4513 Air Courier Services
49221 Local Messengers & Local Delivery
SIC 4215 Courier Services, Except by Air
49311 General Warehousing & Storage Facilities
SIC 4225 General Warehousing & Storage
SIC 4226 Special Warehousing & Storage, nec
49312 Refrigerated Storage Facilities
SIC 4222 Refrigerated Warehousing & Storage
SIC 4226 Special Warehousing & Storage, nec
49313 Farm Product Storage Facilities
SIC 4221 Farm Product Warehousing & Storage
49319 Other Warehousing & Storage Facilities
SIC 4226 Special Warehousing & Storage, nec

INFORMATION

51111 Newspaper Publishers
SIC 2711 Newspapers: Publishing or Publishing & Printing
51112 Periodical Publishers
SIC 2721 Periodicals: Publishing or Publishing & Printing
51113 Book Publishers
SIC 2731 Books: Publishing or Publishing & Printing
51114 Database & Directory Publishers
SIC 2741 Miscellaneous Publishing
511191 Greeting Card Publishers
SIC 2771 Greeting Cards
511199 All Other Publishers
SIC 2741 Miscellaneous Publishing
51121 Software Publishers
SIC 7372 Prepackaged Software
51211 Motion Picture & Video Production
SIC 7812 Motion Picture & Video Tape Production
51212 Motion Picture & Video Distribution
SIC 7822 Motion Picture & Video Tape Distribution
SIC 7829 Services Allied to Motion Picture Distribution
512131 Motion Picture Theaters, Except Drive-Ins.
SIC 7832 Motion Picture Theaters, Except Drive-In
512132 Drive-In Motion Picture Theaters
SIC 7833 Drive-In Motion Picture Theaters
512191 Teleproduction & Other Post-Production Services
SIC 7819 Services Allied to Motion Picture Production
512199 Other Motion Picture & Video Industries
SIC 7819 Services Allied to Motion Picture Production
SIC 7829 Services Allied to Motion Picture Distribution
51221 Record Production
SIC 8999 Services, nec
51222 Integrated Record Production/Distribution
SIC 3652 Phonograph Records & Prerecorded Audio Tapes & Disks
51223 Music Publishers
SIC 2731 Books: Publishing or Publishing & Printing
SIC 2741 Miscellaneous Publishing
SIC 8999 Services, nec
51224 Sound Recording Studios
SIC 7389 Business Services, nec
51229 Other Sound Recording Industries
SIC 7389 Business Services, nec
SIC 7922 Theatrical Producers & Miscellaneous Theatrical Services
513111 Radio Networks
SIC 4832 Radio Broadcasting Stations
513112 Radio Stations
SIC 4832 Radio Broadcasting Stations
51312 Television Broadcasting
SIC 4833 Television Broadcasting Stations
51321 Cable Networks
SIC 4841 Cable & Other Pay Television Services
51322 Cable & Other Program Distribution
SIC 4841 Cable & Other Pay Television Services
51331 Wired Telecommunications Carriers
SIC 4813 Telephone Communications, Except Radiotelephone
SIC 4822 Telegraph & Other Message Communications
513321 Paging
SIC 4812 Radiotelephone Communications
513322 Cellular & Other Wireless Telecommunications
SIC 4812 Radiotelephone Communications
SIC 4899 Communications Services, nec

51333 Telecommunications Resellers
SIC 4812 Radio Communications
SIC 4813 Telephone Communications, Except Radiotelephone
51334 Satellite Telecommunications
SIC 4899 Communications Services, NEC
51339 Other Telecommunications
SIC 4899 Communications Services, NEC
51411 News Syndicates
SIC 7383 News Syndicates
51412 Libraries & Archives
SIC 8231 Libraries
514191 On-Line Information Services
SIC 7375 Information Retrieval Services
514199 All Other Information Services
SIC 8999 Services, nec
51421 Data Processing Services
SIC 7374 Computer Processing & Data Preparation & Processing Services

FINANCE & INSURANCE

52111 Monetary Authorities - Central Bank
SIC 6011 Federal Reserve Banks
52211 Commercial Banking
SIC 6021 National Commercial Banks
SIC 6022 State Commercial Banks
SIC 6029 Commercial Banks, nec
SIC 6081 Branches & Agencies of Foreign Banks
52212 Savings Institutions
SIC 6035 Savings Institutions, Federally Chartered
SIC 6036 Savings Institutions, Not Federally Chartered
52213 Credit Unions
SIC 6061 Credit Unions, Federally Chartered
SIC 6062 Credit Unions, Not Federally Chartered
52219 Other Depository Credit Intermediation
SIC 6022 State Commercial Banks
52221 Credit Card Issuing
SIC 6021 National Commercial Banks
SIC 6022 State Commercial Banks
SIC 6141 Personal Credit Institutions
52222 Sales Financing
SIC 6141 Personal Credit Institutions
SIC 6153 Short-Term Business Credit Institutions, Except Agricultural .
SIC 6159 Miscellaneous Business Credit Institutions
522291 Consumer Lending
SIC 6141 Personal Credit Institutions
522292 Real Estate Credit
SIC 6162 Mortgage Bankers & Loan Correspondents
522293 International Trade Financing
SIC 6081 Branches & Agencies of Foreign Banks
SIC 6082 Foreign Trade & International Banking Institutions
SIC 6111 Federal & Federally-Sponsored Credit Agencies
SIC 6159 Miscellaneous Business Credit Institutions
522294 Secondary Market Financing
SIC 6111 Federal & Federally Sponsored Credit Agencies
522298 All Other Nondepository Credit Intermediation
SIC 5932 Used Merchandise Stores
SIC 6081 Branches & Agencies of Foreign Banks
SIC 6111 Federal & Federally-Sponsored Credit Agencies
SIC 6153 Short-Term Business Credit Institutions, Except Agricultural
SIC 6159 Miscellaneous Business Credit Institutions

52231 Mortgage & Other Loan Brokers
SIC 6163 Loan Brokers
52232 Financial Transactions Processing, Reserve, & Clearing House Activities
SIC 6019 Central Reserve Depository Institutions, nec
SIC 6099 Functions Related to Depository Banking, nec
SIC 6153 Short-Term Business Credit Institutions, Except Agricultural
SIC 7389 Business Services, nec
52239 Other Activities Related to Credit Intermediation
SIC 6099 Functions Related to Depository Banking, nec
SIC 6162 Mortgage Bankers & Loan Correspondents
52311 Investment Banking & Securities Dealing
SIC 6211 Security Brokers, Dealers, & Flotation Companies
52312 Securities Brokerage
SIC 6211 Security Brokers, Dealers, & Flotation Companies
52313 Commodity Contracts Dealing
SIC 6099 Functions Related to depository Banking, nec
SIC 6799 Investors, nec
SIC 6221 Commodity Contracts Brokers & Dealers
52314 Commodity Brokerage
SIC 6221 Commodity Contracts Brokers & Dealers
52321 Securities & Commodity Exchanges
SIC 6231 Security & Commodity Exchanges
52391 Miscellaneous Intermediation
SIC 6211 Securities Brokers, Dealers & Flotation Companies
SIC 6799 Investors, nec
52392 Portfolio Management
SIC 6282 Investment Advice
SIC 6371 Pension, Health, & Welfare Funds
SIC 6733 Trust, Except Educational, Religious, & Charitable
SIC 6799 Investors, nec
52393 Investment Advice
SIC 6282 Investment Advice
523991 Trust, Fiduciary & Custody Activities
SIC 6021 National Commercial Banks
SIC 6022 State Commercial Banks
SIC 6091 Nondepository Trust Facilities
SIC 6099 Functions Related to Depository Banking, nec
SIC 6289 Services Allied With the Exchange of Securities or Commodities, nec
SIC 6733 Trusts, Except Educational, Religious, & Charitable
523999 Miscellaneous Financial Investment Activities
SIC 6099 Functions Related to Depository Banking, nec
SIC 6211 Security Brokers, Dealers, & Flotation Companies
SIC 6289 Services Allied With the Exchange of Securities or Commodities, nec
SIC 6799 Investors, nec
SIC 6792 Oil Royalty Traders
524113 Direct Life Insurance Carriers
SIC 6311 Life Insurance
524114 Direct Health & Medical Insurance Carriers
SIC 6324 Hospital & Medical Service Plans
SIC 6321 Accident & Health Insurance
524126 Direct Property & Casualty Insurance Carriers
SIC 6331 Fire, Marine, & Casualty Insurance
SIC 6351 Surety Insurance
524127 Direct Title Insurance Carriers
SIC 6361 Title Insurance
524128 Other Direct Insurance Carriers
SIC 6399 Insurance Carriers, nec
52413 Reinsurance Carriers
SIC 6311 Life Insurance
SIC 6321 Accident & Health Insurance

SIC 6324 Hospital & Medical Service Plans
SIC 6331 Fire, Marine, & Casualty Insurance
SIC 6351 Surety Insurance
SIC 6361 Title Insurance
52421 Insurance Agencies & Brokerages
SIC 6411 Insurance Agents, Brokers & Service
524291 Claims Adjusters
SIC 6411 Insurance Agents, Brokers & Service
524292 Third Party Administration for Insurance & Pension Funds
SIC 6371 Pension, Health, & Welfare Funds
SIC 6411 Insurance Agents, Brokers & Service
524298 All Other Insurance Related Activities
SIC 6411 Insurance Agents, Brokers & Service
52511 Pension Funds
SIC 6371 Pension, Health, & Welfare Funds
52512 Health & Welfare Funds
SIC 6371 Pension, Health, & Welfare Funds
52519 Other Insurance Funds
SIC 6321 Accident & Health Insurance
SIC 6324 Hospital & Medical Service Plans
SIC 6331 Fire, Marine, & Casualty Insurance
SIC 6733 Trusts, Except Educational, Religious, & Charitable
52591 Open-End Investment Funds
SIC 6722 Management Investment Offices, Open-End
52592 Trusts, Estates, & Agency Accounts
SIC 6733 Trusts, Except Educational, Religious, & Charitable
52593 Real Estate Investment Trusts
SIC 6798 Real Estate Investment Trusts
52599 Other Financial Vehicles
SIC 6726 Unit Investment Trusts, Face-Amount Certificate Offices, & Closed-End Management Investment Offices

REAL ESTATE & RENTAL & LEASING

53111 Lessors of Residential Buildings & Dwellings
SIC 6513 Operators of Apartment Buildings
SIC 6514 Operators of Dwellings Other Than Apartment Buildings
53112 Lessors of Nonresidential Buildings
SIC 6512 Operators of Nonresidential Buildings
53113 Lessors of Miniwarehouses & Self Storage Units
SIC 4225 General Warehousing & Storage
53119 Lessors of Other Real Estate Property
SIC 6515 Operators of Residential Mobile Home Sites
SIC 6517 Lessors of Railroad Property
SIC 6519 Lessors of Real Property, nec
53121 Offices of Real Estate Agents & Brokers
SIC 6531 Real Estate Agents Managers
531311 Residential Property Managers
SIC 6531 Real Estate Agents & Managers
531312 Nonresidential Property Managers
SIC 6531 Real Estate Agents & Managers
53132 Offices of Real Estate Appraisers
SIC 6531 Real Estate Agents & Managers
531399 All Other Activities Related to Real Estate
SIC 6531 Real Estate Agents & Managers
532111 Passenger Car Rental
SIC 7514 Passenger Car Rental
532112 Passenger Car Leasing
SIC 7515 Passenger Car Leasing

53212　Truck, Utility Trailer, & RV Rental & Leasing
SIC 7513 Truck Rental & Leasing Without Drivers
SIC 7519 Utility Trailers & Recreational Vehicle Rental

53221　Consumer Electronics & Appliances Rental
SIC 7359 Equipment Rental & Leasing, nec

53222　Formal Wear & Costume Rental
SIC 7299 Miscellaneous Personal Services, nec
SIC 7819 Services Allied to Motion Picture Production

53223　Video Tape & Disc Rental
SIC 7841 Video Tape Rental

532291 Home Health Equipment Rental
SIC 7352 Medical Equipment Rental & Leasing

532292 Recreational Goods Rental
SIC 7999 Amusement & Recreation Services, nec

532299 All Other Consumer Goods Rental
SIC 7359 Equipment Rental & Leasing, nec

53231　General Rental Centers
SIC 7359 Equipment Rental & Leasing, nec

532411 Commercial Air, Rail, & Water Transportation
　　　　Equipment Rental & Leasing
SIC 4499 Water Transportation Services, nec
SIC 4741 Rental of Railroad Cars
SIC 7359 Equipment Rental & Leasing, nec

532412 Construction, Mining & Forestry Machinery &
　　　　Equipment Rental & Leasing
SIC 7353 Heavy Construction Equipment Rental & Leasing
SIC 7359 Equipment Rental & Leasing, nec

53242　Office Machinery & Equipment Rental & Leasing
SIC 7359 Equipment Rental & Leasing
SIC 7377 Computer Rental & Leasing

53249　Other Commercial & Industrial Machinery &
　　　　Equipment Rental & Leasing
SIC 7352 Medical Equipment Rental & Leasing
SIC 7359 Equipment Rental & Leasing, nec
SIC 7819 Services Allied to Motion Picture Production
SIC 7922 Theatrical Producers & Miscellaneous Theatrical
　　　　Services

53311　Owners & Lessors of Other Nonfinancial Assets
SIC 6792 Oil Royalty Traders
SIC 6794 Patent Owners & Lessors

PROFESSIONAL, SCIENTIFIC, & TECHNICAL SERVICES

54111　Offices of Lawyers
SIC 8111 Legal Services
541191 Title Abstract & Settlement Offices
SIC 6541 Title Abstract Offices
541199 All Other Legal Services
SIC 7389 Business Services, nec
541211 Offices of Certified Public Accountants
SIC 8721 Accounting, Auditing, & Bookkeeping Services
541213 Tax Preparation Services
SIC 7291 Tax Return Preparation Services
541214 Payroll Services
SIC 7819 Services Allied to Motion Picture Production
SIC 8721 Accounting, Auditing, & Bookkeeping Services
541219 Other Accounting Services
SIC 8721 Accounting, Auditing, & Bookkeeping Services
54131　Architectural Services
SIC 8712 Architectural Services

54132　Landscape Architectural Services
SIC 0781 Landscape Counseling & Planning
54133　Engineering Services
SIC 8711 Engineering Services
54134　Drafting Services
SIC 7389 Business Services, nec
54135　Building Inspection Services
SIC 7389 Business Services, nec
54136　Geophysical Surveying & Mapping Services
SIC 8713 Surveying Services
SIC 1081 Metal Mining Services
SIC 1382 Oil & Gas Field Exploration Services
SIC 1481 Nonmetallic Minerals Services, Except Fuels
54137　Surveying & Mapping Services
SIC 7389 Business Services, nec
SIC 8713 Surveying Services
54138　Testing Laboratories
SIC 8734 Testing Laboratories
54141　Interior Design Services
SIC 7389 Business Services, nec
54142　Industrial Design Services
SIC 7389 Business Services, nec
54143　Commercial Art & Graphic Design Services
SIC 7336 Commercial Art & Graphic Design
SIC 8099 Health & Allied Services, nec
54149　Other Specialized Design Services
SIC 7389 Business Services, nec
541511 Custom Computer Programming Services
SIC 7371 Computer Programming Services
541512 Computer Systems Design Services
SIC 7373 Computer Integrated Systems Design
SIC 7379 Computer Related Services, nec
541513 Computer Facilities Management Services
SIC 7376 Computer Facilities Management Services
541519 Other Computer Related Services
SIC 7379 Computer Related Services, nec
541611 Administrative Management & General Management
　　　　Consulting Services
SIC 8742 Management Consulting Services
541612 Human Resources & Executive Search Consulting
　　　　Services
SIC 8742 Management Consulting Services
SIC 7361 Employment Agencies
SIC 8999 Services, nec
541613 Marketing Consulting Services
SIC 8742 Management Consulting Services
541614 Process, Physical, Distribution & Logistics Consulting
　　　　Services
SIC 8742 Management Consulting Services
541618 Other Management Consulting Services
SIC 4731 Arrangement of Transportation of Freight & Cargo
SIC 8748 Business Consulting Services, nec
54162　Environmental Consulting Services
SIC 8999 Services, nec
54169　Other Scientific & Technical Consulting Services
SIC 0781 Landscape Counseling & Planning
SIC 8748 Business Consulting Services, nec
SIC 8999 Services, nec
54171　Research & Development in the Physical Sciences &
　　　　Engineering Sciences
SIC 8731 Commercial Physical & Biological Research
SIC 8733 Noncommercial Research Organizations

54172   Research & Development in the Life Sciences
SIC 8731 Commercial Physical & Biological Research
SIC 8733 Noncommercial Research Organizations

54173   Research & Development in the Social Sciences & Humanities
SIC 8732 Commercial Economic, Sociological, & Educational Research
SIC 8733 Noncommercial Research Organizations

54181   Advertising Agencies
SIC 7311 Advertising Agencies

54182   Public Relations Agencies
SIC 8743 Public Relations Services

54183   Media Buying Agencies
SIC 7319 Advertising, nec

54184   Media Representatives
SIC 7313 Radio, Television, & Publishers' Advertising Representatives

54185   Display Advertising
SIC 7312 Outdoor Advertising Services
SIC 7319 Advertising, nec

54186   Direct Mail Advertising
SIC 7331 Direct Mail Advertising Services

54187   Advertising Material Distribution Services
SIC 7319 Advertising, NEC

54189   Other Services Related to Advertising
SIC 7319 Advertising, nec
SIC 5199 Nondurable Goods, nec
SIC 7389 Business Services, nec

54191   Marketing Research & Public Opinion Polling
SIC 8732 Commercial Economic, Sociological, & Educational Research

541921 Photography Studios, Portrait
SIC 7221 Photographic Studios, Portrait

541922 Commercial Photography
SIC 7335 Commercial Photography
SIC 8099 Health & Allied Services, nec

54193   Translation & Interpretation Services
SIC 7389 Business Services, NEC

54194   Veterinary Services
SIC 0741 Veterinary Services for Livestock
SIC 0742 Veterinary Services for Animal Specialties
SIC 8734 Testing Laboratories

54199   All Other Professional, Scientific & Technical Services
SIC 7389 Business Services

MANAGEMENT OF COMPANIES & ENTERPRISES

551111 Offices of Bank Holding Companies
SIC 6712 Offices of Bank Holding Companies

551112 Offices of Other Holding Companies
SIC 6719 Offices of Holding Companies, nec

551114 Corporate, Subsidiary, & Regional Managing Offices
No SIC equivalent

ADMINISTRATIVE & SUPPORT, WASTE MANAGEMENT & REMEDIATION SERVICES

56111   Office Administrative Services
SIC 8741 Management Services

56121   Facilities Support Services
SIC 8744 Facilities Support Management Services

56131   Employment Placement Agencies
SIC 7361 Employment Agencies
SIC 7819 Services Allied to Motion Pictures Production
SIC 7922 Theatrical Producers & Miscellaneous Theatrical Services

56132   Temporary Help Services
SIC 7363 Help Supply Services

56133   Employee Leasing Services
SIC 7363 Help Supply Services

56141   Document Preparation Services
SIC 7338 Secretarial & Court Reporting

561421 Telephone Answering Services
SIC 7389 Business Services, nec

561422 Telemarketing Bureaus
SIC 7389 Business Services, nec

561431 Photocopying & Duplicating Services
SIC 7334 Photocopying & Duplicating Services

561432 Private Mail Centers
SIC 7389 Business Services, nec

561439 Other Business Service Centers
SIC 7334 Photocopying & Duplicating Services
SIC 7389 Business Services, nec

56144   Collection Agencies
SIC 7322 Adjustment & Collection Services

56145   Credit Bureaus
SIC 7323 Credit Reporting Services

561491 Repossession Services
SIC 7322 Adjustment & Collection
SIC 7389 Business Services, nec

561492 Court Reporting & Stenotype Services
SIC 7338 Secretarial & Court Reporting

561499 All Other Business Support Services
SIC 7389 Business Services, NEC

56151   Travel Agencies
SIC 4724 Travel Agencies

56152   Tour Operators
SIC 4725 Tour Operators

561591 Convention & Visitors Bureaus
SIC 7389 Business Services, nec

561599 All Other Travel Arrangement & Reservation Services
SIC 4729 Arrangement of Passenger Transportation, nec
SIC 7389 Business Services, nec
SIC 7999 Amusement & Recreation Services, nec
SIC 8699 Membership Organizations, nec

561611 Investigation Services
SIC 7381 Detective, Guard, & Armored Car Services

561612 Security Guards & Patrol Services
SIC 7381 Detective, Guard, & Armored Car Services

561613 Armored Car Services
SIC 7381 Detective, Guard, & Armored Car Services

561621 Security Systems Services
SIC 7382 Security Systems Services
SIC 1731 Electrical Work

561622 Locksmiths
SIC 7699 Repair Shops & Related Services, nec

56171   Exterminating & Pest Control Services
SIC 4959 Sanitary Services, NEC
SIC 7342 Disinfecting & Pest Control Services

56172   Janitorial Services
SIC 7342 Disinfecting & Pest Control Services
SIC 7349 Building Cleaning & Maintenance Services, nec
SIC 4581 Airports, Flying Fields, & Airport Terminal Services

56173   Landscaping Services
SIC 0782 Lawn & Garden Services
SIC 0783 Ornamental Shrub & Tree Services
56174   Carpet & Upholstery Cleaning Services
SIC 7217 Carpet & Upholstery Cleaning
56179   Other Services to Buildings & Dwellings
SIC 7389 Business Services, nec
SIC 7699 Repair Shops & Related Services, nec
56191   Packaging & Labeling Services
SIC 7389 Business Services, nec
56192   Convention & Trade Show Organizers
SIC 7389 Business Services, NEC
56199   All Other Support Services
SIC 7389 Business Services, nec
562111 Solid Waste Collection
SIC 4212 Local Trucking Without Storage
SIC 4953 Refuse Systems
562112 Hazardous Waste Collection
SIC 4212 Local Trucking Without Storage
SIC 4953 Refuse Systems
562119 Other Waste Collection
SIC 4212 Local Trucking Without Storage
SIC 4953 Refuse Systems
562211 Hazardous Waste Treatment & Disposal
SIC 4953 Refuse Systems
562212 Solid Waste Landfill
SIC 4953 Refuse Systems
562213 Solid Waste Combustors & Incinerators
SIC 4953 Refuse Systems
562219 Other Nonhazardous Waste Treatment & Disposal
SIC 4953 Refuse Systems
56291   Remediation Services
SIC 1799 Special Trade Contractors, nec
SIC 4959 Sanitary Services, nec
56292   Materials Recovery Facilities
SIC 4953 Refuse Systems
562991 Septic Tank & Related Services
SIC 7359 Equipment Rental & Leasing, nec
SIC 7699 Repair Shops & Related Services, nec
562998 All Other Miscellaneous Waste Management Services
SIC 4959 Sanitary Services, nec

EDUCATIONAL SERVICES

61111   Elementary & Secondary Schools
SIC 8211 Elementary & Secondary Schools
61121   Junior Colleges
SIC 8222 Junior Colleges & Technical Institutes
61131   Colleges, Universities & Professional Schools
SIC 8221 Colleges, Universities, & Professional Schools
61141   Business & Secretarial Schools
SIC 8244 Business & Secretarial Schools
61142   Computer Training
SIC 8243 Data Processing Schools
**61143   Professional & Management Development Training
        Schools**
SIC 8299 Schools & Educational Services, nec
611511 Cosmetology & Barber Schools
SIC 7231 Beauty Shops
SIC 7241 Barber Shops
611512 Flight Training
SIC 8249 Vocational Schools, nec
SIC 8299 Schools & Educational Services, nec

611513 Apprenticeship Training
SIC 8249 Vocational Schools, nec
611519 Other Technical & Trade Schools
SIC 8249 Vocational Schools, NEC
SIC 8243 Data Processing Schools
61161   Fine Arts Schools
SIC 8299 Schools & Educational Services, nec
SIC 7911 Dance Studios, Schools, & Halls
61162   Sports & Recreation Instruction
SIC 7999 Amusement & Recreation Services, nec
61163   Language Schools
SIC 8299 Schools & Educational Services, nec
611691 Exam Preparation & Tutoring
SIC 8299 Schools & Educational Services, nec
611692 Automobile Driving Schools
SIC 8299 Schools & Educational Services, nec
611699 All Other Miscellaneous Schools & Instruction
SIC 8299 Schools & Educational Services, nec
61171   Educational Support Services
SIC 8299 Schools & Educational Services nec
SIC 8748 Business Consulting Services, nec

HEALTH CARE & SOCIAL ASSISTANCE

621111 Offices of Physicians
SIC 8011 Offices & Clinics of Doctors of Medicine
SIC 8031 Offices & Clinics of Doctors of Osteopathy
621112 Offices of Physicians, Mental Health Specialists
SIC 8011 Offices & Clinics of Doctors of Medicine
SIC 8031 Offices & Clinics of Doctors of Osteopathy
62121   Offices of Dentists
SIC 8021 Offices & Clinics of Dentists
62131   Offices of Chiropractors
SIC 8041 Offices & Clinics of Chiropractors
62132   Offices of Optometrists
SIC 8042 Offices & Clinics of Optometrists
62133   Offices of Mental Health Practitioners
SIC 8049 Offices & Clinics of Health Practitioners, nec
**62134   Offices of Physical, Occupational & Speech Therapists &
        Audiologists**
SIC 8049 Offices & Clinics of Health Practitioners, nec
621391 Offices of Podiatrists
SIC 8043 Offices & Clinics of Podiatrists
621399 Offices of All Other Miscellaneous Health Practitioners
SIC 8049 Offices & Clinics of Health Practitioners, nec
62141   Family Planning Centers
SIC 8093 Speciality Outpatient Facilities, NEC
SIC 8099 Health & Allied Services, nec
62142   Outpatient Mental Health & Substance Abuse Centers
SIC 8093 Specialty Outpatient Facilities, nec
621491 HMO Medical Centers
SIC 8011 Offices & Clinics of Doctors of Medicine
621492 Kidney Dialysis Centers
SIC 8092 Kidney Dialysis Centers
621493 Freestanding Ambulatory Surgical & Emergency Centers
SIC 8011 Offices & Clinics of Doctors of Medicine
621498 All Other Outpatient Care Centers
SIC 8093 Specialty Outpatient Facilities, nec
621511 Medical Laboratories
SIC 8071 Medical Laboratories
621512 Diagnostic Imaging Centers
SIC 8071 Medical Laboratories

62161 Home Health Care Services
SIC 8082 Home Health Care Services
62191 Ambulance Services
SIC 4119 Local Passenger Transportation, nec
SIC 4522 Air Transportation, Nonscheduled
621991 Blood & Organ Banks
SIC 8099 Health & Allied Services, nec
**621999 All Other Miscellaneous Ambulatory Health Care
Services**
SIC 8099 Health & Allied Services, nec
62211 General Medical & Surgical Hospitals
SIC 8062 General Medical & Surgical Hospitals
SIC 8069 Specialty Hospitals, Except Psychiatric
62221 Psychiatric & Substance Abuse Hospitals
SIC 8063 Psychiatric Hospitals
SIC 8069 Specialty Hospitals, Except Psychiatric
62231 Specialty Hospitals
SIC 8069 Specialty Hospitals, Except Psychiatric
62311 Nursing Care Facilities
SIC 8051 Skilled Nursing Care Facilities
SIC 8052 Intermediate Care Facilities
SIC 8059 Nursing & Personal Care Facilities, nec
62321 Residential Mental Retardation Facilities
SIC 8052 Intermediate Care Facilities
62322 Residential Mental Health & Substance Abuse Facilities
SIC 8361 Residential Care
623311 Continuing Care Retirement Communities
SIC 8051 Skilled Nursing Care Facilities
SIC 8052 Intermediate Care Facilities
SIC 8059 Nursing & Personal Care Facilities, nec
623312 Homes for the Elderly
SIC 8361 Residential Care
62399 Other Residential Care Facilities
SIC 8361 Residential Care
62411 Child & Youth Services
SIC 8322 Individual & Family Social Services
SIC 8641 Civic, Social, & Fraternal Organizations
62412 Services for the Elderly & Persons with Disabilities
SIC 8322 Individual & Family Social Services
62419 Other Individual & Family Services
SIC 8322 Individual & Family Social Services
62421 Community Food Services
SIC 8322 Individual & Family Social Services
624221 Temporary Shelters
SIC 8322 Individual & Family Social Services
624229 Other Community Housing Services
SIC 8322 Individual & Family Social Services
62423 Emergency & Other Relief Services
SIC 8322 Individual & Family Social Services
62431 Vocational Rehabilitation Services
SIC 8331 Job Training & Vocational Rehabilitation Services
62441 Child Day Care Services
SIC 8351 Child Day Care Services
SIC 7299 Miscellaneous Personal Services, nec

ARTS, ENTERTAINMENT, & RECREATION

71111 Theater Companies & Dinner Theaters
SIC 5812 Eating Places
SIC 7922 Theatrical Producers & Miscellaneous Theatrical
Services

71112 Dance Companies
SIC 7922 Theatrical Producers & Miscellaneous Theatrical
Services
71113 Musical Groups & Artists
SIC 7929 Bands, Orchestras, Actors, & Entertainment Groups
71119 Other Performing Arts Companies
SIC 7929 Bands, Orchestras, Actors, & Entertainment Groups
SIC 7999 Amusement & Recreation Services, nec
711211 Sports Teams & Clubs
SIC 7941 Professional Sports Clubs & Promoters
711212 Race Tracks
SIC 7948 Racing, Including Track Operations
711219 Other Spectator Sports
SIC 7941 Professional Sports Clubs & Promoters
SIC 7948 Racing, Including Track Operations
SIC 7999 Amusement & Recreation Services, nec
**71131 Promoters of Performing Arts, Sports & Similar Events
with Facilities**
SIC 6512 Operators of Nonresidential Buildings
SIC 7922 Theatrical Procedures & Miscellaneous Theatrical
Services
SIC 7941 Professional Sports Clubs & Promoters
**71132 Promoters of Performing Arts, Sports & Similar Events
without Facilities**
SIC 7922 Theatrical Producers & Miscellaneous Theatrical
Services
SIC 7941 Professional Sports Clubs & Promoters
**71141 Agents & Managers for Artists, Athletes, Entertainers &
Other Public Figures**
SIC 7389 Business Services, nec
SIC 7922 Theatrical Producers & Miscellaneous Theatrical
Services
SIC 7941 Professional Sports Clubs & Promoters
71151 Independent Artists, Writers, & Performers
SIC 7819 Services Allied to Motion Picture Production
SIC 7929 Bands, Orchestras, Actors, & Other Entertainers &
Entertainment Services
SIC 8999 Services, nec
71211 Museums
SIC 8412 Museums & Art Galleries
71212 Historical Sites
SIC 8412 Museums & Art Galleries
71213 Zoos & Botanical Gardens
SIC 8422 Arboreta & Botanical & Zoological Gardens
71219 Nature Parks & Other Similar Institutions
SIC 7999 Amusement & Recreation Services, nec
SIC 8422 Arboreta & Botanical & Zoological Gardens
71311 Amusement & Theme Parks
SIC 7996 Amusement Parks
71312 Amusement Arcades
SIC 7993 Coin-Operated Amusement Devices
71321 Casinos
SIC 7999 Amusement & Recreation Services, nec
71329 Other Gambling Industries
SIC 7993 Coin-Operated Amusement Devices
SIC 7999 Amusement & Recreation Services, nec
71391 Golf Courses & Country Clubs
SIC 7992 Public Golf Courses
SIC 7997 Membership Sports & Recreation Clubs
71392 Skiing Facilities
SIC 7999 Amusement & Recreation Services, nec
71393 Marinas
SIC 4493 Marinas

71394   Fitness & Recreational Sports Centers
SIC 7991 Physical Fitness Facilities
SIC 7997 Membership Sports & Recreation Clubs
SIC 7999 Amusement & Recreation Services, nec
71395   Bowling Centers
SIC 7933 Bowling Centers
71399   All Other Amusement & Recreation Industries
SIC 7911 Dance Studios, Schools, & Halls
SIC 7993 Amusement & Recreation Services, nec
SIC 7997 Membership Sports & Recreation Clubs
SIC 7999 Amusement & Recreation Services, nec

ACCOMMODATION & FOODSERVICES

72111   Hotels & Motels
SIC 7011 Hotels & Motels
SIC 7041 Organization Hotels & Lodging Houses, on
          Membership Basis
72112   Casino Hotels
SIC 7011 Hotels & Motels
721191 Bed & Breakfast Inns
SIC 7011 Hotels & Motels
721199 All Other Traveler Accommodation
SIC 7011 Hotels & Motels
721211 RV Parks & Campgrounds
SIC 7033 Recreational Vehicle Parks & Campgrounds
721214 Recreational & Vacation Camps
SIC 7032 Sporting & Recreational Camps
72131   Rooming & Boarding Houses
SIC 7021 Rooming & Boarding Houses
SIC 7041 Organization Hotels & Lodging Houses, on
          Membership Basis
72211   Full-Service Restaurants
SIC 5812 Eating Places
722211 Limited-Service Restaurants
SIC 5812 Eating Places
SIC 5499 Miscellaneous Food Stores
722212 Cafeterias
SIC 5812 Eating Places
722213 Snack & Nonalcoholic Beverage Bars
SIC 5812 Eating Places
SIC 5461 Retail Bakeries
72231   Foodservice Contractors
SIC 5812 Eating Places
72232   Caterers
SIC 5812 Eating Places
72233   Mobile Caterers
SIC 5963 Direct Selling Establishments
72241   Drinking Places
SIC 5813 Drinking Places

OTHER SERVICES

811111 General Automotive Repair
SIC 7538 General Automotive Repair Shops
811112 Automotive Exhaust System Repair
SIC 7533 Automotive Exhaust System Repair Shops
811113 Automotive Transmission Repair
SIC 7537 Automotive Transmission Repair Shops

**811118 Other Automotive Mechanical & Electrical Repair &
          Maintenance**
SIC 7539 Automotive Repair Shops, nec
**811121 Automotive Body, Paint & Upholstery Repair &
          Maintenance**
SIC 7532 Top, Body, & Upholstery Repair Shops & Paint
          Shops
811122 Automotive Glass Replacement Shops
SIC 7536 Automotive Glass Replacement Shops
811191 Automotive Oil Change & Lubrication Shops
SIC 7549 Automotive Services, Except Repair & Carwashes
811192 Car Washes
SIC 7542 Carwashes
811198 All Other Automotive Repair & Maintenance
SIC 7534 Tire Retreading & Repair Shops
SIC 7549 Automotive Services, Except Repair & Carwashes
811211 Consumer Electronics Repair & Maintenance
SIC 7622 Radio & Television Repair Shops
SIC 7629 Electrical & Electronic Repair Shops, nec
811212 Computer & Office Machine Repair & Maintenance
SIC 7378 Computer Maintenance & Repair
SIC 7629 Electrical & Electronic Repair Shops, nec
SIC 7699 Repair Shops & Related Services, nec
811213 Communication Equipment Repair & Maintenance
SIC 7622 Radio & Television Repair Shops
SIC 7629 Electrical & Electronic Repair Shops, nec
**811219 Other Electronic & Precision Equipment Repair &
          Maintenance**
SIC 7629 Electrical & Electronic Repair Shops, nec
SIC 7699 Repair Shops & Related Services, NEC
**81131   Commercial & Industrial Machinery & Equipment
          Repair & Maintenance**
SIC 7699 Repair Shops & Related Services, nec
SIC 7623 Refrigerator & Air-Conditioning Service & Repair
          Shops
SIC 7694 Armature Rewinding Shops
811411 Home & Garden Equipment Repair & Maintenance
SIC 7699 Repair Shops & Related Services, nec
811412 Appliance Repair & Maintenance
SIC 7623 Refrigeration & Air-Conditioning Service & Repair
          Shops
SIC 7629 Electrical & Electronic Repair Shops, NEC
SIC 7699 Repairs Shops & Related Services, nec
81142   Reupholstery & Furniture Repair
SIC 7641 Reupholstery & Furniture Repair
81143   Footwear & Leather Goods Repair
SIC 7251 Shoe Repair & Shoeshine Parlors
SIC 7699 Repair Shops & Related Services
**81149   Other Personal & Household Goods Repair &
          Maintenance**
SIC 3732 Boat Building & Repairing
SIC 7219 Laundry & Garment Services, nec
SIC 7631 Watch, Clock, & Jewelry Repair
SIC 7692 Welding Repair
SIC 7699 Repair Shops & Related Services, nec
812111 Barber Shops
SIC 7241 Barber Shops
812112 Beauty Salons
SIC 7231 Beauty Shops
812113 Nail Salons
SIC 7231 Beauty Shops
812191 Diet & Weight Reducing Centers
SIC 7299 Miscellaneous Personal Services, nec

812199 Other Personal Care Services
SIC 7299 Miscellaneous Personal Services, nec,
81221 Funeral Homes
SIC 7261 Funeral Services & Crematories
81222 Cemeteries & Crematories
SIC 6531 Real Estate Agents & Managers
SIC 6553 Cemetery Subdividers & Developers
SIC 7261 Funeral Services & Crematories
81231 Coin-Operated Laundries & Drycleaners
SIC 7215 Coin-Operated Laundry & Drycleaning
812321 Laundries, Family & Commercial
SIC 7211 Power Laundries, Family & Commercial
812322 Drycleaning Plants
SIC 7216 Drycleaning Plants, Except Rug Cleaning
812331 Linen Supply
SIC 7213 Linen Supply
SIC 7219 Laundry & Garment Services, nec,
812332 Industrial Launderers
SIC 7218 Industrial Launderers
812391 Garment Pressing, & Agents for Laundries
SIC 7212 Garment Pressing & Agents for Laundries
812399 All Other Laundry Services
SIC 7219 Laundry & Garment Services, NEC
81291 Pet Care Services
SIC 0752 Animal Speciality Services, Except Veterinary
812921 Photo Finishing Laboratories
SIC 7384 Photofinishing Laboratories
812922 One-Hour Photo Finishing
SIC 7384 Photofinishing Laboratories
81293 Parking Lots & Garages
SIC 7521 Automobile Parking
81299 All Other Personal Services
SIC 7299 Miscellaneous Personal Services, nec
SIC 7389 Miscellaneous Business Services
81311 Religious Organizations
SIC 8661 Religious Organizations
813211 Grantmaking Foundations
SIC 6732 Educational, Religious, & Charitable Trust
813212 Voluntary Health Organizations
SIC 8399 Social Services, nec
813219 Other Grantmaking & Giving Services
SIC 8399 Social Services, NEC
813311 Human Rights Organizations
SIC 8399 Social Services, nec
813312 Environment, Conservation & Wildlife Organizations
SIC 8399 Social Services, nec
SIC 8699 Membership Organizations, nec
813319 Other Social Advocacy Organizations
SIC 8399 Social Services, NEC
81341 Civic & Social Organizations
SIC 8641 Civic, Social, & Fraternal Organizations
SIC 8699 Membership Organizations, nec
81391 Business Associations
SIC 8611 Business Associations
SIC 8699 Membership Organizations, nec
81392 Professional Organizations
SIC 8621 Professional Membership Organizations
81393 Labor Unions & Similar Labor Organizations
SIC 8631 Labor Unions & Similar Labor Organizations
81394 Political Organizations
SIC 8651 Political Organizations
81399 Other Similar Organizations
SIC 6531 Real Estate Agents & Managers
SIC 8641 Civic, Social, & Fraternal Organizations

SIC 8699 Membership Organizations, nec
81411 Private Households
SIC 8811 Private Households

PUBLIC ADMINISTRATION

92111 Executive Offices
SIC 9111 Executive Offices
92112 Legislative Bodies
SIC 9121 Legislative Bodies
92113 Public Finance
SIC 9311 Public Finance, Taxation, & Monetary Policy
92114 Executive & Legislative Offices, Combined
SIC 9131 Executive & Legislative Offices, Combined
92115 American Indian & Alaska Native Tribal Governments
SIC 8641 Civic, Social, & Fraternal Organizations
92119 All Other General Government
SIC 9199 General Government, nec
92211 Courts
SIC 9211 Courts
92212 Police Protection
SIC 9221 Police Protection
92213 Legal Counsel & Prosecution
SIC 9222 Legal Counsel & Prosecution
92214 Correctional Institutions
SIC 9223 Correctional Institutions
92215 Parole Offices & Probation Offices
SIC 8322 Individual & Family Social Services
92216 Fire Protection
SIC 9224 Fire Protection
92219 All Other Justice, Public Order, & Safety
SIC 9229 Public Order & Safety, nec
92311 Administration of Education Programs
SIC 9411 Administration of Educational Programs
92312 Administration of Public Health Programs
SIC 9431 Administration of Public Health Programs
92313 Administration of Social, Human Resource & Income Maintenance Programs
SIC 9441 Administration of Social, Human Resource & Income Maintenance Programs
92314 Administration of Veteran's Affairs
SIC 9451 Administration of Veteran's Affairs, Except Health Insurance
92411 Air & Water Resource & Solid Waste Management
SIC 9511 Air & Water Resource & Solid Waste Management
92412 Land, Mineral, Wildlife, & Forest Conservation
SIC 9512 Land, Mineral, Wildlife, & Forest Conservation
92511 Administration of Housing Programs
SIC 9531 Administration of Housing Programs
92512 Administration of Urban Planning & Community & Rural Development
SIC 9532 Administration of Urban Planning & Community & Rural Development
92611 Administration of General Economic Programs
SIC 9611 Administration of General Economic Programs
92612 Regulation & Administration of Transportation Programs
SIC 9621 Regulations & Administration of Transportation Programs
92613 Regulation & Administration of Communications, Electric, Gas, & Other Utilities
SIC 9631 Regulation & Administration of Communications, Electric, Gas, & Other Utilities

92614 Regulation of Agricultural Marketing & Commodities
  SIC 9641 Regulation of Agricultural Marketing & Commodities
**92615 Regulation, Licensing, & Inspection of Miscellaneous
       Commercial Sectors**
  SIC 9651 Regulation, Licensing, & Inspection of Miscellaneous
        Commercial Sectors
92711 Space Research & Technology
  SIC 9661 Space Research & Technology
92811 National Security
  SIC 9711 National Security
92812 International Affairs
  SIC 9721 International Affairs
99999 Unclassified Establishments
  SIC 9999 Nonclassifiable Establishments

Appendix: NAICS/SIC Conversion

APPENDIX III

ANNOTATED SOURCE LIST

The following listing provides the names, publishers, addresses, telephone and fax numbers (if available), and frequency of publications for the primary sources used in *Market Share Reporter*.

20/20 Magazine, Jobson Publishing Corp., 100 Avenue of the Americas, 9th Floor, New York, NY 10013, *Telephone:* (212) 274-7000, *Fax:* (212) 431-0500, *Published:* monthly.

ABA Banking Journal, Simmons-Boardman Publishing Corp., 345 Hudson St., New York, NY 10014-4502, *Telephone:* (212) 620-7200.

The Accountant, Lafferty Publications Ltd., IDA Tower, Pearse Street, Dublin 2, Ireland, *Telephone:* (353-1) 671-8022, *Fax:* (353-1) 671-8520, *Published:* monthly.

Adhesives Age, Communication Channels Inc., 6255 Barfield Rd., Atlanta, GA 30328, *Telephone:* (404) 256-9800, *Fax:* (404) 256-3116, *Published::* monthly.

Adhesive Technology, Communication Channels Inc., 6255 Barfield Rd., Atlanta, GA 30328, *Telephone:* (404) 256-9800, *Fax:* (404) 256-3116.

Advertising Age, Crain Communications, Inc., 220 E. 42nd St., New York, NY 10017, *Telephone:* (212) 210-0725, *Fax:* (212) 210-0111, *Published:* weekly.

Aftermarket Business, Advanstar Communications, Inc., 7500 Old Oak Blvd., Cleveland, OH 44130-3343, *Published:* monthly.

Ag Lender, 11701 BoormanDrive, St. Louis, MO 63146, *Telephone:* (800) 535-2342.

Agri Marketing, Century Communications, 6201 Howard Street, Niles, IL 60714, *Telephone:* (708) 657-1200, *Fax:* (708) 647-7055, *Published:* 11x/monthly.

Air Cargo World, Journal of Commerce Inc., 1230 National Press Building, Washington D.C. 20045, *Telephone*: (202) 783-1148, *Published*: monthly.

Air Transport World, 600 Summer St., PO Box 1361, Stamfort, CT 06904, *Telephone:* (203) 348-7531, *Fax*: (203) 348-4023.

Airline Business, Reed Elsevier, PO Box 302, Haywards Heath, West Sussex England, RH 16 3YY.

Akron Beacon Journal, Knight-Ridder Inc., 1 Herald Plaza, Miami FL 33132, *Telephone:* (305) 376-3800.

American Banker, American Banker Inc., 1 State St, New York, NY 10023, *Telephone:* (212) 408-1480, *Fax:* (212) 943-2984, *Published:* Mon. - Fri.

American Ceramic Society Bulletin, American Ceramic Society, 735 Ceramic Place, Westerville, OH 43081-8720, Published: monthly, Price: $50 per year for nonmembers and libraries.

American City and County, Communication Channels Inc., 6255 Barfield Rd., Atlanta, GA 30328,

Telephone: (404) 256-9800, *Fax:* (404) 256-3116, *Published:* monthly.

American Drycleaner, American Trade Magazines Division, 500 N Dearborn St., Ste. 110, Chicago, IL 60610, *Telephone:* (312) 337-7700, *Fax:* (312) 337-8654, *Published:* monthly.

American Ink Maker, MacNair-Dorland Co., 445 Broadhollow Rd., Melville, NY 11747, *Telephone:* (212) 279-4456. *Published:* monthly.

American Laboratory, International Scientific Communications Inc., 30 Controls Drive, P.O. Box 870, Shelton, CT 06484-0870, *Telephone*: (203) 926-9300, *Fax:* (203) 926-9310.

The American Lawyer, 600 3rd Avenue, New York, NY 10016, *Telephone:* (212) 973-2800, *Fax:* (212) 972-6258, *Published:* monthly, with combined issues, *Price:* $135, $265, home; $525 office.

American Machinist, Penton Publishing, 1100 Superior Ave., Cleveland, OH 44114, *Telephone:* (216) 696-7000, *Fax:* (216) 696-0836, *Published:* monthly.

American Metal Market, Capital Cities Media Inc., 825 7th Avenue, New York, NY 10019, *Telephone:* (800) 360-7600, *Published:* daily, except Saturdays, Sundays, and holidays, *Price:* $560 per year (U.S., Canada, and Mexico).

American Printer, Maclean Hunter Publishing Co., 29 N. Wacker Dr., Chicago, IL 60606. *Published:* monthly.

Amusement Business, BPI Communications Inc., Box 24970, Nashville, TN 37202, *Telephone:* (615)321-4250, *Fax:* (615) 327-1575. *Published:* weekly.

Apparel Industry, Shore Communications, 180 Allen Rd., NE, Building N, Ste. 300, Atlanta, GA 30328, *Telephone:* (404) 252-8831, *Fax:* (404) 252-4436, *Published:* monthly, *Price:* $48.

Appliance, Dana Chase Publications Inc., 1110 Jorie Blvd., CS 9019, Ste. 203, Hinsdale, IL 60521, *Telephone:* (708) 990 - 3484, *Fax:* (708) 990 - 0078, *Published:* monthly, *Price:* $60.

Appliance Manufacturer, Business News Publishing Co., 755 W. Big Beaver Rd., Ste. 1000, Troy, MI 48084-4900, *Telephone:* (313) 362-3700, *Fax:* (313) 244-6439, *Published:* monthly.

Arizona Republic, Phoenix Newspaper Inc., P.O. Box 1950, Phoenix, AZ 85001, *Telephone:* (602) 271-8000, *Fax:* (602) 271-8500, *Published:* daily.

Arkansas Business, 201 E. Markham, P.O. Box 3686, Little Rock, AR 72203, *Telephone:* (501)372-1443 Fax: (501) 375-3623, *Published:* weekly, *Price:* $38 per year.

Arkansas Democrat-Gazette, Little Rock Newspapers Inc., Capitol Ave.& Scott St., P.O. Box 2221, Little Rock, AR 72203, *Telephone:* (501) 378-3400, *Fax:* (501) 372-3908, *Published:* daily.

Assembly, Hitchcock Publishing Co., 191 S. Gary Ave., Carol Stream, IL 60188, *Telephone:* (708) 665 - 1000, *Fax:* (708) 462 - 2225.

Asset Sales Report, American Banker Inc., 1 State St, New York, NY 10023, *Telephone:* (212) 408-1480, *Fax:* (212) 943-2984.

ATI, Billian Publishing, 2100 Powers Ferry NW, Ste. 300, Atlanta, GA 30339, *Telephone:* (404) 955-5656, *Fax:* (404) 952-0669, *Published:* monthly.

Atlanta Business Chronicle, American City Business Journals, 1801 Peachtree NE, Suite 15D, Atlanta, GA 30309, *Telephone:* (404) 249-1000, *Fax:* (404) 249-1048, *Published:* weekly, *Price:* $44.

Atlanta Journal-Constitution, 72 Marietta St., NW Atlanta, GA 30303, *Telephone:* (404) 526 - 5151, *Published:* daily.

Audioweek, Waaren Communications News, 2115 Ward CT, NW, Washington D.C. 20037.

Automatic Merchandiser, Johnson Hill Press Inc., 1233 Janesville Ave., Fort Atkinson, WI 53538, *Telephone:* (414) 563-6388, *Fax:* (414) 563-1699, *Published:* monthly.

Automotive Industries, Capital Cities/ABC/Chilton Co., Chilton Way, Radnor PA 19089, *Telephone:* (215) 961-4255, *Fax:* (215) 964 -4251.

Automotive Manufacturing & Production, 851 South Main St, Suite A, Plymouth, MI 48170, *Telephone:* (734) 416-9705, *Fax:* (734) 416-9707.

Automotive Marketing, Capital Cities/ABC/Chilton Co., Chilton Way, Radnor, PA 19089, *Telephone:* (215) 964-4000, *Fax:* (215) 964-4981, *Published:* monthly.

Automotive News, Crain Communications Inc., 380 Woodbridge, Detroit, MI 48207, *Telephone:* (313) 446-6000, *Fax:* (313) 446-0347.

Autoparts Report, Internationak Trade Services, *Published:* biweekly.

Aviation Week & Space Technology, McGraw Hill Inc., 1221 Avenue of the Americas, New York, NY 10020, *Telephone:* (212) 512-2294, *Fax:* (212) 869-7799, *Published:* weekly.

Baking & Snack, Sosland Publishing Co., 4800 Main St., Ste 100, Kansas City, MO 64112, *Telephone:* (816) 756-1000.

Baltimore Business Journal, American City Business Journals, 117 Water St., Baltimore, MD 21202, *Telephone:* (410) 576-1161, *Fax:* (301) 383-321, *Published:* weekly.

Bangkok Post, Post Publishing Company Ltd., Bangkok Post Building, 136 Na Ranong Road, Office Kosa Road, Klong Toei, Bangkok Thailand 10110.

Bank Loan Report, One North Franklin, Suite 1000, Chicago, IL 60606.

Bank Network News, Miller Freeman Inc., 1515 Broadway, New York, NY 10036, *Telephone:* (212) 869-1300.

Banking Strategies, Bank Administration Institute, One North Franklin, Chicago, IL 60606, *Telephone:* (312) 553-4600, *Price:* $59.

The BBI Newsletter, AHC, P.O. Box 740058, Atlanta, GA 30374.

Bee Culture, Dadant & Sons Inc., 51 S. 2nd T., Hamilton, IL 62341, *Telephone:* (217) 847-3324, *Fax:* (217) 847-3660, *Published:* monthly.

Best's Review, A.M. Best Co. Inc., Ambest Rd., Oldwick, NJ 08858, *Telephone:* (908) 439-2200, *Fax:* (908) 439-3363, *Published:* monthly.

Beverage Aisle, Advanstar Communications, Inc., 7500 Old Oak Blvd., Cleveland OH 44130.

Beverage Dynamics, Jobson Publishing Corp., 100 Avenues of the Americas, 9th Floor, New York, NY 10013, *Telephone:* (212) 274-7000, *Fax:* (212) 431-0500.

Beverage Industry, Advanstar Communications, Inc., 7500 Old Oak Blvd., Cleveland OH 44130, *Telephone:* (216) 243-8100, *Fax:* (216) 891-2651, *Published:* monthly, *Price:* $40 per year.

Beverage World, Keller International Publishing Corp., 150 Great Neck Rd., Great Neck, NY 11021, *Telephone:* (516) 829-9210, *Fax:* (516) 829-5414, *Published:* monthly.

Bicycle Retailer & Industry News, 502 W. Cordova Rd., Santa Fe, NM 87501, *Telephone:* (505) 988-5099, *Fax:* (505) 988-7224, *Published:* monthly.

Billboard, BPI Communications, 1515 Broadway, 14th FL, New York, NY 10036, *Telephone:* (212) 764-7300, *Fax:* (212) 536-5358.

Bobbin, Bobbin Blenheim Media Corp., 1110 Shop Rd, Columbia, SC 29202.

Body Fashions and Intimate Apparel, Advanstar Communications, 7500 Old Oak Blvd, Cleveland, OH 44130, Telephone: (212) 826-2839, Fax: (212) 891-2726.

Bond Buyer, American Banker Inc., 1 State St, New York, NY 10023.

Boston Business Journal, MCP Inc., 200 High St., Boston, MA 02110, Telephone: (617) 330-1000, Fax: (617) 330-1016, Published: weekly, Price: $54.

Brand Packaging, Stagnito Communications Inc., 155 Pfingsten Road, Suite 205, Deerfield, IL 60015, *Telephone:* (847) 205-5660, *Fax:* (847) 205-5680.

Brandweek, Adweek L.P., 1515 Broadway, New York, NY 10036, *Telephone:* (212) 536-5336. *Published:* weekly, except no issue in the last week of Dec.

Broadcasting & Cable, Cahners Publishing Co., 1705 DeSales Street, N.W., Washington, DC 20036, *Telephone:* (800) 554-5729 or (202) 659-2340, *Fax:* (202) 331-1732.

Broward Daily Business Review, 633 South Andrews Avenue, Fort Lauderdale, FL 33301, Telephone: (954) 468-2600.

BtoB, Crain Communications, Inc., 220 E. 42nd St., New York, NY 10017, *Telephone:* (212) 210-0725, *Fax:* (212) 210-0111.

Builder, Hanley-Wood Inc., 655 15th St. N.W., Ste. 475, Washington, D.C. 20005, *Telephone:* (202) 737-0717, *Fax:* (202) 737-2439, *Published:* monthly.

Building Material Dealer, 1405 Lilac Drive N, No 131, Minneapolis, MN 55422.

Business 2.0, 5 Thomas Mellon Circle, Suite 305, San Francisco, CA 94134.

Business Communications Review, BCR Enterprises, Inc., 950 York Rd., Hinsdale, IL 60521, *Telephone:* (800) 227-1324, *Published:* monthly.

Business Courier Serving Cincinnati, Standard Publishing, 4500 Carew Tower, Cincinnati, OH 45202.

Business First Columbus, 200 E. Rich St., Columbus, OH 43215, *Telephone:* (614) 461-4040.

Business First - Great Columbus Business Authority, 471 Broad Street, Suite 1500, Columbus, OH 043215.

Business First - Louisville, 501 South 4 Street, Suite 130, Louisville, KY 40202.

Business Forms, Labels & Systems, North American Publishing Co., 401 N Broad Street, Philadelphia, PA 19108, *Telephone:* (215) 238-5300, *Fax:* (215) 238-5457, *Published:* 2x/mo, *Price:* $24.

Business Insurance, Crain Communications, Inc., 740 N. Rush St., Chicago IL 60611, *Published:* monthly.

The Business Journal, American City Business Journals, 2025 N. Summit Ave., Milwaukee, WI 53202. *Telephone:* (414) 278- 7788, *Fax:* (414) 278-7028.

The Business Journal (North Carolina), 1305 Navaho Drive, Suite 401, Raleigh, NC 27609.

The Business Journal - Portland, 851 SW Sizth Ave., Ste 500, nertland, OR 97204.

The Business Journal - Serving Charlotte, 120 W. Morehead St., Suite 200, Charlotte, NC 28202.

The Business Journal - Serving Phoenix and the Valley of the Sun, 3737 N. 7th St., Ste. 200, Phoenix, AZ 85014, *Telephone:* (602) 230-8400, *Fax:* (602) 230-0955, *Published:* weekly, *Cost:* $46.

Business North Carolina, 5435 77 Center Dr., No. 50, Charlotte, NC 28217-0711 *Telephone:* (704) 523-6987 *Published:* monthly.

Business Week, McGraw-Hill Inc., 1221 Avenue of the Americas, New York, NY 10020. *Published:* weekly, *Price:* U.S.: $46.95 per year; Canada: $69 CDN per year.

C&EN, American Chemical Society, Dept. L-0011, Columbus, OH 43210, *Telephone:* (800) 333-9511 or (614) 447-3776. *Published:* weekly, except last week in December, *Price:* U.S.: $100 per year, $198 for 2 years; elsewhere: $148 per year, $274 for 2 years.

Cablevision, Chilton Publications, P.O. Box 7698, Riverton, NJ 08077-7698, *Telephone:* (609) 786-0501. *Published:* twice monthly, *Price:* U.S.: $55 per year, $99 for 2 years; Elsewhere via surface mail: $85 per year, $159 for 2 years.

Canadian Business, CB Media Limited, 70 Esplanade, Second Floor, Toronto MSE IR2 Canada, *Telephone:* (416) 364-4266, *Fax:* (416) 364-2783. *Published:* monthly, *Price:* Canada: $24 per year, $60 for 3 years; Elsewhere: $40 per year, $100 for 3 years.

Canadian Grocer, Maclean Hunter, 777 Bay St., Toronto, ON Canada, *Telephone:* (416) 596-5772, *Fax:* (416) 593-3162, *Published:* monthly.

Canadian Machinery and Metalworking, Maclean Hunter, 777 Bay St., Toronto, ON Canada, *Telephone:* (416) 596-5772, *Fax:* (416) 593-3162, *Published:* monthly.

Canadian Packaging, Maclean Hunter, 777 Bay St., Toronto, ON Canada, *Telephone:* (416) 596-5772, *Fax:* (416) 593-3162, *Published:* monthly.

Canadian Plastics, Maclean Hunter, 777 Bay St., Toronto, ON Canada, *Telephone:* (416) 596-5772, *Fax:* (416) 593-3162, *Published:* monthly.

Candy Industry, Advanstar Communications Inc., 7500 Old Oak Blvd, Cleveland, OH 44130, *Teelphone:* (216) 891-2612, *Fax:* (216) 891-2651, *Published:* monthly.

Capital Times, Penn State Univ., Penn State, Middletown, PA 17057, *Telephone:* (717) 944-0461, *Fax:* (717) 944-3107.

Cardfax, Faulkner & Grey, Eleven Penn Plaza, 17th Floor, New York, NY 10001, *Telephone:* (800)535-8403.

Ceramic Industry, Business News Publishing Co., 5900 Harper Road, Suite 109, Solon, OH 44139, *Telephone:* (216) 498-9214, *Fax:* (216) 498-9121. *Published:* monthly, *Price:* U.S.: $53 per year; Mexico: $63; Canada: $66.71 (includes postage & GST).

Chain Drug Review, Racher Press, 220 5th Ave, New York, NY 10001, *Telephone:* (212) 213-6000, *Fax:* (212) 725-3961.

Chain Leader, Attn: Reader Services, 1350 E. Touhy Ave, PO Box 5080, Des Plaines, IL 60017-5080.

Chain Store Age, Lebhar-Friedman Inc., 425 Park Ave., New York, NY 10022, *Telephone:* (212) 371-9400, *Fax:* (212) 319-4129. *Published:* monthly.

Charleston Gazette, 1001 Virginia St., E, Charleston, WV 25301, *Telephone:* (304) 348-5105, *Fax:* (304) 348-5133.

Chemical Market Reporter, Schnell Publishing Co., Inc., 80 Broad St., New York, NY 1004-2203, *Telephone:* (212) 248-4177, *Fax:* (212) 248-4903, *Published:* weekly.

Chemical News & Intelligence, CNI, Ste. 300, 3730 Kirby Drive, Houston, TX 77098, *Telephone:* (713) 525-2653.

Chemical Week, Chemical Week Associates, P.O. Box 7721, Riverton, NJ 08077-7721, *Telephone:* (609) 786-0401, *Published:* weekly, except four combination issues (total of 49 issues), *Price:* U.S.: $99 per year; Canada: $129 per year. Single copies $8 in U.S. and $10 elsewhere.

The Chicago Tribune, 435 N. Michigan Ave., Chicago, IL 60611, *Telephone:* (312) 222-3232. *Published:* daily.

Child Care Information Exchange, Exchange Press Inc., P.O. 2890, Redmond, WA 98073, *Telephone:* (800) 221-2864, *Published:* bimonthly, *Price:* $35 per year.

Children's Business, Fairchild Publications, 7 W 34th St., New York, NY 10001, *Telephone:* (212) 630-4520, *Fax:* (212) 630-4511.

The Christian Science Monitor, Christian Science Publishing Society, One Norway St., Boston, MA 02115, *Telephone:* (800) 456-2220, *Published:* daily, except weekends and holidays.

CircuiTree, BNP, 755 West Big Beaver, Ste 100, Troy, MI 48084, *Telephone:* (248)362-3700.

CMR Focus, Schnell Publishing Co., Inc., 80 Broad St., New York, NY 1004-2203, *Telephone:* (212) 248-4177, *Fax:* (212) 248-4903, *Published:* weekly.

Coatings World, 70 Hilltop Road, Ramsey, NJ 07446.

Collections & Credit Risk, Faulkner & Grey, Eleven Penn Plaza, 17th Floor, New York, NY 10001, *Telephone:* (800)535-8403.

Columbus Dispatch, 34 S. Third Street, Columbus, OH 43215.

Commercial Appeal, Memphis Publishing Co., 495 Union Ave., Memphis, TN 38103, *Telephone:* (901) 529-2211, *Fax:* (901) 529-2522, *Published:* daily.

Commercial Carrier Journal, Capital Cities/ABC/Chilton Co., Chilton Way, Radnor, PA 19089, *Telephone:* (215) 964-4000, *Fax:* (215) 964-4981.

Computer Reseller News, CMP Media Inc., One Jericho Plaza, Jericho, New York 11753, *Published:* weekly, *Pricet*: $199; Canada $224

Computing Canada, Plesman Publications Ltd., 2005 Sheppard Ave. E., 4th Fl., Willowsdale, ON, Canada M2J 5B1, *Telephone:* (416) 497-9562, *Fax:* (416) 497-9427. *Published:* biweekly.

Confectioner, American Publishing Corp., 17400 Dallas Pkway, Number 121, Dallas, TX 752-7305, *Telephone:* (214) 250-3630, *Fax:* (214) 250-3733.

Contra Costa Times, 2640 Shadelands Drive, PO Box 5088, Walnut Creek, CA 94596-1087, *Telephones*: (510) 935-2525, *Fax:* (510) 943-8362.

Contractor, Cahners Publishing Co., 44 Cook St., Denver, CO. 80206-5800, *Telephone:* (708) 390-2676, *Fax:* (708) 390-2690, *Published:* monthly.

Contractor's Business Management Report, IOMA, 29 West 35th Street, New York, NY 10001-2299.

Control Engineering, Cahners Publishing Co., 1350 E. Touhy Ave., Des Plaines, IL 60018, *Telephone*: (708) 635-8800, *Fax:* (708) 390-2618.

Convenience Store News, BMT Publications Inc., 7 Penn Plaza, New York, NY 10001-3900, *Telephone:* (212) 594-4120, *Fax:* (212) 714-0514, *Published:* 16x/yr.

Crain's Chicago Business, Crain Communications Inc., 740 N. Rush St., Chicago, IL 60611, *Telephone:* (312) 649-5411.

Crain's Cleveland Business, Crain Communications, Inc., 1725 Merriman Rd., Ste. 300, Akron, OH 44313-5251, *Telephone:* (216) 836-9180, *Fax:* (216) 836-1005, *Published:* weekly.

Crain's Detroit Business, Crain Communications Inc., 1400 Woodbridge, Detroit, MI 48207-3187, *Telephone:* (313) 446-6000. *Published:* weekly, except semiweekly the fourth week in May.

Crain's New York Business, Crain Communications, Inc., 220 E. 42nd St., New York, NY 10017, *Telephone:* (212) 210-0100, *Fax:* (212) 210-0799. *Published:* weekly.

Credit & Collections News, Faulkner & Gray Inc., 11 Penn Plaza, 17th FL, New York, NY 10001, *Telephone:* (212) 766-7800, *Fax:* (212) 766-0142.

Credit Card Management, Faulkner & Gray Inc., 11 Penn Plaza, 17th FL, New York, NY 10001, *Telephone:* (212) 766-7800, *Fax:* (212) 766-0142.

Credit Card News, Faulkner & Grey, Eleven Penn Plaza, 17th Floor, New York, NY 10001, *Telephone:* (800)535-8403.

Credit Union Journal, American Banker Inc., 1 State St, New York, NY 10023, *Telephone:* (212) 408-1480, *Fax:* (212) 943-2984.

Critical Mass, P.O. Box 10048, Des Moines, IA 50340-0048, *Telephone:* (800) 888-9896.

Daily News Record, Cahners Publishing Co., 275 Washington St., Newton, MA 02158, *Telephone:* (617) 558-4243, *Fax:* (617) 558-4759, *Published:* 2x/mo.

The Daily Telegraph, Telegraph Group Limited, 1 Canada Square, Canary Wharf, London E14 5DT, United Kingdom.

Dairy Field, Stagnito Communications Inc., 155 Pfingsten Road, Suite 205, Deerfield, IL 60015, *Telephone:* (847) 205-5660, *Fax:* (847) 205-5680.

Dairy Foods, Gorman Publishing Co., 8750 W. Bryn Mawr Ave., Chicago, IL 60062, *Telephone:* (312) 693-3200. *Published:* monthly, except semimonthly in Aug.

Dairy Herd Management, Miller Publishing, 12400 Whitewater Dr., Minnetonka, MD 55345.

Dallas Morning News, 508 Young St., P.O. Box 655237, Dallas, TX 75265, *Telephone:* (214) 977-8222, *Fax:* (214) 977-8776, *Published:* daily.

Dayton Daily News, Dayton Newspapers Inc., 45 S. Ludlow St., Dayton, OH 45402, *Telephone:* (513) 225-2335, *Fax:* (513) 225-2489, *Price:* $130.

Dealernews, Advanstar Communications Inc., 1700 E Dyer Rd., Ste. 250, Santa Ana, CA 92705, *Telephone:*

(714) 252-5300, *Fax:* (714) 261-9790, *Published:* monthly.

Dealerscope, North American Publishing Co., 401 N Broad St, Philadelphia, PA 19108.

Dental Economics, PennWell Publishing Co., 1421 S. Sheridan, P.O. Box 3408, Tulsa, OK 74101, *Telephone:* (918) 835-3161, *Fax:* (918) 831-9804, *Published:* monthly, *Price:* free to qualified subscribers.

Denver Business Journal, 1700 Broadway, Ste. 515, Denver, CO 80290, Telephone: (303) 837-3500, Fax: (303) 837-3535, *Published:* weekly.

The Denver Post, MediaNews Group Inc., 1560 Broadway, Denver, CO 80202, *Telephone:* (303) 820-1010, *Fax:* (303) 820-1406, *Published:* daily.

Design News, McGraw-Hill, Two Penn Plaza, New York, NY 10121-2298, *Telephone:* (212) 904-2000, *Published:* quarterly.

Detroit Free Press, Knight-Ridder, Inc., 1 Herald Plaza, Miami, FL 33132, *Telephone:* (305) 376-3800, *Published:* daily.

Diesel Progress, Diesel & Gas Turbine Publications, 13555 Bishop Ct., Brookfield, WI 53005-6286.

DigitalImager, Photo Marketing Association International, 3000 Picture Place, Jackson, MI 49201, *Telephone:* (517) 788-8100, *Fax:* (517) 788-8371.

Direct Marketing, Hoke Communications Inc., 224 7th St., Garden City, NY 11530, *Telephone:* (516) 746-6700, *Fax:* (516) 294-8141, *Published:* monthly, *Cost:* $56.

Discount Store News, Lebhar-Friedman Inc., 425 Park Ave, New York, NY 10022, *Telephone:* (212) 756-5100, *Fax:* (212) 756-5125, *Published:* weekly.

Display & Design Ideas, VNU Media, 770 Broadway, 6th Floor, New York, NY 10003.

DNR, Cahners Publishing Co., 275 Washington St., Newton, MA 02158, *Telephone:* (617) 558-4243, *Fax:* (617) 558-4759, *Published:* 2x/mo.

Do-It-Yourself-Retailing, National Retail Hardware Assn., 5822 W. 74th St., Indianapolis, IN 46278-1756, *Telephone:* (317) 297-1190, *Fax:* (317) 328-4354, *Published:* monthly, *Price: $8; $2 single issue.*

Drug Store News, Lehbhar-Friedman Inc., 425 Park Ave, New York, NY 10022, *Telephone:* (212) 756-5000, *Fax:* (212) 838-9487, *Published:* 2x/mo.

Drug Topics, Medical Economics Publishing, 5 Paragon Drive, Montvale, NJ 07645-1742, *Telephone:* (201) 358-7200, *Fax:* (201) 573-1045.

DSN Retailing Today, Lebharr-Friedmann Inc., 425 Park Ave., New York, NY 10022, *Telephone:* (212) 756-5100, *Fax:* (212) 756-5125.

DSN Supercenter & Club Business, Lebharr-Friedmann Inc., 425 Park Ave., New York, NY 10022, *Telephone:* (212) 756-5100, *Fax:* (212) 756-5125.

Duty-Free News International, Eurmoney Institutional Investor, Nestor Hosue, Playhouse Yard, London EC4V 5EX, UK.

DVD Report, PBI Media, 1201 Seven Locks Road, Suite 300, Potomac, MD 20854.

E Week, ZDNet, 650 Townsend Street, San Frnacisco, CA 94103, *Telephone:* (415) 551-4800, *Fax:* (415) 551-4813.

EC World, EC Media, Thomson Financial, 300 S. Wacker Drive, 18th Floor, Chicago, IL 60606.

The Economist, The Economist Bldg, 111 W. 57th St., New York, NY 10019, *Telephone:* (212) 541-5730, *Fax:* (212) 541-9378, *Published:* weekly, *Cost:* $110; $3.50 per single issue.

Editor & Publisher, Editor & Publisher Co., 11 W 19th St., New York, NY 10011, *Telephone:* (212) 675-4380, *Fax:* (212) 929-1259, *Published*: weekly.

Educational Marketer, Simba Information, PO Box 4234, 11 River Bend Drive South, Stamford, CT 06907-0234.

Egg Industry, Watt Publishing Co., 122 S. Wesley Ave., Mount Morris, IL 61054-1497, *Telephone:* (815) 734-4171, *Fax:* (815) 734-4201, *Published:* bi-monthly.

Electric Perspectives, 701 Pennsylvania Ave, NW, Washington D.C. 20004-2696.

Electro Manufacturing, CMP Media, 600 Community Drive, Manhasset, NY 11030.

Electronic Buyers News, CMP Media, 600 Community Drive, Manhasset, NY 11030.

Electronic Education Report, Simba Information, PO Box 4234, 11 River Bend Drive South, Stamford, CT 06907-0234.

Electronic Information Report, Simba Information, PO Box 4234, 11 River Bend Drive South, Stamford, CT 06907-0234.

Electronic Media, 488 Madison Ave., New York, NY 10022.

Electronic News, Electronic News Publishing Corp., 488 Madison Ave., New York, NY 10022, *Telephone:* (212) 909-5924, *Published:* weekly, except last week of Dec.

Electronic Publishing, Penn Well, PO Box 1260, Tulsa, OK 74101.

Electronic Times, CMP Media, 600 Community Drive, Manhasset, NY 11030.

Engineering & Mining Journal, Maclean Hunter Publishing Co., 29 Wacker Dr., Chicago, IL 60606, *Fax:* (312) 726-2574, *Published:* monthly.

ENR , McGraw-Hill Inc., Fulfillment Manager, ENR, P.O. Box 518, Highstown, NJ 08520, *Telephone:* (609) 426-7070 or (212) 512-3549, *Fax:* (212) 512-3150, *Published:* weekly, *Price:* U.S.: $89 per year; Canada: $75 per year. Single copies $5 in U.S.

Equus, Fleet Street Publishing Corp., 656 Quince Orchard Rd., Gaithersburg, MD 20878, *Telephones*: (301) 977-3900, *Fax:* (301) 990-9015.

Excelsior, 417 Thompson Ave., PO Box 70, Excelsior Springs, MO 64024.

Feedstuffs, Miller Publishing Co., 12400 Whitewater Dr., Ste. 1600, Minnetonka, MN 55343, *Telephone:* (612) 931-0211.

Financial Times, FT Publications Inc., 14 East 60th Street, New York, NY 21002, *Telephone:* (212) 752-4500, *Fax:* (212) 319-0704, *Published:* daily, except for Sundays and holidays, *Price:* $425.

Flight International, Reed Elsevier, PO Box 302, Haywards Heath, West Sussex England, RH 16 3YY.

Floor Covering Weekly, Hearst Business Communications, 60 E 42nd St., Ste. 234, New York, NY 10165-0006, *Telephone:* (212) 541-4080, *Fax:* (212) 541-4699.

Floor Focus, 28 Old Stone Hill, Pound Ridge, NY 10576, *Telephone:* (914) 764-0556, *Fax:* (914) 764-0560.

Florida Times-Union, Morris Communications, PO Box 936, Augusta, GA 30913-0936.

Florida Trend, Trend Magazines, PO Box 611, Saint Petersburg, FL 33731.

Folio, Cowles Business Media, 911 Hope St, PO Box Stamford, CT 06907-0949, *Telephone:* (203) 358-9900.

Food & Beverage Report, Stagnito Communications Inc., 155 Pfingsten Road, Suite 205, Deerfield, IL

60015, *Telephone:* (847) 205-5660, *Fax:* (847) 205-5680.

Food Institute Report, Food Insitute, Elwood Park, New Jersey.

Food Processing, Putnam Media, 555 W Pierce Road, Ste. 301, Itasca, IL 60143.

Food Service Director, Bill Communciations, 355 Park Ave., S, New York, NY 10010, *Published*: monthly.

Footwear News, Fairchild Publications, 7 W. 34th Street, New York, NY 10001, *Telephone:* (212) 630-4000, *Published:* weekly.

Forbes, Forbes, Inc., P.O. Box 10048, Des Moines, IA 50340-0048, *Telephone:* (800) 888-9896, *Published:* 27 issues per year, *Price:* U.S.: $54 per year; Canada: $95 per year (includes GST).

Forest Products Journal, Forest Products Society, 2801 Marshall Court, Madison, WI 53705-2295, *Published:* monthly, except combined issues in July/August and November/December, *Price:* U.S.: $115 per year; Canada/Mexico: $125; single copies $12 each plus shipping and handling.

Fortune, Time Inc., Time & Life Building, Rockefeller Center, New York, NY 10020-1393, *Published:* twice monthly, except two issues combined into a single issue at year-end, *Price:* U.S.: $57 per year; Canada: $65 per year.

Frozen Food Age, Maclean Hunter, 4 Stamford Four, Stamford, CT 06901-1201, *Telephone*: (203) 325-3500, *Published:* weekly.

Fruit Grower, Meister Publishing Co., 37733 Euclid Ave., Willoughsby, OH 44094-5992.

Furniture Today, Cahners Publishing Co., 200 S. Main St., P.O. Box 2754, High Point, NC 27261, *Telephone:* (919) 889-0113, *Published:* weekly.

Global Cosmetic Industry, Advanstar Communications Inc., 270 madison Ave., New York, NY 10016.

Global Positioning & Navigation News, Phillips Business Information, 1201 Seven Locks Road, Suite 300, Potomac, MD 20854.

Globe and Mail, 444 Front St. W., Toronto, ON, Canada M5V 2S9, *Telephone:* (416) 585-5000, *Fax:* (416) 585-5085, *Published:* Mon.-Sat. (Morn.).

Golf Magazine, Times Mirror Magazines, 2 Park Ave., New York, NY 10016, *Telephone:* (212) 779-5000, *Fax:* (212) 481-8085.

Golf Week, Golfweek, PO Box 1458, Winter Haven FL, 33882, Telephone: (813) 294-5511.

Golf World, Billian Publishing, 2100 Powers Ferry Rd, Ste. 300, Atlanta, GA 30339.

Gourmet News, United Publications, 106 Lafayette Street, P.O. Box 995, Yarmouth, Maine 04096, *Telephone:* (207) 846-0600, *Fax:* (207) 846-0657.

Government Executive Procurement Review, National Journal Inc., 1730 M. NW, Ste 1100, Washington D.C. 20036, *Telephone:* (202) 862-0600.

Graphic Arts Monthly, Cahners Publishing Company, 44 Cook St., Denver, CO 80206-5800, *Telephone:* (800) 637-6089.

Greenhouse Insider, Meister Publishing Co., 37733 Euclid Ave., Willoughby, OH 44094-5992.

Grocery Headquarters, Delta Communications Inc., 455 N. Cityfront Plaza Drive, Chicago, IL 60611, *Telephone:* (312) 222-2000, *Fax:* (312) 222-2026, *Published:* monthly.

Grok, Internet Industy Publishing, 315 Pacific Ave., San Francisco, CA 94111-1701, *Telephone:* (415) 733-5400, *Fax:* (415) 733-5401, *Published:* weekly.

Hawaii Business, Hawaii Business Publishing Corp., 825 Keeaumoku St., PO Box 913, Honolulu, HI

96808, *Telephone:* (808) 946-3978, *Fax:* (808) 947-8498, *Price*: $18.

Healthcare Informatics, Wiesner Inc., Englewood, CO 80112, *Published:* monthly.

Healthcare Purchasing News, Nelson Publishing, 2500 Tamiami Trial, Nokomis, FL 34275.

HFN, 7 E. 12th St., New York, NY 10003. *Published:* weekly.

Hollywood Reporter, 5055 Wilshire Blvd, 6th Fl, Los Angeles, CA 90036, *Telephone:* (213) 525-2000, *Fax:* (213) 525-2377, *Published:* weekdays.

Home Accents Today, 1350 E. Touhy Ave, PO Box 5080, Des Plaines, IL 60017-5080.

Home Textiles Today, Cahners Publishing Co., 249 W 17th St., New York, NY 10011, *Telephone:* (212) 337-6900.

Hospital Material Management, Aspen Publishers, 200 Orchard Ridge Dr., Ste. 200, Gaithersburg, MD 20878, Telephone: (301) 417-7500, Fax: (301) 417-7550.

Hotel & Motel Management, Advanstar Communications, Inc., 7500 Old Oak Blvd., Cleveland, OH 44130, *Telephone:* (216) 826-2839.

Household and Personal Products Industry, Rodman Publishing, 17 S. Franklin Turnpike, Box 555, Ramsey, NJ 07446, *Telephone:* (201) 825-2552, *Fax:* (201) 825-0553, *Published:* monthly.

Houston Chronicle, 801 Texas Ave., Houston, TX 77002, *Telephone*: (713) 220-7171, *Fax:* (713) 220-6677.

Implement & Tractor, Farm Press Publications, Inc., PO Box 1420, Clarksdale, MS 38614, *Telephone:* (601) 624-8503, *Fax:* (601) 627-1977. *Published:* monthly, *Price:* $15 per year.

The Indianapolis Star, Indianapolis Newspapers Inc., 307 N. Pennsylvania St., Indianapolis, IN 46204, *Telephone:* (317) 633-1157, *Fax:* (317) 633-1174.

Industrial Ceramics, Cahners Publishing Company, 275 Washington Street, Newton, MA 02158.

The Industry Standard, Internet Industy Publishing, 315 Pacific Ave., San Francisco, CA 94111-1701, *Telephone:* (415) 733-5400, *Fax:* (415) 733-5401, *Published:* weekly.

Infoworld, Infoworld Publishing Co., 155 Bovet Rd., Ste. 800, San Mateo, CA 94402, *Telephone:* (415) 572-7341, *Published:* weekly.

Ink World, 70 Hilltop Road, Ramsey NJ 07446.

Inside, 601 West 26th Street, 13th Floor, New York, NY 10001.

Interavia, Swissair Centre, 31 Route de l'Aeroport, P.O. Box 437, 1215 Geneva 15, Switzerland, Switzerland, *Telephone*: (902) 788-2788, *Published:* monthly, Price: $128 per year.

International Accounting Bulletin, Lafferty Publications, 1422 W Peachtree Blvd., Atlanta, GA 30309.

Internetweek, CMP Media, 600 Community Drive, Manhasset, NY 11030.

Investor's Business Daily, P.O. Box 661750, Los Angeles, CA 90066-8950, *Published:* daily, except weekends and holidays, *Price:* $128 per year.

Kansas City Business Journal, 1101 Walnut St, Suite 800, Kansas City, MO 64106.

Kansas City Star, Kansas City Star Co., 1729 Grand Ave., Kansas City, NB, 64108, *Telephone:* (816) 234-4141, *Fax:* (816) 234-4926.

Landscape Management, Advanstar Communications, 7500 Old Oak Blvd, Cleveland, OH 44130, *Telephone:* (216) 243-8100, *Fax:* (216) 891-2675.

Las Vegas Review Journal, 1111 W Bonanza Road, PO Box 70, Las Vegas, NV 89125.

Latin Trade, Freedom Communications Inc., 200 South Bicauyne Blvd., Suite 1150, Miami, FL 33131, *Published:* monthly.

Lawn & Landscape, GIE Publishing Co., 4012 Bridge Ave., Clevalnd, OH 44113, *Telephone:* (216) 961-4130, *Fax:* (216) 961-0364.

*LG-CG North America, Adv*anstar Communications Sandpointe Ave, Santa Ana, CA.

Licensing Letter, EPM Communications, 160 Mercer Street, 3rd Floor, New York, NY 10012.

Limousine & Chauffered Transportation, 21061 S Western Wve., Torrance, CA 90501, *Telephone*: (310) 533-2400.

Los Angeles Business Journal, Los Angeles, CA 92005-0001, Telephone: (800) 404-5225.

Los Angeles Times, The Times Mirror Company, Times Mirror Square, Los Angeles, CA 90053, *Telephone:* (800) LA TIMES.

Lubricants World, Chemical Week Associates, 110 William Street, New York, NY 10138, *Telephone:* (212) 621-4900, *Fax:* (212) 621-4949.

M Business, CMP Media, 600 Harrison St., San Francisco, CA 94107, *Telephone:* (415) 905-2200.

Magazine & Bookseller, Baker's Garden, 26 North orchard Farms Avenue, Simpsonville, SC 26981-1937, Telephone: (864) 329-1937.

Macleans, 7th Floor, 777 Bay Street, Toronto, ON M5W 1A7.

The Manufacturing Chemist, Miller Freeman, City Reach, 5 Greenwich View Place, Milharbour, London E14 9NN.

The Manufacturing Confectioner, The Manufacturing Confectioner Publishing Company, 175 Rock Rd., Glen Rock, NJ 07452, *Telephone:* (201) 652-2655, *Fax:* (201) 652-3419, *Published:* 12 times per year, *Price:* $25 per year, single copies $10 each, except $25 for April and July issues.

Marketing Magazine, Maclean Hunter Canadian Publishing, P.O. Box 4541, Buffalo, NY 14240-4541, *Telephone:* (800) 567-0444, *Fax:* (416) 946-1679, *Price:* Canada: $59.50 per year, $98.50 for 2 years, $125 for 3 years; U.S.: $90 per year.

MB, 3033 Chimey Rd., Suite 300, Houston, TX 77056, *Published:* monthly, combined issues in Jan./Feb. and July/Aug.

Med Ad News, Engel Communications Inc., 820 Bear Tavern Rd., Ste. 302, West Trenton, NJ 08628, Telephone: (609) 530-0044, Fax: (609) 530-0207.

Media Industry Newsletter, P&A House, Alma Road, Chesham Bucks, HP 5 3HB, UK.

Mediaweek, Adweek, LP, PO Box 1976, Danbury, CT 06813-1976, *Telephone:* (800) 722-6658, *Published:* weekly.

Medical Marketing & Media, CPS Communications, 7200 West Camino Real, Ste. 215, Boca Raton, FL 33433, *Telephone:* (407) 368-9301, *Fax:* (407) 368-7870, *Published:* monthly, *Price:* $75 per year.

Membrane & Separation Technology News, BCC Inc., 25 Van Zant, Norwalk, CT 06855-1781.

Mergers & Acquisitions, 195 Broadway, 10th Floor, New York, NY 10007, Telephone: (646) 822-2000.

Metal Center News, 2000 Clearwater Dr., Oak Brook, IL 60523.

Michigan Retailer, Michigan Retailers Association, 221 North Pine Street, Lansing, MI 48933, *Published:* 10x/yr. *Pricet:* $20.

Microwave Journal, Horzon House Publications, 685 Canton St., Norwood, MA 02062.

Milling & Baking News, Sosland Publishing Co., 4800 Main St., Ste. 100, Kansas City, MO 64112, Telephone: (816) 756-1000, Fax: (816) 756-0494.

Milwaukee Journal-Sentinel, Journal/Sentinel Inc., P.O. Box 371, 53201, *Telephone:* (414) 224-2000, *Published:* Mon-Sat.

Mining Engineering, Society for Mining, Metallurgy and Exploration Inc., 8307 Shaffer Parkway, Littleton CO 80127-5002, *Telephone:* (303) 973-9550, *Fax:* (303) 973-3845, *Published*: monthly.

MMR, Racher Press, 220 5th Ave., New York, NY 1001, *Telephone:* (212) 213-6000, *Fax:* (212) 213-6101, *Published:* biweekly.

Modern Brewery Age, Business Journals Inc., 50 Day St., PB Box 5550, Norwalk, CT 06856, *Telephone:* (203) 853-6015, *Fax:* (203) 852-8175.

Modern Casting, American Foundrymen's Society, 505 State St., Des Plaines, IL 60016-8399, *Telephone:* (708) 824-0181.

Modern Healthcare, Crain Communications, 740 N Rush, Chicago, IL 60611-2590, *Telephone:* (312) 649-5350, *Fax:* (312) 280-3189.

Modern Physician, Crain Communications Inc., 740 N. Rush St., Chicago, IL 60611-2590.

Modern Tire Dealer, Bill Communications Inc., PO Box 3599, Akron, OH 44309-3599, *Telephone:* (216) 867-4401, *Fax:* (216) 867-0019, *Published*: 14x/yr.

Monterey County Herald, Monterey Pensinsula Herald Co., PO Box 271, Monterey, CA 93942.

Mortgage Banking, Mortgage Banekrs Assn of America, 1125 15th St. NW, Washington D.C. 20005, *Telephone*: (202) 861-6500, *Fax:* (202) 872-0186, *Published:* monthly.

Mortgage Servicing News, Thomas Financial Mortgage Publications.

Music Trades, P.O. Box 432, 80 West St., Englewood, NJ 07631, *Telephone:* (201) 871-1965, *Fax:* (201) 871-0455, *Published:* monthly.

Nashville Business Journal, PO Box 23229, Nashville, TN 37202-3229, *Telephone:* (615) 254-9154.

National Fisherman, 120 Tillson Ave., PO Box 908, Rockland, ME 04841, *Telephone:* (207) 594-6222.

National Home Center News, Lebhar-Friedman Inc., 425 Park Ave., New York, NY 10022, *Telephone:* (212) 756-5151, Fax: (212) 756-5295, *Published:* 2x/mo.

National Mortgage News, Natioanl Thrift News Inc., 212 W. 35th St., 13th FL, New York, NY 10001, *Telephone:* (212) 563-4008, *Fax:* (212) 564-8879, *Published:* 39x/yr.

National Real Estate Investor, Communications Channels Inc., 6255 Barfield Rd., Atlanta, GA 30328, *Telephone:* (404) 256-9800, *Published:* monthly.

National Underwriter, The National Underwriter Co., 505 Gest St., Cincinnati, OH 45203, *Telephone:* (800) 543-0874, *Fax:* (800) 874-1916, *Published:* weekly, except last week in December, *Price:* U.S.: $77 per year, $130 for 2 years; Canada: $112 per year, $130 for 2 years.

Nation's Restaurant News, Lebhar-Friedman, Inc., Subscription Dept., P.O. Box 31179, Tampa, FL 33631-3179, *Telephone:* (800) 447-7133. *Published:* weekly on Mondays, except the first Monday in July and the last Monday in December, *Price:* $34.50 per year and $55 for 2 years for professionals in the field; $89 per year for those allied to field.

Natural Gas Week, Energy Intelligence, 5 East 37th Street, 5th Floor, New York, NY 10016.

Network World, Network World, Inc., 161 Worcester Rd., Framingham, MA 01701-9172, *Telephone:* (508) 875-6400, *Published:* weekly.

New Orleans City Business, New Orleans Publishing Group, 111 Veterans Blvd., Ste. 1810, Metairie, LA 70005, *Telephone:* (504) 834-9292, *Fax:* (504) 837-2258.

The New York Times, New York Times Co., 229 W. 43rd St., New York, NY 10036, *Telephone:* (212) 556-1234. *Published:* daily.

News & Observer, 215 S. McDowell, Raleigh, NC 27601, PO Box 191, Raleigh, NC 27602.

News & Record, Landmark Communications, 150 W. Brambleton Ave., Norfolk, VA 23501.

Nikkei Weekly, 1-9-5 Otemachi, Chiyoda-ku, Tokyo, 100-66 Japan.

Nursery Retailer, Brantwood Publications, Inc., 3023 Eastland Blvd., Ste. 103, Clearwater, FL 34621-4106, *Telephone:* (813) 796-3877, *Fax:* (813) 791-4126, *Published:* 6x/yr.

Nutraceuticals World, 70 Hilltop Road, Ramsey, NJ 07446, *Telephone:* (201) 825-2552, *Fax:* (201) 825-0553.

Official Board Markets, Packaging Info., Advanstar Communications, 131 West Firth Street, Duluth, MN 55802.

Oil & Gas Journal, PennWell Publishing CO., PO Box 2002, Tulsa, OK 74101, *Telephone:* (800) 633-1656, *Published:* weekly.

Ophthalmology Times, Advanstar Health Care Communications, 270 Madison Ave., New York, NY 10016-0695, *Published:* 2x/mo.

Origination News, Thomas Financial Mortgage Publications.

Paint & Coatings Industry, 755 W Big Bewaver Rd, Ste. 1000, Troy, MI 48083.

Paperboard Packaging, Advanstar Communications Inc., 131 West First Street, Duluth, MN 55802, *Telephone:* (218) 723-9477, *Fax:* (218) 723-9437, *Published:* monthly, *Price:* U.S.: $39 per year, $58 for 2 years; Canada: $59 per year, $88 for 2 years.

PC Magazine, 28 E 28th St., New York, NY 10016-7930, *Telephone:* (212) 503-5255, *Published:* weekly.

Pest Control, Advanstar Communications Inc., 7500 Old Oak Blvd., Cleveland, OH 44130.

Pet Product News, Fancy Publications, P.O. Box 6050, Mission Viejo, CA 92690, *Telephone:* (213) 385-2222.

Philadelphia Inquirer, Philadelphia Newspapers Inc., 400 N. Broad St., Box 8263, Philadelphia, PA 19101, *Telephone:* (215) 854-2000, *Published:* daily.

Photo Marketing, Photo Marketing Association International, 3000 Picture Place, Jackson, MI 49201, *Telephone:* (517) 788-8100, *Fax:* (517) 788-8371. *Published:* monthly, *Price:* U.S.: $35 per year/with Newsline $50, $55 for 2 years/$65 with Newsline; Canada: $35 per year/$50 with Newsline, $55 for 2 years/$70 with Newsline (payable in Canadian funds plus GST).

Pipeline & Gas Journal, Oildom Publishing Co. of Texas, Inc., 3314 Mercer St., Houston, TX 77027, *Telephone:* (713) 622-0676, *Fax:* (713) 623-4768, *Published:* monthly, *Price:* free to qualitifed subscribers; all others $15 per year.

Plastics News, Crain Communications, 965 E. Jefferson, Detroit, MI 48207-3185, *Published:* weekly.

Playthings, Geyer-McAllister Publications, Inc., 51 Madison Ave., New York, NY 10010, *Telephone:* (212) 689-4411, *Fax:* (212) 683-7929, *Published:* monthly, except semimonthly in May.

Point of Purchase, VNU Media, 770 Broadway, 6th Floor, New York, NY 10003.

Pork, National Pork Producers Council, P.O. Box10383, Des Moines, IA 50306, *Telephone:* (515) 223-2600.

PR Week, PR Publications Ltd., 220 Fifth Ave., New York, NY 10001, *Telephone:* (212) 532-9200, *Fax:* (212) 532-9200, *Published:* 49x/yr.

Practical Accountant, Faulkner & Gray, Inc., 11 Penn Plaza, 17th Floor, New York, NY 10001, *Telephone:* (800) 535-8403 or (212) 967-7060, *Published:* monthly, *Price:* U.S.: $60 per year; Elsewhere: $79 per year.

Prepared Foods, Cahners Publishing Company, 44 Cook St., Denver, CO 80217-3377, *Telephone:* (303) 388-4511, *Published:* monthly.

Printing Impressions, North American Publishing Co., 401 N Broad St., Philadelphia, PA 19108, *Telephone:* (215) 238-5300, *Fax:* (215) 238-5457.

Private Label Buyer, Stagnito Communications Inc., 155 Pfingsten Road, Suite 205, Deerfield, IL 60015, *Telephone:* (847) 205-5660, *Fax:* (847) 205-5680.

Produce Business, Multipress International, 301 Yamato Rd, Ste. 4110, Boca Raton, FL 33431.

Professional Candy Buyer, Adams Business Media, 2101 S. Arlington Heights Rd., Arlington Heights, IL 60005-4142.

Professional Jeweler, 1500 Walnut St, Ste 1200, Philadelphia, PA 19102, *Telephone:* (215) 567-0727, *Fax:* (215) 545-9629.

Progressive Grocer, 263 Tresser Blvd., Stamford, CT 06901, *Telephone:* (203) 325-3500, *Published:* monthly, *Price:* U.S.: $75 per year; Canada: $86 per year; single copies $9 each.

Providence Business News, 300 Richmond St., Ste 202, Providence, RI 02903, *Telephone:* (401) 273-2201, *Fax:* (401) 274-0670.

Provider, American Health Care Association, 5615 W. Cermak Rd., Cicero, IL 60650, *Published:* monthly.

Publishers Weekly, Cahners Publishing Company, ESP Computer Services, 19110 Van Ness Ave., Torrance, CA 90501-1170, *Telephone:* (800) 278-2991, *Published:* weekly, *Price:* U.S.: $129 per year; Canada: $177 per year (includes GST).

Pulp & Paper, Miller Freeman Inc., P.O. Box 1065, Skokie, IL 60076-8065, *Telephone:* (800) 682-8297, *Published:* monthly, *Price:* free to those in pulp, paper, and board manufacturing and paper converting firms; Others in U.S.: $100 per year.

Purchasing, Cahners Publishing Company, 44 Cook St., Denver, CO 80217-3377, *Telephone:* (303) 388-4511. *Published:* semimonthly, except monthly in January, February, July, August, December, and one extra issue in March and September, *Price:* U.S.: $84.95 per year; Canada: $133.95 per year; Mexico: $124.95 per year.

Quick Frozen Foods International, EW Williams Publishing Co., 2125 Center Ave., Ste. 305, Fort Lee, NJ 07024, *Telephone:* (201) 592-7007, *Fax:* (201) 592-7171, *Published:* monthly.

R&D Magazine, Cahners Publishing Company, 275 Washington St, Newton, MA 02158, Telephone: (708) 635-8800, Fax: (708) 390-2618, Published: monthly.

Railway Age, Simmons-Boardman Publishing, 345 Hudson St., New York, NY 10014, *Telephone:* (212) 620-7200, *Fax:* (212) 633-1165, *Published:* monthly.

RCR, RCR Publications, 777 East Speer Blvd., Denver, CO 80203.

Real Estate Alert, 5 Marine View Plaza, Ste. 301, Hoboken, NJ 07030-5795, *Telephone:* (201) 659-1700, *Fax:* (201) 659-4141.

Realtor, 430 N. Michigan Ave., Chicago, Il 60611-4087.

Research Alert, EPM Communications, 160 Mercer Street, 3rd Floor, New York, NY 10012.

Research Studies, BCC Inc., 25 Van Zant, Norwalk, CT 06855-1781.

Research Studies, Freedonia Group, 767 Beta Drive, Cleveland, OH 44143, Telephone: (440) 684-9600.

The Record, 150 River St., Hackensack, NJ 07601.

Refrigerated & Frozen Foods, Stagnito Communications, 1935 Sherman Rd., Northbrook, IL 60062, *Telephone:* (847) 205-5660, *Fax:* (847) 205-5680.

Report/ Magazine (Alberta Edition), 17327, 106A, Edmonton, Alberta, CA.

Restaurant Business, Penton Publishing, 1100 Superior Ave, Cleveland, OH 44114, *Telephone:* (216) 696-7000.

Restaurant Hospitality, Penton Media, 1300 E 9th Street, Cleveland, OH 44111.

Restaurants & Institutions, Cahners Publishing Co., 1350 Touhy Ave., Cahners Plaza, Des Plaines, IL 60017-5080, *Telephone:* (312) 635-8800.

Retail Merchandiser, Schwartz Publications, 233 Park Ave, New York, NY 1003, *Telephone:* (212) 979-4860.

Rock Products, Maclean Hunter Publishing Co., 29 N Wacker Drive, Chicago, IL 60606, *Telephone:* (312) 726-2802, *Fax:* (312) 726-2574.

Roofing Contractor, BNP, 755 West Big Beaver, Suite 1000, Troy, MI 48084, *Telephone:* (248) 362-3700, *Fax:* (248) 362-0317.

Rubber & Plastics News, Crain Communications, 1725 Merriman Road, Ste. 300, Akron, OH 44313,

Telephone: (330) 836-9180, *Fax:* (33) 836-1005, *Published:* weekly.

Rural Builder, Krause Publications, 700 E State St., Iola, WI 54990, *Telephone:* (715) 445-2214, *Fax:* (715) 445-4087.

Sacramento Business Journal, 1401 21st St., Sacramento, CA 95814-5221, *Telephone:* (916) 447-7661, *Fax:* (916) 444-7779, *Published:* weekly.

St. Louis Business Journal, American City Business Journals, 1 Metropolitan Square, PO Box 647, Saint Louis, MO 63188, *Telephone*: (314) 421-6200, *Fax:* (314) 621-5031.

St. Louis Post Dispatch, 400 South 4th Street, Ste 1200, St. Louis, MO 63102.

St. Petersburg Times, Times Publishing Co., 490 1st Ave., PO Box 1121, St. Petersburg, FL 33731.

Sales & Marketing Management, Times Mirror Magazines, Inc., 2 Park Ave., New York, NY 10016, *Telephone:* (212) 592-6300, *Fax:* (212) 592-6300, Published: 15x/yr.

San Antonio Business Journal, American City Business Journal, 82001H 10 W, Ste. 300, San Antonio, TX 78230-4819, *Telephone:* (512) 341-3202.

San Jose Mercury News, Knight-Ridder Inc., 1 Herald Plaza, Miami, Fl 33132, *Published:* daily.

Sarasota Herald-Tribune, 801 S. Tamiami Trail, Sarasota, FL 34236, *Telephone:* (813) 953-7755, *Fax:* (813) 957-5235.

Screen International, EMAP Media, 33-39 Bowling Green Lane, London EC1R ODA, *Telephone:* 44 (0)171 396-8000, *Published:* weekly.

SDM, Cahners Publishing Co., 1350 E. Touhy Ave., Des Plaines, IL 60018, *Telephone:* (708) 635—8800, *Fax:* (708) 299-8622.

Seattle Post-Intelligencer, 101 Elliott Ave, Seattle, WA 98119, *Published:* daily.

The Shepard, Sheep & Farm Life, 5696 Johnson Rd., New Washington, OH 44854, *Published*: monthly.

Shopping Center World, Communications Channels, Inc., 6255 Barfield Rd., Altanta, GA 30328, *Telephone:* (404) 256-9800.

Signs of the Times, Pacific Press Publishing, PO Box 7000, Boise, ID 83707-1000, *Telephone:* (208) 465-2500, *Fax:* (208) 465-2531.

Small Business Banker, American Banker Inc., 1 State St, New York, NY 10023, *Telephone:* (212) 408-1480, *Fax:* (212) 943-2984.

Smart Business, ZDNet, 650 Townsend Street, San Francisco, CA 94103.

Snack Food & Wholesale Bakery, Stagnito Publishing Co., 1935 Shermer Rd., Ste. 100, Northbrook, IL 60062-5354, *Telephone:* (708) 205-5660, *Fax:* (708) 205-5680, *Published:* monthly, *Price:* free to qualified subscribers; $45 per year to all others.

Soap & Cosmetics, 455 Broad Hollow Road, Melville, NY 11747-4722, *Published:* monthly.

South Florida Business Journal, American City Business Journals, 7950 NW 53 St., Ste. 210, Miami, FL 33166, *Telephone:* (305) 594-2100, *Fax:* (305) 594-1892.

Sporting Goods Business, Gralla Publications, Inc., 1515 Broadway, New York, NY 10036, *Telephone:* (212) 869-1300.

Sports Marketing, the Courtyard, Wisley, Surrey GU23 6QL, England.

Star Tribune, 425 Portland Ave., Minneapolis, MN 55488, *Telephone:* (612) 673-4000.

The State, Knight-Ridder Inc., 1 Herald Plaza, Miami, FL 33132.

Stores, NRF Enterprises Inc., 100 West 31st St., New York, NY 10001, *Published:* monthly, *Price:* U.S./Canada: $49 per year, $80 for 2 years, $120 for 3 years.

Strategy, Brunico Communications, Ste. 500, 366 Adelaide St., Weest, Toronto, ON M5V 1R9.

Supermarket Business, Howfrey Communications, Inc., 1086 Teaneck Rd., Teaneck, NJ 07666, *Telephone:* (201) 833-1900, *Published:* monthly.

Supermarket News, Fairchild Publications, 7 W. 34th St., New York, NY 10001, *Telephone:* (212) 630-4750, *Fax:* (212) 630-4760.

Supply House Times, Horton Publishing, 1350 Touhy Ave, Ste. 100E, Rosemont, IL 60018-3358.

Tampa Bay Business Journal, American City Business Journals, 405 Reo St. Ste 210, Tampa, FL 33609, *Telephone:* (813) 289-8225, *Published*: weekly, *Price*: $42.

The Tampa Tribune, PO Box 191, Tampa, FL 33601, *Telephone:* (813) 259-7711, *Fax:* (813) 259-7823.

Telephony, Intersec Publishing Corp., 9800 Metcalf, Overland Park, KS 66282-2960, *Published:* monthly.

Textile World, Maclean Hunter Publishing Co., Circulation Dept., 29 N. Wacker Dr., Chicago, IL 60606, *Price:* U.S./Canada: $45 per year, $75 for 2 years, $105 for 3 years.

Time, Time, Inc., Time & Life Bldg., Rockefeller Center, New York, NY 10020-1393, *Telephone:* (800) 843-8463, *Published:* weekly.

Tire Business, Crain Communcations, Inc., 1725 Merriman Rd., Ste. 300, Akron, OH 44313-5251, *Telephone:* (216) 836-9180, *Fax:* (216) 836-1005.

Toronto Star, One Yong Street, Toronto, Ontario M5E 1E6, Telephone: (416) 367-2000, *Published:* daily.

Tradeshow Week, 5700 Wilshire Blvd, Ste 120, Los Angeles, CA 90036, *Telephone:* (323) 965-2437, *Fax:* (323) 965-2407.

Trailer/Body Builders, Tunnell Publications, PO Box 66010, Houston, TX 77266.

Transport Topics, American Trucking Assn., 2200 Mill Road, Alexandria, VA 22314, *Telephone*: (703) 838-1770.

TV Intl, Warren Publishing, 215 Ward Ct., NW, Washington D.C., 20037.

U.S. Banker, Kalo Communications, 60 E. 42nd St., Ste. 3810, New York, NY 10165, Telephone: (212) 599-3310.

U.S. News & World Report, 2400 N. St. NW, Washington, D.C. 20037, *Telephone:* (202) 955-2000, *Published:* weekly.

Underground Construction, Oldom Publishing, PO. Box 219368, Houston, TX 77218-9368, *Telephone:* (281) 558-6930, *Fax:* (281) 558-7029.

Upside, Upside Media Inc., 2015 Pioneer Court, San Mateo, CA 94403, *Telephone:* (650) 377-0950, *Fax:* (650) 377-1962, *Published*: monthly.

Urethane Technology, Crain Communications Inc., 1725 Merriman Rd., Ste. 300, Akron, OH 44313-5251, *Telephone:* (216) 836-9180, *Fax:* (216) 836-1005, *Published:* 6x/yr, Price: $83.

USA TODAY, Gannett Co., Inc., 1000 Wilson Blvd., Arlington, VA 22229, *Telephone:* (703) 276-3400. *Published:* Mon.-Fri.

Utah Business, 85 E Fort Union Blvd, Midvale, UT 84047, Telephone: (801) 568-0114.

Utility Business, Intertec Publishing, 707 Westchester, White Plains, NY.

VAR Business, CMP Media Inc., 1 Jericho Plaza A, Jericho NY 11753, *Telephone:* (516) 733-6700, *Published:* weekly.

Variety, 475 Park Ave., South, New York, NY 10016, *Telephone:* (212) 779-1100, *Fax:* (212) 779-0026. *Published:* weekly.

Video Business, Capital Cities/ABC/Chilton CO., Chilton Way, Radnor, PA 19089, *Telephone:* (215) 964-4000, *Fax:* (215) 964-4285, *Published:* weekly.

Video Store, Advanstar Communications Inc., 1700 E. Dyer Rd., Ste 250, Santa Ana, CA 92705, *Telephone:* (714) 252-5300.

Video Week, Advanstar Communications Inc., 1700 E. Dyer Rd., Ste 250, Santa Ana, CA 92705, *Telephone:* (714) 252-5300, *Published:* monthly.

Wall Street Journal, Dow Jones & Co. Inc., 200 Liberty St., New York, NY 10281, *Telephone:* (212) 416-2000. *Published:* Mon.-Fri.

WARD's Auto World, Ward's Communications, 28 W. Adams, Detroit, MI 48226, *Telephone:* (313) 962-4456. *Published:* monthly.

WARD's Dealer Business, Ward's Communications, 28 W. Adams, Detroit, MI 48226, *Telephone:* (313) 962-4456. *Published:* monthly.

Warren's Cable Regulation Market, 2115 Ward CT, NW, Washington D.C. 20037.

Washington Business Journal, American City Business Journals, 2000 14th St, Ste. 500, Arlington, VA 22201.

The Washington Post, The Washington Post, 1150 15th St., N.W., Washington, DC 20071, *Published:* weekly.

Washington Technology, Tech News Inc., 1953 Gallows Road, Ste. 130, Vienna, VA 22182.

The Washington Times, News World Communications, 3600 New York Ave., NE, Washington D.C. 20002, *Telephone:* (202) 636-3028, *Fax:* (202)526-9348.

Waste Age, National Solid Waste Management Assn, 1730 Rhode Island Ave., NW, Ste. 100, Washington D.C. 20036.

Waste News, 1725 Merriman Road, Akron, OH 44313.

Wearable Business, Intertec Publishing, 707 Westchester, White Plains, NY, *Published:* monthly.

Wichita Business Journals, American City Business Journals, 110 S. Main St., Ste. 200, Wichita, KS 67202.

Wines & Vines, Hiaring Co., 1800 Lincoln Ave., San Rafael, CA 94901-1298, *Telephone:* (415) 453-9700, *Fax:* (415) 453-2517, *Published:* monthly, *Price:* $32 per year without directory; $77.50 per year including directory.

Wired, 520 3rd St., 4th Fl., San Francisco, CA 94107-1815, Telephone: (415) 276-5000, *Published:* monthly, *Price:* $39.95; Corporate: $80.

Women's Wear Daily , Fairchild Publications, 7 E. 12th St., New York, NY 10003, *Telephone:* (212) 741-4000, *Fax:* (212) 337-3225. *Published:* weekly.

Wood & Wood Products, Vance Publishing Corp., 400 Knightsbridge Pkway., Lincolnshire, IL 60069, *Telephone:* (708) 634-4347, *Fax:* (708) 634-4379, Published: monthly, except semimonthly in March.

Wood Digest, Johnson Hill Press, 1233 Janesville Ave., Fort Atkinson, WI 53538, *Telephone:* (414) 563-6388, *Fax*: (414) 563-1702.

World Oil, Gulf Publishing, 3301 Allen Pkway, PO Box 2608, Houston, TX 77242, *Telephone:* (713) 529-4301, *Fax:* (713) 520-4433.

Yahoo!Internet Life, Ziff Davis Inc., Ona Park Ave., New York, NY 10016, Published: monthly.

Youth Markets Alert, EPM Communications, 160 Mercer Street, 3rd Floor, New York, NY 10012.

Ziff Davis Smart Business for the New Economy, ZDNet, 650 Townsend Street, San Francisco, CA 94103.

MARKET
SHARE
REPORTER

ISSN 1052-9578

MARKET SHARE REPORTER

AN ANNUAL COMPILATION

OF REPORTED MARKET SHARE

DATA ON COMPANIES,

PRODUCTS, AND SERVICES

2 0 0 2

ROBERT S. LAZICH, Editor

GALE GROUP

THOMSON LEARNING

Detroit • New York • San Diego • San Francisco
Boston • New Haven, Conn. • Waterville, Maine
London • Munich

Robert S. Lazich, *Editor*

Editorial Code & Data Inc. Staff

Susan Turner, *Contributing Editor*
Joyce Piwowarski, *Programmer/Analyst*

Gale Group Staff

Eric Hoss, *Coordinating Editor*

Mary Beth Trimper, *Composition Manager*
Wendy Blurton, *Senior Buyer*
Nekita McKee, *Buyer*

Gary Leach, *Graphics Artist*
Cindy Baldwin, *Production Design Manager*

Copyright © 2001
The Gale Group
27500 Drake Rd.
Farmington Hills, MI 48331-3535

ISBN 0-7876-3348-8
ISSN 1052-9578

Printed in the United States of America

TABLE OF CONTENTS

TABLE OF TOPICS

The *Table of Topics* lists all topics used in *Market Share Reporter* in alphabetical order. One or more page references follow each topic; the page references identify the starting point where the topic is shown. The same topic name may be used under different SICs; therefore, in some cases, more than one page reference is provided.